A FIERY S(

Hirsch in rehearsal, mid-1950s.
University of Manitoba Archives

Published with the generous assistance of The Canada Council for the Arts and the Canada Book Fund of the Department of Canadian Heritage.

The authors and the publisher wish to thank the following for their kind permission to use images in the book: Fernand R. Leclair for the photo of John Hirsch with Pierre Elliott Trudeau and Pierre Juneau; Sylvie Drake for the caricature of Hirsch; Charles Pachter for his charcoal drawing of Hirsch, the Archives of Manitoba, University of Manitoba Archives, Library and Archives Canada, and the Stratford Shakespeare Festival.

Cover design: David Drummond
Cover photo: David Street
Chronology tables: Irving Dardick
Set in Adobe Minion by Simon Garamond
Printed by Marquis Book Printing Inc.

LIBRARY AND ARCHIVES CANADA CATALOGUING IN PUBLICATION
Martz, Fraidie
A fiery soul : the life and theatrical times of John Hirsch / Fraidie Martz and Andrew Wilson.

Includes bibliographical references and index.
ISBN 978-1-55065-319-9

1. Hirsch, John, 1930-1989. 2. Theatrical producers and directors—Canada—Biography. I. Wilson, Andrew, 1956 Apr. 29- II. Title.

PN2308.H57M37 2011   792.02'33092   C2011-905454-X

Published by Véhicule Press, Montréal, Québec, Canada
www.vehiculepress.com

Distribution in Canada by LitDistCo
www.litdistco.ca

Distribution in U.S. by Independent Publishers Group
www.ipgbook.com

Printed in Canada on FSC certified paper.

A Fiery Soul

The Life and Theatrical Times
of John Hirsch

Fraidie Martz
and Andrew Wilson

Véhicule Press

For Sam Martz

and for

David and Hugh Wilson

Contents

A fiery soul, which working out its way
Fretted the pigmy-body to decay
And o'er inform'd the tenement of clay

–John Dryden, "Absalom and Achitophel," 1681

I am a member of four mafias: Hungarian, Jewish,
homosexual and Winnipeg.

–John Hirsch

During the 1980s, North American actors had to bring three
things to any audition: a classical piece, a contemporary piece,
and a John Hirsch story.

–Daniel Sullivan

Preface

BOTH AUTHORS of this biography regret never having met John Hirsch. Fraidie Martz became interested in Hirsch when she was researching her book *Open Your Hearts: The Story of the Jewish War Orphans in Canada*. During that time she became friends with Hirsch's adoptive sister Sybil Shack, and visited the Shacks' home in Winnipeg where Hirsch lived for many years. After *Open Your Hearts* was published in 1996, she continued to collect material on Hirsch – the most famous of the war orphans – and began to draft this biography. Andrew Wilson, who had done the substantive editing on *Open Your Hearts*, came on board the Hirsch project after doing some interviews in England on Fraidie's behalf. Andrew remembers being "hooked" while arranging his first interview, when a long-time friend and colleague of Hirsch's said, "John Hirsch was a monster – but I loved him. What do you want to know?"

Whether they loved or hated Hirsch, the people contacted during the preparation for this book were wonderfully generous with their descriptions of the man and of the times he lived through. The authors wish to thank the following for generously sharing their memories and materials or helping with contacts: Evelyne Anderson, Louis Bako, David Bassuk, Susan Benson, Elke Bidner, James Blendick, John Bluethner, Thomas Bohdanetzky, Tibor Bolgar, Doreen Brownstone, Shieky Brownstone, Douglas Campbell, Heather and Len Cariou, Antoni Cimolino, Joy Coghill, Christopher Dafoe, Gordon Davidson, Richard Dennison, Garth Drabinsky, Sylvie Drake, Chris Durang, David Ehrlich, Larry Enkin, John Erkel, Edward Evanko, Robert Farley, Anna Fried, Keith Garebian, Eddie and

Deborah Gilbert, Andras Hamori, Glen and Margaret Harrison, Desmond Heeley, Paul Hecht, Jane Heffelfinger, David Helwig, Judith and Tom Hendry, Martha Henry, Paul Henteleff, Peter Herrndorf, Linda Intaschi, Steven Jack, George Jonas, Robert Kalfin, John Kennedy, Martin, Josh and Sara Knelman, Daphne Korol, Martin Lager, John Lahr, Alan Laing, Robert Lantos, Ming Cho Lee, Susan Lemenchick, James Leverett, Marilyn Lightstone, Leon Major, Alan Mandell, Marti Maraden, Ora Markstein, Des McAnuff, Catherine McCartney, Catherine McKeehan, Seana McKenna, Joey Miller, Larry Mirkin, Peter Molnar Gal, Mavor Moore, Arnold Naimark, Mark Negin, Elizabeth Osborn, Adam and Sylvia Ostry, Stephen Ouimette, Charles Pachter, Ted Patterson, Peter Pearson, Robin Phillips, Gordon Pinsent, Priscilla Pointer, Anna and Julian Porter, Aaron Posner, Peter Raby, Brian Rintoul, Perry Rosemond, Julius Rudel, Celeste Sansregret, Frank Savino, Steven Schipper, Michal Schonberg, Desmond Scott, Sybil Shack, Robert Sherrin, David Silcox, Stanley Silverman, Gail Singer, Reg Skene, Eoin and Susan Sprott, Guy Sprung, Daniel Sullivan, Gary Thomas, Ralph Thomas, Paul Thompson, Bryan Trottier, Keith Turnbull, Jay Turton, Kenneth Welsh, Susan Wilcox, Joy Wishart, Betty Jane Wylie, Sarah Yates, and Magda Zalán.

For help with Hungarian sources and translation we thank Hanna Heffner, Zeev Oren, and Sebestyén József Matyikó. We also thank Rachel Joyce and Christine Kaleeba for their transcriptions of recorded interviews.

For help with documentation or photos we thank the following: Elsie Douglas, Volunteer Archivist, Manitoba Theatre Centre; Roberta Kremer, UBC; Chris Kotecki, Archives of Manitoba; Gina Morham; Michelle Strutt, University of Manitoba Archives; Sophie Tellier and Theo Martin, Library and Archives Canada; Francesca Marini and Nora Polley, Stratford Shakespeare Festival Archives; John Calhoun, Billy Rose Theatre Division, New York Public Library; Laurie Lam, Manitoba Theatre Centre; Maia-Mari Sutnik, Art Gallery of Ontario.

Thanks to people who read drafts of individual chapters: Anna Fried, Martha Henry, Peter Herrndorf, Martin Knelman, Larry Mirkin,

Alon Nashman, Mark Negin, Michal Schonberg, Gail Singer, Reg Skene, Paul Thompson and Betty Jane Wylie.

Special thanks to: Alon Nashman and Paul Thompson for sharing material from their own project on Hirsch, as well as their invaluable insider's point of view; Malcolm Page for advice and a critical eye along the way; Michal Schonberg, Hirsch's literary executor, for providing access to material held by Library and Archives Canada and for many other forms of assistance; Gail Singer for her memories, amazing contacts and sense of humour. Warm thanks also to Simon Dardick and Nancy Marrelli of Véhicule Press for keeping faith.

Extra special thanks to Bryan Trottier, for enduring endless questions with good humour and unflinching candour.

We of course take full responsibility for any errors that might appear in the book.

Finally, from the bottom of our hearts, we thank the following for reading, encouraging, sheltering and sundry assistance: Stuart Adams, Judy Blankenship, Scott Harker, Blanche Howard, Barbara Tessman and Ed Toombs. Andrew Wilson thanks Claire Bolderson, as ever, and more and more.

One

A Hungarian Childhood, Interrupted

IN THE DAWN of an early spring day in the mid-1930s, an old man and a boy walk hand in hand in the green Hungarian countryside near the town of Siófok. Passing newly sown wheat fields, they climb a small hill to the Jewish cemetery, entering through wrought-iron gates as black as the old man's overcoat and bowler hat. There they stop to watch the sun rise, and stand briefly before the twin headstones of the grave where the old man's wife lies buried, and where he intends to join her when the time comes. From the south comes the sound of a small steam engine chuffing its way towards Ádánd, the village where the old man was born eight decades before. Singing a prayer under his breath, the old man places a pebble on his wife's grave, and tells the boy:

Here will I rest
your dad and you too
when our time will come.
And your son and his will stand
putting pebbles on our graves
and if there will be enough sons
and sons of sons
the pebbles will grow
like small pyramids
you read about in the Bible.

The words are from a poem called "My Grandfather," which John Hirsch published in the literary journal *Alphabet Magazine* in 1966. The poem concludes:

He said it
and it had to be so;
the world was safe
the future was firm in my mind
as my hand in his warm hand.

The future, so secure in the young boy's mind, could not have turned out to be more different. No sons, no pyramids, not even a graveyard. Mór Hirsch would die of malnutrition in the Budapest ghetto in 1944. John's brother, father and mother, and the rest of Siófok's Jewish citizens, were transported to Auschwitz, where most perished. When John wrote those words, he was thousands of miles from his native soil, and as a gay man he knew he would never have children. All that remained to him from that time of comfort and safety were thirty-year-old memories.

It is said that refugees can be divided into two categories: those who arrive with photographs and those who have none. Hirsch believed he had a photographic memory of his early years, but even minimal research reveals his reminiscences to be riddled with pitfalls for the unwary biographer. He was terrible with dates (for instance, his writings contain three different years for his bar mitzvah), careless about names of persons and places, and capable of both embellishment and outright fabrication. He once told a journalist that he never took photographs, nor kept a diary, saying breezily that, "I rely on my memory of images, and those erased were not worth preserving." It is hard to know if he meant this – he may have done at that time he said it – but equally, it would have been in keeping for him to have said it for effect.

Noted as a director for his visual imagination and sense of history, it is certain that Hirsch drew on his early memories to populate and dress his productions. But it is equally certain that they were essential to his survival, nourishing and sustaining him through years of great loss and deprivation. He once said, "The memories of my childhood gave me shelter all my life. All the people I knew were strong characters as if drawn by a single stroke of charcoal on a white page."

It was a typical Hirsch statement: a vivid metaphor framing a psychological truth. The principal characters from his childhood – mostly family members, many of them women – were indeed strong personalities, but his memories of them and the places they lived were far from "single strokes on a white page." His early life exposed him to a vivid cross-section of *Mitteleuropean* society, with all its contradictions and colour. Certain figures in his family embody different aspects of that society, like symbolic characters in a staged allegory: a proudly nationalist father versus a skeptical, cosmopolitan mother; a sharp-tongued secular grandmother versus a Tevye-like grandfather; the provincial paternal family in Siófok versus the sophisticated maternal family in Budapest. These themes, and some of the characters, would appear again and again in his work as a director, writer and (though he would have hated the term) cultural bureaucrat. They also very much shaped the man he became.

If *Mitteleuropa* is as much a state of mind as of political geography, John – János, as his name appeared on his birth certificate, and Jancsi to his family and friends – was born almost at its centre. The date was May 1, 1930; the place was Siófok, which was and remains today a popular resort town on the shores of Lake Balaton, Hungary's "Inland Sea." Located about one hundred kilometres southwest of Budapest, Siófok's beaches and spas drew tens of thousands of pleasure seekers during the summer holiday season. To accommodate the visitors a variety of hotels, pensions and private villas sprang up around the railway station, with its twin roof peaks standing up like bull's horns. Surrounding the town were vineyards and orchards, with a large peasant population scattered in villages and large estates. Starting in the 1870s, artists began to build villas in the area, finding inspiration in the gently rolling countryside and the ever-changing lake. The town itself was dominated by the neo-Romanesque Catholic Church and an octagonal water tower resembling a beach house on stilts, which has been Siófok's best-known feature since it was built in 1912.

Almost all of the images that John retained of Siófok until 1940 were happy, and he wrote about them with both colour and detail. For instance, the young John always looked forward to late spring when, with the ripening of the first cherries, "horses with red ribbons woven into their manes pulling peasant-carts down from the hills into town, brought pennies-a-bunch cherries and fresh butter wrapped in large leaves." And to the autumn, when attics "cradled red apples in straw, and pantries hung heavy with grapes strung up on twine stretched between rough shelves, with rows of jars of unripe melons floating in brine." Years later, he would work closely with set and costume designers to conjure that sense of closely observed and deeply felt reality in his productions.

As permanent residents, the Hirsch family lived in the town proper. The house John grew up in was one of the largest in Siófok, located across the street from the water tower. Built around a courtyard with a tree-filled garden, the house was always full of people, not only the immediate family of mother, father, grandfather and brother István (Stephen), two years younger, but an extended family of about twenty-five members, including a great many aunts, uncles and cousins.

His paternal roots can be traced to the environs of Bratislava, once the capital of Hungary. At some point in the late eighteenth or early nineteenth century the family moved south to the village of Ádánd, nestled in the rich farmland of the Balaton region. Originally they were country people who farmed, but subsequently they went into the grain business and moved into the larger centre of Siófok. In return for his support to the Hungarian government during the complicated politics of the late nineteenth century, John's grandfather acquired a license to sell tobacco, salt and kerosene, which he parlayed into a successful retail business. Other family members became manufacturers and industrialists. At the time John was born the family had been financially secure for decades, yet remained very much rooted in the land and local villages. John always thought of them as *Cherry Orchard* people, and spoke often of how they served as prototypes in his productions of Chekhov's plays.

John's father József was one of four sons, and the only one to stay in Siófok and work in the business. Over the years he and Mór Hirsch expanded it to include hardware, construction and building supplies, which provided a comfortable living for his family. In written reminiscences of his childhood John had relatively little to say about his father's personality, other than he "was a laughing fellow full of jokes to swap with travelling men who came to sell him hardware for the store." He chose to accent how handsome his father was: "Six-foot-three and some, he looked like all the heroes of Viennese operettas. Well-built with a little moustache, dark hair and flashing eyes."

József had been wounded in the First World War and took great pride in having served as an officer. On national holidays he would put on his uniform with all his medals, and march in the parade with the other veterans. Like most Hungarian Jews, he and his family were fervent patriots, despite their somewhat precarious and frequently changing status within it. For a few decades following the First Law of Emancipation in 1867, Jews enjoyed full civil and political rights. Once treated as second-class citizens (and even subject to a special "toleration tax"), the legislation meant that Jews were not only allowed but encouraged to participate in the modernization and industrialization of Hungary. Over the following decades, they contributed substantially to the country's development, politically, economically and culturally, and Jewish assimilation happened faster in Hungary than almost anywhere else in Europe.

By the time John was born, the family's Jewish identity fit comfortably with life in Siófok. Theirs was a liberal stream of Judaism, very different from the inward-looking *shtetl* (village) tradition or the rigorous Orthodoxy found in many other parts of Europe. John's grandfather prayed every day at sunrise and sunset wearing his *tallit* (prayer shawl), but although the Hirsches kept a kosher household, eating non-kosher foods out of the house was not prohibited. They were proud of being Jews in a Catholic town and equally proud of being Hungarian citizens.

Small wonder, then, that the Hirsches strove to equal or outdo their gentile countrymen in displays of Magyar nationalism. Love of country was expressed very differently to the restrained British style that John would meet later among English-Canadians, and which would often infuriate him. The patriotism he grew up with was on display everywhere one looked, starting with the large photograph of József in officer's uniform which dominated the hall of the house. Another source of pride was being related to Siófok's most famous son, Emmerich (Imre) Kálmán, the composer of such operettas as *The Gay Hussars* and *Countess Maritza*. Those who later criticized John Hirsch's penchant for frothy musical confections might perhaps have been a bit more forgiving, for cabarets, operettas and musical comedies were in his blood.

John's mother, Ilona, brought a note of urban sophistication to the small-town earthiness of the Hirsch clan. Her family, the Horváts, lived in Budapest, and boasted a circle of friends that included many of the foremost opera singers and actors of the day. One family legend – there were many – told of an ancestor whose company of five actors had performed across the length and breadth of Hungary. Another spoke of a family member who had been elected to the legislature – dizzying heights for a Jew, even in the relatively liberal Hungary of the late nineteenth century – only to be forced to leave the country after an *affaire d'honneur* fought with sabres.

Bringing Ilona into the family was a step up, socially and culturally, for the Hirsches. She spoke five languages, played piano and painted well, loved the theatre, and was an avid reader. The family's library was full of her art books, the latest novels from Budapest and Vienna, and favourite Hungarian classics. Pride of place went to the works of Mór Jókai (known in English translation as Maurus Jókai), the nineteenth-century novelist and journalist who, in the national imagination, is a mix of Charles Dickens, Victor Hugo and Walter Scott. While many of Jókai's bestselling books were swashbuckling tales of legendary Magyar heroes, he also wrote short stories set around Lake Balaton, where he settled in later life. (It would have been important to the Hirsches that Jókai depicted Jews sympathetically in his writing; his first published play was *Zsidó fiú* – The Jewish Boy).

Ilona was also an accomplished conversationalist and cook. She cultivated a wide circle of friends – many of them musicians, actors and writers drawn to Siófok during the *saison* – who came to eat at her table and mingle in her salon.

Some of the guests were very distinguished indeed. John often told the story of having danced, as a three-year-old, for the most celebrated male dancer of the twentieth century, Vaslav Nijinsky, whose wife, Countess Romola de Pulszky, was Hungarian. One summer day in 1933, a musical friend of Ilona's brought the great dancer and his wife to the Hirsch home. Nijinsky had last danced in 1919, and had been in and out of asylums and cure homes for over a decade. Among John's stock of childhood images was that of the "peacefully insane, fat, bald, immobile" Nijinsky wearing a long, black overcoat in the heat of July. With his mother's friend accompanying on piano, the little boy danced impromptu in the middle of the salon to the tune of *Who's Afraid of the Big Bad Wolf.*

The salon was central to his memories, the place where family and friends gathered regularly for conversation and entertainment. The room was furnished with a large, intricately patterned Persian rug and heavy Empire-style furniture, the latter a wedding gift from his maternal grandfather. On its walls hung Meissen mirrors adorned with cherubs and tiny violets, and intricately framed paintings by contemporary Hungarian painters. Reflecting a trend from atelier work to *plein-air* painting at the time, many of these paintings featured large vistas of the Magyar countryside under masses of frothy grey and white clouds. John adored them – while he appreciated and understood fine art he had an abiding affection for kitsch – but it isn't clear whose taste these landscapes actually reflected. One influence was certainly József's brother, John's Uncle Lajos, a bookkeeper-accountant at a textile firm in Budapest, who was a passionate art collector. Having spent a lifetime, and much of his money, collecting contemporary Hungarian art and befriending Hungarian artists, he seems to have talked John's parents into supporting at least some of his favourite painters.

In contrast to his admiring but distant relationship with his father, John was very close to his mother. He spent a lot of time with her: they played piano together, and she helped him construct the puppet theatres that became a fixture of his childhood. He inherited his interest in fine cooking from her, eventually becoming an expert, if spectacularly disorganized, chef and host of memorable dinner parties.

The one male in the household with whom John had a deep connection was his gentle paternal grandfather, Mór Hirsch. As an adult, John would call Mór Hirsch the centre of his childhood world. His grandfather's black bowler hat, like the local rabbi's cap, was for the boy "a symbol of the roundness and the rightness of the world." The bond was formed early. When John was two years old, his brother István was born, and the Hirshes moved John's bed into his grandfather's room. John would insist in later life that he remembered the trauma of being "exiled from Eden," but equally that it had turned out to be another kind of paradise. Every night, until he was eight, he fell asleep listening to fairy tales and folk legends, of which Hungarian folklore has an immense store. Certain characters – wily brigands, beautiful princesses and heroic aristocrats – appeared over and over again, and the young John was certain that his grandfather had actually known some of them.

John later learned that his mother had worried about the effect of this storytelling on him, and actually consulted a family member who was a psychoanalyst. In the end, John's bed stayed where it was. As an adult John frequently argued that storytelling and fantasy were essential not just to his but to any child's development. John would act on this premise throughout his artistic life, writing and producing dozens of plays for children, and taking theatre to the schools. He speculated that the evening ritual with his grandfather might have been the source of his attachment to Shakespeare's late comedies, especially *The Tempest*.

"Jancsi." John Hirsch as little boy in the town of
Siófok, Hungary, mid-1930s.
University of Manitoba Archives

The connection was not confined to the nighttime or the house.
No day felt complete without a walk with his grandfather along the
Sió canal, built in the 1860s to connect Lake Balaton with the
Danube, or along the waterfront. A favourite destination was a tavern
(John became Canadian enough to refer to it as a "beer parlour" in
his reminiscences) where his grandfather took his afternoon tipple.
Here more rituals were played out: John was allowed to drink the
head, never the beer; and at the coffee house the foam and whipped
cream, never the coffee. Another destination was the store that Mór
Hirsch had established when he first moved to Siófok. The Grand
Tobacco was located on the main square and fulfilled an important
social as well as economic function. In John's memory there were

always dozens of people sitting around talking animatedly, from the priest and the mayor to the peasants who came to town to buy nails by the keg and kerosene by the gallon. Though his father had taken over the business by this time, both grandparents continued to work in the shop well into old age (his grandmother died when John was very small and he had few memories of her). The place was dark and full of scents "like a rum-soaked rich cake." In the winter it was warmed by the stove where Mór Hirsch would roast chestnuts, adding their aroma to the mix. John's memories made it into a sort of Aladdin's cave:

> In this Grand Tobacco shop sat my grandfather, on a throne gilded by tobacco leaves counting the green hand rolled cigars. And amid pyramids of matches, cigarettes from Turkey, Egypt, and some even from India, my grandmother added up the silver of the day.

In the late months of spring, a favourite treat was a visit to the market, where the first cherries of the season were sold in little clusters placed on green leaves. But before John could grab a cherry to pop into his mouth, his grandfather insisted he say a prayer thanking God for the cherries growing once again on the trees. While Mór Hirsch was not strict or pedantic about religion, John was in no doubt about how important it was to his grandfather. Watching the old man say a prayer before he ate a piece of bread or drank a glass of water, John came to understand that his grandfather's whole day was an ongoing thanksgiving.

The Judaism that John absorbed in Siófok was essentially personal. Neither the synagogue nor the religious curriculum at the local Jewish primary school he attended (along with a number of children from other faiths, whose parents sent them because of the quality of the education offered there) seems to have made much impression on him, except for the stars that adorned the blue ceiling of the synagogue. Christianity was a very different matter, and he later on traced a significant part of his stage influences to the Catholicism he saw practiced in his hometown. It was in Siófok that he first saw theatre in religion and religion in theatre, a correlation that merged in his imagination and was to find diverse expressions in his career as a director.

The church in the centre of Siófok towered over John's imagination as it did over the town. The peal of its bells woke him in the morning, signalled the start of the mid-day meal and accompanied him to bed in the evening. Every morning on his way to school, and every afternoon on his way home, he passed the huge church doors – open always, even to the poorest, shoeless peasant boys, but closed forever to him as a Jew. Forbidden to enter, he was still able to peer into the interior from the threshold, drinking in the smell of incense and dreaming of pulling the bell ropes himself. The church, actually a fairly modest one appropriate to a town the size of Siófok, assumed the grandeur of St. Peter's in his imagination, forever leaving him with the vision of its gold and silver interior lit by the radiant light streaming from the huge stained-glass windows. Candles, statues and the constant movement of clergy and worshippers completed the picture, and were added to his growing stock of visual treasures.

Of all the annual religious events celebrated in Siófok, the one which drew John most was All Saints Day on the first of November. Called Halottak Napja (literally the day of the dead), this holy day is taken very seriously in Hungary. In John's memory, All Saints began with the peasants burning dried twigs and stalks, making the night fog grow thick and grey. The old women of the town had already been to the market to purchase coloured candles; as night fell, their candles in hand, they walked along the road that turned toward the river and continued on until they reached the cemetery at the top of the hill. The women then covered their heads with large woollen shawls and moved through the dark to find the graves of their loved ones, where they lit their candles, knelt and prayed. John never dared go by himself, but persuaded the family's Catholic maid to take him. He would forever remember the women at the gravesides, "as if their feet were sunken in the earth and some magnet deep down was drawing them on. The whole cemetery buzzed and droned with prayers in the night, as if the dead insects of the summer had returned to sing."

Exclusion from the mysterious and theatrical religion of the majority was a great stimulus to his imagination. As he put it later, "Most of the ritualistic elements of my productions of Shakespeare's works are really my way of becoming a Catholic."

So it was that at the age of five John Hirsch decided to mount his own version of All Saints Day. With the pocket money his grandfather gave him to buy sweets, John bought a box of candles exactly like the ones he had seen the women buy in the market (in another version of the story, he said he used candle stubs from the graveyard after Halottak Napja). He then took a large wooden butter-box and lined it with pieces of an old green velvet drape, which once hung in his grandfather's room. Set on its side, so that the opening formed a proscenium (the arch at the front of the stage, through which the audience views the play), the box became John's first theatre, with actors made out of wire, wool and bits of cork. He locked the doors of his room, drew the blinds, and arranged all the candles in a circle in the box so that the actors stood like Roman players in front of coloured columns. All was ready. John lit the candles and sang "Deo, Deo," followed by "St. Theresa, save us!" Alas, the velvet caught fire. In John's wry words, "The wooden box burned like Rome while Nero yelled for help, which was held up by the locked door."

The near disaster in no way dampened his interest. Rather, it started the exploration of different forms of theatre that continued throughout his career. Puppetry was the first stop on this voyage. At Christmas, he and Éva Weinberger, a girl two years his senior from a neighbouring house, decided to put on their own puppet show in the Hirsch salon. They invited all the children they knew to see their first play, *Hansel and Gretel*, for which John painted sets featuring huge candies and pieces of gingerbread. The first one was a triumph and was repeated year after year, with more friends drafted to participate. Over time the puppet theatre became more and more sophisticated. Candles were soon replaced by electric bulbs dipped into coloured lamp paint, which gave off a pleasant odour and dried quickly. He learned how to construct an apparatus that produced lightning and a floor that revolved like a carousel.

In the future he would always highlight his years of self-apprenticeship in puppetry, an art that demands many skills from the artist, from the plethora of technical know-how needed to mount a production to working the puppets themselves. Equally, he would maintain that introducing children to puppet theatre was the best education for appreciating live drama as adults. "Here illusion is all," he would argue, "and the reality of illusion, which is so important in adult theatre, must be accepted. With an audience which has had the experience of the puppet theatre in childhood, you have no trouble when you try to present a play which has not the reality of the movies, which does not try to give you slices of life with chunks of baloney in between."

His increasing sophistication in the practice of puppetry was fed by visits to Budapest, where puppetry of a very high standard was part of both popular and high culture. Hungary, like much of Eastern Europe, had an old and honoured tradition of puppet artistry. In Budapest, he often saw open-air shows like *Paprika Jancsi Szinhaz* (Mr. Punch's Theatre), or the venues dedicated to puppetry and marionettes like the National Puppet Theatre.

These early visits to Budapest brought him closer to his maternal family and to the other great childhood influence in both his professional and personal life. This was Tekla Weisz, John's maternal grandmother. It is hard to imagine a more striking contrast to the genial small-town merchant Mór Hirsch than the fiercely intellectual, fiery-tempered Tekla. In a high school essay written in Winnipeg, probably in early 1949, John described his grandmother's appearance (the passage, spelling errors and all, shows the progress John made in English during the short time he had been in Canada):

A flat, tallish woman with the face of a Roman bust... some ancient Patrician with short iron grey hair, a sharp nose that cut the air ahead of her, eyes that were brilliant and flashing to see, to cut to the heart of the matter like two tiny falcons that struke [struck] out and returned to their sockets and there they perched tied to her brain by the vital leashes of her nerves. The mouth was wide with thin lips

that turned down at the corners in mockery of the world
from which she carried [cared] not a pfenning [penny].

John called his grandmother "a bluestocking ... with a mind as
alive as a cage of vultures." Tekla had been frustrated in her early
hopes of studying political science. By the time John knew her she
was focused almost entirely on intellectual matters, with little interest
in domestic concerns like cooking or housekeeping. The daughter
of a proud Viennese family that revered Schiller, Beethoven and
Mozart rather than Mór Hirsch's Jehovah, she regarded living in
Hungary as the equivalent to exile among barbarians. It was disappointing to her that her talented daughter, John's mother, had married into a small-town Philistine family. But at least the Hirsches
were reasonably presentable in her mind. When one of her sons
married the daughter of Polish Jews who kept a kosher house, Tekla
practically froze her son and his new family out of her social life.

Tekla was fluent in Hungarian but never thought it a civilized
language and spoke it as little as possible. She preferred to speak
German – or French when discussing fashion, food or literature. A
bookseller in Vienna regularly sent her the latest books and newspapers, which she carried in an overflowing carpetbag wherever she
went. Even the daily newspaper she favoured, the *Pester Lloyd*, was a
German-language paper printed in Budapest, a kind of *Wall Street
Journal* of the time, liberal in its politics and with a wide circulation.

By the time John knew her, she had become an intimidating
and decidedly eccentric character. Her dress sense was singular; he
remembered "her ramrod straight body in a black coat that went
straight down to her ankles, wearing a pair of Wellington boots and
a mannish suit, and carrying fifteen newspapers and a black
umbrella." In a city that valued fashion, she always wore the same
clothing on all occasions, even to weddings. She also was famously
undiplomatic in her speech, "with language often peppered with
words never uttered by a lady of her age and station."

A widow since 1933, Tekla resided in a large flat on the second
floor of a large block of flats in an upper-middle-class neighbour-

(Left) John's father, József, was a decorated veteran of
the Austro-Hungarian Army. *University of Manitoba Archives*
(Right) John walking with his grandmother Tekla and
mother Ilona, late 1930s. *Courtesy of Anna Fried*

hood. John remembered it as a cold, dark and gloomy apartment
with high ceilings and walls lined with bookcases. Heating was
provided by a green porcelain stove, which John remembered as
never supplying enough heat to "warm up the wooden cherubs
forever flying above the oak doors." Hanging above the divan where
John slept was an oil painting of Romeo in a boat and Juliet on the
balcony, and Venetian mirrors encircled by glass flowers. The kitchen
intrigued him. Painted battleship grey, it was always full of steam.
Tekla hated cooking and housework, and the kitchen utensils were
battered and bent, the dishes chipped, and the cutlery ill-assorted.
Yet John could also see that the credenza in the dining room was
full of fine Rosenthal dinnerware, the drawers crammed with exquisite table linen, and the shelves heavy with boxes containing the fine
silver cutlery. Like the house in Siófok, the Budapest apartment supplied
him with visual templates for his productions of Chekhov's plays.

Tekla appears to have doted on John, treating him more like an intimate friend than a grandson. He remembered "her heavy black skirt, and the boots underneath which I always helped her put on, and the long pink flannel underwear." She, too, was a performer, but unlike John she was content with an audience of one. He had a strong memory of lying on his divan in the darkened living room, wrapped in blankets and his grandmother's old housecoats for added warmth, with his head resting on a huge feather pillow. Before him, his grandmother stood on a chair with her long white hair hanging down on both sides of her face, singing a saucy vaudeville song about Fanny Schneider's red petticoat (Schneider was a famous cabaret dancer of the time):

>...Schneider Fáni de azt mondta / nem kell néki piros szoknya / inkább kell néki gigerli / aki őtet ingerli. (...But Fanny Schneider up and said / She'd have no petticoat of red /A gigolo she'd have instead / The very thing to turn her head.)

Tekla had two sons, Gyuri and Pál, who lived at home when John first came to visit. When their father died in the mid-1930s, the two took over the chemicals business that was the source of the family's income, and were able to move out. However, John was aware of another presence in the apartment: the shadow of Tekla's youngest son, Rező, who had died by his own hand. An artist who became successful in his early twenties, Rezső had been invited to exhibit his sculptures in Rome, where he fell in love with an older married woman. The passion was reciprocated, and the two travelled around Italy as Rezső exhibited in Milan, Naples and Genoa. It was in Genoa that his beloved suddenly announced that she was returning to her husband, and swore she would never again see him. That evening, Rezső threw himself under the wheels of the Genoa-Budapest express train. Back in Budapest, Tekla went nearly mad with grief when she heard the news. Rezső was buried in a cemetery at Como with one of his own angel sculptures standing over his grave. Every year a member of the family had to visit the cemetery in order to reassure Tekla that the money she sent to the cemetery gardener was actually used for planting fresh flowers at the gravesite. (When John's cousin, Anna Fried, the daughter of Gyuri, visited the cemetery in the 1980s, she found the records relating to Rezső's burial, but the grave itself was no longer marked and the statue had been stolen.)

John was reminded of the tragic story every time he entered the apartment, where plaster-of-paris busts that Rezső had made of the family stood on the top of the wardrobes lining the hall. John also discovered drawings of the *femme fatale*, hidden away in a portfolio of sketches tied with a black ribbon.

But the departed uncle had an additional effect on John, both as a person and as an artist. He would eventually tell the story – and possibly convince himself – that he had been born on the same day that Rezső died. The idea that the soul of the departed had entered his body just as he was taking his first breath is strongly reminiscent of the Jewish folk belief portrayed in *The Dybbuk*, one of John's greatest triumphs as a director. (In fact, Anna Fried asserts that Rezső died in 1933, three years after John was born.)

While John felt the shadow of Rezső in his grandmother's affection, the bond between grandmother and grandson was not just based in grief for a dead child. There seems also to have been a meeting of mind and temperament. Even when very young, John always had the feeling that she was treating him with the respect due an intelligent adult; later on in his life, it was how he would treat children himself.

When he visited her in Budapest John loved to accompany her to the Café Cairo, a coffee house distinguished by its faux-Egyptian décor, where she had her own *stammtisch* (an earmarked table for what John called her "table-tribe"). She walked there every afternoon around five o'clock. There as many as fifteen women of about her age would be waiting for her to hold court on politics and literature, interpreting the day's events and everything else. In contrast to Tekla, these women wore smart black hats with tidy veils, white lace blouses and small gold chains. John felt as welcome there as he did when visiting a Siófok tavern with his grandfather. "I always got the whipped cream from her coffee," he recalled, "and ended up with a Swiss newspaper which I pretended to read."

John's exposure to his grandmother's preference for German and European culture did nothing to diminish the patriotism he had learned at home in Siófok. The radio was full of patriotic poems, often set to music like Sándor Petőfi's "Ha a föld Isten kalapja, úgy hazánk bokréta rajta" ("If the world is God's hat, our country is the bouquet on top") and popular songs evoking favourite locations like "Hétre ma várom a Nemzetinél" ("Meet Me at Seven in Front of the National" – the reference being to the National Theatre). There was also the influence of the local school, with its whitewashed walls and hard chairs that left red welts on the back of the students' legs, where nationalistic poems were a staple of the academic diet. There John learned that Hungarians were morally superior to Serbs, smarter than Romanians, more trustworthy than Poles, more intelligent than Czechs, and more industrious than Germans. He also experienced a peculiarly Hungarian form of celebrity appropriation. Shakespeare was really Hungarian, he learned, and even Adam and Eve spoke Hungarian in Eden.

Hungarian nationalism permeated even his earliest experiences of theatre. By the age of seven or eight, theatre was already his major interest. At an age when most young boys are playing with building blocks and trains, John was busily writing and putting on plays and puppet shows in the family garden, and saving his pocket money for theatre tickets. The first play he ever saw, in the hotel near his house in Siófok, was performed by one of the many touring companies that criss-crossed Hungary, playing in the small towns and provincial centres. János Vitéz (translated variously as "John Hero" or "Sir John"), was a swashbuckling musical of war, foreign travel and magic based on an epic poem composed in 1845 by Sándor Petőfi. The young John was entranced by the story of another young János, the Hungarian shepherd who joins the Hussars, battles his way across Europe, loses and then resurrects his childhood love, and turns down immortality to return to his homeland. But as well as revelling in the pure entertainment of the moment, he was also clearly drinking in the *life* of the theatre – the comportment of the actors offstage, the technical work, even the essential but unsung job of marketing. In a speech he gave years later he described the excitement of the touring company's arrival in Siófok:

> A week before the players arrived the advance man came to town, usually from the south, on the 7:30 train. He was a large man with a heavy cloth coat, his neck circled by a red fox fur collar and he wore a green Borsalino hat with small yellow feathers stuck in the back. He came with a shiny black briefcase. In it he had the posters which he distributed among the local merchants, giving them season tickets for putting these posters in their windows.
>
> The actors arrived a week later. They came dressed in citified dresses and suits. The women wore large hats in which birds nestled. Around their necks were red feather boas. They wore a great deal of make-up and smiled sweetly at everyone. The actors addressed all ladies as Madame or Mademoiselle and Fräulein and Gnädige Frau (if they were German-style actors) – they called even the peasant women so. And the tickets went quickly.
>
> They performed in a beery hotel ballroom where there were large mirrors all around and long red drapes hung in front of the windows – drawn for the performance. At one end of this hall the stage was set up with electric cords running in all directions and all the boards and ropes visible. The curtains were red and mended in spots. The pianist, who also took in the money at the door, played the overture. The light switches clicked one by one, the squabbling behind the curtain ended, the audience was silent and in the darkness the piano player struck a magnificent chord, played a couple of marches which were applauded thunderously. More switches were clicked. The curtain was flooded with light, it parted and revealed yet another curtain made of black material with gold stars and moons, magic numbers and signs, and in the middle sat a huge painted green toad. This was my very first play.

Theatre was forever connected in John's mind with his Hungarian identity. He often fielded questions about his influences as a theatre director by declaring that he came from a country where theatre was not only important but "essential." He would also quote a popular saying that every Hungarian is born with Act One in his head, and spends the rest of his life working on Acts Two and Three. Again, this type of sweeping statement, so characteristic of Hirsch's public utterances, had a great deal of truth to it. When Hirsch was young, theatre was everywhere in Hungary and attended by all classes. The country had for many years the highest concentration of theatre and cabarets on the continent, and boasted a distinctive form of folk theatre called the *népszinmû*, which drew its themes and speech forms from village life – or at least, village life as imagined by an urban playwright. Starting in the 1800s, Magyar-language theatre was a major instrument of national revival. Magnificent theatre buildings were built even in medium-size provincial centres with government support. Streets and public squares were often named after actors and actresses. It seemed to John, particularly from the table talk he heard while accompanying his grandmother, that the lives of actors supplied much of the daily gossip and that everybody from maids to politicians liked to know which actors were performing in what plays.

It was a huge source of pride that an almost endless number of Hungarians gained international success in films, theatre and music. John grew up proud of the fact that Leslie Howard, the archetypal English film star, was the son of a Hungarian Jewish tailor (which was true) and that the majority of Hollywood films were created by Hungarians (partly true). The Korda brothers Alexander, Vincent and Zoltán had huge success in both Britain and the U.S. during John's childhood, directing and producing films such as *The Private Life of Henry VIII* and *Sanders of the River*. John also took pride in knowing that Hungary had produced a remarkable galaxy of great scientists and entrepreneurs. In short, much of the country's culture was for John an ongoing rejoicing in being part of a uniquely talented community.

John, Ilona, József and István (Stephen) Hirsch in the mid-1930s.
University of Manitoba Archives

It didn't seem strange to John that Hungary was (as a widely repeated joke had it) a kingdom without a king, ruled by an admiral without a navy or a coastline. Only as an adult did he become aware that Hungary was never really a great power in the world of international affairs, and appreciate the flourishing theatre of chauvinistic propaganda to which he had been exposed by the *népszinmü* puppets. None of this dampened his love for Hungary, and he cherished his Hungarian heritage all his life.

Despite his privileged relationship with many grownups, John had no awareness of the unease his parents and grandparents must have felt about events both inside and outside Hungary. This may be attributed to his age and to the grownups' wish to spare him from their worries. Yet in some ways his memories were in keeping with the security that many Hungarian Jews felt – or persuaded themselves to feel – at the time. Even after the Nazi repression of Jews began in Germany after 1933, many Hungarian Jews told themselves that "it couldn't happen here." Coffee house life went on as before, and his grandmother's beloved *Pester Lloyd* proudly published German-language writers, Jewish and gentile, who were banned in Germany. On March 12, 1938, when the German army marched down the Kärtnerstrasse in Vienna, many Jews consoled themselves with the idea that perhaps Hitler would be satisfied with Austria and stay out of Hungary.

But the noose was tightening. In May 1938, the Hungarian government bowed to pressure from Berlin and enacted the first of what became a series of anti-Jewish laws. The first of these set quotas of twenty per cent for Jews in many professions. The second, promulgated in May 1939, banned Jews from most government jobs and from editing newspapers, and restricted the number of employees in any commercial enterprise. The curtailment of civil rights did not preclude the conscription of men aged eighteen to twenty-five for labour service. The wish of the anti-Semites to separate Jews from other Hungarians became a humiliating reality. Venomous anti-Semitic rhetoric appeared in the press and in public discourse.

Even then, many Jews retained faith in Hungary and particularly in the father figure of the Regent, Admiral Miklós Horthy. Although as head of state Horthy had authorized the anti-Jewish laws, it was generally understood that he had resisted Nazi pressures to impose even harsher measures. When Germany attacked Poland on September 1, 1939, Horthy refused the German army passage across Hungarian soil. When Britain and France declared war on Germany, Hungary still clung to its illusion of neutrality. Even after Hungary officially joined in Germany's war in June 1940, Jews escaping from other countries were given protection in the kingdom.

Slowly but surely, however, the secure foundations of John's happy childhood were being knocked away. The first shock came in the summer of 1940, when he learned he was to be sent away from Siófok to attend school in Budapest. As a Jewish child, he could only attend a Jewish *gimnázium* (high school). No such school existed in Siófok.

It was a terrible time for the ten-year-old John, and he reacted to it with all the pathos of his dramatic soul. He cried all summer at the thought of being sent away and separated from his family and home. He threatened to commit suicide, to burn the house down. Nothing worked. As September drew near, his grandfather gave him a ten-*pengő* note – the first paper money he had ever possessed – to spend on sweets and books. He gravely advised John not to go to the movies too often, to behave and to be polite to the people with whom he was to board (he could no longer stay with his grandmother, who had died earlier that year). Other relatives pressed money and advice on him. His mother found a different outlet for her anguish, packing and repacking his luggage dozens of times in the weeks before he left Siófok.

His departure left him with a jumble of images, full of both pain and melodrama. A substantial crowd – immediate family, aunts and great-aunts, a gaggle of cousins, the faithful maid, and many townspeople who knew the Hirsches – went to the station to see him off. By the time the train arrived everyone was crying. The terrible truth suddenly dawned on him: their happiness had been an act, a terrible deception to cover up their true feelings about the crime of sending him away! Devastated, he allowed himself to be put on the train and watched as the conductor was given a tip to keep an eye on him.

And yet, the next two years turned out not to be the nightmare he had expected. They were to be an important part of his education, although not his formal education since he spent as little time as possible at school. Instead, he found great solace and pleasure in Budapest's many cinemas and theatres. His grandfather's ten-*pengő* note (worth about three U.S. dollars at the time – a lot of money) bought him a season ticket to the National Theatre and the Opera. The money from uncles and aunts allowed him to pick and choose between about thirty venues catering to a wide variety of tastes. In venues ranging from cabarets to open-air theatres in public parks he saw brilliant political satires, nationalist "folk theatre," Viennese farces and even – as he later put it – a few downright vulgar spectacles. In the traditional establishments like the magnificent Madách Theatre (now the home of Lloyd Webber musicals), he admired translations of classical French dramas, and was fired up by contemporary Hungarian plays.

Most impressive of all was the National Theatre of Hungary, which in John's time was housed downtown in a graceful nineteenth century building on Blaha Lujza Square. One of the best-appointed theatres in Europe, with plush red carpets and ornate seats, gilded panels and oversize chandeliers, its main stage featured the great works of Shakespeare, Schiller and Lessing, as well as Hungarian classics and contemporary plays. All of this was performed in the grand style, with "acting that matched the size of the theatre," in John's memory. It also had a smaller *Kammer* (chamber) theatre, where he saw more intimate modern plays by Cocteau, Ibsen and Shaw. The National Theatre indelibly shaped John's sense of excellence in theatre:

> I knew when I came into contact with something great. I worshipped the great actress Gizi Bajor, whom I saw in *Camille*. I still recall the scene when she was standing silently in the middle of the great stage, her long white dress spreading around her like frozen waves. The gambling casino with its green velvet tables was ablaze with lights. Her lover, furious at her, paced up and down clutching a handful of banknotes. He turned, and threw the money at her. It flew around her like dirty paper in the wind, and the whole theatre was hushed with a silence which rang with the words of his anger. Then a small cry as she turned quickly, and the one big rose on her breast flashed and seemed to spread like blood as she fell onto the blue carpet, and the curtain came down.

Another powerful memory was furnished by Harald Kreutzberg, the German dancer. Although past his dancing prime at forty, Kreutzberg still shone with greatness. John was mesmerized:

> He [was] a short, stocky man with a completely bald head. He always danced alone. In the recital he was accompanied only by a piano player. Then I saw what pantomime could do on stage, and how much more effective it can be, at times, than the spoken word.

He did a dance, or rather a dance pantomime, after the Dürer Totentanz series of woodcuts. With the twist of a scarf, the changing of a cap, he became the peasant, the merchant, the whore, the scholar and the king…and always Death lurked on the stage, now sitting just over the footlights, now crouching behind a wing, now sitting up with dangling legs…the Death which was not there but was as real as the peasant and the whore. He danced a Spanish troubadour song and never again have I heard such singing of a love song, such playing of a guitar, as when no one sang and no one played, but only Kreutzberg, the short, bald dancer moved.

As well as the theatre, some of his happiest moments were spent in cinemas, where he fell under the spell of American movies. Though inspired by the grandeur of films like *Gone with the Wind* and the action scenes in Westerns, his imagination was most captured by the sophisticated fare served up by directors like Frank Capra and Ernst Lubitsch. His perfect America was that of Carole Lombard and William Powell in *My Man Godfrey* – one of fine mansions, elegant clothes and witty repartee.

The theatre and cinema may have helped him avoid thinking about the worsening position of Jews in Hungary, which was readily apparent to anyone reading the newspapers. The third of the "Jewish Laws" was passed by the legislature in mid-1941 and followed Germany's Nuremberg Laws in defining Jews by race rather than religion. Jewish rights to property and work were increasingly curtailed. Less available was news about the massacres and deportations of Jews in the territories annexed by Hungary in Slovakia, Ruthenia and Transylvania by agreement with Germany and Italy. But in Budapest, Jewish students like John continued to go to school and Jewish social programs sprang up to assist those who could no longer seek help from the state or traditional institutions. All was not right in Hungary, but enough was right for him to continue a life that suited him, with theatre and cinema providing both escape and an education.

A further blow to John's foundations occurred in 1942 when the Jewish *gimnázium* was closed, and he returned to Siófok. The old, secure life was gone. Sixty Jewish men – about one-quarter of the town's Jewish population – had been sent into the forced labour corps in late 1940, although those over the age of forty were soon allowed to come home. The repression does not appear to have been uniform or whole-hearted on the part of local authorities: some Jewish properties were confiscated, others not; economic and cultural activities were restricted but not forbidden. As a decorated veteran of the First World War, John's father (and one other Jewish veteran in town, a plumber) was spared some of the repressive measures visited on other Jews in town, and was convinced that this would continue to be so.

Some of the townspeople embraced the official anti-Semitism. The family's windows were hit by the occasional stone, and cries of "bastard Jew" and "Christ-killer" began to follow John when he walked through the town. Years later, John would describe a growing sense of shame and self-hatred inflicted by the daily accusation of crimes he knew he hadn't committed, yet which some part of him believed.

Despite threats and humiliations, and the departure of some Jews who were able to secure visas to other countries, the Hirsch family and hundreds of thousands like them continued to hope that events would eventually change in their favour. They had weathered bad times before, and God willing they would do so now. Mór Hirsch continued to pray each day. John watched with increasing anger and incredulity as his grandfather put on his phylacteries in the morning and in the evening, blessing the sunrise and the sunset and the bread that was increasingly scarce. One day John screamed at him, "Why are you praying, what's the point in praying?" Yet still Mór Hirsch prayed.

John's mother Ilona, with her Germanophile background, retained a stubborn measure of faith that the nation that had produced Beethoven and Goethe would come to its senses. For his part, John's father took refuge in patriotism. Leave the country? Never. He was a Hungarian, he insisted, as had been his whole family for hundreds of years, and he could not believe that his homeland would harm him or his children. Events gave just enough support to that faith to sustain them for another year or two. By now an Axis satellite, Hungary nonetheless retained a considerable degree of independence and was thus Jewry's last place of safety during the Holocaust. For the first four years of the war, some 800,000 Jews continued to live there in relative security, more so than in almost any other German-occupied or -allied state in Europe. Under Admiral Horthy and Prime Minister Miklós Kállay, the government paid elaborate lip service to Hitler's demands to eliminate Hungarian Jews, but in reality dragged their feet. Nazi demands for mass deportations were rejected on the grounds that the economic effects on Hungary would be too heavy and the time was not yet ripe. There was food rationing, but shortages were few. There was censorship, but some of the newspapers and journals hardly disguised the anti-Nazi opinions of their editors and contributors. Books were published and plays staged in Budapest whose themes openly decried Nazi ideology. Besides, everyone knew that the Allied forces were advancing and the war would end soon.

The foundations were utterly smashed in mid-March 1944. Frustrated by Kállay and Horthy's prevarication, and with Soviet forces about to enter Hungary, the Germans decided to take the country in hand. In the early morning hours of Sunday, March 19, 1944 the German army, without firing a shot, overran the country. In short order Prime Minister Kállay was replaced and Admiral Horthy sidelined. On March 31, the new regime decreed that Jews would wear the yellow star. Other decrees definitively banned all Jews from the public services and professions, and authorized confiscation of major and minor assets, from businesses to bicycles. At the same time, a Special Operational Commando arrived to organize mass deportations under the personal supervision of Adolf Eichmann. Throughout May and June the deportations were carried out systematically from region to region, with the exception of Budapest, where they were scheduled to occur after the provinces had been cleared. By the end of June about 400,000 Jews had been deported.

In Siófok, the Hirschs' various business licences were revoked in March, like those of all the town's Jewish merchants. On April 5 they were ordered to wear the yellow star and to fire any Christian servants. The confiscation of houses and apartments began soon after, and the Jewish primary school was closed on April 19. John's father was arrested and sent to work camp in Germany, where he died, possibly shot during the course of a forced march. On June 29 Hungarian gendarmes supervised by German soldiers put 135 women, 62 men and an unknown number of children on a train bound for an improvised camp in nearby Veszprém, where they stayed a few weeks. John's mother and eight-year-old brother István, and most of his young friends – including his sixteen-year-old fellow puppeteer, Éva Weinberger – were in that group. The stay in Veszprém lasted only a few weeks before they were again herded onto a train, this time bound for Auschwitz where Ilona and István perished.

Of the 550 Jews living in Siófok in 1939, a total of 79 survived the war. John was one of them, for the very simple reason that his parents had sent him back to Budapest the previous year.

John had celebrated his bar mitzvah on his thirteenth birthday in a hurried backyard ceremony. A few days later, in the early morning, he was whisked away from home by an old friend, his grandmother's former maid. Another departure from Siófok:

> It was very early in the morning, and the train was leaving around 6:30. Most of the people in the house were still asleep so there was no way of saying goodbye to anyone. My father was up, and he ran to the baker and bought two rolls which my mother stuck into my pockets. I remember they were still hot. My mother and father kissed me goodbye and that was the last I saw of them.

John's mother Ilona, evidently less trusting than her patriotic husband, had devised the plan, hoping that in Budapest there would be a greater possibility of anonymity (she was not alone, for several thousand other Jews from the provinces also took up this strategy, including an estimated fifty people from Siófok). John's grandfather, now eighty-five, had already been sent to Budapest separately, where he lived with John's paternal uncle Lajos.

The last message John received from any of his family came in the form of a postcard, which found its way to him in Budapest. It was from his mother: Ilona had thrown it off the cattle car taking her to Auschwitz. As John recounted later, "She had scrawled ten lines on that postcard, nine of them in Hungarian and one in French. The French line was a joke about the situation she found herself in. I kept the card for years and lost it when I was mugged in N.Y. When that happened I did my best to remember her tip that it's best to laugh in the face of absurd tragedy because you have no other recourse."

The story of the postcard sounds improbable, and John himself referred to it as a "miracle." Yet we know that during this period, when Hungarian Jewry were being destroyed and Europe was burning outside the country's borders, the Hungarian postal system was functioning normally. An eyewitness who was in the camp in Veszprém at the same time as the Hirsches remembered Hungarian gendarmes cooperating with inmates to send their mail for them – at the same time that they were divesting them of wedding rings and money. Ilona Hirsch, like everyone else, would had been allowed to take some personal belongings and supplies with her, part of the subterfuge used by Eichmann to convince deportees that they were going to new homes, not their deaths. It is perfectly plausible for her to have thrown a stamped postcard from the train and for some civic-minded soul to have picked it up and posted it for her. The history of the Holocaust is full of such improbable events. As the Nobel Prize laureate Czeslaw Milosz said in his essay defending the implausible number of coincidental meetings in Pasternak's *Dr. Zhivago*: "Anyone who has lived through wars and revolutions knows that in a human anthill on fire the numbers of extraordinary meetings and unbelievable coincidences multiplies tremendously in comparison with periods of peace and everyday routine." In Hungary, the anthill was truly on fire.

In Budapest John lived with his uncle, Pál Horvát, at 44 Hernád Street in an old corner apartment building they shared with several other families. Budapest Jews had by this time been concentrated in an area comprising about 2,000 buildings, each marked by a yellow star. Admiral Horthy was removed from office in October while trying to negotiate Hungary's surrender with the Soviets, and the fascist Arrow Cross party took power in Budapest with the support of the German occupiers. In collaboration with Eichmann's organization, the new authorities organized new deportations from Budapest. Yet even then, the Final Solution didn't run according to plan in Hungary. The deportations were delayed by pressure from both international and national sources, notably the Catholic Primate and several prominent Protestant churchmen. Several thousand Jews were placed under the protection of the Portuguese, Swedish and Swiss diplomatic missions. But as the year drew to an end, the situation grew ever more desperate. Within the city, gangs of Arrow Cross members and Hungarian army deserters made sporadic raids, shooting and assaulting Jews. On November 2 shells began to rain on Budapest as the Russians arrived on the city's outskirts. John remembered the terrible winter days when the Red Army had besieged the city: "There was no light, no water, no food. During the day we were allowed to go out into the streets for an hour or two. I used to take a big kitchen knife and a basket and look for dead horses so that we cut some meat off their carcasses. Corpses were piled up all winter like cordwood."

After fierce fighting, the Soviet forces took the city on February 13, 1945. About 100,000 Jews remained in the city, which had suffered widespread damage from Soviet bombing and artillery, as well as demolition carried out by the retreating Germans.

The Red Army victory came too late for Mór Hirsch. Weeks before Russian soldiers entered Budapest, the old man died in a makeshift ghetto hospital, crying out in his delirium for a piece of bread. John Hirsch was fourteen years old, and the world he had known and loved was gone.

Two

Adrift in Europe

IN THE EARLY DAYS after the fall of Budapest, John's priority was survival. During this period he did and saw things that haunted him in later life, surfacing occasionally in dreams, poems and other writings:

> I looted with the grownups
> Packed my baskets with food
> Stole a renaissance portrait and gave it to my dying aunt
> Followed a Russian soldier
> Into a bombed out house
> And took home a loaf of bread.

Food was the priority. Marianne Guttman, who lived in the apartment next to John and his uncle, remembered living mostly on dried green peas begged from friends and neighbours. The result was scurvy, with bleeding gums and sores on her skin that wouldn't heal. There was also the cold to contend with, since fuel was scarce and expensive. Trips to the Városliget park in the centre of Budapest yielded kindling if one had the strength to go and collect it, but more often it was the family furniture – chairs, tables, whatever could be cut up – that went into the stove. Many years later, John would remember sitting in his freezing bedroom, huddled under a rug, listening to Ella Fitzgerald on the American Armed Forces Radio Service. It was the beginning of a love affair with the American singer that would last the rest of his life. "Her English words, peppered with the static of my ancient radio, were like strange food to me, and being half-starved, it didn't matter to me what these strange hors d'oeuvres were. They were extraordinarily nourishing." Her voice, light and playful, spoke to him of hope and freedom, a total contrast to the patriotic marches played incessantly by the Russians over the loudspeakers they set up in different parts of the city.

As the winter gave way to spring of 1945, the fifteen-year-old roamed the city and its environs, looking for food and opportunities to buy, sell, or sometimes steal something of value. A day could be called good when he was able to lay his hands on two boxes of shoe polish, which he could barter for food. But the next day was bad: the polish was ruined when he was forced to hand over his belongings to be processed through a disinfecting chamber. Some days were mixed, like the day he met a soldier willing to trade a container of sugar for a packet of salt; a few hours later, he discovered that the container had a false bottom. And then there was the excellent day when he not only acquired some eggs during one of his forays outside the city but also found a bicycle that allowed him to ride back to Budapest, where he swapped the eggs for other foodstuffs.

Like so many other lost souls in any war's aftermath, he desperately wanted to go home. One day he set off westwards towards Siófok, a hundred kilometres away across the flat Hungarian landscape. The bicycle fell apart and he walked, occasionally hitching rides in peasants' carts, sleeping wherever he could. Finally he reached the Sió canal where it opened onto the lake.

It was a beautiful sunny day in early spring, but still cool. John walked along the canal he knew so well, stepping carefully to avoid crushing small patches of yellow and purple wild flowers. Even though he knew by now what had happened to his family, he was under the sway of a "phantasmagorical belief" that when he got home he would find his mother, father and various relatives sitting under the trees in the courtyard, talking and laughing as they always did. They would all have dinner together and then he would sleep in his own bed.

The reality could not have been more cruel. Before he even reached his house, a passerby yelled at him, "So, you've come back, you dirty Jew!" Panicking, he ran the rest of the way only to find devastation. The windows on the family home were all broken and he could barely make out the name József Hirsch engraved on the open iron gates. The courtyard was now a haven for feral cats. Under the flowering spring trees, the once beautiful garden had become a junkyard, having been used as the dumping ground for furniture seized from other Jewish homes. Despite the mess, it didn't take long for John to recognize the pieces of furniture he'd known in vivid detail ever since he was little: the headboard of his parents' bed, the family piano lying on its side, its strings tangled on the ground. There was the dining room table, always highly polished, now with its patterns of inlaid wood ruined by rain and snow. He looked closer. The gilded claws that had graced the table's ornate legs, which he had always imagined to be mythical sphinxes, were missing.

In his parents' bedroom, exposed to the elements through the broken windows, he found a mountain of books "emptied like a load of manure on the filthy floor…some torn, some shut, some, like turtles turned upside down, deprived of cover, rotten with rain, huddled in silence like children on the cattle trains." Rummaging in the pile, he managed to unearth some beloved old friends: gold-lettered books of Hungarian history; the yellow, canvas-covered art books of Impressionist painters sent from Paris by one of his mother's admirers; his favourite novel, *The Man with the Golden Touch*, from the multi-volume collected works of Mór Jókai. Sick at heart, he sat down on a heap of books and stayed there. In a poem written much later, he described crying through the night, "with the books under my lice-ridden head."

It was only in the morning that he fully accepted that no one would be coming home. There was nothing left for him in Siófok.

Back in Budapest, things started to look up when his uncles Pál and Gyuri were able to return to the factory that had been the family business. At some point during the early 1940s, many of the assets from this side of family had been transferred to John's father, who because of his status as an Austro-Hungarian military veteran was not subject to the same restrictions as other Jews. During this time, John had to go through numerous legal hoops to establish his rights to his father's property, as well as to transfer back some of it to his uncles.

On an immediate, practical level, a dramatic improvement to their situation came when Pál brought home from the factory a candle mould and some paraffin, and set up a makeshift business in their apartment with John and their neighbours, the Guttmans. Candles proved to be in demand, particularly with the peasants who came into the City to sell their produce, and the small business meant that the diet at 44 Hernád Street improved substantially. There was also a little cash, which allowed John to get back to the theatre for the first time, when he and Marianne Guttman – by now close friends – attended a production of Shaw's *Saint Joan* at the National Theatre. Later, Marianne recalled that theatre was still the thing that most interested John, and he talked continually about making his career in it someday.

The Jewish high school re-opened, and both John and Marianne attended. The school was a fertile recruiting ground for Zionist organizations including one called Hanoar Hazioni (Zionist Youth), which was preparing to take Jewish orphans to Palestine. John and Marianne decided that Palestine sounded like a much better option than staying in Budapest, and after much discussion with their respective families, decided to emigrate. They and several other friends from the school joined a group of about one hundred young people, mostly orphans, who left Budapest on January 30, 1946. They travelled west through Austria, arriving some weeks later at a camp for displaced persons in Aschau, Upper Bavaria. The camp was one of hundreds set up by the United Nations Relief and Rehabilitation Administration (UNRRA) to deal with the millions of people displaced by the war. There they would wait until travel could be arranged to Palestine.

Marianne, who died in May 2001 in Montreal, left behind an unpublished memoir, which describes her time in Aschau. In contrast to the usual depictions of such camps, she remembered it as a beautiful place surrounded by forest-covered mountains, well equipped with a large, modern kitchen, a dining hall, and a small hospital. Her overall impression was one of camaraderie between the staff and the young people who came from all over Central Europe. Outside the camp, things were different. The faces of the local population clearly betrayed their hatred of the camp's Jewish inhabitants.

Marianne's memoir describes a warm August evening when John, who had been leaning against the window frame in his dormitory, straightened up, and walked to the door. Taking a pencil from his pocket, he drew a rectangle on the upper half of the door and told her, "If we cut out this rectangle," he said, "we can have the stage for the puppet theatre." Marianne was delighted to help him, and with some other Hungarian friends was able to obtain materials to make the puppets and paint the sets. One of these friends was Ora Markstein, with whom Marianne had attended art classes in happier times. A survivor of Auschwitz, as was her young husband Francis (Ferenc, in Hungarian), Ora was pregnant when she arrived in Aschau and gave birth to a son in July. Painting backdrops for the puppet theatre was a welcome diversion to her as a young mother, and she and the others put their hearts into it as John prepared his first production.

He quickly wrote a script about a boy named Peter, his friend the Snowman and a wicked witch. The plotline revolved around the theft of the witch's broom and involved chases, several changes of scenery, and a lot of audience participation – a bit of a gamble, since they were doing it in Hungarian. Marianne describes the cast and crew's nervousness before "opening night," but *Peter and the Snowman* was a hit with the camp inhabitants and staff. Impressed with the production and with the young people's enterprise, the head of the camp directed the carpentry shop to make a bigger and better-equipped puppet theatre according to John's specifications. Other successful shows followed, notably a colourful *Ali Baba and the Forty Thieves*, but *Peter and the Snowman* remained the camp favourite. The witch's line, "Oh, you broom thief, just you wait!" became a byword in Camp Aschau.

Like everyone else in the camp, John was all too aware that Aschau was but a temporary stopover on the way to somewhere else. But it was now very difficult to get into Palestine, and the stay in Aschau stretched on into the winter of 1946-47. Some of the camp inhabitants found other places to go. Marianne obtained a visa to Norway, while Ora Markstein and her husband, desperate to leave Germany, used the last of their funds to buy French visas on the black market, and left for Paris soon after.

John stayed on at the camp until the Hanoar Hazioni announced in early 1947 that the final stage in the *aliyah* (literally the "ascent" to Eretz Israel) was ready. The next stop was Marseilles, where a ship would be waiting to take them to Palestine. As it turned out, there were more delays, but in July the *Exodus* sailed from Marseilles with 4,500 passengers aboard, most of them Holocaust survivors. Before it reached Palestine, however, the ship was seized by the British navy and forced to return to France. The passengers refused to get off the ship in France, and the French would not allow them to be disembarked by force. Weeks later they were finally forced off the ship in Hamburg, where most of them ended up again in camps for displaced persons in Northern Germany. The massively reported incident did much to turn world opinion against Britain's restrictive Jewish immigration policy regarding Palestine.

But John was not aboard the *Exodus*. Although he left Aschau with the Hanoar Hazioni group and crossed into France with them, he changed his mind while on the train for Marseilles. Neither a pioneering life in Palestine nor Judaism itself sounded like safe bets – or particularly attractive ones. Instead, he decided to go to Paris, thinking there was plenty of time in the future to go to Palestine should he have no other choice. Paris had long been idealized by Hungarian writers and artists as a cultural and intellectual mecca where living itself was an art form. He waited for the right moment to change trains and made his way to Paris, arriving shortly before his seventeenth birthday. He spent his first days wandering the streets, living on tomatoes scavenged from markets and sleeping on the benches of Boulevard de Strasbourg in the 10th arrondissement.

He quickly found that life was difficult for displaced persons, who were constantly at risk of detention by the police; in fact, he spent the night in jail at least once. Yet he also met other people in similar circumstances and discovered the "kindness of strangers." Constant alertness was the key. If he managed to spend a night in a hotel courtesy of a new friend, he had to make a fast getaway at dawn before officials arrived to check the occupants' papers. Tapping into the city's lively trade in bogus documents was another survival strategy that required making friends. He soon acquired a poorly forged Chilean passport, which gave him more confidence as he went from one soup kitchen to another and registered at all charitable organizations – Catholic, Lutheran, Unitarian and Jewish – for food packages and clothing.

Being in Paris did have its compensations. Although he didn't have the money to go to the theatre or museums, Pigalle could always be relied on for sideshows to watch in the street. Even the shop windows held a fascination. For years he would remember the simple yet dramatic beauty of a shop-front display in which a solitary rose, suspended on a background of midnight-blue velvet, adorned a single bottle of perfume. He often referred to it as a model of how much can be achieved with so little.

He met up again with Ora and Francis Markstein, who were living in a cheap hotel with their young son and Ora's parents. Life was hard for the young couple. Though Francis spoke several languages, including French, he had not been able to find work and Ora kept the family going by painting glassware on a piecework basis. "John's eyes were popping out of his head with hunger when he first found us," she remembers. He often dropped in around dinner time: "We didn't really have enough to feed ourselves but I couldn't send him away, so we shared what we had."

Letters to and from his relatives in Hungary in this period suggest that he somehow found a place to stay and was no longer on the street. Although his uncles suggested he might do better to return to Budapest and learn a trade, the news from Budapest was mostly bad. There were "proletarian" squatters in one of the family properties, and the courts had been no help in dislodging them. Moreover, the Communists were slowly taking more and more power, despite repeated defeats in the polls. It all confirmed John's feeling that there was no future for him back in Budapest.

A large part of his time was spent waiting in queues as he visited the embassies of various countries to put his name on lists for immigration. He remembered the oft-repeated drill:

> You had to fill out dozens of forms, and if they were interested in you, a few weeks later, you were called for a medical examination at which they took a blood test. After going through half a dozen of these medicals, you had to lay off for a while. I had to go to bed for a week because I could hardly walk…[I was] in no condition to be *that* generous with my blood, even though my future depended on it.

The drill always resulted in rejection. He was too young for Brazil, Argentina was interested only in lumberjacks, Mexico needed dental technicians, Guatemala gold miners, and the U.S. rejected him because he was underweight.

There finally came a day when he joined a long line-up he thought was for free shoes but which turned out to be for immigration to Canada. His luck had finally turned. It was the right queue at exactly the right time. The government of Canada, after many years of urging by the Canadian Jewish Congress (CJC), had just passed Privy Council Order 1647 authorizing the immigration of five hundred orphaned Jewish child survivors of the Holocaust. He was the right age (the limit was eighteen). Documents – real ones this time – from UNRRA confirmed his status as an orphan. Even his blood was judged acceptable, though only on the third test. A great deal of paperwork remained to be done, but he was in.

Ora Markstein remembers the joy in John's voice when he told her about it. Acceptance into the program gave him entry into a makeshift orphanage just outside Paris, 4 rue St-Hubert, in the town of Chelles (Seine-et-Marne). An elegant chateau with spacious grounds and shrubbery pruned to look like peacocks, fawns and elephants, the orphanage was in effect a holding station for the War

Orphans Project, which was still waiting for the Canadian government to authorize the orphans' entry into Canada.

John spent the next five months there, along with about forty other boys. By now a tall, thin figure, he stood out from the others not only physically but in other ways as well. All the other boys concentrated a great deal of effort on regaining their strength through swimming and other sports, but John showed no interest at all. He was the only one in the group who couldn't throw a ball, and it bothered him not a whit. Yet he was also popular, entertaining the others by playing the piano and doing impersonations of movie stars and the orphanage staff.

It was at the Chelles orphanage that John made a life-long friend, a stocky, good-looking Romanian refugee named David Ehrlich. Today a grandfather living comfortably in Vancouver, David has the number A-12373 tattooed on his arm, identifying him as a former prisoner of Auschwitz. He had survived his time there – April 1944 to January 1945 – by claiming to be an experienced carpenter, a lie that saved him from immediate selection for the gas chambers and instead secured him a job in one of the forced-labour factories staffed by concentration camp inmates. Though three years older than John – he'd had to lie about his age in order to be accepted by the War Orphans Project – David was drawn to the orphanage's oddball intellectual precisely because of their differences. Though fluent in German, Hungarian, Romanian and Yiddish (the result of Transylvania's multi-ethnic makeup and his own gift for languages), David was painfully aware of his lack of education and hoped that some of John's erudition and social graces would rub off on him. Unlike most of the other boys, John seemed to have a plan and was always able to make smart decisions when faced with choices. It struck David that it would be a good idea to stick close to him.

It was also clear to David that John had another significant difference from the other boys: he had no interest in girls. There was a nightclub near the orphanage where David and the older boys spent as much time as they could, dancing until all hours with local girls. John never went along. Nevertheless, David found him to be good company, and the two spent a lot of time together waiting for the next stage in the War Orphans Project to start.

Some of the unpublished poems and documents in various archives suggest, however, that John did have at least one love interest during this period, though probably an unrequited one. A short story, written in John's university days, describes two young men getting ready to go to sleep in the same bed. The setting sounds like the orphanage, and though not explicit, the first-person narrative is clearly full of sexual longing. Another manuscript, this time a poem, describes one of the older boys resident at the orphanage, whom he nicknamed "gorilla" for his strong physique and ugly face, and who counter-nicknamed John "owl ... because I hooted my despair/ cried at night like a child." Ugly or not, the young man had a girlfriend whom he used to smuggle into the orphanage and have sex with while John pretended to sleep. Yet the tough guy cries when John eventually leaves the orphanage, and the memory was clearly important to John.

It took months, but eventually the long-awaited authorizations for the orphans to enter Canada were given. The entire orphanage emptied in late September, and the boys embarked at the Gare du Nord for London. There they stayed for a couple of days at another Jewish charitable organization, during which time John and David explored London on foot. Finally, on September 30, 1947, the boys embarked at Southampton on the S.S. *Aquitania*, bound for Halifax, Nova Scotia.

The *Aquitania* was a splendid four-stacker ocean liner that had seen service as a troopship in both world wars. Now she had been chartered by the Canadian government to take returning soldiers, war brides and immigrants to Canada. David had a great time, enjoying the sea air and the novel experience of dining at tables with white tablecloths. John, in contrast, was horribly seasick.

Midway across the Atlantic, the chaperones spread a map out in front of the boys, and asked where they would like to go in Canada. The choices seemed to be Halifax, Winnipeg and Vancouver. Neither John nor David knew much about Canada, and David didn't have a clear preference. But as David expected, John did.

"I chose Winnipeg," he said many years later, "the spot in the centre, remembering my mother's words to avoid extremes – the middle being the safest." It seemed like good advice. And besides, wasn't it a good bet that the city nearest the middle of the continent would also be at the centre of everything else?

[Three]

Our Bird of Paradise

ACROSS THE OCEAN and thousands of miles inland, Pauline Shack picked up the telephone in her North Winnipeg home. On the line was a social worker from the Canadian Jewish Congress (CJC) urgently seeking homes for six – or possibly eight – Jewish orphans who were to arrive in a few days. The situation was critical. The children had disembarked in Halifax on October 6 and were already on the train to Winnipeg. Despite a strong campaign by the CJC, not enough families had yet been found to take them in.

Could the Shacks take a child for a couple of weeks, just until a permanent placement could be arranged? Pauline consulted her husband Alex and daughter Sybil, a school teacher who was living with them at the time. It wasn't the first time the question had come up. In fact, the Shacks had been on a CJC list for almost a decade. Back in 1938, when there seemed a possibility of Hitler allowing some Jewish children to leave Germany, the CJC had canvassed Canada's Jewish communities for homes, and the Shacks had indicated they would like to adopt a little girl. In the end, however, the Canadian government proved unwilling to provide a safe haven for Jewish children, unlike Great Britain, which accepted about ten thousand under the Kindertransport program in the nine months preceding the outbreak of war in Europe.

Now, in 1947, a long-term commitment did not seem feasible for the Shacks. The time was no longer right, at their age, to undertake the raising of a young child. Pauline had barely recovered from a long illness and Alex was only a few months away from retirement on a small pension. Still, they had the spare room vacated years ago

A FIERY SOUL

by their other daughter, Freda, and they wanted to help out. In the
end, they told the CJC they would be happy to take a little girl for a
couple of weeks, just until an adoptive home could be found for
her. Almost immediately, two grateful social workers visited the
Shacks to assess the house and room, and went away satisfied.

A day later they called to say there were no little girls among
the group arriving in Winnipeg, only boys.

Fine, the Shacks said, they would manage.

Then another call. The boys were not little. They were all in
their teens.

Okay, said the Shacks, maybe that would be even better. During
the war years Pauline Shack had kept a virtual open house, feeding
and mothering young trainees from England and New Zealand who
came to Manitoba for the British Commonwealth Air Training Plan.
Some had stayed a night or two in the spare bedroom before returning to their training schools in communities as far afield as Gimli,
Brandon, or Carberry, as well as Winnipeg itself.

The day before the orphans were to arrive, the pair of social
workers returned to the Shacks with another request they clearly
feared would meet with rejection: Could the Shacks possibly take
two teenage boys for a very short period?

Since pairs of airmen guests had occasionally shared the double
bed in the spare bedroom, and since the situation was desperate,
once more the Shacks accepted. They would take in two orphans
for a couple of weeks, until adoptive parents could be found. As
Sybil later summed up the story, "And that is how the 'little girl'
turned out to be two boys in their late teens, and the 'couple of
weeks' into a lifetime."

The impression of chaos provided by this story does an injustice
to the Jewish War Orphans Project. The orphans' arrival was the
culmination of long years of political representation and manoeuv-
ring by the CJC. According to the conditions attached to the Government's permission for the project, all costs for the orphans – housing,
food, clothing, education, medical and social services – were to be
assumed by the Jewish community. Despite the contributions of a few

57

wealthy Jewish families (as well as donating money, Sam Bronfman had lobbied to break down the government's resistance to the project), the funding came largely from personal donations of people of modest means, enabling the CJC to contribute $35 per week towards the costs assumed by adoptive families.

It was not possible to know in advance who the children were and when they would arrive. Delays frequently occurred at the point of embarkation, and local committees which had prepared home placements were confronted at the last minute with news of change. There were many instances of people spending futile hours at railway stations and finally returning home – only to be called by baffled station masters and told that a group of foreign boys and girls had unexpectedly arrived. The one constant was urgency. Under these conditions, finding the right home to meet the needs of any one youngster was at best a haphazard venture. Inevitably, many of the pairings were less than ideal, and some were tragic mismatches. As the youngsters struggled to adjust to a strange family, a new country, new expectations, a new culture and a new language, they upset many a well-meaning home.

The whole enterprise was actually a huge gamble. There was no model to guide the people running the project, nor the foster families, in caring for the young Holocaust survivors about to arrive in Canada. Most had witnessed unspeakable events. Many had seen their parents beaten and murdered, and had themselves been systematically terrorized and humiliated. No one could predict what kinds of emotional problems and needs would well up to challenge the peace of a Canadian home as they struggled to adjust to a new country; some people quietly wondered whether these children would *ever* recover from their experiences, despite everyone's kindest efforts. However, supporters of the War Orphans Project chose to believe that landing on Canadian soil would bring the young newcomers a complete break with the past – wipe the slate clean and enable them to begin all over again.

To the social workers, the Shacks seemed a pretty good bet. They were exactly the sort of the "salt of the earth" people the CJC had hoped to find, and, except for their age, could have been a poster family for the War Orphans Project. Both having been born in Ukraine before the turn of the century, Alex and Pauline Shack loved Canada and Winnipeg with an intensity that characterizes many immigrants.

Economically, they were solid working class. Alex (Sasha) Shack spent most of his working life tending to the Winnipeg Hydro steam-heating system, proud of both his job and his status as a rank-and-file union man. Politically the Shacks were dedicated to the principles of J.S. Woodsworth (for years the MP for Winnipeg North) and the Cooperative Commonwealth Federation, the forerunner of today's New Democratic Party. Pauline's pragmatic management of the family finances had allowed them to raise two daughters, Sybil and Freda, and send both of them to university. Sybil was already well on her way to becoming a distinguished educator, author and human-rights advocate, for which she was recognized by her appointment to the Order of Canada in 1984.

It was a cold, crisp Thanksgiving Monday when Sybil and Alex Shack drove to the Young Men's Hebrew Association (YMHA) on Albert Street to meet the two boys and bring them to their new home. Their initial impression was of great contrast between the two teenagers. The solid, good-looking David Ehrlich seemed calm but cautious as he waited to see how things would turn out. His companion, John, was several inches taller, beanpole-thin, and couldn't keep still for a minute. Sybil thought he moved like a marionette on a string, jumping and dancing around in his excitement. Many years later she would reminisce:

> Who could have possibly dreamt at the time that this lanky boy whose black curly hair stood up on end like wire all over his head, and whose pale white wrists and ankles sticking out from his too-short sleeves and trousers, would become our bird of paradise to bring light and colour to the sparrows whose lives he graced.

Back at 148 Polson Avenue, one of a row of modest brick houses packed closely together on the street, Pauline – as would be the case so often in the future – was waiting with food prepared for the two guests. As the boys looked around, they noticed that the house was like a small jungle, with plants on every window ledge. Some of them were decades old, a legacy from Pauline's mother to be passed on with love from one generation to another. (Years later, John's Toronto home would also be filled with plants, and he would proudly tell his visitors that many were offshoots of plants given him by his "mother," as he always referred to Pauline.)

Pauline – known to friends, relatives and her community as "Ma Shack" – was another of the strong women who had such a profound impact on John Hirsch's development. John saw her as "Tolstoy *sans* the beard." He loved everything about her, including (and perhaps especially) her contradictions. She was a dedicated socialist. During the 1919 Winnipeg General Strike, Pauline had carried her own soapbox to address the strikers in front of Winnipeg City Hall. Later on, during the Depression, her house was marked as a place where the men who rode the rails in search of work could always find a meal. Yet she was also an ardent Royalist and hung the Queens' pictures – going back to Queen Mary – all over the house. In her later years she became a devoted fan of professional wrestling, which John would join her to watch on television during his intermittent visits.

Pauline Shack was, as John would describe her many years later, a deeply religious agnostic who refused to go to synagogue because she didn't believe in priests and rabbis, yet she was also a lifelong vegetarian who kept a strictly kosher kitchen. Although she never ate meat herself she cooked it for the rest of the family and the many she welcomed to her table. Food and feeding people was a strong part of her identity. The downstairs fridge and freezer were filled with things put away for the winter, for the family and for "anyone who dropped by." A typical meal Ma produced had several courses: bread baked that day, chopped liver, chicken soup, a solid main course, compote, and one or two or three desserts. Two weeks before she died, she was still baking bread while confined to a wheelchair.

"Tolstoy sans the beard." Hirsch's adoptive mother, Pauline Shack,
in the 1970s.
University of Manitoba Archives

Communication in the first few days was difficult, but helped along by goodwill and a sense of humour on both sides. Neither boy had any English beyond a few unacceptable words John had picked up during his wanderings in Europe. The multilingual David initially spoke French to Sybil and Yiddish to Alex. Both boys learned English rapidly, helped by a one-month course at St. John's Technical School. Sybil's memoirs relate that two weeks after arriving in Winnipeg, John missed getting off at his streetcar stop because he had become engrossed in reading *The Saturday Evening Post*. Even with his limited English, John had opinions on just about everything, and rudimentary conversations were soon replaced by real discussions of culture, current events and – always a favourite topic – cooking.

Outside of the house things could be more difficult. The newcomers spent many of their early days in Winnipeg at the YMHA, and one day at the lunch counter a gentleman brought John a Coca-Cola. John was enjoying the drink – much prized in Europe – when out of the blue, a little old man "looking like Rumpelstiltskin" stormed up to him, tore the bottle out of his hands and unleashed an incomprehensible tirade in Yiddish before storming off again. As John described the scene, "There I was, skinny as a plucked chicken, pulling down over my bird-like wrist my jacket made out of an old American army blanket, sipping away on the nectar of this new world, and being yelled at."

A Hungarian-speaking onlooker explained that the old man, a Mr. Boroditsky, had called John insolent and ungrateful, and cursed the day he had contributed to the fund that enabled the CJC to bring orphans to Canada. Jacob Boroditsky was (and still is, many years after his death) part of Winnipeg's local history. He owned the Bell Bottling Company, whose crowning glory was a soft drink called Wynola, the staple thirst quencher and the champagne of the North End. John told and retold the story for years as a hilarious anecdote, but at the time the experience was intimidating and the incident was never forgotten. It was also John's first run-in with Canadian Jews' expectation that he would understand Yiddish, a language entirely strange to him. "This always upset them," he said,

Soon after arriving in Winnipeg 1947. Social worker Thelma Tessler with orphans David Ehrlich, Anton Deutsch, Ernest Green, László Greenspan, Eugene Josef, John Hirsch. *Archives of Manitoba*

"because they thought they had been cheated and I probably wasn't a Jewish orphan at all."

Such isolated incidents aside, Winnipeg's Jewish community treated the orphans with great kindness and generosity. That generosity was a pragmatic one, however, typical of the times. As designed by the CJC, the War Orphans Project emphasized the promotion of independence and self-sufficiency among its young charges. Each youngster was expected to go to work as soon as possible after arrival. Only those few with a demonstrable special talent would be able to resume their educations, and then only if funds from private benefactors could be found. This was very disappointing to the many who had dreamed of continuing their studies in Canada. In fact, there was no alternative, given the Project's limited resources, but the policy also reflected the assumption that each youngster was healthy and capable of determining his or her own life.

While David worked in a furniture factory, John was given a job in the office of Aronovitch & Leipsic, a large insurance and real-estate firm with offices on the corner of Portage Avenue and Main Street. The business was established in 1905 by Russian-born Abraham Herman Aronovitch, who was the CJC's Western representative for some years. John later described his duties:

> I went to work as an office boy where every morning at 7:00 o'clock. I changed the calendars on the desks, cleaned the ash trays, filled the water cooler with the block of ice left at the door which I broke into large chunks with a long ice pick, dusted the desk tops, and stood in line at the main post office with all the other file boys to pick up the mail, and said "Good morning" to Jimmy, the old man in the wicket – practically my only English phrase. After all the bundled stenographers arrived at 8:00, I started my rounds delivering letters to other insurance companies and banks on the bone-chilling February streets....
>
> Ma and Pa Shack and Sybil were working people, and they did not believe in charity. I had to earn my keep so I could feel independent. And so the central European boy became a worker, and I learned what that was. On Sundays, the boys whom I envied because they worked in the general factories where they could earn lots of money, went to St. John's Park. They had bicycles and bought clothes for themselves, but I was a "white collar" worker and earned $11 a week, out of which I paid $6 for room and board.

John made a good impression with the firm and continued to work there on weekends, holidays and summers for several years. He also provided many stories for people to talk about, the most memorable being his first office Christmas party. Rather than attempt a monologue in his still uncertain English, he drew on his skills as a mime, seating himself on a chair in front of his audience and running the gamut of emotions – laughter, anger, grief, and back again – as he watched an imaginary film.

It was as obvious to the Shacks as to everyone else that John was not destined to work forever in an insurance office. Sybil was well connected with the local educational authorities, having recently completed a Master's degree in Education at the University of Manitoba, and she made it her mission to get him back into school. Within weeks of John's arrival, she prevailed upon Dr. Harry Stein, a professor at the university, to do a psychological assessment of John. After the test, Stein told Sybil, "You have a genius on your hands," which did not surprise her in the least.

In the spring of 1948, with Sybil's support, John approached the Manitoba Department of Education to find out what credit he could be given towards high school standing. He had no papers to show what schooling he had had, and in fact his formal schooling had ended not long after his bar mitzvah at age thirteen. Nonetheless, officials at the Department seemed to have no difficulty assessing John and said that if he could pass an examination in Canadian history in August, he would be given junior matriculation (Grade 11 standing). With coaching from Sybil during May and June, and substantial reading on his own, he wrote and passed the exam with a mark of sixty-nine per cent. That fall, less than a year after his arrival in Winnipeg, John enrolled in Grade 12 at St. John's Technical High School, where he had taken his first English course. At that time Jewish pupils formed a large part of the school's enrolment. Academic standards were high, and the list of alumni who have gone on to prominence in Canada is long. John did poorly in chemistry and mathematics, but shone in history and English. A year later, he was accepted as an Arts student at the University of Manitoba.

At Polson Avenue, weeks turned into months and the promised alternative home never materialized. Both the Shacks and the two young men silently agreed that there was no need for one. The double bed was replaced with two single beds, and John's book collection grew with each passing week.

As time went on, the Shacks felt their way into the bedevilling question that all foster families in the Jewish War Orphans Project faced: how – or whether – to address the orphans' past. Again, there was no model. The scars of the Holocaust were still raw, and for the most part survivors seemed to have blotted it out. Not wanting to pry or stir up terrible memories, the Shacks watched carefully and took their cues from the boys themselves. John didn't talk about his experiences in the early days. It was only later that he would describe feeling "as though he was broken into a thousand pieces and needed to burrow into the ground to try to put himself together." Some of the signs of trauma were only too clear, however. John was racked by horrifying nightmares during his first months in Winnipeg. David suffered less from his memories, saying today that he was blessed with a less active imagination than John. Other signs of trauma were more subtle. Sybil noted that John took to drawing stick men hanging from lamppost gallows. It took more than a year for the bodies to be transformed into intricate designs of flowers, fruits and abstract forms. If there was a piece of paper and pencil at hand, John decorated it – a habit he never relinquished. As time went on, Sybil learned more about John's experiences and realized that he carried around a terrible sense of guilt about his grandfather. When John had first spoken about the death of his grandfather he had given the impression that he was with Mór Hirsch when he died. The truth, it seems, was that he had avoided the old man in his final days, unable to bear the pain of the situation. Sybil commented, "Over the years I was able to hear several versions of his grandfather's death, until he finally found himself able to deal with his feelings, and admit to himself what had really happened."

Like all good families, the Shacks comforted and scolded, lectured and defended John. But they could only really deal with the things that came to the surface, and much of it remained buried until years in the future. It is striking to see how often he used the word "terrified" in his reminiscences about his first years in Canada. The peaceful world he had come to often didn't feel real, and he waited for the bombs to fall to turn it into a world he knew. Sometimes he put his feelings down on paper, as in a poem called "On the Anniversary of My Escape," written in the late 1940s or early

1950s, which expresses a kind of desolate alienation from the God-fearing, decent folk of his new homeland. Beginning with the line, "It is an accident that I am here," it concludes with John's feeling that he had been "overlooked by the real Lord: / Death" and that he would forever be a "transient among people / who still believe in prayers."

Beneath the surface John was struggling with the fallout of his past. Although he came to appreciate and even love Winnipeg, he frequently felt a terrible anger:

> I cried going to work on the yellow Main Street streetcar
> from north Polson, and sat talking in my head that soon
> enough planes will come and bomb these smug people, so
> well fed and so full of industry and prudence.

His rapid progress in English, which was such a source of pride to the Shacks and astonishment to his teachers, was another source of internal conflict. One poem, titled "About English," weaves together several strands of anguish: his loss of Hungarian, his humiliation at having to learn the child-like basics of another language and his guilt over being a survivor:

> Every day, not being able to speak out,
> I mutter a thousand jeremiads to myself
> In an already fading language.
> I curse and in night classes
> Learn how the cow jumped over the moon
> And the cat climbed the tree.
> The red-haired Scottish teacher
> Gentle and patient
> Teaching the th's
> So I will speak well,
> So I will speak for the silenced ones.
> Th, th put your tongue forward
> And push against your teeth,

Not de, de but the, the.
I see mountains of false teeth
Tongues bitten and choked,
Ashes and silence,
Ashes and silence.

Sybil, an astute observer of young people, reflected later that, "He came to us as a boy aged beyond his years, but in many ways he was a man who wanted to find his childhood." Like a child, his moods could swing wildly. A failed high school friendship could send him to his bed in floods of tears, and the stress of exams sometimes led to panic attacks. His life, she thought, was "all peaks and valleys; by comparison ours were flat prairies." Many of the peaks were active volcanoes and when they exploded there was no telling where the lava would flow or the ash fall. Occasionally the Shacks caught some of the heat and dust, but more often it was left to them to help him and others bear the aftershocks.

Later on, they had to cope with the wilfulness and eccentricities of the budding artist. Sybil recalled Ma Shack serving coffee and cinnamon rolls to two policemen who came to arrest John one morning because he had not only overlooked several parking tickets but, more importantly, a court summons. John's excuse was that he had been rehearsing and couldn't be expected to remember such trifles. Similarly, he remained oblivious to the need to do anything around the house, except for the kitchen. Snow was an inconvenience to be tramped through, not shovelled, at least not by him. He also made the Shacks' home a gathering place for his friends and the unfinished basement a workshop for making puppets, costumes and props.

When John needed something for his work, that need came before all else. On one occasion Ma found that she had unknowingly donated the satin skirt of her forty-year-old wedding gown for costumes for his puppets. She accepted the loss without reproach. She wasn't the only one. David, who had learned his carpentry skills in Auschwitz as a survival strategy, found himself donating his time to John's projects. During their first year in Winnipeg John revived his idea of producing puppet theatre and decided that he needed a portable puppet theatre that could be carried on the city streetcars. David not only built the theatre but found himself pressed into service as a roadie, carrying and setting up the theatre in schools and private homes.

David's earlier observation that John didn't seem interested in the opposite sex was reinforced early on in Winnipeg, when John climbed into his bed one night – and just as quickly climbed out. David remembers, "There was a kind of standoff that lasted about a month when we couldn't look each other in the eye. Then it was over and things went back to normal." At the same time, John was close to several girls during this period, and later described himself as having "gone out with" a girl from the North End while in high school. Sybil remembered him as having been heartbroken when it ended.

David stayed with the Shacks until 1951, when he was able to bring his surviving sister Rose and her husband over from Europe, and found a place where they could live together. Eventually David married and moved to Yorkton, Saskatchewan, where he ran a dry-cleaning business and raised a family of three sons. He stayed in close touch with the Shacks as the years passed, and with John. When John's first Broadway production, Joseph Heller's *We Bombed in New Haven*, opened in 1968, David drove the nearly two thousand miles to see it.

Surrounded by a new family that loved and accepted him, it was easy for John to feel safe and welcome at Polson Avenue, but the surrounding neighbourhood and the city beyond took a bit more time. He had been told that Winnipeg was home to almost a half million people, yet the straight, wide and almost empty streets didn't seem to fit the description – where was everyone? Ugly signs and billboards covered graceless buildings, few of them with any appearance of age or history. The impression of implacable, freezing strangeness and of endless winter remained with him. A poem in a school notebook begins with a flight of Cold War fancy:

By March
your nails turn purple,
and some begin
to hallucinate
about the Russians fiddling with the weather over in
Siberia, like huge underground vacuum cleaners
sucking away every breath of warmth from Manitoba,
and that's how they melt those icebergs to make good vodka.

The poem describes the sun as buried in the prairie earth, "weighed down by all this infinite winter / never to wake."

As the months passed he began to see beauty in the silent emptiness of winter. Years later, John wrote:

Winnipeg is winter. Columns of snow rising 100 feet high on a windless night, cutting through the dry, 40-below weather. White headlights of cars. Red, green and amber flash from the monster snow-clearing Caterpillars. The soft snow falls. You hear no footsteps, the snow muffles houses and sounds, the silence falls in flakes like the snow and covers everything. The black, scrawny branches fatten with white, fill out like old ladies; everyone grows round and bundled, and their faces look like McIntosh apples wrapped in sheepskin. The sun is up all the long day, the snow sparkles like ground glass, the light bounces, skips, the air is cut sharp with specks of diamond, the sky is a blinding summer blue.

A human as well as geographic landscape emerged as he became acquainted with the people who lived and worked in the long rows of working-class houses of Winnipeg's North End. There he began to see something like the Central European mix of his childhood, a place of cultural diversity but without the demons of ethnic hatred that had surfaced in the 1930s. Spring arrived, and faces emerged from behind turned-up fur collars and heavy scarves. As people no longer hurried to get out of the cold but had time to chat, the diversity became clearer. He couldn't believe it: Ukrainians, Poles, Germans, Lithuanians, Russians and Jews living side-by-side and not killing one another. He could look into the eyes of people and not feel uneasy about being Jewish – or worry about having the correct identity papers. Memories of uniformed authorities at borders or in the streets of Paris died hard. The Shacks' next-door neighbour, a policeman, tried to be friendly and always said hello when their paths crossed, but it took John months to be able to reply.

He soon came to know the shops and small businesses that were such an important part of the North End. One important landmark for an always-hungry teenager was Kelekis Restaurant on Main Street, which sold French fries in a paper bag for a nickel. Originally from Greece, the Kelekis family had started out in Winnipeg with a fruit stand before the First World War, graduated to a chip wagon that was a familiar sight in the city during the 1930s, and eventually opened the restaurant in the 1940s. The restaurant became a hangout for people who worked in the theatre and other entertainment industries, and over the years has collected a huge number of photographs of famous Winnipeggers who were patrons. Hirsch always had great affection for the place, and for the three Kelekis sisters who served the customers.

In the fall of 1949 John entered the University of Manitoba. Glen Harrison, who would work with John many times in the future, became aware of him in that first year during a History of Fine Arts class, remembering him as "a very intense young man who always seemed to be standing at the back of the room, never sitting like the rest of us." He did well academically at university, though not without some moments of emotional drama. Essay-type exams he handled with ease, even with his newly acquired English, but he never became comfortable with multiple-choice tests. He panicked when faced with a hundred multiple-choice questions on his first psychology test. How could only one answer be acceptable when he could see several plausible approaches to each question? Only minutes after opening the exam book he ran out of the classroom and arrived home in a terrible state. Fortunately the psychology professor agreed to pass him on the basis of his year's work.

John created a strong rapport with some of his teachers, who thought it worth their while to invest extra time in him. One such was Lloyd Wheeler, the Scottish head of the English department, who spent hours helping John to make his Hungarian accent less pronounced. Another was Victor Cowie, whom John would eventually direct as an actor in several professional productions, including the 1973 *Dybbuk*.

John's university essays show both his interests and his abilities. In a paper written for the drama course taught by Professor George Broderson (who also ran the city's Little Theatre), John provided an early indication of the eclectic stance he would take as a director. It begins boldly: "In this essay I will approach a play, a character, [or] a tone as a Marxist, a Freudian or a 'stream of consciousness' critic would. But at all times I shall remember that no one approach will or can tell the whole truth." The twenty pages bubble over with ideas and opinions, as well as a fascination with Chekhov. At times the language is grandiloquent and full of intellectual bravado, yet the ending sounds heartfelt:

> I felt humble and inadequate when I began this essay. The feeling is still with me. I feel as one who was sent out to catch a will o' the wisp or the mist which rises from one of Chekhov's lakes in the dawn.... But if I have failed to catch the mist, this mist which is the elusive essence of all Chekhovian plays, I think I can at least claim that I have touched it. I can claim that I have felt it rise around me and encompass me. If there is a word which can describe its indescribable quality may I suggest that word to be: humanity.

Socially, he presented an exotic figure, this strange bird with the heavy Hungarian accent, who waved his arms wildly and declaimed his opinion on anything and everything. Normally, especially in places with a strong British influence, this type of individual would be written off as a tiresome show-off, but John had the talent to back up the apparent overconfidence. He could sing (or at least, he knew a lot of songs by heart) and dance, improvise on the piano, and write idiosyncratic yet clearly sophisticated poetry and prose. He gathered around himself a group of young men and women who shared and sharpened one another's ideas in heated debate, and threw himself into student parties. With a few of them he ventured into Winnipeg's nightlife, visiting Charlie Mazzoni's Don Carlos Casino on Pembina Highway. With its bullfighting posters on the wall and straw-covered chianti bottles with candles on the tables, the Casino (where you couldn't gamble, that being illegal in Manitoba) did not serve alcohol: you brought your own, usually a bottle of rye in a paper bag, and spiked the expensive ginger ale that could be bought from the waiters. The main attraction was the musicians who came through, including some of the major jazz artists of the time. It was there that John first saw his favourite singer, Ella Fitzgerald, and got her autograph, barely five years after first hearing her over the U.S. Armed Forces radio in Budapest.

While in university John started to date a young woman named Gloria Knight, who was part of the crowd of campus intellectuals that John socialized with. The relationship lasted a couple of years, but in December 1951 Hirsch wrote to a friend, "Gloria and I are all finished. I wanted to get rid of her but another man appeared on the horizon. My little lady fell for him. I was the one who introduced them to each other. But when she fell I felt awful about it and I still do, but what can I do? So it is pretty rotten. She is very nice to me. So is he. But all finished." John and Gloria stayed in touch for many years, even after Gloria married the "other man" – writer and CBC broadcaster Norman Newton – and moved to Vancouver.

As John's circle of friends and acquaintances expanded, he began to understand the larger divisions within Winnipeg. The social pecking order was still headed by Anglo-Scots families, and other ethnic groups (not just Jews but Ukrainians, Poles and other sizeable minorities in town) were not welcome at many of the city's top clubs, businesses and even certain faculties at the university. There was a major divide between the multicultural North End and the largely British South End. One of the friends he made at this time was the poet Arthur Adamson, who once wrote that "until I came to university, the North End was a foreign domain.... John Hirsch would wryly refer to my background as 'pukka sahib.'" When John invited him to dinner at the Shacks', it was the first time Adamson had been in a North End home. Adamson was intrigued by John's mercurial personality, which could change in minutes from gleeful amusement to cascades of indignation, and was reminded of Dryden's lines: "A fiery soul, which working out its way / Fretted the pigmy-body to decay / And o'er inform'd the tenement of clay."

John's energy and industriousness were notable, even by student standards. He published poetry and short stories in *The Manitoban*, the campus newspaper, wrote and produced plays for university drama groups, and got involved with the Winnipeg Little Theatre. He made a bit of extra cash painting wall decorations at the Glendale Country Club (a golf club started by Winnipeg Jews, who were excluded from the long-established St. Charles Country Club) while still working part-time at Aronovitch & Leipsic. And he seems to have acquired a persona as an off-the-wall campus celebrity. In an interview with the student newspaper, John replied to stock questions with a Wildean relish.

His favourite dish? "Caviar sandwiches soaked in champagne and served on orchid petals."

His plans for the future? "When the Russians withdraw from Hungary I plan to re-occupy my ancestral castles, take over my oil well, gold mines and forests, and restore the crown jewels to myself. But my plans for the immediate future, however, are to buy a new pair of shoes."

Five years after his arrival in Canada with no English, and now aged twenty-two, John graduated from the University of Manitoba with an Honours B.A. in English literature and philosophy. He got the highest marks in English that year and won the McLean Scholarship, the Chancellor's Prize for Fiction, and the Winnipeg Society Prize for poetry. As well, he was awarded a fellowship to continue in a graduate English program.

The fellowship carried with it the requirement that he teach English to students in the Agriculture program. This was a source of ongoing frustration mounting almost to agony, as he tried to teach native-born Canadians some appreciation of English literature, the basics of writing a coherent sentence, and the beauty of one of their official languages. As he would prove for the rest of his life, John could empathize with people with limitations and disabilities but found it impossible to tolerate those he perceived as *stupid*. Equally, one can easily imagine what the "Aggies" – forced to fulfil an academic requirement in which they had no interest, taught by someone with whom they had nothing in common – thought of their tutor.

During these years, the surrounding prairie opened itself to John and despite his hyperbolic description of himself as a refugee from a "handkerchief-size country whose ancestors for the last three hundred years hadn't even walked on grass," he began to feel a connection with the countryside surrounding Winnipeg. He spent one Labour Day weekend with a couple of university friends in Whiteshell Provincial Park, a hundred kilometres east of the city on the Trans-Canada Highway.

At night we sit in the cottage by the fire. There is little talk. We get up early before the sun, row across fields of water lilies in the blue mist of the lake, going fishing for pickerel. The sky turns pink. For the first time I hear a loon's cry. The silence, a silence I have never experienced before, is suddenly defined, clean, fresh and clear as the water on my trailing hand. We go past green islands, barely visible – just the scent of rotting wood, moss, ferns, grey mushrooms.... It begins to rain. The lake sizzles like a frying pan.

I felt very small and at the same time could touch the sky. The prairie, the pines, the rocks, the white shells, the endless lakes healed me, liberated and shaped me in a new way. The slow awesome feeling that all this was now my country – that I was a co-proprietor of the land. I loved the place.

He even reached an accommodation with the fearsome prairie winter. In a written fragment about driving home at night from Brandon to Winnipeg – just over two hundred kilometres – in the dead of winter, he describes himself as both frightened and thrilled by the feeling of being lost in space. Driving seemed like sailing a plank across a frozen sea with no light, no signpost, only snow swirling across the headlights of the car. As the hours passed, he became terrified that he would never reach the city.

And the joy when the first faint lights appeared on the horizon when driving down Pembina Highway across the Osborne Bridge, past the snow-covered Legislature Building at Portage and Main; the old yellow streetcars empty but for the driver and perhaps a sleeping passenger; past the Royal Alexandra Hotel, the North Main underpass, Nordic Pool Hall, and down my street.

Finally home, with the memory of the incredible endless road, straight as an arrow in my head.

Summer jobs during his university years allowed him to see other parts of Canada, particularly working as a porter on the Canadian National Railway. He hated making up berths and cleaning lavatories – the required professional subservience – and the all-too-frequent drunken passengers, but was grateful for the chance to see the country as a whole. He swam in the Pacific, breathed in the mountain air of the Rockies, and found welcome echoes of Europe in the smells and sounds of Montreal. In an ode to his new country, he thanked Canada for providing him with a new home when he had lost his own:

And I am now,
in your light,
in your waters,
in your peace,
in your desert

a husk and yet fuller than I've ever been,
knowing myself like the rocks around me.

The sense of home was fragile. John was deeply affected when
Pa Shack, only recently retired, died in 1950. Bored in retirement,
he had hired on as a timekeeper on a road gang, and suffered a massive heart attack while on the job. Though closer to Ma and Sybil,
John mourned the death of this gentle, good-humoured man. This
blow was amplified by Ma and Sybil's subsequent decision to sell
the house at Polson Avenue and buy a bungalow on Churchill Drive
at the other end of the city, facing the Red River. John raged at them,
accusing them of abandoning the North End and its diverse, unpre-
tentious community. But it was the loss of the house, where he had
put down his first tentative roots in Canada, which hurt most. His
sense of betrayal didn't abate until the autumn day when he walked
home along the river and noticed, as if for the first time, the
wildflowers growing on the river banks, birds congregating in
preparation for their migration south, and the squirrels gathering
acorns for the winter.

According to Sybil, who saw him that evening, the change was
marked and immediate: John had stopped grieving for the North
End, and re-centred his world. He soon had his own private sanctu-
ary when a suite in the basement of the new house was finished. It
had a separate entrance, which allowed John to come and go at all
hours without disturbing Sybil and Ma. The bungalow remained
home for him until 1975, when he made his permanent move to
Toronto.

In the early years, John took pleasure bringing his university
friends home, as he now had complete faith in Ma's ability to cope
with any demands involving food. In the first of many occasions
remembered by Sybil, he called at five o'clock in the afternoon to
ask whether he could bring a couple – three or four, possibly more,
he wasn't sure yet – students from Africa for dinner. By the time the
young men arrived she was ready for them with a pot of meatballs,
chili con carne, or cabbage rolls simmering on the back burner. Sybil

continued to help him with many practical questions over the years. She taught him to drive and also introduced him to the mysteries of financial investment and money management. (Both proved to be canny investors, leaving substantial financial bequests to carefully chosen charities at the ends of their respective lives.)

For the rest of his life, scarcely a Sunday passed without a phone call home to Ma and Sybil from wherever in the world he happened to be. As he shuttled back and forth across the continent to fulfil commitments in New York, New Haven, Dallas, Seattle, Los Angeles or San Diego, he would stop off in Winnipeg – hardly a convenient stopover – often on the same short notice he had given Ma when he brought friends home for dinner. Sybil remembered one such phone call: "I have to be in Toronto by tomorrow afternoon. Right now I'm in San Francisco and I'll be in Winnipeg around 6:00 o'clock. Tell Ma I'll be home for supper, and I'm bringing a friend." Late in the evening, Ma and John would sit across from each other at the kitchen table and talk as though not a day had passed since they had last seen one another. The next morning he would depart, laden with jars of pickles and borscht, and leaving behind him some new memento from his travels.

Ma Shack died in 1989 at the age of ninety-eight, four months to the day after John died at age fifty-nine. Sybil died in 2004. To both of them, John was forever the boy who looked to them for trust and love, and was in return, as Sybil put it, "a son to my mother, a brother to me." John was intensely aware of the debt he owed his adopted family and never tired of saying that the Shacks had put his shattered life back together with their care, "the only glue that can put human beings together." He concluded, "You don't lose faith in humanity, and in yourself if you experience goodness in your life. All you have to know is that it exists."

Four

Apprenticeship: From *Child's* to *Chu Chin Chow*

IT WASN'T A BUDAPEST coffee house, still less a Paris café. But Child's Restaurant was, as John's friend Tom Hendry put it, "headquarters ...for a few harried souls then manning the cultural ramparts out here in the Artistic Outback." These few harried souls would, in coming decades, reveal themselves to be an impressively talented and productive generation of born, adopted and temporary Winnipeggers.

Located in one of the city's tallest buildings at the windswept corner of Portage and Main, Child's was part of a well-known chain established in the United States in the 1890s. (Rodgers and Hart gave it a mention in the song "Manhattan": We'll go to Yonkers / Where true love conquers / In the wilds. / And starve together, dear / In Child's....) Looking back many years later, Hendry makes it sound Runyon-esque, a place where, "under the death-dealing gaze of a permanently furious hostess," gamblers showed up for pancakes and sausages at 2:00 in the morning after finishing their card games, a pornography dealer named Detroit arrived at 3:00 in search of a philosophical debate, and would-be writers who were Not Able to Work (Hendry's capitals) sat over ten-cent cups of coffee until chucking-out time at 4:00.

John had inevitably gravitated there in the months following his arrival in Winnipeg, sensing it was the nearest thing he would find to the Budapest coffee house where his bluestocking grand-mother had taken him, with its elegant chat about culture and politics. Physically there was little resemblance. Most Budapest coffee houses were furnished with luxurious furniture, gilt mirrors and giant chandeliers; one could while away entire afternoons reading local and foreign newspapers and journals that hung from bamboo racks. In contrast, Child's reminded him of a railway station's warm waiting room. The place was cavernous, with high ceilings and black-and-white tile floors, and rows of thick, square pillars covered with the plainest of mirrors. Its ice-frosted front windows shone on the city-block-long marble counter, while the North End waitresses in black uniforms with white aprons and caps scurried around carrying plates of thick cinnamon pancakes and countless large cups of coffee. But the "intelligentsia," the intellectual community he felt an almost physical need to find, were there. Even with his minimal English he recognized them before he knew their names.

And before long, he did know their names – and their stories, some of which he would follow for decades, either personally or through the press. At a nearby table one might find graduate philosophy student Roman Kroitor, who would become both an award-winning documentary filmmaker and co-inventor of the IMAX cinema technology (as well as many National Film Board documentaries, he co-directed the 1990 *Rolling Stones: At the Max*). At another, art student Takao Tanabe, who would win the Governor General's award for his landscapes. Future diplomat Dorothy Armstrong usually sat surrounded by male undergraduates looking, in Tom's amused memory, like "a belle who had decided to hell with the ball that she happened that day to be the belle of." There were the writers like Adele Wiseman, a regular who was in danger of becoming a bit of a joke: everyone knew she was working on a huge novel, but no one had ever seen it. Or her friend Margaret Laurence, a recent graduate of the University of Winnipeg, who was writing news stories and reviews for *The Winnipeg Citizen*. Both women would go on to win the Governor General's Award for Fiction. There was already a theatre crowd, many of them fresh from the University of Manitoba Dramatic Society. Among them was Douglas Rain, already confident of the talent that would establish him as one of North America's finest actors, and plotting his imminent escape to the Old Vic Theatre School in England. Members of the Winnipeg

Little Theatre often made up a lively table headed by Peggy Green, who would prove an important collaborator of John's in the early days of his career.

Another Child's regular was James Reaney, often to be found late at night writing poems in a school exercise book, his boiled eggs on toast going cold. The future playwright, children's writer, professor and literary critic migrated from the East to be an English lecturer at the University of Manitoba. Years later, John wrote:

> James Reaney was a very young man at the time, from Stratford, Ontario, whose mother took him to a blind tailor before he was sent out to the West and ordered him a blue serge suit, and in that blue serge suit and a raincoat, with an alarm clock under his arm, Jamie arrived in Winnipeg. The alarm clock was brought because he hated teaching so much that he couldn't trust the alarm system at the university, and every time he walked into a lecture hall he'd set his clock exactly to forty-five minutes, and when the bell rang, he walked out.

In 1967 John would direct Reaney's play *Colours in the Dark*, the second Canadian play ever produced at Stratford.

And then there was Tom Hendry. A year older than John, Tom was an occasional student at University of Manitoba, forever changing courses or dropping out or being expelled, but always drawn back to the library, cafeteria, campus activities and what were then known as "co-eds." They first met in the university canteen when Tom borrowed two cents for coffee from John, who asked for repayment when they met again a couple of days later. The two got to chatting a bit later at Child's when Adele Wiseman introduced them formally. It turned out that Tom was an actor who at the time was rehearsing *Eros at Breakfast*, a wordy drama by Robertson Davies that was to be entered in a campus drama festival. And not just an amateur actor: like so many theatre people of his generation, Tom got his first paycheque as an artist from the CBC's drama department.

The speaking part – Buddy Jackson, a farm boy on the Winnipeg-based segments of CBC's long-running Farm Radio Dramas – helped Tom pay his way through several years of university. They talked some more; Tom invited John to the *Eros at Breakfast* cast party (where John "endeared himself to one and all during the festivities by getting terribly drunk, going to sleep behind some velvet drapes and awakening in time to recite poetry in Hungarian"); John invited Tom to the Shacks' to meet Ma and Sybil; John invited Tom to act in his first directorial effort at the university, a one-act play by poet and CBC drama producer Norman Newton...and so was born a partnership that would change the face of Canadian theatre.

In some ways, it was hard to imagine a less likely pair. Tom was born and bred in Winnipeg of Scots-Irish stock. Boyishly handsome, and with an easy charm leavened by a mordant sense of humour, Tom had his own sense of style, eschewing the popular zoot-suit for an English tweed jacket. Later on he would drive a Jaguar, a highly impractical car for Winnipeg's winter conditions. Tom had the classic dilettante's problem of possessing many talents yet having no driving passion or direction. Although he had never actually seen a fully professional stage company at work (theatre in Winnipeg had largely gone into hibernation during the war years) he enjoyed acting and was good at it; he dabbled in writing fiction and drama, and showed promise; he could more than hold his own in intellectual and political debates. Yet he also had a talent for organization and numbers. When he and John first met in the winter of 1949-50, Tom had just embarked on a course in accounting, from which he would eventually graduate as a Certified Chartered Accountant.

After a long dormancy during the war years, theatre was beginning to stir again in Winnipeg. The most obvious signs of life were at the newly resurrected Winnipeg Little Theatre, and the two got involved with it.

However, their first enterprise was not theatre, but film. Both felt keenly the lack of access to foreign films in Winnipeg, where it was nearly impossible to see even the classics of non-English cinema. Learning of a distributor that could supply such films, they organized a film society and proceeded to order whatever interested them. One year, for instance, they gluttonously caught up on all the Russian films they had ever read about.

The friendship deepened over many evenings at the Shacks', where Tom spent much of his time lying on the living room floor "endlessly engaged in three-cornered debates ... on every imaginable subject" with John and Sybil. Sometimes when the two were alone, John's fears and darker feelings emerged. On one of these occasions Tom remembers John saying he wished he weren't Jewish, as all it had ever brought him was misfortune. Another conversation began when John asked, "Tom, what would you do if I got sick?" Tom replied, "I'd bring you food and anything else you needed to comfort you." John paused, and said, "If you were sick, I'd steal your food. That's how we survived during the war."

But the late-night talkfests at Child's Restaurant were central to these years, and it is interesting to see the way the two talented, ambitious young men thought about them. Tom's writings about the period seem typical of his pretention-piercing sense of humour, and possibly, too, of a certain Anglo-Scots disapproval of ambition worn too openly on the sleeve: "Epitaphs should be written for all the works of Art discussed in Child's planned parenthood fashion but all aborted or stillborn. All the stories told to death, the novels analyzed-before-written to death, the Little Magazines that never got beyond a Table of Contents (everything by Us), the plays never put on, the painting never begun, and the poems never sung."

John participated in the same conversations but "read" them differently. He, too, saw an irony in the endless talk, but found it normal and even desirable that people should have dreams. What bothered him was what he later called the "lack of arrogance" exhibited at Child's. It was a time when the diaries and letters of Virginia Woolf and the Bloomsbury Group were being published, as were those of Gertrude Stein's expatriate "crowd" in 1930s Paris, and everyone was talking about them (Hendry once signed off a letter to John with "Love to all au coté de Chez Infant," an ironic if misspelled reference to Proust). For the bright, talented people around the marble-topped tables at Child's, history and culture were things that happened elsewhere, in London or Paris or New York, or even Toronto. Certainly not in Winnipeg, which many of them thought of as "nowheresville." John found this hard to take:

> I had just arrived, and I got into Child's restaurant, where people were sitting around planning to go to London, and I couldn't [stand it]. This was just too much. I had been wandering around long enough. I could not understand why all these people wanted to go. No one wanted to stay. They kept running down the place, they kept saying how terrible it was and how everything that was worthwhile, everything that was to be emulated, was in London. No one wanted to stay in Winnipeg, ever. And that was terrible because I had just got there. And I also knew that I had to stay there.

But to stay there, John had to put in place the final building block of a new identity. He had to make a career for himself in theatre, in a city where professional theatre had little history and no present.

As the psychiatrist Vivian Rakoff has observed, "Every act of immigration is like suffering a brain stroke: One has to learn to walk again, to talk again, to move around the world again and, probably most difficult of all, one has to learn to re-establish a sense of community." For John, a life in the theatre – one of the most intense professional communities to exist – was the final building block in his recovery from his shattered childhood. "My effort to create a theatre," he said, "was not only to be accepted in Winnipeg, but also to re-create, to renew myself. Winnipeg and I came together in a fortuitous confluence of motives."

Whereas Tom Hendry did theatre because he could (one can imagine him having succeeded in any number of fields), John did theatre because he had to. Work in the theatre was literally his salvation. One cannot imagine where else he could have found the mixture of catharsis and community that theatre provided. After years of being blown about by events beyond his control, directing plays brought John into a world in which he was in control. As Maggie Smith, whom John would direct during his tenure at Stratford, wrote in her autobiography:

> It's a world whose timetable is more precise than anything else on earth. Outside, the trains can run late. But trains in the theatre are always on time – it's strict, it's secure. The theatre is full of people looking for fabricated security. They find it there. Nowhere else.

Even death, a subject that obsessed John in the early years and which surfaced frequently both in his poems and nightmares, is within the theatre director's control. However dark the story, the cast's appearance at the curtain call is a kind of resurrection.

John was fully aware of his need for theatre and used it to build his public persona as an artist with dramatic pronouncements like "I am at home everywhere in this world and nowhere…[except] in my own head and in my art." There were other motivations, however, like the one shared with many other survivors of the Holocaust: a feeling that he was carrying out a kind of penance. "I know what it means," he said, "to be engulfed by a sense of loss and by a sense of guilt. Somehow you feel responsible that others have died and you feel guilty that you're alive." He often said he had to achieve great things on behalf of those who did not live to use their talents.

Finally, he had to build something for himself in the place to which fate (and a lucky decision) had brought him. "I could see that there were not enough activities there in theatre which could provide me with a living," he wrote later on. "The only way to become a professional in the theatre in Winnipeg at that time was to start a theatre….So one had to convince the community to support what was really a very personal and private obsession and need, and actually one had to gather other people around oneself to achieve that end because you cannot do anything on your own."

His reasons were not all egocentric or therapeutic. Yes, he needed theatre, but in his estimation so did Winnipeg. Sybil Shack maintained

FRAIDIE MARTZ AND ANDREW WILSON

that some of what drove John was the feeling that he owed a debt to the community that had adopted him. The only way he could repay that debt was to offer it – and if necessary force-feed it – the cultural riches of his lost childhood that lived still in his memory and imagination.

He knew it wouldn't be easy. For the most part mainstream theatre in Winnipeg – and indeed in Canada – was either imported or amateur. (Ethnic and political theatre were something else again. There was some tradition of both in the city, notably language-based productions from the francophone, Jewish and Ukrainian communities, but at this stage John was interested in integrating, not separating himself from the mainstream.) If Canadian business invested at all in theatre, it was not in local talent but in theatres that foreigners could play in. In Winnipeg some impressive buildings like the Dominion Theatre (constructed in 1904) and the Pantages (1914) were built by Canadian interests. Others, like the Walker Theatre (1906, renamed the Burton Cummings Theatre in 2002), were built by American companies. For many years Western Canada's largest and most opulent theatre, the two-thousand-seat Walker, was the northernmost stop for touring shows promoted by the New York-based Theatrical Syndicate.

Although during the early part of the century these theatres had brought some of the greatest international stars to Winnipeg, a combination of the Depression and the cinema had by the 1930s reduced the quality and quantity of live theatre offered to Winnipeggers. Tom Hendry would describe himself as "part of a generation to whom the classics meant a week of Donald Wolfit every five years; contemporary drama meant tired touring troupes doing *The Hasty Heart* on the last long leg back to New York; and to whom local productions meant practically nothing."

Part of the problem, as John began to see it, was simply the reigning idea of culture: what was "serious" and therefore worthy, versus what was not. Classical music was worthy because it was somehow related to church and education; ballet was odd but somehow pure, and in any case rich people paid for it; paintings and sculptures made sense because they covered walls and filled up empty spaces in parks and city squares. And always, the feeling that England – not the real country with its post-war rationing and rapid social change but an imagined England of garden parties and Noel Coward-style repartee – was the source of all cultural validity. He and Tom laughed at what was considered "cultural" in Winnipeg: "three thousand school children, all singing one after the other 'Hark, Hark, Hear the Lark' at a three-week long music festival adjudicated, of course, by some organist from the Royal Academy of Music, London, England."

More specifically, he found a puritanical tradition in Winnipeg that held theatre in a sort of benign contempt: whatever else might be said for it, strutting about on stage was not an activity people ought to be paid for. It looked too much like fun, and fun was certainly not something you paid people to have. He knew that even more than by his accent, he was marked as an outsider by his determination "to earn a living doing something I loved and was fun, when work was considered punishment, and only suffering was rewarded with money."

Amateur theatre was a different matter. It was a sociable form of entertainment in the years before radio was widely available and in the many places not served by a nearby cinema. In 1930, for example, the Manitoba Drama League had ninety member groups around the province. Not only did amateur theatre have the virtue of costing nothing, but it often had the support of the top people in society – or at least their wives. Across Canada performances of suitable plays by men and women who were not motivated by commercial gain were tolerated and even encouraged. The Winnipeg Little Theatre, established in 1921 as the Winnipeg Community Players, was one of the country's best and most successful. It flourished for many years under the direction of John Craig but died in 1938 after it lost the support of crucial society figures such as Lady Tupper (granddaughter by marriage of the former prime minister, she had been one of the founders and had both acted and directed there) and the wealthy Richardson family.

The Winnipeg Little Theatre had come back to life just after John arrived in Canada, under the gentlemanly direction of one of John's University of Manitoba professors, the Oxford-educated George Broderson, and the province's Supervisor of Physical Education, Leeds-born Robert Jarman. The venue was the former Pantages Theatre, which had been bought by the city and renamed the Playhouse.

John began by hanging around the Little Theatre rehearsals, volunteering for any work they cared to give him like painting and designing sets, doing odd jobs and playing small parts. His first stage appearance came in October 1950. The role was a one-line part in a production of Sheridan's comedy *The Rivals*, directed by Peggy Green, which required him to wear purple tights. Looking back, he would write: "The audience wasn't listening. They were looking at my tights. Besides, my strong Hungarian accent didn't fit very well with the eighteenth century English atmosphere."

Much of what John wrote about this period is highly critical. The Winnipeg Little Theatre put on four shows a year for two nights each. He was incredulous. How could it be that Budapest, a city of one million, had supported twenty professional theatres in the 1930s, while Winnipeg with half a million couldn't support a single one? The audience of about seven hundred faithful souls who turned out for each show came under his critical scrutiny: "Even the most dedicated theatre-goers in the group could be spotted wearing the same moth-eaten pieces of fur with the same flowered hats, gloves and reticules. They regarded theatre as a social obligation and paraded about in their well-brushed tuxedos as further proof of their devotion to culture."

He didn't much care for the Playhouse as a space (he thought its acoustics muddy), or for many of the people who trod its forty-year-old boards. Or rather, he didn't care for their attitude toward theatre, specifically their lack of professional aspiration: "... all the housewives that used to act once a year and thought they were Sarah Bernhardt" and "all those, bless their hearts, professors of English at universities who were really Peter Brook underneath it all."

He was unimpressed by the choice of plays, which tended to focus on well-known British authors like Shaw, Priestly, and Coward, along with the occasional Broadway success. Outside of the one-act plays written especially for the Dominion Drama Festival, no Canadian plays were staged. (In fact, the only full-length Canadian play he saw performed during his first decade in Canada was a University of Manitoba production of *Dark Harvest* by Gwen Pharis Ringwood. The director was George Broderson, whom John held in some respect despite the above-quoted remark about professors of English.)

But his strongest criticism was for the annual Dominion Drama Festival. The DDF was a national institution that ran from 1932 to 1978, with a break for the war years. It was created under the patronage of Vere Brabazon Ponsonby, the Ninth Earl of Bessborough (an Irish peer, rather than an English one), who was Governor General from 1931 to 1935. The major theatrical event of the year in Winnipeg, as in many cities and towns across the country, was the province-level adjudication of the Festival. John found the gatherings in the lobby of the Playhouse laughably pretentious, particularly the entrance of the "little god" – the adjudicator, almost always an Englishman. While some of the adjudicators, particularly at the national level, were indeed knowledgeable (including stars like Michel Saint-Denis, director of the Old Vic and eventual founder of the National Theatre School of Canada in 1960), others were experts only by virtue of their accent:

....Little Theatre groups from Brandon, Flin Flon, and Dauphin came to Winnipeg to put on their plays in front of this out-of-work British actor in a tuxedo hired by the Dominion Drama Festival to come across the ocean to pass judgment. The adjudicators were colourful people who regaled us with anecdotes about Noel, Gertie, Binky and John. We were duly impressed. When they adjudicated they spoke like Professor Higgins, but after the show in the bar of the Marlborough Hotel they became more and more like Mr. Doolittle.

Nonetheless, the DDF was important to anyone interested in the theatre, and John played the game. In 1952, for instance, the Little Theatre entered John's production of *Pussycat, Pussycat, Where Have You Been?*, a one-act farce by Norman Newton (the "other man" who had married John's former girlfriend, Gloria) with Tom Hendry in the lead as an over-sexed tomcat facing castration.

As well as their activities at the Little Theatre, both young men were busy with their studies and other activities in the early 1950s. Yet both were determined to make at least part of their living from the theatre. They eventually hit on the idea of forming a puppet theatre. This was something that John had always loved, but they also reasoned that it might be easier to find financial support for a project aimed at children than one for adult audiences.

They were right. Financial support was obtained from the Junior League, a women's service group John would refer to as "the girls with their cashmere sweaters and pearls." The Junior League had been established in 1928 and already had a long history of fund-raising and volunteer work. John approached the group and made his pitch: if the Junior League would provide $200, he and his colleagues would start a puppet theatre and take it from school to school. The Junior League members were delighted. They not only provided the money, but it was frequently one or another of them who ended up driving the Muddiwater Puppets Theatre to its performances, most of which were on Saturday mornings (the artistic director still being a student). The "girls" at that time included Kathleen Richardson and Jane Heffelfinger, both of whom would be important supporters of John and his projects for years to come. The Richardson family was one of the wealthiest in the city, while Jane Heffelfinger's husband George was president of the National Grain Company.

Muddiwater's first production was *Peter and the Snowman*, a somewhat modified version of the script John had written in the displaced persons camp at Aschau, Germany. The troupe comprised three other members including, in the role of the Snowman, an eighteen-year-old designer named Mark Negin who also created the sets and costumes. (At the time Negin was known by his first name, Louis. He later changed his name to Mark, his middle name, in order to avoid confusion with his cousin Louis Negin, the actor.) Negin, who would work several times with John in the future, including on his celebrated 1973 production of *The Dybbuk*, had studied stage design at the Willesden School of Art in his native London. On arrival in Winnipeg he had quickly found paid employment at Eaton's department store creating decorations for the annual Santa Claus parade, and volunteered at the Little Theatre. The Little Theatre connection was a useful one. Negin's occasional late arrivals at work were accepted when he explained that he had been up late at rehearsals the night before. Now retired from the theatre (though still active as an artist), he remembers the Muddiwater/Children's Theatre period between 1953 and 1955 as great fun: "We were all doing what we wanted to be doing. And the Junior League were marvellous to us. John pretty much left me alone to do the sets and costumes, while he and Tom shared the writing."

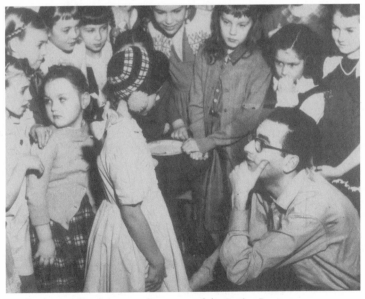

Hirsch at a performance of the Junior League
Children's Theatre, mid-1950s.
Archives of Manitoba

Part of the fun was the furious activity in the Muddiwater workshop – the basement of the Shacks' house on Churchill Drive. As usual, John pulled in whomever he thought could contribute to his projects. For example, some of the puppet costumes were sewn by Chaika Wiseman, Adele's mother, who later became well known for making exquisite cloth dolls derived from her Ukrainian childhood memories (Chaika and her doll-making provide the focus of her daughter's 1978 book *Old Woman at Play*.) David Ehrlich was once again drafted as a free source of carpentry, constructing a light theatre that could be transported easily in a station wagon.

The puppet theatre played in schools and community centres all around the city. A newspaper article at the time provides a schedule of six performances in venues ranging from St Paul's United Church to the clubhouse of the Canadian Ukrainian Athletic Club.

With the success of this first venture, John again approached the Junior League in late 1953 with the idea of writing new plays for the Junior League Children's Theatre program. This time he was given $300, and he began to write plays for it, with Tom adding song lyrics in several productions. Four of the scripts have survived, all strongly marked by the theme of children reversing misfortune (and often oppression) through a mixture of their own efforts and a little help from magical friends. The first play was *Sauerkringle*, in which three youngsters named Hopeless, Hapless and Anne dream of freedom from drudgery in the bakeshop run by Mr. and Mrs. Sauerkringle. Salvation comes through their own imagination and the arrival of a magician who, with audience help, transforms Anne into a witch and Hopeless and Hapless into a two-headed dragon, allowing them to take revenge on the Sauerkringles and their adult associates.

The most ambitious play was *The Box of Smiles*, a circus play with jugglers, clowns and ballerinas. The plot is set in the court of King Hugo and Queen Ingry, who own a box that contains all the smiles in the country and is guarded by two children, once again named Hopeless and Hapless. Enter Bernard, a melancholy magician who steals the box, captures Hopeless and Hapless with a magic rope, and – the play's cliff-hanger – threatens to pickle them in vinegar. The script encourages audience participation and features wordplay calculated to amuse both children and adults, including a swipe at civil service bureaucratic procedures.

In April 1953 the Little Theatre's director Robert Jarman died of a heart attack while adjudicating a DDF round in Pilot Mound, a small town south of Winnipeg. The job was as much administration as actual directing, but John applied for it. His application was eventually accepted, but only after a great deal of discussion. It seemed more than a little brash – the word *chutzpah* was not yet current in Winnipeg – for a 23-year-old undergraduate with a heavy Hungarian accent to expect to replace Robert Jarman's shoes. Jarman had been a fixture in Winnipeg society ever since he and his wife Bertha had arrived from England in 1929. He even had a hand in the creation of the Royal Winnipeg Ballet, having introduced founders Gweneth Lloyd and Betty Farrally (themselves newly arrived from Britain in 1939 and desperate for useful social contacts) to Lady Tupper, who became an indispensable support to the ballet. One might forgive the Little Theatre Board for its hesitation, but John took it as evidence of prejudice. Still, it meant that John walked straight into a paying, if only part-time, theatre job directly upon graduation, at a salary of $1,000 for the year.

The job at the Little Theatre also increased his access to the overlapping social and cultural power structures in Winnipeg. But that caused some questions to be asked back at Churchill Drive. Ma Shack's socialist principles, class consciousness and sense of proper hospitality were disturbed as John came home with stories about the people he was meeting. John wrote some years later: "Ma usually asked where I was going when I went out. If it happened that I had been invited to dinner at some rich people's home on Wellington Crescent she would invariably say 'You had better eat something before you go. Believe me, all you're going to get is a bit of ham, and some celery and olives.' She was always right."

John was aware that as a Jew and a foreigner he was not welcome in some of the city's exclusive clubs. But he was now mixing with important people in the city who recognized his talent and did not care about his religion or ethnic origin. The Junior League "girls" like Kathleen Richardson and Jane Heffelfinger were influential allies to have in one's corner.

The first full-length play John directed for the Little Theatre was William Saroyan's *The Time of Your Life*. Though *The Time of Your Life* had won the 1940 Pulitzer Prize for Drama, it was a brave choice for a fledgling director. Set in a San Francisco bar, it has twenty-four speaking parts – including labourers, barflies, a prostitute and a burned-out cop – and little in the way of plot. Tom Hendry played a pinball fanatic and several actors (Helene Winston, Ramona McBean, Sid Perlmutter and Murray Senens among them) would work with John frequently over the coming decade. The reviews for the December 1953 opening performance were excellent, with the *Winnipeg Free Press* calling the new director "gifted" and commending his handling of the large cast: "There was a unity in this play that made for the kind of an evening that the Little Theatre should give us."

In 1953 the intellectual and theatre crowd at Child's Restaurant were all talking about the news from Stratford, where Tyrone Guthrie was directing the Festival's first summer season in a tent theatre. Alec Guinness had the title role of *Richard III*, and, while most of the lead thespian and technical duties were to be carried out by people imported from England, there were real opportunities for Canadians to work and learn there. Some of the Child's crowd eventually made the trip eastward, and Douglas Rain made it into the Stratford company for that first season with a speaking role as the Marquis of Dorset and the job of understudy to Alec Guinness. Another was Mark Negin, who left a bit later to work in the Stratford props department, starting out on the 1955 production of Christopher Marlowe's *Tamburlaine*.

It wasn't just Stratford that was creating a buzz, however. Cultural life in Canada seemed to be stirring, if not quite taking off, with brave attempts to create professional theatre companies. Vancouver had already seen the creation and demise of the Everyman Theatre Company (1946-51), from whose ashes had risen the Totem Theatre. The creation of the Crest Theatre in Toronto was announced in 1953;

it began its first season of professional productions in January 1954. Closer to home, the Winnipeg Ballet had received its Royal imprimatur in 1953, providing, in John's words, "a model of two people cropping up from nowhere starting a ballet of all things, in the middle of the prairies, and it was a professional organization by then." The Winnipeg Symphony was being re-energized under the baton of Prague-born conductor and composer Walter Kaufman. Kaufman created an original musical score for John's Children's Theatre play *Rupert the Great,* featuring piano and a lot of percussion (the score calls for "timpani, 4 gongs, side drum, bass drum, cymbals, triangle, and ratchet").

Some of this was the aftermath of the 1951 report by the Royal Commission on National Development in the Arts, Letters and Sciences, now remembered by most English-Canadians as the Massey Commission. The Commission had deplored the fact that facilities for advanced training in the arts were almost non-existent. It had also noted (as John would find himself arguing years later) that Canada was not deficient in acting or playwriting talent, but that this talent found little encouragement apart from the Canadian Broadcasting Corporation.

John had already benefited from CBC's support for drama. CBWT, the CBC affiliate radio station based in the Telephone Building on Portage Avenue East, had broadcasted his play *The Magnificent Infant* as part of its Winnipeg Drama Series while he was in his fourth year at university.

When CBC television arrived in Winnipeg in 1954, John brashly applied for a job. His application was successful and he became CBWT's first and youngest staff producer in the newly constructed building at 541 Portage Avenue. The job covered everything from educational and literary programs to ice-skating spectacles and *Pets Corner.* The most popular programs were a half-hour discussion group called *Round Table,* a monthly children's natural history program called *Take a Look* and the ethnic dance program *Dances of the Nations.* Occasionally he managed to work in some drama, one of which was Chekhov's *The Anniversary,* a one-act play adapted

Hirsch in rehearsal, mid-1950s.
University of Manitoba Archives

for television by Tom Hendry, who had directed it at the Little Theatre. John's most elaborate production was the Royal Winnipeg Ballet's setting of Robert Service's *The Shooting of Dan McGrew*, which he co-produced with the Ballet's Gweneth Lloyd. The ballet aired in March 1956.

Initially excited, he soon became disenchanted with CBC television. The bureaucracy, even at the small regional station, was stultifying and the national network showed no interest in the work being done there. He found this out firsthand during a visit to CBC headquarters in Toronto, as he indicated when he wrote to Tom, "Winnipeg does not exist as far as these people are concerned. No one looks at the CBWT exports." He added, "If you are from London, Eng. you are better off."

In addition to all of these activities, John read widely about theatre – everything from reviews of current productions in world capitals to heavy treatises on theatre theory. He was particularly interested in the politics of culture and the proper role of the state in supporting it. A 1954 interview with *Winnipeg Tribune* theatre critic Ann Henry shows that he was heavily influenced by events in the European theatre. In particular he described his vision of publicly funded theatre centres across the country, following existing models in France and Germany. He felt strongly that something similar could and should happen in Canada and that he would have an important part in it, starting in Winnipeg. He put this all in a speech to the Junior League in October 1954, laying out his vision of what could be achieved in the city: "If you and I and a few more people like us come along and feel the same need we might in time, in a few years convince the city fathers that Winnipeg would benefit at least as much from a theatre as from a two million dollar hockey arena. God almighty! Two million dollars! And with ten thousand, what a theatre we could have." He ended the speech with the provocative thought that "this dream could become a reality in five years."

According to Winnipeg theatre historian Reg Skene, John had by this time "built for himself a formidable reputation as a theatrical miracle-worker. He had seemed that year to be everywhere, doing everything, and always with astonishing success." Yet John also understood that despite his recent reading and production experience he was not yet equipped to take on the necessary leadership role.

He therefore took any opportunity to increase his practical experience of directing, and in any form that presented itself. He and Tom continued their association with the Little Theatre, where John directed Jean Giraudoux's *The Enchanted* and Tom directed John in Gogol's political satire *The Government Inspector*. The latter was the final production in the Little Theatre's 1954-55 season, and received excellent reviews. A review in the *Tribune* mentioned John as a standout in the role of the postmaster: "Hirsch's slender frame, his superbly made up face which presented him as a sort of fawning ghoul, his exquisite costume, all combined to present a personality that was missed when he was off stage."

Also mentioned in the review were the sets designed by Taras "Ted" Korol, which the reviewer described as having "touches of brilliance." Ted Korol was one of the Winnipeggers who were drawn into John's directorial orbit in the Little Theatre and worked with him for many years. Growing up in extreme poverty and roughly discouraged from his interest in art at young age by a domineering father, Ted had become a schoolteacher. Given an opportunity to express his creativity at the Little Theatre, however, he became a brilliant set and costume designer. He and John also became intermittent lovers, something John didn't have a problem with but which weighed heavily on Ted over the years. Ted was a tormented soul who craved respectability, which neither his artistic talent nor his attraction to men could give him: public knowledge of the latter would almost certainly have lost him his teaching job. Moreover, Ted was actually part of a straight couple. His wife, Daphne Stanley-Harris, began as a dancer with Royal Winnipeg Ballet and was one of the most capable actresses in the city. The Korols had a child together and their marriage survived until Ted's death in 1998. The two were a formidable creative force, Ted with his design work and Daphne as a dance teacher, actress, and theatre director in her own right. (In 1994 the City of Winnipeg recognized the couple's lifelong dedication to the arts by naming the Pantages Playhouse rehearsal studio in their honour.)

Daphne didn't particularly like John, though she recognized his talent. But she was devoted to Ted and felt strongly that he and John sparked each other creatively; their affair was something she could tolerate. In her memory of the time, homosexuality was accepted among the older or more sophisticated members of dance and theatre communities. Her memories fit with those of Mark Negin, who remembers that there was indeed a gay scene in Winnipeg, but a very discreet one within tightly closed circles. "It was the old thing," he recalled: "You didn't 'frighten the horses.' The important thing was that you didn't get caught and you didn't do anything to shock people." In fact John was so discreet about his homosexuality in the early days that it was only in the latter part of the 1950s that Sybil found out he was gay. Negin remembers that the news was hard on her; quite apart from her own innocence of the matter, male homosexuality was effectively illegal at the time. Eventually she and Ma accepted it, but it took time.

In the mid-fifties John became friends with James Duncan, a public school music teacher and an enthusiastic singer who loved Broadway musicals and had directed several for the University of Manitoba Glee Club. Duncan was convinced that Winnipeggers would come out to see big, well-performed productions. It was a fairly safe bet. Musical theatre in various forms had been popular with Canadian audiences since the nineteenth century and musicals were much produced by high schools and amateur groups. Moreover, Winnipeg had the perfect venue for open-air summer musicals in the North End's Kildonan Municipal Park. There, among the park's magnificent elm and oak trees, the city had recently built the two-thousand-seat Rainbow Stage to replace the old bandstand that had been washed out when the Red River flooded in 1950. The city's original intention was to provide a summer stage for anything "cultural," from church choirs to Ukrainian dancing and variety shows. Duncan had co-ordinated Rainbow Stage's official opening concert in July 1954 and directed its first full musical, *Brigadoon*. John got his first chance to direct a full musical, *The Wizard of Oz*, in July 1956, under the auspices of the newly formed Winnipeg Summer Theatre Association.

All these activities – the full-time job at CBC, the Little Theatre, the Children's Theatre and the Rainbow Stage – kept John busy, and solvent. His income tax statement for 1956 shows an income of just over $5,000 from CBC, plus $550 for his work at Rainbow Stage and $50 from the Junior League for *The Box of Smiles*. But it did not add up to a satisfying whole. Nor did it bring his dream of a professional theatre for Winnipeg any closer. The most exciting mainstream theatre in Canada was happening two thousand kilometres east in Stratford, Ontario (twenty hours straight driving, via Minneapolis and Chicago) but there was no chance of his directing there. Chutzpah was one thing, solid training in classical theatre was entirely another. He simply wasn't ready, and he knew it. It was all very well to pontificate about Stanislavsky and Samuel Beckett and Artaud's Theatre of Cruelty to the cognoscenti at Child's, and to move under-rehearsed amateurs around hastily-constructed sets in a two-night run, but he needed more experience and formal training.

The obvious place to go was England, but to do so required funding. Here the DDF connection seemed the best card to play. He applied to the Canadian Foundation in Ottawa for a grant to take him to England, with the support of several DDF officials. Children's theatre would be his focus, he wrote in his proposal: "I have the ideas, but am cramped by not knowing what has been done and learned elsewhere. A year abroad would enable me to go ahead with my plans with assurance and the confidence which knowledge alone can bring."

The grant came through. In autumn 1956 John left Winnipeg for his first trip back across the Atlantic, and enrolled as a part-time student in London's Central School of Speech and Drama, a good choice for solid grounding in classical theatre techniques. The first weeks in London were difficult, as he wrote afterwards:

I once again underwent the traumatic experience of finding myself in a new land with a map in my pocket and realizing that though the map was of the right country, the terrain did not correspond to it. I was bewildered almost to the point of wanting to go home. But I had saved for this trip and instead of going home I decided to throw away the map, forget about Margaret Rutherford and Alec Guinness as the archetypes of Br. middle class; decided not to see another Noel Coward play ever again – unless given free tickets – and began to live in London and tried to find out for myself the Britain of 1957, the Britain after Suez.

Writing home to Ma Shack and Sybil from the Shaftesbury Hotel on Monmouth Street, where he initially rented a room including breakfast for twenty-five shillings a day, he wrote about how poor everyone was, and how down-at-the-heels even the venerable Old Vic Theatre looked. Still, by November he would write to Tom that he was seeing lots of theatre, loving the cultural life and living well on $100 a month. He added, "I am saying 'CAHNT' already. Shocking."

He was there at a time when the British stage was being knocked off its comfortable axis. The shock waves from the first English production of *Waiting for Godot* in August 1955 had not yet dissipated. In the East End Joan Littlewood's Theatre Workshop was bringing new methods of rehearsing and writing to the English stage and had recently given the first performance of a Brecht play, *Mother Courage and Her Children*. As far as playwriting itself went, Coward and Rattigan were still filling theatres, but 1956 was the year that the so-called "Angry Young Men" of British theatre first made themselves heard, beginning most famously with John Osborne's *Look Back in Anger* at the Royal Court Theatre.

Of all the plays John saw in London, Osborne's *The Entertainer* made the greatest impression. With Laurence Olivier in the title role, the play opened at the Royal Court in April 1957 to great controversy. At the performance he attended John watched one of his Central School teachers leave ostentatiously during the intermission. John thought the play gave real insight into English life as he was seeing it, and felt he had to send a letter to the playwright. Osborne replied, saying he "was most thrilled to read that at last somebody had 'got through' to what I was saying – very few people have, and at first this is rather depressing – but letters like yours can be tremendously encouraging."

John also spent time exploring professional possibilities in London. Through his DDF connections he got to meet John Allen, a pioneer in children's theatre in Britain. In a letter to Sybil and Pauline he wrote, "I met John Allen and had a nice chat with him. He showed me around his dep't. We went out to Putney where he is giving a series of lectures on the American Theatre. He ended up the lecture by repeating large chunks of my conversation with him. I didn't mind." Allen took him to see some children's plays performed, which John judged to be "just a bit more literate than mine, but it used basically the same ideas and methods of presentation as I do." He also went to interviews at the BBC and received some encouragement about work in children's television, but nothing came of it. He had lunch with at least one other well-known director, André van Gyseghem, another former Dominion Drama Festival adjudicator. Van Gyseghem put him in touch with the management of the Unity Theatre, a well-established socialist theatre in St. Pancras, about directing a play, but again it came to naught.

His letters home certainly show that Winnipeg was in his thoughts and the idea of establishing a theatre company there was still strong, including among some of the expatriate Winnipeggers also seeking their theatrical fortunes in England: "I saw Evy Anderson. She is doing well but would like to act in Wpg. if someone would give her some money for it. So would Behrens and Peter. Anyone, any money for a Manitoba Repertory Theatre?" (The people referred to were Evelyne Anderson, Bernard Behrens and Peter Boretski, all of whom went on to professional careers in acting.)

Moreover, in contrast to the vague "possibilities" in London, there was a real opportunity on offer at Winnipeg's Rainbow Stage. A letter to Sybil and Ma says, "Jim Duncan wrote that he wants me back by the middle of May…. He offered a 1,000 and I wrote back that I cannot do it for less than 1,200. He wants me to do 4 shows – and to do it in such a short period will be murder." Murder or not, John accepted the job and prepared to go home. Before leaving, however, he treated himself to a week visiting some of the historic towns in Southern England, and reported to Sybil that he'd had a "glorious" time in Bath, Salisbury, Dorset and Oxford.

Back in Winnipeg, John found not much had changed since he'd left. Child's was still the place to hang out and dream about being elsewhere. The Little Theatre was still on simmer, happily getting on with its occasional productions. Tom, who by this time had finished his accountancy degree, was working half days in his new profession and spending the rest of the time writing. The Winnipeg Summer Theatre Association's working relationship with the municipality was still unclear, and the largely amateur "cultural events" on offer at Rainbow Stage were not attracting the hoped-for crowds. Nonetheless, Tom put together a budget for productions he hoped would be big and colourful enough to draw large audiences. The numbers more or less added up, assuming bad weather didn't keep the crowds away.

As he was so often to do in the future, John went public with a challenge to the municipal government: if the municipality would provide $2,000 as working capital, he would provide the organization to put on a full summer season. After many meetings and much paper-work, the City declined the request. Aldermen Douglas Chisholm, who was responsible for the municipal treasury, told them they would get the money when they could prove that they could get as many people to a musical comedy "as I can to a Yo-Yo contest."

With their own money and that of a few friends, they went ahead anyway and had a resoundingly successful season. The out-standing production that summer was a musical comedy written for the London stage during the First World War, *Chu Chin Chow*. The comedy is loosely based on the plot of Ali Baba and the Forty Thieves with a complex plot, slapstick comedy, lively songs (from "The Song of the Scimitar" to "Any Time's Kissing Time") and lots of parts for extras (thieves and slave girls abound).

John and his team pulled out all the stops for their production. The starring roles featured some of Winnipeg's best performers and several members of the Royal Winnipeg Ballet figured in the more intricate dance numbers. Among the sixty extras were a group of

Hirsch rehearsing the cast of *Chu Chin Chow*
at Rainbow Stage, August 1957.

waiters recruited from the Shanghai and New Nanking restaurants, making it difficult to get a Chinese meal during the run of the show. In one of his first reviews for the *Winnipeg Free Press*, Chris Dafoe wrote, "John Hirsch and his crew of assistants have given us a show that has almost everything: colour, wild and tame animals, a gala parade, lascivious slaves, danced by some of the best dancers in Canada, and other numerous surprises. The costumes were a sight to behold. Anybody who stays home to watch TV this week is crazy." Extra atmosphere was provided by City Hall's contribution of the Christmas lights that normally decorated Portage Avenue in winter time, which were placed behind and above the stage on the Park's stately oak trees. The finale concluded with a blaze of fireworks and sent 2,000 satisfied Winnipeggers home almost every night of its run.

The season also featured two plays, one of them a melodrama written by Tom Hendry called *The Pitfalls of Pauline*. The latter's hero was played by a young Newfoundlander named Gordon Pinsent, who today still delights in uttering his ultimate line: "Go now! I shall remain to see that he expiates his diabolic depravity!" Pinsent, whose path would cross with Hirsch's many times, had come West during a stint with the armed forces and was now keeping himself alive by working as an advertising agency graphic artist and teaching ballroom dancing at the local Arthur Murray Studio.

Despite the crowds, the season again lost money, but John had proved his point. If the quality of the production was high, Winnipeggers would come in their thousands to see locally produced musicals with local talent. Alderman Chisholm had to eat his words in public about the yo-yo contest, but the Rainbow Stage never got its subsidy. John and Tom continued to be make the Rainbow Stage their main summer job for the next three years, allowing John to familiarize himself with the canon of Broadway musicals from *Carousel* to *The Wizard of Oz*. Costs were kept low by keeping the productions largely amateur, with most of the singers, dancers and bit parts taken up by high school and university students. Many went on to successful acting and technical careers both in Winnipeg and further afield.

Ed Evanko was one of the high school students whom John directed at the Rainbow Stage and who went on to an international career as a singer and actor. The son of Ukrainian immigrants, he grew up singing at weddings and in choirs, and was well aware of the city's North/South divide. He remembers John as a bridge across that divide: "At Rainbow Stage, you'd expect to have people like James Duncan and Daphne Stanley-Harris from the Gilbert and Sullivan tradition. But then there were the Ukrainians, myself and Joanie Karasevich and Ted Korol, and people like Len Cariou, and the children of the Jewish community, who didn't have the WASP box around us." John had a kind of mystique for Evanko and the other youngsters: "He had all this Old World knowledge and this passion for live theatre, and we were wide-eyed, trying so hard to do more for him. It's one of the things that makes a great director. In that way he was not unlike Tyrone Guthrie in that he saw the whole stage and everything on it, so no matter how small your part, you felt 'What I'm doing, he's *seeing*.' You had to be good, and you wanted to be."

John was already a serious, exacting director, which was one of the things that contributed to his mystique. Glen Harrison, who had known John from his first days at university and was now chorus master at the Rainbow Stage, remembers the discipline but also John's sense of fun:

One of my best memories of *Chu Chin Chow* came about on the Sunday night after our final rehearsal at the Dominion Theatre before moving back to the Rainbow Stage. It had been a long and strenuous week of rehearsals, so John said he would cut the rehearsal "a bit" so the cast could have a picnic and fire out at Bird's Hill Park sand pits. Great! About 9 p.m., props etc. were loaded into everyone's car trunks, and away we went. Unfortunately, neither John nor his driver knew exactly where they were headed. We all reached our desti-nation, a fire was started, food ready to cook, but no John! They were lost. Finally they sighted a fire and people down at the bottom of hill, and grabbing swords and sabres from their car, the two charged down to the fire, brandishing their swords and shouting "Allah bid thee good sweating" and others phrases from the show. Unfortunately, the group at the bottom of the hill was a Christian Church group quietly enjoying a summer campfire. After much apologizing, the two men did finally find our group, and the cast certainly had a new opinion of John after that.

The essential elements were adding up in John's vision of a professional repertory company for the city. A corps of capable actors, designers and stage personnel had been building up, with many champing at their artistic bits to go professional. His own prestige was high after the success of the Little Theatre, Children's Theatre and Rainbow Stage productions, as well as his CBC work. Obviously money was a big impediment, but then it always was. The most glaring lack, symbolic as well as practical, was a space in which a professional company could make its home.

Even before the summer season of 1957 was underway, John and Tom had been mulling over an important opportunity. The old Dominion Theatre had been purchased by a mystery buyer (subsequently revealed to be the Richardson family) and a lease for its use granted to the Winnipeg Little Theatre. Since the Little Theatre was not expected to fill the Dominion with its own productions, it was expected that the theatre would be rented out to other arts groups.

According to Tom, the professional die was cast at a party as the two were complaining to whoever would listen about the Little Theatre's limitations. Tired of the familiar litany, someone said, "All you people ever do is bitch. Why don't you start a theatre?" John and Tom talked it over in earnest, and agreed that the availability of the Dominion Theatre had provided a real opportunity on which everything else could be built – if they could get a reasonable rent agreement. They spoke to the Dominion's outgoing administrators and, getting what they felt was an excellent deal on the rent, they started to plan a complete season for 1957-58.

But several issues needed to be dealt with first. One, of course, was money. Another was Tom's status in the enterprise. Recently married (he'd met his wife-to-be, naturally, at Child's in 1955), he was happy with his routine of half-days at his accountancy practice and half-days spent writing. John originally asked him to take on the new theatre company as an accountancy client, but the money issue quickly forced a re-think. Ever cautious, Tom was adamant that they needed to be able to pay for the first show fully even if they didn't sell a single ticket. He calculated that they'd need a minimum of $6,000 to mount the first play, and without a backer they would have to supply that money themselves. That made them partners, which both realized would only work if (a) they divided the responsibilities clearly between the artistic and the administrative and (b) they got equal salaries. And that meant Tom would have to work in the company full time.

They decided to go ahead. The company needed a name and they decided on Theatre 77, because the Dominion Theatre was, in Tom's words, "77 good-size steps from Portage and Main." Each put up $2,000 and the remainder came in the form of a bank guarantee from a lawyer friend. Rather than fold his healthy accounting business, Tom took on a partner to look after his clients.

It is hard to emphasize enough the importance of Tom's part in this arrangement. If Winnipeg, and indeed Canada, had little tradition of home-grown professionalism in direction and acting, it had even less in theatre management. Without Tom's contribution in the next few years John Hirsch's career would likely have had to develop elsewhere and Winnipeg would have lost its place in Canadian theatre history.

Having created the company, the first order of business was to decide on a program. As would continue to be John's policy in future years, they tried to be ambitious but also realistic about what the company could do justice to in terms of production quality. The initial publicity for Theatre 77 announced a line-up of four plays for the 1957-58 season: Eugene Labiche's light comedy *The Italian Straw Hat*, S. Ansky's Jewish folk play *The Dybbuk*, a stage adaptation of Lewis Carroll's *Alice in Wonderland*, and Harold Brighouse's *Hobson's Choice*. The schedule had to take into account the Little Theatre's season, which had precedence as the tenant of the Dominion Theatre.

John began rehearsals for *The Italian Straw Hat* in September, on the second floor of a semi-derelict building near the Dominion Theatre above Jimmy's Cafe. One entered via a flight of steep, dimly-lit stairs and emerged into a vast, unheated space strewn with piles of lumber. The space was used both for rehearsals and for set building. As the weather got colder male members of the cast had to manhandle containers of oil from the building's basement to keep a heater going – never enough to make the place truly warm – and it was impossible to work there during the coldest weeks of the year.

The company reflected the changing state of theatre in Winnipeg at the time. While most had established careers in other fields (many were teachers and salespeople), a few were already making at least part of their living through CBC radio drama. The core was composed of Little Theatre actors, along with some from its francophone equivalent, the Cercle Molière. Some of the older actors were former members of the city's political theatre companies. A few were already highly skilled, others raw but desperate to learn and practice their art. In reality the company could be called professional only to the extent that everyone received some payment. The stipends were not enough to let the cast give up their day jobs, and rehearsals therefore took place in the evening. Nonetheless, the infrastructure of a professional theatre was beginning to be put into place, with activities like publicity, costumes and set construction carried out during the day.

The Italian Straw Hat was a safe choice to begin with. Premiered in 1851, the five-act play involves a bridegroom trying to get to his own wedding and having to deal with all manner of obstacles, which are set in motion when his horse eats a straw hat belonging to someone having an adulterous affair. As opening night approached, expectations were high and there was a bit of competitive edge in the atmosphere since the Little Theatre had done well with its first offering in September, another farce called *The Remarkable Mr. Pennypacker*. The new theatre group had an extra impetus for feeling competitive as the Little Theatre's Board had recently hired a Yale Drama School graduate named Arthur Zigouras as artistic director and drama teacher. John was hurt that the Little Theatre hadn't even considered him for the job, and many of the Theatre 77 company felt resentful on his behalf.

A CBC radio interview recorded by reporter Warner Troyer three days before *The Italian Straw Hat* opened reveals John both as a young man with a mission and as someone with a sure-footed sense of publicity. His accent, though not thick, is audible: "We" comes out as "ve." The interviewer lobs him a soft question about his background and ambitions, and John smoothly establishes that he came only ten years ago from Hungary and is hugely grateful to Winnipeg for its warmth and welcome. Why does he stay? "I don't believe that anywhere else in Canada I would have the same opportunities as I have in Winnipeg." He states his confidence that there are enough talented people in the city to at least "form a nucleus" for a professional theatre, and brushes aside Troyer's suggestion that once people are good enough to go professional, they'll leave for the East or the United States. "I think that is all right," he replies, explaining that it is natural for people to pursue their own careers. "The point is that you have to ensure that the talented people, the talented youngsters who are growing up are going to get good training and that they are going to have some opportunities right in their home town."

Troyer asks almost apprehensively if John intends to put on "very heavy plays with great social significance" or if he'll stick to "the frothy stuff." John patiently reassures listeners that he won't start with the great classics and that he believes in variety: they'll do entertaining plays, as well as educational ones and those of social significance. The interview ends with Troyer listing the competition *The Italian Straw Hat* faced – a WIFU football game, a visit from a "name band" and even Hallowe'en – while offering a ponderous "Hats off to John Hirsh and to all the members of Theatre 77."

The play got bad reviews in both local papers but sold out anyway and was even held over. While some of this had to do with Tom's aggressive pre-selling of the show, word of mouth did the rest.

The next show was *Alice in Wonderland*, produced in co-operation with the Women's Committee of the Winnipeg Symphony, another of the city's service organizations. The show broke even for Theatre 77 and made money for the Committee's charities, which pleased everyone. By this time, however, John had realized that he couldn't put together a cast capable of pulling off *The Dybbuk*. He had been talked into it initially by George Werier, one of the city's more experienced actors. Werier had acted in the play during the 1930s in a political theatre group and was convinced that the city's Jewish population would come out to see it in a new production. However, John was adamant that they couldn't do plays that were beyond their creative reach – and this one was just too *big* a play. George Werier was bitterly disappointed, but in December came back with the suggestion that Theatre 77 do Arthur Miller's *Death of a Salesman*. Again, competition came into the equation. The Little Theatre's second offering of the year had been a solid production of Miller's *The Crucible*. Tom and John were skeptical at first but finally decided that if the Little Theatre could do Arthur Miller successfully then Theatre 77 had to do it too – and better.

They announced the change in the season and began rehearsals, giving it a solid two months. January and February 1958 were so cold that the only place to work was in the building's coal basement, with the actors emerging from rehearsals looking like minstrel-show performers in blackface. As with most of the Theatre 77 productions, Ted Korol designed the sets.

The production was a triumph and for the first time both of the city's theatre critics praised the show unreservedly. The final offering of the season was *Arsenic and Old Lace*, which was substituted for the originally scheduled *Hobson's Choice*. Again, Gordon Pinsent shone as Mortimer Brewster, the theatre critic who actually hates theatre, and the company handled the fast-paced business with aplomb. Though well received, the play did less business than expected due to a minor Canadian phenomenon: the arrival in town of *My Fur Lady*, a student review from McGill University, which satirized just about everything worth satirizing in Canada at the time (the flag debate, the DEW line, the Canadian "establishment," even the worrying teenage preoccupation with Elvis). Nonetheless, *Arsenic and Old Lace* looked and sounded good, and the box office returns were respectable. It wrapped up a season that had proved its point: a professional approach not only resulted in better shows but would be supported by Winnipeg audiences. Over ten thousand people had come to Theatre 77's shows during the course of the year.

The experience also cemented John's status among many in the theatre community as a charismatic visionary. It is hard, sixty years later, to imagine the esteem in which many, particularly the younger members of the local theatre community, held him. Gordon Pinsent wrote in his autobiography about being swept up by John's enthusiasm about the possibilities of a life in the theatre: "I recall each detail still. John, in the low-ceilinged basement of the old Dominion Theatre, dwarfing us, wiping dripping water off his neck from the bandaged pipes while he directed us out of our minds and into a lifelong love of work and dedication to a life in the arts made possible through him to us." He also described the way Hirsch would cut loose at cast parties on the warped boards of the Dominion stage, dancing so wildly on the stage that he occasionally put his foot through the scenery. "It was all feeling and joy, a freeing of each moment that might otherwise go unused," Pinsent remembered.

The Theatre 77 season had not yet ended before Jim Duncan

was back to John and Tom, urging them to take on the Rainbow Stage again. They agreed, but insisted on greater autonomy from the City this time with a revised pricing structure. They chose a new summer season of musicals and Tom once again prepared a budget. But then he had to drop out on doctor's orders, exhausted after the strain of running Theatre 77. He passed the administrative duties over to someone else and took the summer off to recover.

Once again the season went well for John, culminating in a production of *The King and I* that was as spectacular as *Chu Chin Chow*. Attendance was excellent, and for the first time the Rainbow Stage came close to breaking even.

As with the previous summer, there was news of change at the Little Theatre. The artistic director, Arthur Zigouras, was moving onto the CBC. Don Campbell, the chairman of the WLT's Board, put out feelers to John to see if he was interested in the job. John didn't find the offer either flattering or interesting, particularly since Tom wasn't included. If Theatre 77 had taught him anything it was the value of having a capable manager behind him. He was inclined to turn it down flat. Tom agreed that it would be a step backwards to return to amateur theatre, but also understood that the Little Theatre had an important bargaining chip: as the Dominion Theatre's tenant, it was within the Little Theatre's power to kill Theatre 77 by simply refusing to rent the space to them. A better response was to make them a bigger, bolder offer. What did they really want to do?

Their opportunity came soon enough, when Don Campbell invited John and Tom to meet with the Little Theatre Board at his house in Tuxedo, then, as now, the wealthiest Winnipeg suburb.

Five

Growing an Orange on the Prairie

IN TOM HENDRY'S MEMORY the Tuxedo meeting was a relaxed affair:

> We presented our proposals, they presented their proposals,
> everybody had a drink, and before the afternoon was over,
> the rough shape of the centre had been hammered out.
> The Board of Directors of the Winnipeg Little Theatre had
> become the Board of Directors of the Manitoba Theatre
> Centre (MTC) and had acquired to their surprise, an artistic
> director and an administrator who, to their surprise, had
> just accepted a 50% drop in income, and taken the jobs."
> On July 16 the new organization issued its inaugural press
> statement, announcing that the new theatre would be "a
> non-profit organization to promote both amateur and pro-
> fessional theatre, and to operate a theatre school, starting
> in the next season."

In fact, this was only one of many meetings that took place
between Theatre 77 and the Winnipeg Little Theatre over the course
of that summer, and possibly not even the most important of them.
But it is a good place to start in order to understand how the MTC
began. Hirsch and Hendry were sharing drinks with important
representatives of both "town and gown," some of whom they
already knew well. Donald Campbell was a partner in the accounting
firm Price-Waterhouse, and Tom had articled for him as a student
earlier in the decade. Gordon Horner was a member of the Grain
Exchange, one of the most important businesses in the province
and one with which the MTC would carefully maintain a relationship

in future years. David Jones was a prominent local solicitor, there to dot the i's and cross the t's of any agreement.

"Gown" was represented by professors Bill Stobie and Ogden Turner, both from the English Department of the University of Manitoba. Stobie was a benign, modest presence whose wife Margaret – also a professor of English – frequently acted in Little Theatre productions. Turner, on the other hand, was a critical, somewhat distant character whom Hirsch and Hendry found hard to take, at least initially.

The Little Theatre board members were only thinking about hiring a director, and on much the same terms as Hirsch had run the Little Theatre in the early 1950s. They didn't want the sardonic Hendry as part of a package. But Hirsch was adamant: it was both of them or nothing. Moreover, the initial offer from the Little Theatre was a kind of sharing arrangement, with two separate organizations sharing the Dominion Theatre and an artistic director. That, too, was unacceptable to Hirsch. He was willing to tolerate some kind of accommodation with amateur theatre, and even to help improve it, but his ultimate goal was a fully professional organization. That would take money and a kind of organization that didn't yet exist.

He did have a model in mind: the late Roger Planchon's recently established Théâtre de la Cité, in France. Planchon had built an international reputation blowing the cobwebs off Molière and Shakespeare and was Brecht's best-known exponent in France, working from a small, semi-professional theatre in the heart of Lyon. In 1957 Planchon had moved to a bigger building in Lyon's industrial suburb, Villeurbanne, with the idea of creating a new type of regional theatre expressly designed as a public service. Théâtre de la Cité not only sought to attract a working-class audience, but to develop such an audience through theatre courses aimed specifically at factory workers. It eventually obtained the support of the national government. Hirsch argued that a theatre school would be a valuable addition to Winnipeg, both to train young actors and to educate the local audience. He also wanted a touring company, which would not only find new audiences in Manitoba and neighbouring provinces but attract funding from the provincial government.

Both sides agreed that the Winnipeg theatre scene should try to tap into Canada Council funding and that a single organization – particularly one called a provincial theatre centre rather than a theatre pure and simple – was far more likely to achieve this. A major sticking point, however, was how to accommodate both professionals and amateurs in one organization, with Turner especially skeptical about Winnipeg's ability to sustain a fully professional theatre. Equally important, the Little Theatre board members worried about the local actors – many of them personal friends or relatives – being pushed off the local stage by professional actors hired from outside. The compromise was to run two separate series, one with paid actors and one with amateurs, under the overall banner of the Manitoba Theatre Centre. A season ticket would provide entry to all eight shows.

One of the first tasks, therefore, was to plan an eight-play season that would attract solid audiences while balancing Hirsch's artistic ambitions, the abilities of the pool of actors available in Winnipeg and a $60,000 budget (with $7,000 in the bank). Hirsch would direct the paid series productions, while another director had to be found for the unpaid shows.

A brief search found no Canadian candidates willing to move to Winnipeg and resulted in the hiring of Zara Shakow. A New Yorker, Shakow had a solid background in commercial theatre, not only directing but as a talent scout and coach. Hirsch prudently gave her two popular plays from the New York stage almost guaranteed to sell well if the productions were good. Garson Kanin's *Born Yesterday*, the story of a crooked businessman and his scatter-brained-but-loveable showgirl mistress, had been a huge hit on Broadway, running from 1946 to 1950 in its original production, and had also done well as a Hollywood film. More serious but also a good bet for Winnipeg, was *The Diary of Anne Frank*, which had won the 1956 New York Drama Critics Circle award for best play in its original production.

For himself, Hirsch took on *A Hatful of Rain* as his first MTC production. Like *Born Yesterday*, the play had had a long run in New York after its premiere in 1955 and been turned into a Hollywood movie. Choosing a play about drug addiction was risky, as was

Hirsch's decision to stage a Canadian play, *Teach Me How to Cry*, by the late Alberta-born playwright, Patricia Joudry. Hirsch would also direct three other well-known plays in the paid actors' series: Tennessee Williams' *The Glass Menagerie*, Jean Anouilh's *Ring Around the Moon*, and John Steinbeck's *Of Mice and Men*.

Tom Hendry threw himself into selling season tickets and beefing up the administrative end of the theatre. Having no money to pay anyone else for the moment, he enlisted the help of volunteers, mostly from the Little Theatre, and got them phoning both the existing subscribers to the two organizations and a new list he drew up of potential audience members. It was the first of the September telephone campaigns that became part of the early MTC folklore. He began sending out large quantities of free tickets to different organizations like social clubs, student groups and trade unions to try to entice people into the theatre. He devised the early MTC slogan, "The only professional theatre between Toronto and Yokohama," which he later defended, tongue firmly in cheek, as mostly true. There was nothing else resembling a professional theatre company west of Winnipeg except for the Totem Theatre in Vancouver, which was on its last legs. Finally, he and Hirsch continued their policy of speaking to any and all community groups that might provide an audience or material support for their productions.

Otherwise, the process of producing plays went on much as before. Rehearsals continued to run from 7:00 'til 11:00 in the evenings upstairs at the Playhouse to allow everyone to work at their day jobs. Male actors continued to carry cans of oil upstairs for the heater each time they reported for work.

In *A Hatful of Rain* Gordon Pinsent played the lead part and Doreen Brownstone his pregnant wife. Brownstone, who had three small children and a husband who disapproved of her theatrical ambitions, remembers that Hirsch managed to make use of the fact that both she and Pinsent had "real lives" outside of the theatre. Before starting rehearsal, Hirsch would send them into a separate room to sit quietly and talk about their days, like husband and wife: "I would come in all shaken from rushing away from getting the children to bed and arguing with my husband. Gordon had a wife and a small child. We'd calm each other down and get to where we were comfortable, to live that life together and be those people, not the people we came into the rehearsal as." (Brownstone was still a working actor fifty years later, playing Yente in MTC's 2008 production of *Fiddler on the Roof* for the Centre's fiftieth anniversary.)

On the evening of October 28, 1958, young women in black dresses and white gloves guided formally dressed audience members to their seats for the opening performance of *A Hatful of Rain*. The production was well received and provided further proof that Gordon Pinsent was coming into his own as an actor. Pinsent also shone in the season's later productions as Jim, the "gentleman caller" in *The Glass Menagerie*, and as the cynical but tender-hearted George in *Of Mice and Men*, with Jane Heffelfinger as Curley's Wife. *The Glass Menagerie*, though presented in the middle of a particularly bitter January, was also held over for a second week. The rest of the professional series also got good notices, as did the amateur shows. Zara Shakow had proved a sound choice as the Centre's second director, particularly in her production of *Anne Frank* towards the end of the season in April. In Hendry's memory, the play "sold itself," particularly among the city's Jewish population, which he described as providing a faithful "audience-foundation" for the theatre in its early days.

When the dust had finally settled on the Dominion stage at the end of the season, Hendry was able to report to the Board that the season had been a success. Compared to the attendance achieved by the Little Theatre and Theatre 77 separately in the previous year, the MTC's first season had more than doubled its audiences. The season had resulted in a $1,800 deficit, but that was hardly a disaster. The MTC concept had been proven and – crucially – Hirsch and Hendry's standing with the Board was strengthened. The two-series approach was dropped. From now it would all be MTC, pure and simple.

The summer kept both busy with Rainbow Stage. This was a source of income for both and, at least for Hirsch, a source of some pleasure. Hendry worked on the administration again and ran himself ragged. But the two were also working on the next MTC season, encouraged not only by the previous season's success but also by some new sources of funding.

After years of public and private ranting about the need for government subsidies Hirsch was more than pleased when the Canada Council awarded MTC $12,000. This was the beginning of what became a regular program of support for regional theatres. Hirsch finally had some money to pay union-scale salaries rather than stipends to actors and other staff.

September found him in Toronto looking to do some hiring. In what was to become typical of Hirsch, he turned it into a media event: "Young Toronto Actors Money-Hungry" read the top headline on the *Star's* entertainment section, with the kicker, "Spurn Training, They Prefer Fast Buck Hirsch Claims." Hirsch told the reporter that after a week in Toronto he was in despair about the future of Canadian theatre. Young actors in Toronto, the centre of Canadian theatre, were more interested in "sitting around the CBC cafeteria hoping to see producers and other big shots" than in gaining experience with steady work in Winnipeg. The article was full of Hirsch's provocative quotes:

> "We're not asking them to come out for nothing," he laments. "We're offering them $60 a week, an opportunity to learn, and a chance for people to share in the building of a theatre....They say that Toronto is a theatrical centre. What's it the centre of? You can't develop a centre, without it being the centre of something."

Threatening to look elsewhere, particularly the United States, Hirsch returned to Winnipeg and preparations for the second season.

Zara Shakow having returned to New York, the theatre needed a second director, and that, too, proved hard to find in Canada, until Desmond Scott appeared. An English actor and director with over ten years' professional experience in British theatre and broadcasting, Scott had been working in Canada since 1957 with organizations like Toronto's Crest Theatre and the Canadian Players touring company. He had heard about Hirsch's difficulties in finding directors and actors willing to go to Winnipeg. But more important, he had seen that the playbill for the next MTC season included John Osborne's *Look Back in Anger* and Ben Jonson's *Volpone*. Intrigued, he applied for an interview and arranged to stop off in Winnipeg while heading to a job in summer theatre in B.C.

The interview with Hirsch took place in the bar of the Marlborough Hotel where Scott found "this long, lanky Jewish character folded despondently over the bar." Hirsch was in a state of deep gloom over the news that two of his best actors – one of them Gordon Pinsent – were leaving Winnipeg to pursue their careers in Toronto. Hirsch asked a few questions about Scott's background and prospects, but did most of the talking. He also took Scott out to meet Hendry at Rainbow Stage. In the end, Hirsch offered Scott the post of "resident director" beginning in September at $125 a week.

Scott returned to Winnipeg at the end of the summer wondering if he still had a job, having been told by a fellow passenger on the train that the roof had fallen in on the Dominion Theatre. In fact, the roof was still standing, but the MTC was in danger of becoming homeless. The building inspectors had been to visit and informed Tom Hendry – shortly after he and his team of volunteers had presold a record 16,000 seats – that the roof needed $100,000 in repairs, which would take a year to carry out.

Hendry spent a couple of frantic weeks hunting for a new venue, and finally found one in the Beacon Theatre. A former vaudeville theatre on the tougher end of Main Street, it at least had a workable stage. But as Hendry reflected on his first visit, surveying an eight-foot high "Fuck You" someone had scrawled on a wall, it was going to be a tough sell to many Winnipeggers. He held off announcing the move until the last minute, but ticket sales slowed down immediately. Equally worrying was the future of the Dominion Theatre. Would its mysterious owner pay for the repairs, or might it be the end of the building altogether? As it happened, the owner was seriously annoyed: years later Kathleen Richardson commented, "The ink was hardly dry on my having bought the wretched thing when the roof needed to be replaced." Through her representative, however, she agreed to rebuild the roof.

The 1959-60 season fit with the MTC's general strategy of presenting a range of plays to the Winnipeg audience, with a couple of reasonably "challenging" productions among the more popular choices. The challenging ones this season were the very ones that had attracted Scott. The harshly realistic *Look Back in Anger* had divided the London critics when it premiered in 1956, while *Volpone* had served up a bawdy satire when it opened at the Globe Theatre exactly 350 years earlier (more recently Joan Littlewood's Theatre Workshop – another model for Hirsch – had produced a modern-dress version of the play in 1955). With its large cast of fourteen and its archaic dialogue, *Volpone* would stretch the capabilities of the company, and in fact, Scott had to take on one of the important roles as Mosca, the perfidious accomplice of the lead character. But the other six plays seemed to offer surefire success. Five of them had already made the trip from Broadway stage to Hollywood screen, most of them during the 1950s. Hendry argued that name recognition was, in a population not in the habit of attending live theatre, a powerful selling point: "If they've even heard it or seen it on the marquee at the movies, they'll come and see it in the theatre." Ibsen and Chekhov would have to wait a little longer.

Desmond Scott proved a fortunate addition to the MTC. In contrast to Hirsch's excitability and interest in experimentation, actors from that period remember Scott as orderly and precise in his directing; in a peculiar way they complemented each other. For his part, Scott remembers Hirsch as being kind to him on a personal level, inviting him home to dinner at the Shacks' several times, but also generous in the directing opportunities he gave him. As well as *Look Back in Anger*, Scott would direct *The Caretaker* and Canada's first professional production of *Waiting for Godot* while at the MTC.

Hendry's fears about the Beacon's location and reputation had been well founded. Ticket sales were lower than hoped. This continued through the year despite good reviews for most of the plays. It was frustrating for all concerned but also a spur to fundraising efforts. Board members Albert Cohen and James Russell worked hard at getting donations, using Cohen's contacts among business people and Russell's with the Conservative Party, which had taken over the provincial government. They managed to raise a little over $25,000 from private and corporate donors and – a first – $7,300 from the province and the city.

Hirsch was central to the fundraising as the MTC's public face, popping up frequently at events around town. Newspaper clippings show him doing everything from organizing an ethnic pageant for the Royal Visit of 1959 to judging a children's fingerpainting contest with Mayor Stephen Juba. Hirsch and Juba got along well. Of Ukrainian extraction and elected in 1956 as the city's first "ethnic" mayor, Juba was also a believer in feeding the press material they could turn into headlines. He would be a supporter of the MTC for the rest of Hirsch's time in the city.

The Junior League was still an important supporter of Hirsch's – in cash, kind and volunteers – and in 1960 Hirsch spoke to them at a luncheon about his hopes for the next phase of theatre in Winnipeg. Noting that the Canada Council had begun to support the MTC, Hirsch challenged local businessmen (i.e. the husbands of many of those in attendance) to follow suit. In doing so he may have added a touch of bad karma by invoking the example of Stratford, "the sleepiest and dullest town in the world," which nonetheless attracted tens of thousands of visitors to its festival. A bit of vision and faith would be repaid many times over, he suggested. But his strongest message was that theatre in Winnipeg could only advance if those who worked in it were paid decent wages. He spoke of the local designers, their sets drawing applause the moment the curtain rises, yet earning less than junior office clerks. Acting, he said, was still seen as less than respectable, compared to the work of other artists:

> The public accepts now without the blink of an eye that in our Symphony we have full-time musicians who don't just drop in to play and rush back to their butcher shops after the rehearsal. And believe me this makes a difference. To be an actor you must concentrate and believe in the reality you are creating. This cannot be done on three hours a day or a late evening basis, when the brain and body are tired and the imagination functions at zero.

He looked forward to the discovery and support of new play-wrights to tell their stories to future generations because "only then can we say that we have really lived here on this prairie, because to leave behind washing machines, cars, old rubber tires and count-less adding machines which will all be dug up by future archaeolo-gists, and to be judged purely by the junk would be a great shame." He teased, cajoled, even gently scolded his audience, but – mindful that the Junior League had given him more support than any other group – closed by inviting them to continue helping to create metaphorical buildings of lasting value, "as fine as cobwebs and strong as steel, treasures for the minds of the sons of the sons of the children you have."

Hirsch's drive to improve the quality of actors and technical staff was actually making some headway. Some of the people hired in these early years would play a recurring part in Hirsch's future career and personal life. In the second half of the 1959-60 season MTC hired another young British theatre professional, Eoin Sprott, to design sets on a full-time basis. Originally from Dundee, Scotland, Sprott was very young and had limited experience, but he had done a summer at Stratford, Ontario, as well as some shows at the Red Barn Theatre on Lake Simcoe. Hirsch hired him sight unseen on the Red Barn's recommendation to design the "big" productions of *Anastasia* and *Teahouse of the August Moon*. Sprott found the atmosphere exhilarating despite the difficulties of working at the Beacon, the low budgets and – in his memory the main limitation of MTC in those days – the quality of the actors available in Winni-peg. He liked Hirsch and Hendry and was delighted when they offered him a permanent position with the company during the regular season, allowing him to continue working at Stratford during the summers. Sprott's professional association with Hirsch would stretch into the 1970s, in New York and at the CBC.

Another longstanding professional relationship began in the summer of 1960 when a young clothing salesman named Len Cariou approached Tom Hendry and asked to audition for the Rainbow Stage. The future Broadway star was twenty, with no particular qualifications and no background in theatre. His wife was pregnant with their first child and he was grateful to have recently landed a job selling bespoke suits at the shop of Ernie Gould on Portage Avenue. When he auditioned for Hirsch he was at first alarmed by Hirsch's Hungarian accent, worrying that he couldn't understand him. But the audition went well and the kindly Gould was willing to release him from the shop for the summer (Cariou remembers that in addition to his apprentice's stipend from the Rainbow Stage he made a little money on commissions from well-heeled clients he met through Hirsch and Hendry.) Cariou had an excellent season at the Rainbow Stage in shows like *The Pajama Game* and *Damn Yankees*, learning to "lay it on with a trowel just for anything to register past the fifth row" in outdoor theatre. As well as a powerful baritone singing voice, he clearly had that "something" which even without any formal training drew one's eye to him on stage. At the end of the summer Hirsch offered him the role of Ensign Pulver in *Mister Roberts*, one of the planned productions for the 1960-61 season. Cariou was delighted to be asked. He'd been bitten by the theatre bug during the summer but was now the father of a baby girl and needed steady work. He laid this out to Hirsch who, he remembers, told him, "Don't worry, kid – he always called me kid – I'll give you work." Cariou signed on at $65 a week and worked at MTC for the next five seasons.

Hirsch was able to assure Cariou a regular salary because even after the Beacon disaster MTC was in surprisingly good shape. Hirsch had another, larger Canada Council grant in hand, and his board was having increasing success with private fundraising. Despite his criticism of Toronto actors the year before, Hirsch was now able to lure small numbers of professional actors to Winnipeg as permanent members of the company, where they were often assigned smaller but pivotal "character" parts. This in turn allowed Hirsch and Hendry to ratchet the company up towards the next level, as a fully professional theatre. Rehearsals would no longer be held at night but during the daytime, in line with the rules of the actor's union, Actor's Equity. *Look Back in Anger*, in February 1960, was the first show in which all of the actors were in the union.

The move toward professionalization was noticed and resented.

There were letters to the editor, public meetings and private accusations, and a lot of hurt feelings as Little Theatre stalwarts found they no longer had their annual turn in front of the spotlights. Nor, as time went on and Hirsch was able to hire more outside talent, did all local actors appreciate the competition. In September 1961 Hendry entered into a very public argument with a Winnipeg actor who, in the pages of the *Winnipeg Free Press*, accused the MTC of having "ballooned with the hot air of professionalism, and will undoubtedly have to fill its concavity with outside talent." As if to underline his point, the writer fulminated that the MTC "hasn't entered a Dominion Drama Festival in three years." In his published reply Hendry ignored the jibe about the drama festival – the last thing he and Hirsch cared about – but noted that out of two hundred roles played by one hundred actors in the 1960-61 season, only fifteen had been played by "imported actors."

Hirsch felt strongly that importing talent was a means both for local actors to improve their skills and for local audiences to become more knowledgeable and demanding of higher standards. He was also conscious that the theatre profession could only rise in Canada if there was a network of theatres for actors to go to, as well as training opportunities. In this, the move towards becoming a "union shop," with actors represented by the New York-based Actors Equity, strengthened his hand. Stratford had been organized by Equity since the mid-1950s and its actors were not permitted under union rules to work in amateur theatre. In Winnipeg actors eventually had to choose whether to join the union and work according to its rules or to keep theatre as a hobby and social activity.

Hirsch's relationship with the MTC Board was occasionally fractious but essentially constructive. He and Hendry won more battles than they lost (an ongoing deficit may be testament to this), but at least one loss – when they lobbied in vain to prevent Ogden Turner being elected president – turned out to be fortuitous. They had been slowly easing out the remnants of the Little Theatre and recruiting individuals they thought would open up new sources of funding, as well as support their ideas. Hendry remembers, "We just looked for people who were smart and progressive. But we had inherited Ogden, and he had just hung on and was a pain in the ass." Turner won, and even today Hendry sounds incredulous when he says that Turner turned out to be one of the best presidents they ever dealt with. He didn't attempt to interfere with Hirsch's artistic direction and provided strong support for outreach projects like the theatre school and the touring company.

. For by this time the MTC had made good on its early promise to create its own theatre school. The school opened in January 1960 at 91 Albert Street, a short distance from the Dominion. In keeping with the model borrowed from the Théâtre de la Cité in France, Hirsch saw this more as a way of building the audience rather than training future professionals. The MTC also began a Studio Theatre series in the same space as the school. In it, they planned to run more experimental or controversial plays, including locally written ones, while leaving the main stage (the Beacon or the Dominion when it was finished) free for productions that could be expected to attract bigger audiences. In its early years of operation the "theatre across the street" would allow the MTC to flex its creative muscles on plays like Ionesco's *The Lesson*, Chekhov's *The Marriage Proposal* and Dylan Thomas' *Under Milk Wood* without incurring serious financial risk.

The touring company came next, which began taking a production called *Shakespeare Goes to School* into local high schools. When MTC first proposed the tour at the Winnipeg School Board for funding, the Communist member Joe Zuken supported it so enthusiastically that the rest of the Board all voted against it. The following year, after Hendry quietly asked Zuken to tone down his support, the school board provided the financing. The touring company activities grew in ambition, eventually taking productions around Manitoba and into neighbouring provinces.

The 1960-61 season kept to the formula established previously, relying on recent Broadway productions like *Mr. Roberts* and *The Four Poster*. Greater challenges to both director and actors were posed by Sean O'Casey's *Juno and the Paycock* and particularly Tennessee Williams' *A Streetcar Named Desire*, the former directed by Scott and the latter by Hirsch.

Hirsch's sense of spectacle was on full display in his production of Howard Richardson and William Berney's *Dark of the Moon*. A weird tale of witchcraft and doomed love with a hillbilly setting and matching dialogue ("Lord, they pleasured tharselves in the barn!"), it had had a respectable, seven-month run on Broadway in 1945 and had become a staple of university and amateur theatre, partly because it offers a large number of broadly drawn parts. Hirsch made it a very physical production with the cast in constant motion and a lot of special effects. Rehearsals were so intense that one actor fainted while running through the climactic religious revival scene.

Martin Lager, one of Hirsch's newly hired staff actors, played the "witch boy" who spends a year as a human being. He remembers the audience reaction to the special effects, such as lightning flashing from his hands and an apparently instant transformation back into being the witch boy when his human girlfriend's infidelity is revealed:

> That was done by a momentary black-out and the actresses playing the witch girls pulled this Velcro material off me, so that here I was suddenly in a totally other outfit. The effect would elicit gasps from the audience. But John had a lot of those innovative ideas. He was really good with plays that had that fantastic element to them, and charm.

The play got good reviews and good audiences, but it also provoked a degree of backlash from conservative audience members who were offended by its treatment of religion. Some patrons cancelled season tickets and Hendry received letters accusing the theatre of "godless Communism." Lager also remembers a less attractive aspect of Hirsch that surfaced at this time and continued throughout his career: "He tended to always need, for the lack of a better word, a whipping boy, somebody that he singled out for special derogatory attention. And the only way to defeat that was to just stand up to him and then he would just back off. But if you weren't able to stand up to him – after all he was the director – then you suffered."

Some of Hirsch's trademark idiosyncrasies were set by this time. One was his habit of snapping his fingers if he found the rhythm of a scene flagging. Almost all actors who worked with him remember this. He found other ways of making his displeasure known. Denise Fergusson, who played Raina in *Arms and the Man* at MTC in 1961, remembers: "You knew the rehearsal was going *really* badly when he disappeared into his seat and all you could see were his feet on the top of the row of seats in front of him."

He could be tough on actors, particularly if he felt they hadn't done their homework or were self-indulgent. Len Cariou comments, "He got a reputation with some people as a miserable sonofabitch but I always felt you needed to get some perspective on what he was doing and why. Most people did. If you had a brain in your head, you just had to do the work."

Evelyne Anderson liked and admired Hirsch, but also saw a director with much to learn. One of the first in the long line of native-born Winnipeg actors to train and work in the U.K., Anderson had returned to her hometown to look after her dying mother. Intending to leave again, she had instead gotten married and settled down. The MTC was a godsend, giving her the chance to continue her career. Having worked for three years in English theatre she saw Hirsch's inexperience more clearly than others, and watched as he learned his craft: "When he was young he would sometimes over-produce. He wasn't secure in letting the moment take itself, and always wanted things happening on stage."

The third season saw several major developments on both the artistic and business fronts. One was the establishment of the MTC Young Company, which grew out of Hirsch's long-time interest in "growing" theatre talent in Canada. Both he and Hendry were part of the discussions to create the National Theatre School, attending the 1959 meeting in Stratford where the creation of the school was approved. Once the school opened in November 1960, Hirsch became a visiting teacher there, making quick trips to Montreal to give classes. The job not only paid Hirsch a welcome stipend but gave him a chance to check out the talented young actors who were attending the school. Before long he hired some of the best students from the school's first graduating class for the newly formed MTC

Young Company. The opening play of 1961-62 season, Christopher Fry's *The Lady's Not for Burning*, included Martha Henry, who would work for Hirsch many times in the future. She had found Hirsch inspiring at the National Theatre School but also intimidating, for "although he opened the world of Chekhov, at the same time he lambasted us for our immaturity (some of us were 17)." Nonetheless, she fell for his energy, his eccentricities and his directing style: "In the middle of the prairie there was no one to compare him to and no one tried. He was Hirsch and *he* defined what the theatre was."

By the beginning of the 1961-62 season the Dominion Theatre refurbishment had finally finished. With their offices, rehearsal room and workshops housed in the building next door on the north side of Portage Avenue East, the MTC was now a substantial presence on the block. Nonetheless, the coffee shop on the corner was annexed as the place where staff held many of their meetings. The owner was initially annoyed at this but eventually came to enjoy the presence and ongoing business from the theatre people. Within the Manitoba Theatre Centre the atmosphere was informal. Judith Carr – who would become Tom Hendry's second wife – joined as the centre's first full-time publicity manager at the beginning of the season. She remembers enjoying the open-door policy that reigned in the company. Hirsch would frequently flop down into a chair in her office, distraught with a problem, large or small. A short conversation might lead to a solution and Hirsch would be up and out the door and on to the next thing – or the next office.

The MTC was receiving increasing amounts of notice for its work nationally. In June 1961 the music and drama critic of the *Ottawa Citizen*, Herschel Hardin, prefaced a series of articles on the state of theatre in Ottawa – "and a miserably low state of affairs it is," he said – with the comment, "The only way to lead into such a series is to have an example of something better, namely the Manitoba Theatre Centre."

Much of the growing recognition of the theatre was focused on its artistic director. He already had something of a national profile as a frequent contributor to CBC radio, having begun with the *Assignment* series in 1957. By the early 1960s he was a resident authority on modern theatre, giving talks on playwrights like Tennessee Williams and important historical figures like Konstantin Stanislavski. In 1961 Hirsch was invited to an international conference in Vienna, to which he added an extensive tour of European theatre groups including Brecht's Berliner Ensemble in East Berlin. On his return he used the event as an opportunity for more polemic, telling the *Toronto Star* he was "ashamed and appalled" by Canada's lack of funding of the arts. "The Russians invited us to send an exhibition of Canadian theatre to Russia. What are we going to send? A model of the Stratford stage?" The government subsidized sports to the tune of five million dollars, he said, while the Canada Council received only three million.

Hirsch had access to some good actors by now, and some very promising ones, but he wanted great ones, the best in Canada. That would take more money than the Board was used to paying; instead of $100 a week paid to local Equity members, top Stratford Festival actors could not be lured to Winnipeg for less than $250. He and Hendry strategized with the sympathetic board members, and in the end were able to hire Douglas Rain and Zoe Caldwell to lead the cast of *Playboy of the Western World* in March 1962. Rain – born in Winnipeg and therefore easy to sell to the Board – was one of the best of a very good company at Stratford, while the Australian-born Caldwell was a rising international star, fresh from performances in London and New York. Directed by Des Scott, *Playboy* not only pulled in good audiences but inspired the company. Martin Lager remembers that Caldwell and Rain not only treated the local members of the cast with warmth and kindness but also raised performance standards "a notch or two."

It also began what slowly became a mutually beneficial arrangement with Stratford, giving a winter "home" to some of its actors and staff while introducing some talented Winnipeggers to the Festival. The period corresponded with the Festival's "golden years" of the early to mid-1960s when there was a strong, cohesive sense of the acting ensemble under artistic director Michael Langham.

Playboy was followed by another Hirsch-directed musical, *The*

Boyfriend, with Len Cariou in the lead role. It was by far the MTC's greatest success to date. Some eighteen thousand people flocked to see it and – somewhat to the wonderment of the Board – it actually took in more money than it cost to put on. In addition to being the season's biggest success *The Boyfriend* also saw the beginning of an important friendship for Hirsch. Watching from the balcony during a performance, Hirsch and Hendry noticed a very tall, blond gentleman who seemed to be completely captured by the musical, catching even some of the theatrical "in jokes" that passed by the rest of the audience. Buttonholing him during the intermission, they found he was Jacques Beyderwellen, a visiting businessman from Montreal. Multilingual, sophisticated, and not-so-discreetly gay, Beyderwellen invited both Hirsch and Hendry to visit him in Montreal, where he moved in an exciting circle of artists, writers, theatre people and – to Hirsch's delight – good-looking young men.

The season ended with that rare beast, a new Canadian play. Finding and supporting new Canadian playwrights was proving harder than putting on existing plays from the international repertoire. Nonetheless, Hirsch and Hendry did try. In 1960 they had put out a press release and taken ads in newspapers across the country offering $1,000 for "any playable script." After reading over a hundred scripts they concluded it would be an uphill battle; nothing had arrived that seemed worth the work it would take to bring it to stage. They used the Studio Theatre to put on small productions by people working at the MTC. Martin Lager had his first play produced there, playing on weekends to audiences of fifty (he would go on to become a successful television and movie writer). They commissioned new scripts and adaptations for the school tours and for the Children's Theatre series. However, no new script made it to the main stage until May 1962 when MTC commissioned Toronto-based Len Peterson to write a musical about immigration.

The result was *Look Ahead!* The title is an exhortation from a Canadian government brochure for recent immigrants; the story that finally made it to stage was of the Dapcevic family, who move from Yugoslavia to Ontario. Len Peterson was already a highly experienced writer of television and radio drama, yet despite his bona fides, the potential appeal of the theme in a city built on recent immigration, and Canada Council support for Canadian scripts, the go-ahead was only given after a fierce battle with the more cautious members of the MTC Board. As it turned out, *Look Ahead!* sold well with MTC's growing audience, and was held over.

The *Winnipeg Free Press*'s Chris Dafoe was only partially convinced by this "whirlwind panorama of Canadian life" that attacked a range of evils from advertising to evangelical avarice. "There is a wealth of golden material in *Look Ahead!*," he judged. "The great weakness is that it bogs down in an embarrassment of riches. The editorial blue pencil has been too often spared."

The season finished with another play by Jean Anouilh, the comic *Thieves' Carnival*. Hirsch commented in the program that he'd chosen the play to reassure Winnipeggers that spring had come: "The winter was too long and my nerve edges are raw from it, so a light, pinky-coloured play might very well be the order of the month."

For despite the successes of his theatre company Hirsch's nerve edges needed constant attention. His mood swings were frequent and dramatic, almost part of his Central European *shtick* – the artist's persona he had created for himself. But they were also real, and he used many strategies to maintain his emotional health. One was simply to buy himself flowers. One colleague remembers that a trip to the flower shop, "would feed him – then he would come to rehearsals and yell at everybody."

Another strategy was travel. His colleagues accepted that he *needed* to get out of Winnipeg four or five times a year. He often went to see theatre in New York or other American cities, where he was building a large network of professional contacts. He had his teaching in Montreal. He started making annual trips to Greece, visiting a new island each year.

The 1961-62 season saw MTC's ticket sales jump from 64,000 to 112,000 – part of it attributable to casual ticket sales for *The Boyfriend* – and its operating budget rise to over $200,000. The Canada Council was now providing $30,000 and private fundraising almost $32,000. The Rainbow Stage was still a going concern with its well-attended productions but neither Hirsch nor Hendry had any interest in continuing to devote their summers to musicals. They dropped the Rainbow Stage which struggled for several years to find a stable management structure. Eventually it did, and has continued to be part of Winnipeg's cultural life ever since.

The 1962-63 season was, in Tom Hendry's memory, "a kind of consolidation thing.... It was just slug, slug, slug." Productions included the musical *Pal Joey* and a new play by the young Bernard Slade (long before he created the *Flying Nun* TV series and *Same Time, Next Year*). Des Scott, who had moved back to Toronto to continue his acting and directing career, returned to direct a successful production of *The Caretaker*, the MTC's first Pinter play.

Among the year's productions Hirsch directed Ibsen's *An Enemy of the People*, adapted by a friend from university days, Betty Jane Wylie. Though in love with literature and theatre, she had gotten married in 1952 and started raising a family – "as everyone did, in

1962-63: Hirsch and Tom Hendry flanked by Manitoba Theatre Centre Board president Donald J. Campbell and actor Jean Murray.
University of Manitoba Archives

those days," she remembers. She re-established contact with Hirsch when she and her husband Bill began to go to plays at the MTC. One day, when Hirsch invited her to see a rehearsal, Wylie hired a babysitter and came down to the theatre. She was in Hirsch's office when he took a phone call. "I need a new script for *Enemy of the People* in six weeks," he said after putting down the phone. Wylie hadn't read the play, but did so quickly and returned to tell Hirsch, "I'm going to do your script for you." She had been reading excerpts from Rachel Carson's *Silent Spring* in *The New Yorker* and was fired up by Carson's ground-breaking research on the global impact of pollution. In her mind Carson's warning fit perfectly with the plot of the eighty-year-old play, in which a small-town doctor faces the wrath of his community when he draws attention to the public health risks of a new tourist development. Wylie (whose father was a GP) thought it could be adapted to present-day Canada. Hirsch heard her out but told her he couldn't pay for totally new adaptation. Wylie didn't care; she wanted to write the script. Hirsch told her to give it a try.

Wylie returned in a week with her script, which she set in a fictional town called Venture, Saskatchewan. Hirsch liked it, but delayed telling William Hutt, the rising Stratford star who had been hired to play the protagonist, Dr. Stockman. Wylie remembers, "When Hutt finally found out the script was by a Winnipeg house-wife, he wanted to buy himself out of the contract. But he changed his mind when he read the script, and even apologized to me." The play, with its local references and a solid cast, got good reviews and audiences when it opened, and in Wylie's memory, it changed her life. She did two more adaptations for Hirsch in the next few years, and wrote speeches and promotional material for him – all unpaid. And her husband Bill, an accountant who had a public relations business, was invited to sit on the MTC Board. "That's the way it was, the man would be invited," she comments wryly. Betty Jane's unpaid work at the MTC ceased when her two-year-old son Matthew was diagnosed with brain damage and she needed to devote enormous amounts of time to him (she later wrote *The Book of Matthew*, a pioneering book about raising a child with "special needs"). Her husband went on to become the general manager of the MTC in February 1964.

The rest of the season's offerings also found favour with Winnipeg audiences. The audience and subscriptions list were still growing fast, and the touring company and school and Studio Theatre were all busy. With these successes receiving increasing notice in theatre circles, the biggest guns in Canadian theatre criticism, the *Globe & Mail*'s Herbert Whittaker and the *Toronto Daily Star*'s Nathan Cohen, both made visits to see what all the fuss was about. Cohen, the toughest of the critics – he dismissed all the others as mere "reviewers" – and a national celebrity thanks to the television panel show *Fighting Words*, arrived in Winnipeg on a January day in 1963. The city obliged with classic winter weather and Cohen began his report with, "'Cold? You consider this cold!' exclaimed one of my hosts as I pounded my ears to thaw them out...." (One has the strong sense of locals pulling the "sophisticated" visitor's leg about the rigours of the prairie climate.) Hirsch spent a great deal of time with Cohen during this visit, beginning a prickly relationship that lasted until the latter's death in 1971.

Cohen wrote a highly analytical four-article series on the MTC that not only looked at its productions but at the Winnipeg audience, the organization's finances, and even its pricing policy. Taking note of the size and demographics of the Winnipeg audience, Cohen noted that "the rangy, bearded, impassioned Hirsch and the furrow-faced, quietly loquacious Hendry" were offering a repertoire "plainly designed to cut through commercial and coterie lines to reach a broad cross-section of people, by presenting many forms of dramatic entertainment and by ensuring in each instance a professional' quality of content and presentation." He found "an adventurousness and sensibility of selection" in the recent seasons' playbills, but also looked beyond this to the role of the MTC's various educational and outreach activities in "the forging of a rooted theatre in the stubborn, resistant Canadian soil." He judged that the MTC was "the only truly community theatre we have in Canada" and concluded that the MTC gave him "cause for hope that we will one day have an indigenous and vital English language theatre."

Hirsch enjoyed the celebrity but remembered to give credit to the city. He liked to say that growing an orange in the middle of the Prairies wasn't necessarily easy but could be done if people got behind it. Winnipeg had definitely got behind the Manitoba Theatre Centre.

In much the same way that Planchon's Théâtre de la Cité in France had been a model for Hirsch, the MTC was becoming a model for regional theatre across North America. Hirsch and Hendry were both in demand as consultants, often at the behest of the Canada Council, as the first wave of regional theatres arose in Canada. Both of them visited Vancouver in 1962 as that city's Playhouse began to take shape, while up-and-coming directors like Leon Major frequently came to visit Winnipeg. Another visitor was Robert Kalfin, future director of the Chelsea Theater Center in Manhattan. Kalfin, who toured North American theatres while working out his own ideas for a non-profit cultural centre, found that "the work that John Hirsch was doing captured his imagination more than the rest." Hirsch became a "friend and sounding board" for Kalfin, and would eventually direct an Obie-winning production at the Chelsea Theater Center.

Hirsch was starting to be invited to guest-direct outside of Winnipeg. His first major production in Toronto was at the Crest Theatre in April 1963, when he directed Tennessee Williams' *Cat on a Hot Tin Roof*. Hirsch was greatly interested in Williams, and the MTC had done three of Williams' plays by this time. In a talk he gave on Williams for the CBC radio program *Anthology*, Hirsch recalled one of his early trips to New York, when he had managed to see the sold-out original production of *Cat on a Hot Tin Roof*, directed by Elia Kazan. Hirsch had emerged from the play feeling like "a punching bag in the sweaty corner of a gymnasium after being worked over by some heavy-weight." After the promise of *Streetcar* in the late 1940s, Hirsch said, Williams in the late 1950s had descended "into a world of private phantoms, where castration meets up with cannibalism." It was not violence that bothered Hirsch, he said: "I can stand the sight of Gloucester's eyes being put out, of Lear being battered by the venomous gods, scenes which are at least as violent as the description in *Suddenly Last Summer* where the young woman reports Sebastian's end on the blazing beach where the scrawny black boys, like birds of prey, pin him down and eat his private parts." Nor did he demand spiritual uplift. But he was looking for "affirmation" in the theatre, signs that "despite the sub-conscious death-wish and its conscious manifestations personified in our mass-suicidal leaders, some of us ARE trying to live." He traced that kind of affirmation back to Shakespeare's *Lear* and Brecht's *Mother Courage*, pulling her wagon through a war-torn landscape while singing of spring. At the end of his talk Hirsch denounced the "cul-de-sac of individualism" that the theatre and Williams had fallen into, and called on theatre artists "to resist the 'all is lost' attitude to life on one hand and the escapist, nonsensical on the other. I know these might not be too fashionable demands, but I truly feel that the responsibility of the artist is to provide the balance, to order and communicate. If he fails in this task he ceases to be an artist."

The talk, typed by Hirsch with ellipses and words in capital letters as prompts for timing and emphasis makes strange reading today. At a time when the word "gay" hadn't yet replaced "homosexual" and when the physical expression of homosexuality was illegal in North America, Hirsch had to be careful about what he said. Noting that *Cat on a Hot Tin Roof* was billed as Williams' first work to deal with the problem of homosexuality, Hirsch argued that a fundamental weakness of the play was that

> the writer refuses to treat the problem of homosexuality in an honest way, which he was supposed to have done. (Probably because the public is interested in the sensational aspect of the deviation ... not in its serious implications.)

The parentheses were pencilled in by hand, suggesting Hirsch was undecided about whether to include the sentence. The question of what "implications" is a can of worms he chooses not to open. The next line in the typescript is stroked out, but still readable:

The problem is never resolved, unless you call the scene where the wife gives TEA AND SYMPATHY treatment to the husband with results only to be guessed at…coming as it does…just as the curtain touches the floor at the end of act three."

A gay man's skepticism about the lasting benefits of tea and heterosexual sympathy, or disappointment in Williams' weak resolution? Probably a bit of both.

In his personal life Hirsch was discreet about the "deviation." His straight colleagues often knew but didn't see this side of his life. Evelyne Anderson remembers that in cast parties and socializing at the Shacks' house Hirsch's homosexuality simply didn't figure. "He was very conscious of not displaying that side of his character. He kept his personal life very quiet. It was difficult to be gay in those days."

Difficult, but far from impossible. Hirsch maintained a circle of gay friends, some of whom, like Arnold Spohr, were heavyweights in the city's political and cultural scene. The long-time artistic director of the Royal Winnipeg Ballet and Hirsch were close for many years, and Hirsch served on the RWB's Board of Directors. The city had a few venues close to MTC where gay men could meet safely and comfortably, and Hirsch could be found in all of them— the Mardi Gras bar on Portage Avenue, the Moon Room Chinese restaurant on Main Street and the Grange Hotel just behind the theatre were all spots where the theatre, dance and art crowds met up. But discretion was still the order of the day and most gay socializing had to happen at private parties. When the sexual itch simply needed to be scratched one might make a visit to one or another of Winnipeg's few cruising grounds – notably behind the Legislature – or simply pick up someone late at night on Portage Avenue. That could be risky. In the early 1960s Winnipeg magistrates were happy to impose fines on men caught indulging in, as one magistrate put it publicly, a "revolting and sickening offence." The Shack household was visited at least once by the police following up John's activities, though it does not appear to have resulted in a criminal charge.

He also fell in and out of love. In 1962 he started an affair with a young man named Louis Bako, who was part of two other intersecting circles in Hirsch's life, artists and Hungarians. Thirteen years younger than Hirsch, Bako had arrived in Winnipeg with his family in 1958, part of the wave of refugees who left Hungary after the 1956 popular revolt and its suppression by the Soviet Army. They met at a dinner put on by a Hungarian social organization and soon after Bako came to work backstage at MTC painting sets and eventually moved on to designing shows for the Children's Theatre. He subsequently studied set design at the National Theatre School and worked in both Canada and the United States before devoting himself to a successful career as a painter. Along with his evident talent, friends from the period remember Bako as "beautiful," with a body sculpted by years of water polo. Hungarians have long been a power in the sport, and Bako was a member of a Winnipeg team made up largely of young refugees. The MTC crowd often went to cheer him on.

Hirsch was smitten with Bako. He once wrote to him, "I have never felt so deeply and painfully involved as with you. Partly because you are somehow my lost brother, because we spoke the same language, because we both of us have much in common. We love to cry and fight and yell and love." But he was also smitten with the milieu Bako came from. He was always welcome at the home of Bako's parents, where he revelled in Hungarian food and conversation, and felt comfortable enough to bring "the whole theatre" there for dinner (Mrs. Bako was by several accounts a phenomenal cook). Today Louis Bako is still uncertain as to whether his parents understood that he and Hirsch were lovers. He never talked about it with them, and "if they knew, they pretended not to know." Even after the affair was over Hirsch continued to visit the Bakos in Toronto, where they moved in the late 1960s.

The results of the 1962-63 season were excellent. Attendance continued to climb, and was up by twenty per cent over the previous year. The budget was now almost a quarter of a million dollars, of which about $100,000 was provided by subsidies and donations. Yet the year had ended with a deficit, and Hirsch and Hendry were not looking forward to the inevitable criticism from some board members at the Annual General Meeting in June.

When the meeting came around they had a treat for the Board in the elongated shape of its guest speaker, Sir Tyrone Guthrie. Only two months before the meeting Guthrie had opened the new Minneapolis Theater, a regional theatre dedicated to a classic repertory and based on a resident company. Guthrie had spent four years shepherding it into existence and served as its first artistic director (it was renamed the Guthrie Theater in his honour in 1971). The MTC put Guthrie up at Winnipeg's opulent historic landmark, the Fort Garry Hotel. When Hirsch and Hendry went to fetch him they were in a considerable state of excitement as they crossed the high-beamed lobby with its large, glittering chandelier lighting the grey-and-black marble floor. The excitement gave way to stupe-faction when they knocked on Guthrie's door. The theatrical knight was naked when he answered it and ushered them in as though this was the most usual thing in the world – which it was for Guthrie, who was renowned for his "state of more than gypsy undress." After Guthrie had put on some clothes, they had a chat during which Guthrie listened intently to the duo's description of the business to come. Then Hirsch managed to fold the six-foot-five Guthrie into his Mini Minor and drove him around Winnipeg before taking him to the meeting.

Guthrie gave a speech that elegantly cut the rug out from under those who were exercised about the deficit. Attacking the purely for-profit motive driving much of theatre on the continent, he praised the efforts of MTC both to lead and reflect the interests of the local community, and shamelessly stroked the board members:

> This is what I was so impressed with here, why I was so thrilled at the way the deficit balance sheet was received. There is certainly nothing to panic about here. The important thing is that your attendance figures are so substantially up....

The support of a figure like Guthrie and the excellent attendance figures could not make up for one important loss. In the spring,

Tom Hendry handed in his resignation. There were many reasons, some of long standing. As he put it, "John was in charge of production so I wouldn't think of interfering. I was the administrator, so he meddled all the time." Long working days, endless problem solving, and constant skirmishing with the Board had taken their toll. His marriage had broken down and he was increasingly frustrated with the contradictions of running an artistic business: "Whatever instincts I had about doing more in the way of new work, I could see that it was going to be a long time before the theatre, as I understood it, wanted to do anything much like that.... I found repeatedly that I was tiring of the role which I had previously enjoyed of being Mr. Mean."

He left after a small argument with the Board over charging audiences for programs that normally would have been forgotten. In this case Hirsch sided with the Board and Hendry decided to pack it in. He arranged for a successor to take over his job as general manager, and left Winnipeg with a $4,500 Canada Council grant to visit theatres in other parts of the world. During the trip he sent chatty and affectionate letters to Hirsch and, while spending February 1964 in Malta, he started to send Hirsch installments of a script that would become *Fifteen Miles of Broken Glass*, which Hirsch would direct for CBC television.

Meanwhile the 1963-64 season got under way. In October the theatre premiered *Names and Nicknames*, a children's play by Hirsch's old friend and university mentor James Reaney. Hirsch co-directed with Robert Sherrin, one of his former students from the National Theatre School, and the cast of eight included Heath Lamberts and Martha Henry. The actors took many parts, changing from people to farm animals to alarm clocks, and used a variety of techniques like mime and choral speech. The *Winnipeg Free Press* commented, "Even a stuffy audience of adults at the Theatre Centre Sunday night was charmed and enchanted."

Hirsch followed up with *The Hostage*, by Irish playwright Brendan Behan. Highly influenced by Brechtian ideas, particularly in its use of music and song, it tells the story of a young English soldier kidnapped by the IRA and held in a Dublin brothel in the hours before a young IRA man is scheduled to be executed in Belfast. It was the kind of play Hirsch loved to do, softening up the audience with laughter and gradually moving toward its serious climax. The political element was accentuated by actual events. Ten days before the opening of *The Hostage* Hirsch interrupted rehearsals and told the cast to take three days off. President Kennedy had just been assassinated and he wanted the company to watch television and think about how it related to the play.

Alan Laing, a frequent collaborator with Hirsch for the next two decades, remembers the production as the spark for his future career in theatre (he went on to be musical director at Stratford and the National Arts Centre, and composed music for countless plays across North America). At the time Laing was a young composer and pianist, and had a reputation as a quick study. Hirsch called him less than a week before the play opened to take the on-stage part of the brothel's pianist. He would have four days to learn entrances, exits and some sixty bits of music for a three-hour play. Laing accepted and was swept up in the energy and creativity of the production. He tells a fairly typical anecdote about Hirsch during this period:

> The set was a two-storey house with a piano on stage left, and the actress who was playing the prostitute suggested that at one point I come running down from her upper room doing up my shirt and pants as I ran down, her waving at me from the window. We tried it in John's absence at the Wednesday matinee, and it got a predictably huge laugh, so we kept it in (it was early in the run). John came back some nights later, saw the business and for half an hour lectured the poor stage manager about changing the direction without permission, etc., etc. At the end of this, the SM apologized and told John he'd see it was removed. John replied, "Oh no, keep it in – it's very funny!"

When the season ended Hirsch began a long trip that would take him back to Hungary for the first time. He had stayed in touch with his uncles Gyuri and Lajos over the years, frequently receiving letters about the difficulties of running a business enterprise in a Communist country. Hirsch still owned some property and other assets left by his father, and though blocked from receiving any benefits outside the country, he was able to make occasional disbursements to his family, particularly in times of need.

The trip is sketched in Hirsch's postcards and letters to Ma and Sybil Shack, and to Louis Bako. First a visit to Toronto where he reports being offered the Crest Theatre, with the option of moving into the St. Lawrence Centre later on ("All of these offers are so exciting, such great opportunities, and here I am stupidly bound by all these ties"). Then a stop in Montreal where he finds he has developed two red spots on his body due to anxiety: "Deep down, I don't want to go….20 years ought to be such a long time, but of course it isn't at all. I am ashamed of myself to be so tied to the past. One of the reasons why I AM going is to try to bring about confrontation which might just chase away the ghosts. It is stupid to be afraid but I am not a very courageous person." Montreal had a bright side, though: "The place is full of Hungarians so it might have served, the week, as a bridge." Then Vienna, where Hirsch had to wait while the Hungarian legation processed his visa for Hungary. While there he wrote Louis that he'd had "a little fling" with a young woman, "22 years old, beautiful and thinks I'm the greatest." Bako wasn't entirely surprised by this; Bako knew he sometimes had sex with women.

Finally arriving in Budapest, he had an emotional reunion with the remains of his mother's family: Uncle Lajos ("very old, before his time"), Uncle Gyuri ("good-humoured and stoical about everything"), and his cousin Anna, whom he later helped emigrate to Canada. Their situation saddened him: "Such a damaged bunch we are," he commented. He visited Siófok and found that the family home had become a shabby co-op store and the once-beautiful garden had been replaced by a concrete warehouse – "my Cherry Orchard," he said.

Back in Budapest he met intellectuals and theatre people, and found himself acting almost as a confessor, listening to litanies of hopelessness and cynicism. The city was "peeling," the people shabbily dressed, the "bankruptcy of socialism coupled with inertia quite frightening – yet the ritualistic repetitions of humanistic slogans still go on." The greyness of Budapest also drove home another lesson:

> I became terribly conscious of my need, and I think all men's need, for colour, variety, frivolity, play, decoration, the possibility for moderate waste, luxury. It exists there only when it comes to food and because it is the only reasonably inexpensive colourful sensuous relief people eat like hogs. So even eating becomes an over-done activity.

He returned to North America via New York, too depressed to get back to work immediately. "I'll be fine, but it takes time," he told Sybil and Pauline.

In Winnipeg the Manitoba Theatre Centre was firing on all of the cylinders that had so impressed Nathan Cohen during his visit. A National Film Board documentary made in the autumn of 1964 shows an institution that takes its community responsibilities seriously and has fun doing so. Much of it has to do with the MTC's outreach to young people. Director Mort Ransen takes his cameras into the theatre school, watching teenagers being led through breathing and voice exercises. A troupe of young Québécois actors piles into a station wagon, travelling out to Manitoba high schools in an MTC-sponsored tour; they perform Molière with great panache, then chat with their anglophone counterparts. Another group from the resident Young Company visits a different high school, performing songs and poems ("And the Highwayman came riding, riding, riding...") and giving candid answers to questions about ambition and the chance to act at Stratford. There are beautifully framed shots of kids responding with delight to the slapstick in Hirsch's musical play for children, *The Box of Smiles*.

And through it all there is the clean-shaven, bespectacled Hirsch striding awkwardly down Portage Avenue, talking passionately about

everything from French-English relations in Canada to the importance of theatre in the general education of a child. He makes his
familiar plea for subsidizing theatre in Canada. Subsidy is necessary
everywhere, he argues, but particularly in Canada where physical
distances are so great and the population relatively small. "If people
worry this is socialistic, then fine," he argues, "but the private sector
should come forward as institutions like the Ford Foundation do in
the United States." Again, out comes the metaphor of "a country of
huge muscles and pea-sized brains" and an un-checkable allegation
that the Canadian government spends "five million dollars on military bands" compared to "maybe half a million for the theatre, if
that much." In a more reflective sequence, he describes how subsidized theatre permits a certain amount of failure, which he regards
as essential:

> Because out of the failures and errors of an artist come the
> beautiful things, and the meaningful things and the good
> things....One of the things I hate about working in
> commercial situations is that you are pressed to produce
> something good every day, as if you were a machine. And
> the very thing that makes you a director, that makes you an
> artist is that you are a human, perhaps weaker than most
> people. I really do believe that. Because you can't be asked
> [he makes the gesture of a machine punching downwards]
> to punch the same shape every day....

He talks with pride about how MTC has "infiltrated the school
system" and shown the education authorities the value of their work
in the teaching of English and literature. Part of this is a voice-over of
actors Martha Henry and Paul Hecht performing a scene from *Macbeth*
in a high school gym. He also mentions the growing fame of MTC's
main stage productions, dropping a deadpan "People come *all the way
from Toronto*" into the conversation before breaking into a quick grin.
   One of the film's most striking sequences captures Hirsch
working with Zoe Caldwell in rehearsal for *Mother Courage*. He darts

back and forth from the numbered audience seats to darkened stage, talking Caldwell through a scene with her wagon, how she should think of it at that moment, "like an animal that is going to eat her." Caldwell replies with her deep, sultry voice, holding Hirsch's eye as they speak, then Hirsch is racing back into the stalls to catch the overall effect.

Hyperbolic as it sounds, *Mother Courage* became legendary in Winnipeg. When the MTC mounted a new *Courage* in February 2010, comparisons with 1964 abounded, but a telling comment came from an MTC volunteer: "I've heard about it my entire life, mostly from people who themselves did not see it." Yet it should be remembered that Brecht was a gamble in North America at that time, more talked about by theatre intellectuals (often through their hats, since few of Brecht's writings on theatre had yet been translated) than performed. Hirsch knew he needed an extraordinary actress for the lead and the Australian-born Caldwell was certainly such an actress.

Opening night party for *Mother Courage*, December 1964.
Front row: Thomas Bohdanetzky and Frances Hyland;
Middle: Zoe Caldwell (in hat); Back row: Len Cariou (with cigarette),
John Hirsch, Martha Henry, unknown, Paul Hecht.
University of Manitoba Archives

Just thirty-three at the time and somewhat young for the part, she had shared the stage with Edith Evans, Paul Robeson and Charles Laughton at the Royal Shakespeare Company in England, and was one of the founding members of the company Tyrone Guthrie had recently established in Minneapolis. The supporting cast included a strong representation of Stratford's best including Douglas Rain as the cook, Frances Hyland as the mute daughter Katrin, and Martha Henry as the prostitute Yvette. Years later, the rehearsals are still vivid in the minds of actors and stage crew. Martha Henry remembers, "John drew on his own experiences to illuminate the inner state of the characters of the play." For example, she remembers him describing how his sweater, worn for six months and rotted with sweat, disintegrated in his hands when he took it off. Len Cariou, who played one of Courage's sons, says the rehearsal process was like no other he can recall, with Hirsch pulling up memory after memory:

> In the middle of rehearsals he would stop us and tell us something about how it was for him during the war. And it would just stop. Twenty minutes he would talk, tell us a story. And then 'Okay, let's go again.' He would go back to the scene and we would look at each other, gobsmacked.

The feeling of doing something special was pervasive. Eoin Sprott designed the show, delighted not to be working on living rooms and the other typical sets of commercial theatre. The quality of the set and the dirt-spattered costumes was matched by that of the props, notably the sixteen kosher chickens plucked by Caldwell and beheaded by Rain every night. (Why kosher? Because supermarket chickens were already plucked, beheaded and eviscerated, and the only source the MTC props people could find for what they needed was a little kosher meat market.)

The show sold out each night and reviewers were unanimous in their praise. Herbert Whittaker called the production "a major achievement for a Canadian company. It offers hope for a serious future for our theatre." Hirsch explained its success in an interview published by the *Toronto Daily Star* on the last Saturday of 1964: "I know my actors, I know my play and I know my audience."

In February 1965 Hirsch had to rescue *Irma La Douce* after guest director Rocco Bufano had, improbably, set the musical as a "heavy drama" and left town after opening night. Glen Harrison, who conducted the orchestra, remembers Hirsch stepping in to re-block the show and inject the missing humour and sense of spontaneity, and the show finished its run respectably. Bufano was one of several people the company had invited to guest-direct individual productions since Des Scott had by then left the company to continue his acting and directing career elsewhere. It wasn't apparent to the people at the MTC, but Hirsch was actually looking for someone to take over.

That someone turned out to be twenty-six-year-old Eddie Gilbert, who came to direct George Bernard Shaw's *Heartbreak House* in March 1965. Gilbert, like Des Scott, was British. An Oxford graduate in law ("I got interested in the theatricals that were going on, and my life went into a downward spiral from there"), he had worked at the Oxford Playhouse, Sadler's Wells and the Royal Shakespeare Company, though he had relatively little experience as a director. At the Royal Shakespeare Company he had come to the attention of Michel Saint-Denis, and it was Saint-Denis (founder of the National Theatre School in Montreal) who engineered Gilbert's move to Canada when the National Theatre School needed a new teacher.

Hirsch met Gilbert during one of his periodic teaching gigs at the National Theatre School and soon after invited him to direct a short play at the MTC. Gilbert was impressed with what he found there:

> I was familiar with the repertory scene in Britain and what John was doing was comparable by any measure. And in some cases, superior. What makes a successful theatre is a very, very complicated set of circumstances and also, timing. There are waves, and the Manitoba Theatre Centre was riding a very positive wave, and the work was very good.

The buzz and optimism of the company was attractive and he quickly understood the high level of community support the MTC had built up. Hirsch started taking him to meetings with the Board, and Gilbert observed that Hirsch understood the benefits of a dynamic tension between board and artistic management, with the latter trying to do excellent plays and the former trying to finance it. "The real thing that John had mastered was to brighten their lives," Gilbert recalls.

> They came away from their encounters with John with something to talk about, something that had challenged them or gave them their dinner table conversation for the next month. 'The last time I spent any time with John, we got into a yelling match,' they could say to their banking associates.... He was perfectly aware of the value of pushing the prima donna button – sometimes he couldn't help himself and sometimes he did it on purpose.

Gilbert was delighted when Hirsch asked him to stay on as resident director. It was only later, however, that Gilbert realized Hirsch was preparing his own departure from MTC. Although the time was not yet ripe to leave, he was spending increasing amounts of time on projects outside of Winnipeg.

Hirsch's triumph with *Mother Courage* and the close ties the MTC had built with Stratford had finally resulted in an invitation from Michael Langham to direct a play there. Langham had done a wonderful job as Stratford's second artistic director, building on Guthrie's pioneering work to create a company style and nurture a generation of excellent actors. But "growing" Canadian directors was not one of his priorities. Although Canadians did work as assistant directors during Langham's tenure at Stratford, the only Canadian to whom he had so far offered Stratford's main stage was Jean Gascon, who directed *Comedy of Errors* in 1963 and in 1964 Molière's *Le Bourgeois gentilhomme* there. As founding father of Montreal's Théâtre du Nouveau Monde, Gascon was not only a seasoned director but a splendid old-school actor.

Describing his first impression of Hirsch some years later Langham said, "He wasn't the ordinary, bland, middle-class person that I kept meeting all over Canada. He was something very special and eccentric." Langham offered Hirsch *The Cherry Orchard*, the first Chekhov to be presented on the Festival Stage. This was part of Langham's strategy of broadening the Stratford repertoire, possibly influenced by Guthrie's successful presentations of Chekhov in Minneapolis. The matching of play and director was perfect. Hirsch had been thinking hard about Chekhov since his university days.

The plot of *The Cherry Orchard* is simple: an aristocratic Russian family has come to the end of its wealth and its tether. The family's country estate, which boasts a beautiful cherry orchard, must be sold to pay off its mortgage. A prospective buyer – a prosperous business-man who is the son of one of their serfs – plans to cut down the cherry orchard and build summer cottages on the land. As Hirsch summarized it, "the play chronicles the lives of a group of people during a brief summer just as the rug is about to be pulled from under their feet." In the program notes he said, "I know what it means to lose a home, to be dispossessed. And I know what it means when a whole society disappears. I know all of Chekhov's people – they feel like my contemporaries." Although Chekhov had written *The Cherry Orchard* as a comedy, its first director Konstantin Stanis-lavsky had interpreted it as a tragedy at the Moscow Art Theatre in 1904. Hirsch was looking for a balance between the two. He later said, "If Chekhov doesn't make you laugh, it's a bad production. If Chekhov doesn't make you cry, it's a bad production."

Shortly after Hirsch arrived to begin rehearsals he wrote to Louis Bako that his physical surroundings were fine: he had, he said, a "beautiful cottage in the village with trees all around." But "as usual I am nervous, anxious, full of fears and insecurities, & there is no one here to phone to talk to. Every new beginning is like walking a tightrope without the memory of having walked it before." The first challenge was simply that of producing Chekov in the Festival Theatre. Langham, the acknowledged master of the thrust stage, had taken years to get used to it, while Hirsch would later say that the only directors to whom a thrust stage was "natural" were those with "a choreographic sense, twenty years of repertory experience, and nine *Shrews* and five *Hamlets* behind them."

In preparation Hirsch immersed himself in the Chekhov and came equipped with a library of information. In a conversation with the *Globe & Mail's* Herbert Whittaker a few weeks before the play opened he said, "I even know what kind of scent the characters in the company should wear. We won't use it, that would be gimmicky, but I know that Kate as Madame Ranevskaya should wear a cologne called 4711, while Bruno Gerussi as the valet Yasha should reek of pomade."

Langham gave Hirsch every resource Stratford could offer. Brian Jackson, a fine costume and stage designer, had just returned from a year of study in Italy. Louis Applebaum, who had written the music for Stratford's first productions as well as its famous trumpet fanfares, would take responsibility for music. And the cast was a selection of Stratford's best actors, beginning with Kate Reid as Madame Ranevskaya, William Hutt as her ineffectual brother Gaev and Douglas Campbell as humbly-born entrepreneur Lopakhin. As a group, the cast knew the stage and knew each other, and most had been directed by Hirsch at least once in the recent past.

After having the cast read the play in English three times Hirsch invited the late George Ignatieff to a rehearsal. A Russian aristocrat whose family had fled the Revolution when Ignatieff was ten, Ignatieff was a top Canadian diplomat at the time. Hirsch had him sit in the middle of the stage and read the whole first act in Russian. As Hirsch had intended, the actors laughed in the right places even though no one spoke a word of Russian, while they all got a sense of "the music of the language." Hirsch brought in films like the Soviet adaptation of Chekhov's *A Lady and Her Dog* (1960) and gave each of the actors a "kit" with translations of Chekhov's letters, working notes, diaries and telegrams. William Needles, in the role of the family's clerk Yepihodov, commented on how this depth of information helped him as an actor: "You felt that there was all kinds of activity going on in the house, offstage as well as onstage, and that there was an enormous amount of life and meaning – familial meaning – within this house that included not only the family itself but the servants and everybody in the neighbourhood. This made the ending so much more tragic when the house was denuded of everything."

The rehearsals were not all sweetness and light. A very young Richard Monette, in one of his earliest Stratford roles, watched Hirsch blast Kate Reid as she struggled with three props – a purse, a handkerchief and a piece of paper: "John, watching from the auditorium, was wearing track pants, his usual mode of dress. As Kate fumbled with her purse, John suddenly yelled out: 'Look at her! Look at her! This expensive actress cannot use props! Look at her!' And then he grabbed hold of the waistband of his track pants and pulled it right over his head." It seemed particularly unkind because the highly insecure Reid was battling both alcohol and her weight at the time. Despite such outbursts, however, the cast were able to create an unusual sense of ensemble, while still creating highly individualized performances.

When the play opened on July 26, 1965 the critics – with the exception of the *Star*'s Nathan Cohen, who was increasingly sour about Stratford – were unanimous in their praise of the production. Robertson Davies, writing in the *Peterborough Examiner*, complimented Hirsch as "a Canadian man of the theatre in whom this country has a great possession; let us take care that he is adequately regarded in appreciation and understanding." Comparing *The Cherry Orchard* to the other productions at the Festival the Montreal *Gazette*'s Gordon Jocelyn called it "the most satisfying experience in Stratford this year." For Hirsch the best accolade was a quip by Tyrone Guthrie, whose *Cherry Orchard* with Jessica Tandy and Hume Cronyn had opened on June 15 in Minneapolis. After seeing the Stratford production, Guthrie told Hirsch, "Well, my dear boy, your Act 1 is better than mine." Then he added, "But my Act 2 is better than yours."

Hirsch returned to Winnipeg for the new season feeling good about himself and his career. After the triumph of *Cherry Orchard* Michael Langham had offered him a two-year contract to do three plays, one in 1966 and two in 1967. He also had a contract in hand to do a television play for CBC's "Festival" series, based on the script Tom Hendry had started while travelling in Europe. With queries about work coming in from the United States, he had been taken on by the well-known New York agent Peter Witt, who was urging Hirsch to explore possibilities on Broadway and in Hollywood. In a letter to Louis Bako, who was now working in commercial theatre in Los Angeles, he outlined the different projects he had on the go, saying, "I have a good future my agent tells me and I know it myself."

Working at Stratford had strengthened Hirsch's connections with up-and-coming talent, and he was able to get money from the Canada Council to hire assistants for most MTC departments. His personal reputation as an expert on building institutions like the MTC meant requests for consulting and assistance were frequent. The theatre programs from this period are full of news items about Hirsch, Robert Sherrin (as head of the school and Children's Theatre) and general manager Bill Wylie travelling to help the new regional theatres that were appearing across Canada and the United States.

Hirsch was also astutely building a network of contacts that would serve him well throughout the rest of his career. He was now an important figure in the burgeoning Canadian cultural "scene." A list of his activities in 1965 included: theatre advisor, Canadian Centre for the Performing Arts; vice-president of the Canadian Theatre Centre; member of the advisory committee for Expo 67; and member of the boards of the National Theatre School and the Royal Winnipeg Ballet. He also arranged for the MTC to become the first Canadian institution to join the Theater Communications Group, an organization dedicated to promoting non-profit professional theatre in North America. This connection proved useful to both Hirsch and the MTC over the years.

By the time Hirsch's production of *Andorra* opened on December 18, 1965 he had made his decision to leave the MTC. For a while Hirsch framed his leaving as a kind of sabbatical, but the hardheaded Bill Wylie insisted that the break be a clear one and Eddie Gilbert was formally appointed to succeed Hirsch. Gilbert remembers that "*Andorra* felt like Hirsch's swan song" and that by February Hirsch's production of *The Threepenny Opera* seemed much like that of a guest director.

Hirsch's production of *Andorra* was the Canadian premiere of Max Frisch's play in which the people of a town turn on a boy and surrender him to an invading army because he is Jewish. In the program notes Hirsch highlighted the playwright's point that Andorra is simply a name for any country where there is hatred and prejudice: "For example, Andorra is America where black people are segregated, or Canada where native people are kept on reservations. The play presents simple human beings, people who could be our next door neighbour, who turn into killers." In private Hirsch found it "a harrowing show and very tough on me," and complained of it affecting his nerves.

The cast featured a number of children, including John Bluethner, then a fourteen-year-old taking classes at the MTC Theatre School (he would go on to spend almost two decades as an actor and be Hirsch's assistant director for *Twelfth Night* in Toronto in 1980). Despite the darkness of the play, he remembers enjoying Hirsch's passion about the play and his ability to explain what it meant; he also remembers temper tantrums and language he had never heard an adult use before. The production itself made a huge impression on Bluethner, particularly the culminating invasion by storm troopers in helmets emblazoned with arrows rather than swastikas (Hirsch may have been remembering the Arrow Cross fascists he had seen during wartime Budapest). William Hutt, who played the boy's father, would tell his biographer many years later, "I was *in* it, and it frightened me."

Though outwardly confident, Hirsch was nervous about leaving the MTC and in fact the break wasn't a complete one. He took away with him a small annual stipend as a consulting director, which he retained until the mid-1970s. In an interview with the *Winnipeg Free Press* he maintained his position that the departure was a sabbatical. "I took this sabbatical for two reasons. One is to establish myself as an international director. The second is to get Winnipeg theatre used to the idea that it can exist without me."

He had his Stratford and CBC contracts in hand – and the possibility of work in the United States. Asked in an interview about where he thought he might be in a few years' time he replied with a list of things he would like to do:

FRAIDIE MARTZ AND ANDREW WILSON

I would love to go to Broadway to produce just one play because I would love to have the experience. I would like to go to Hollywood to make films. I would like to go to Africa and work in a country where there is no theatre. I would like to do television. I would like to write plays for children. I would like to write some poetry. I would like to do everything.

He had a strong sense of accomplishment in Winnipeg, of having slain several dragons that had faced him during the 1950s, notably the "puritan ethic" that had cast theatre as trivial and not worthy of support, the idea that the city would not accept Brecht and other challenging playwrights on the international scene, and that Canadian plays would not draw substantial audiences. Artistically Hirsch felt he had "worked out his craft" during his years at the MTC, and it was time to work in a larger arena.

Hirsch's impact on his adopted city was summed up in 1996 by Rory Runnels, founder of the Manitoba Association of Playwrights: "If you are a Winnipegger, in your 40s or older, and especially if, like me, you are involved in some capacity with the theatre here, then John Hirsch has had an impact on you. As a presence, then as a symbol, and, yes, as myth...."

A full history of the Manitoba Theatre Centre has not yet been written and is long overdue. Hirsch looms over that history, along with Tom Hendry. The two were immortalized for the fiftieth anniversary of the MTC's founding in a bronze statue by Ruth Abernathy. When it was unveiled Hendry made a typically self-deprecating crack about becoming a target for pigeons. But John Bluethner, a Winnipegger for most of his life and someone who had worked with Hirsch as both a child actor and assistant director, had a different take. Noting that the statues are supposed to be life-size Bluethner mused, "I think John's is a little small. I remember him as being bigger, somehow."

[Six]

Director at Large

ON THE EVENING of January 2, 1966 Hirsch sat in the audience at Montreal's Théâtre du Nouveau Monde watching Denise Pelletier put her personal stamp on a French-language version of *Mother Courage*. It was one of the Québécoise actress's greatest performances, portraying Courage as a Fury who was "as frightening as war itself." Also on stage was Jean Gascon and an ensemble of the best francophone actors in Canada.

Directing a play in a language he didn't speak was a gamble for Hirsch, but the conditions were those under which he worked best: a script he knew in his bones, first-class actors, and a production team he trusted (the production had essentially been transported from Winnipeg, costumes and all, to Montreal). The gamble paid off handsomely with huge applause and great reviews. It also marked a new high in Hirsch's love affair with the city, with its vibrant nightlife and its Hungarian restaurants where he could play the exiled aristocrat, sweeping in "like an Esterházy" with a retinue of friends.

For a man who intended to make the leap from national to international rank among directors, it was an auspicious start. Still in his mid-thirties, Hirsch had a strong portfolio behind him, no family ties other than the endlessly supportive Shacks back in Winnipeg and boundless enthusiasm for his profession. His timing was also good. With the rise of regional theatres across North America, more and more opportunities were available for freelance directors. After his years of apprenticeship and of running the MTC he had strong skills honed by directing a wide variety of plays and actors.

But freelancing presented Hirsch with challenges that were as much personal as technical. For the better part of the decade he had always been the boss. Now he would be the guest, dropping in to work at institutions with their own histories and ways of working, and with audiences he didn't know. Going freelance held the promise of substantial fees, but to make a living he had to attach himself to more than one theatre organization. Even the MTC, always glad to have him back, now had to think creatively about how to afford him, such as co-productions with other theatres to share the costs.

Stratford was the blue-chip stock in his portfolio. In February he returned there to continue the cycle of Shakespeare's history plays that had begun the previous year. Michael Langham would direct *Henry V* while Hirsch would take on *Henry VI*, the first instalment of the Wars of the Roses trilogy.

Hirsch finally had a whole Shakespeare play to himself, and the formidable acting company that Langham had built up over the years. Yet he felt under-appreciated and vaguely unwelcome in Stratford and was often vocal in his criticisms of the Festival. He freely complained to interviewers that he was treated as "somebody from out West" and faced a certain "Anglo-Saxon disdain" there. However, he had more familiar faces around him this time around as some of his close Winnipeg colleagues were working there for the season. Eoin Sprott was production manager at the Avon Theatre, and a relatively new colleague, a Hungarian of the 1956 generation named Thomas Bohdanetzky, was stage manager for *Henry VI*. The large cast was full of people Hirsch had directed recently and the National Theatre School connection was also apparent. Powys Thomas, a much-loved faculty member and founder of the School, played a notable Winchester and one of Hirsch's recent students, Kenneth Welsh, had landed a part despite what he remembers as a disastrous audition (he "dried" three times in front of Hirsch, and was amazed to be offered a contract).

Hirsch acquitted himself well in the best tradition of the Festival as his beautifully costumed cast spoke their lines clearly and convincingly, and moved efficiently on and off the stage. The reviews were largely favourable, with the *New York Times'* Stanley Kauffman judging that "the success of this production begins with director

John Hirsch....He is highly skilled in the Guthrie-Campbell-Langham vein of pageantry and alarums on the open stage, a style generic to this festival; but he also shows a personal quality of intense subjectivity. For instance, the disputes in the Council Chamber become bruising contests of naked ego." In the wake of such a success, Michael Langham invited Hirsch to come back to Stratford the following year to direct the last of the Wars of the Roses plays, *Richard III*, with Christopher Plummer tentatively cast as the villainous king.

By mid-summer Hirsch's short-term future was falling into place. His ambition to direct at a major theatre in New York was coming closer to realization as his agent finalized a contract with Lincoln Center. At Stratford Langham suggested he direct not only *Richard III* in the following year, but also another play, preferably a Canadian one in honour of the country's upcoming centenary. Hirsch agreed and suggested commissioning a new play from his old friend James Reaney. Although Reaney had now had several plays produced and was a three-time winner of the Governor General's Award for poetry, the Stratford Board wasn't at all confident in the project. They might have been even less confident had they known that Hirsch's only instructions to Reaney were "to do something free form, personal, and using as much material already written as possible." He had also shared with Reaney his interest in the illusions and special effects pioneered in the Czech theatre and the possibility of using movie screens. Beyond that, and a deadline for delivering a script the following spring, Reaney could do what he wanted.

In September Hirsch disappeared to Tunisia for a holiday, missing the broadcast of his first television production in over ten years: Tom Hendry's *15 Miles of Broken Glass*. Hendry had begun the script while travelling in 1965. After several drafts the script had been accepted for broadcast in CBC's "Festival" series of ninety-minute televised films. The story was set in what Hendry described as "the Canada I remember – where everyone had Scottish or Irish names, and governments were made up of people you could like or hate personally because you knew them personally," and centred on a young air cadet on the Prairies in 1945 as he deals with the disappointment of "missing out" on the Second World War. Delighted with Hendry's unforced, naturalistic dialogue and intrigued by a play whose central issue was the *absence* of war, Hirsch told the *Globe & Mail* it was "the first Canadian play I've encountered that has not been self-conscious about being Canadian."

Shot at CBC's old Jarvis Street studios in the spring, the show was broadcast on September 21 and garnered good reviews for its script and the work of actors Heath Lamberts, Gordon Pinsent and another recent National Theatre School graduate, Terence Kelly. It also caught some political flak about its opening scene in which two air cadets – frustrated by the arrival of V-J Day before their seventeenth birthdays – roast potatoes in a bonfire of Union Jacks. This provoked the wrath of former prime minister John Diefenbaker, who asked if it was the policy of the CBC – a favourite Conservative target, then as now – to denigrate Canada's connection with the mother country. CBC's answer was to re-broadcast the show in April, 1967.

By now Hirsch was focused on New York, where he had a contract to open Federico Garcia Lorca's poetic drama *Yerma* in December at Lincoln Center's new Vivian Beaumont Theater. *Yerma* was by anyone's standards a tough assignment: a six-act poem rather than a traditional play. The story, if it can be said to have one, is simple: Yerma is a Spanish peasant, childless because her husband is sterile (or possibly uninterested). Over the course of the play, driven mad by the fecundity of the other women in her village, she laments her plight; in the last act she kills her husband. Hirsch felt considerable affinity for Garcia Lorca, the poet, playwright and director murdered – most probably by Nationalist militia – shortly after the outbreak of the Spanish Civil War in 1936. Like Hirsch, Garcia Lorca was a homosexual in a society where it was impossible to talk openly about sexuality. Even thirty years after the playwright's death it was still impossible for Hirsch to discuss that sexuality in the program notes. "Lorca wrote Yerma as an expression of his own deeply desper-ate need for love, for growth, for freedom," was the best he could manage without any reference to the nature of that love.

Hirsch was enthusiastic about working in New York and felt equal to anything the city could throw at him, but it is hard to imagine conditions further from Hirsch's comfort zone: an unconventional play, a cast of actors he hadn't yet met, and a new stage to get to grips with. Moreover, he was coming to a deeply troubled organization.

The Beaumont's original artistic directors, Elia Kazan and Robert Whitehead, had been fired in 1965. They were replaced by Herbert Blau and Jules Irving from the Actor's Workshop in San Francisco, who brought with them a group of Workshop actors as the core of a reborn repertory company. Blau and Irving came with a hugely ambitious program, not only of changing the repertoire but also of finding a new audience, integrating more black actors, tackling explicitly political themes and eventually creating a national theatre like that in London. As it turned out, the company did not gel as an acting ensemble, the established critics were hostile and the box office disappointing. Blau clashed with the Board and was fired shortly before Hirsch arrived, leaving Jules Irving in command as artistic director, struggling to find a repertoire and a company style.

When Hirsch reported for work at the Beaumont, his accent, intensity and slightly eccentric appearance initially worked well for him. The Lincoln Center publicist wrote that watching him walk down a corridor was an adventure in movement: "With a jerky grace, his head leads, followed by a giraffe neck and a slender torso, all balanced on Ray Bolger legs. He prefaces his talk with a forward thrust of head, an abrupt smile, then a shyer, wider one, quickly wiped away, a bit nervously, a bit shamefacedly. Then a larger laugh."

As a theatre the Beaumont made a less than favourable impression on Hirsch. When the *Globe & Mail*'s Herbert Whittaker visited it, Hirsch had to take Whittaker out to a nearby greasy spoon on 10th Avenue to do the interview. Hirsch commented, "In all that expensive, elaborate building, there's only a machine that deals out cokes."

The cast that Hirsch was given to direct was a mixture of Blau's and Irving's San Francisco company and New Yorkers. The latter included Gloria Foster – one of the just-emerging generation of black leading actors – in the title role, and the young Frank Langella as her husband. Again Hirsch was disappointed. While he found abundant talent among the cast, the actors lacked the technical skills of those he had been working with in Canada. *Yerma* demanded actors who could speak poetry and who understood the chorus function. Hirsch commented that, "Actors who are not used to playing in classical theatre – who are only used to psychological approaches and naturalistic acting – have difficulty," and added, "What I demand are actors capable of a huge, passionate coolness." His demands did not make him popular with many of the cast. He got on well with Frank Langella, whose work he respected, less well with some of the more Method-focused actors, and never quite clicked with Gloria Foster. Daniel Sullivan, one of the Actor's Workshop group, remembers a rehearsal in which Hirsch became frustrated with Foster's emotive approach: "He was shouting from the back row at Gloria, 'Darling, I am already crying and my eyes are watering, I can't even see you. IT'S ONLY 10 MINUTES INTO THE PLAY – why are you forcing it at this point?' It was hilarious, done with humour, not anger."

Hirsch auditioned several composers for *Yerma* and finally chose Stanley Silverman, a young New Yorker with whom he would work many times in the future. Silverman was mainly writing atonal music at the time, and when he brought in his first "sketches" Hirsch commented, "Stanley, these are peasant women. They've never *heard* notes like that." Further work found not only a more folkloric approach – some of it written for two singers who were integrated in the cast – and for guitars and percussion, but also complete sound design that fit with the sets to be created by David Hays. Silverman remembers how he and Hays worked to turn the director's vision – deeply influenced by his many holidays in the Mediterranean region since the early 1960s – into theatrical reality: "You entered the theatre and thought that you were in some sort of rocky Spanish wasteland with a little water flowing through a small brook." Hirsch always loved sounds that represented the elements, and the sounds of water poured into basins and bowls, of wind chimes and sheep bells, featured prominently in *Yerma*.

The music and sets got glowing mentions in reviews when *Yerma* opened, but opinions about the overall production were mixed. The now-defunct *Morning Telegraph* and the *Daily News* liked it; Walter Kerr of the *New York Times* didn't. Hostile or not, there was wide agreement that *Yerma* was the best play yet produced by the company.

The experience forced Hirsch to rethink his often-critical attitude towards Stratford. He recognized the superiority of the Stratford organization, which was able to turn out, in its relatively short season, productions "of a quality which I can see now, after my present experience, are unmatchable in the entire continent.... These are facts – just facts." Nonetheless, he found in New York, "a real appreciation of what you can do," and was pleased to be asked to direct another play (replacing Blau) at the Beaumont in April. This one was more in keeping with his experience and outlook: Brecht's *Galileo*, with an international star, Anthony Quayle, in the title role.

In the meantime the demands of his new life as a freelancer imposed themselves. He had a musical comedy to direct in snow-bound Winnipeg. Hirsch flew home to a warm welcome from the Shacks and his friends, and started to work on a production of *A Funny Thing Happened on the Way to the Forum*. While in Winnipeg he also checked up on a project he had set in motion the previous year, when the MTC received a $10,000 grant from the Imperial Order of the Daughters of the Empire to commission an original script for the 1967 Centennial. The IODE may not have had a play about Winnipeg's 1919 General Strike in mind when they made the grant, but that is what Hirsch had suggested to Ann Henry, a local writer and theatre reviewer whose father had been a leader in the strike. Henry was feeling her way towards a study of a family cracking under the pressure of a civic disaster and of the long-lasting scars left on the citizens and politics of Winnipeg. Hirsch continued to work with Henry, despite the other work on his plate. "John would come over and read it," she remembered, "then go off saying, 'carry on, carry on...' waving his arms and legs like a windmill." In the end, Eddie Gilbert did the detailed dramaturgical work with Henry and directed the premiere of the play, *Lulu Street*. Hirsch would direct it himself five years later at the 1972 Lennoxville Festival, and had the CBC do a televised version a few years later.

In the meantime Hirsch was keeping track of another Centennial script-in-progress. James Reaney was still working on the play Hirsch had commissioned him to write for Stratford, and the news was both good and bad: good because he had plenty of material, bad because it was shaping up into a 400-page script that was hard to describe, save that it was autobiographical and much of the story happened in Stratford. Since tickets and posters had to be printed, Reaney had been forced to give it a name, *Colours in the Dark*, but little else was fixed. Hirsch was nervous but left Reaney to get on with it and trusted him to deliver something workable by the beginning of rehearsals in April. The Festival Board was even more nervous. Although Michael Langham supported the project, a lot of reassurance was necessary with some Board members during the development stages.

Hirsch also found himself putting out a more urgent Stratford fire. Michael Langham's verbal agreement with Christopher Plummer had fallen through, and a new lead, Alan Bates, had agreed to play Richard III in the 1967 season. This was the beginning of a new epoch at Stratford, when the Festival began to bring in international stars for lead roles. Unfortunately Langham had committed an uncharacteristic public relations gaffe, making it sound like Bates had been a desperate second choice, and Bates was threatening to pull out. While Langham telexed a personal apology to Bates, the Festival issued a flattering press release issued under Hirsch's name: "The part is absurd, the melodrama grotesque. Richard is a monster on a huge scale. As wicked as Ivan the Terrible, as satanic as Lucifer. How do you make him human? Only Alan Bates can do it."

Bates, a gentle man who was not inclined towards prima donna turns, was mollified by the Stratford charm offensive, and he and Hirsch hit it off in late March when they met for the first time in New York. The two swapped ideas about the play at The Ginger Man, a British-style pub on West 64th Street, drinking a lot of beer in the process. After the pub closed the discussion continued outside on the sidewalk, with Bates tipsily trying out different variations of the hunchbacked monarch's limp, "beer mug still in hand and oblivious to the stares of late-night pedestrians in the busy district."

By that time Hirsch was deep into rehearsals for *Galileo* at the Beaumont. The play is one of Brecht's best-known, pitting organized religion against scientific method and free inquiry through the story of the great Italian scientist. While intrigued by the play, Hirsch found the production a difficult one. In a letter written in mid-March Hirsch shared his contradictory feelings about it with Tom Hendry: "Terribly excited by the play, so brilliant, so difficult. Such a stupid thing to undertake what with the lack of really good minor players I haven't chosen. Plus all the younger people seem to have no respect for intellect – brains – content. Is it me? The age of McLuhan is *really* here? Training? Tony Quayle very good...." He raged against his own imperfections as well as the working conditions at the Beaumont: "It always just as the end approaches, I clam up and can't communicate with as much ease and love most necessary at this stage. Anyway, it is a misery. The show is huge and I don't see all the physical elements growing around it as one does in a real theatre. Everything is done far away by people I don't know....What is my fault, inability, and how much of it is THEY, the actors, the environment?" His sense of mission is also there: "But this is New York and I keep telling myself that somehow my presence here makes some sense if I can bring them closer to the kind of theatre I know, believe in, with all ITS imperfections."

Although Hirsch enjoyed working with Anthony Quayle, the two had one run-in during the rehearsal. Daniel Sullivan remembers the incident, which stemmed from Hirsch's treatment of one of the cast, a young man named Frank Bayer: "Frank was a stage manager who was thrust into the role of the Young Monk after John fired the original actor. Poor Frank was doing his best but he was, let's face it, a stage manager, not an actor. John grew quickly impatient with Frank and would grumble audibly as Frank tried to get through a treacherously long speech in the second act." Quayle eventually decided that Hirsch was bullying Bayer and threatened to walk out of the theatre if it continued. The grumbling stopped and relative harmony reigned for the rest of the rehearsal period. Sullivan concludes the story: "I was sitting in Frank's dressing room on opening night trying to calm him because he was terrified. John was nervously going to each dressing room to wish the actors good luck and when Frank opened the door to him, John hesitated for a moment and then said 'Frank.... Be better.' He moved quickly onto the next dressing room without any idea of the devastation he had just caused." (Devastated or not, Frank Bayer not only had a long career as a stage manager on both coasts but stayed in touch with Hirsch for many years.)

When it opened in mid-April, *Galileo* won wide critical acclaim and gave the Beaumont its first clear success since opening. Walter Kerr wrote in the *New York Times* that more than anything that had yet been done at the Beaumont Theatre "the production walks the stage unafraid, confident that it will be listened to, conscious of its vocal and visual authority." In April Hirsch was awarded the prize for Best Director by the Outer Critics Circle, which represents critics who review New York productions for out-of-town newspapers and national publications. The good reviews were gratifying but Hirsch was particularly pleased by the celebrity status that a New York success brings. He later wrote of his excitement when Marlene Dietrich came backstage to offer congratulations.

Meanwhile, the 1967 Stratford season was gearing up. By this time Michael Langham had announced that he was leaving Stratford after twelve years as artistic director. In his words, "the Festival had become too big and unwieldy for one man to give to all its varied undertakings the attention they merited.... Obviously, the time had come for the artistic director's responsibilities to be shared." The responsibilities would henceforth be shared by Jean Gascon and John Hirsch, with Gascon as the artistic director and Hirsch (due to his commitments and ambitions elsewhere) as associate director. It was the first time Stratford would try a shared leadership model; what is surprising, given its outcome two years later, was that it was not the last.

Rehearsals for Hirsch's two productions, *Richard III* and *Colours in the Dark*, began in April. The two plays, and the two rehearsal processes, could not have been more different. *Richard* was exactly the type of production that Stratford was designed to do, a classic script with which one might take certain liberties but which would always be judged against previous productions. In contrast, *Colours* had no past and would require an immense effort from the creative team – director, composer, designers and actors – before the script was finalized.

Hirsch's thinking on *Richard III* was strongly influenced by contemporary currents in international theatre, particularly the Polish critic Jan Kott's *Shakespeare, Our Contemporary*, rather than by flags-and-pageantry tradition. Hirsch saw Richard as "a Nietzschean hero, a superman who is daring society and God to see how far he can go…. He creates wilfully – and that's where the hero enters – a greater murderer and greater villain than anyone who came before him." Richard's self-described deformity and joyful villainy – the cornerstones of Laurence Olivier's 1944 performance at London's Old Vic Theatre, which had been the reigning model for the role ever since – were to be downplayed.

As rehearsals advanced Hirsch's vision of this new Richard and his world took shape. Outside in the real world the growing debacle of Vietnam was undermining old attitudes towards the military; inside the Festival theatre Hirsch was replacing the flags and trumpets of old with faceless, robotic soldiers and electronic music. The cast and crew settled into rehearsals well. Bates, happy in a new love affair with a young man he'd just met in Stratford, was a popular figure with his new colleagues. Moreover, he enjoyed working with Hirsch, whom he found refreshingly open to ideas from other people. He later told the story of how his understudy Neil Dainard contributed a novel staging idea in the play's final scene before battle is joined by Richard's and Richmond's opposing forces. Hirsch was having trouble dealing, in staging terms, with the marked similarity between two commanders' speeches, and shared his frustration with the cast. Dainard suggested having both actors on stage at the same time and mixing the speeches, thereby emphasizing the shared rhetoric of the putative good and evil leaders. Hirsch loved it, and the idea was incorporated in the production.

Meanwhile, rehearsals for *Colours in the Dark* were taking place in the Stratford High School auditorium with the portraits of Reaney's old teachers looking down on a somewhat apprehensive cast. The script Reaney had delivered for the first run-through was a scotch-taped collage derived from his poems, diaries and notebooks over the years and inspired by a visual design, Paul Klee's "magic squares" technique. It begins with a children's party on one part of the stage and, next door, a boy confined to bed with measles, his eyes covered to protect them from the light. The boy is Reaney; the play follows his life story from his Stratford childhood to his finding employment and love further afield, in Winnipeg and Toronto, as a young man. Along the way there is a mix of individual experience and local folklore: a fight between hardwood and softwood trees, an old woman – Granny Crack – who hangs on a child's jump rope all the clothes she has ever worn, children shouting anti-Catholic and anti-Protestant jingles, a girl tap dancing in a "superbly horrible" pink dress, a man reciting "An Ode on the Mammoth Cheese" and a riff on the street names of Winnipeg.

The value of knowing and trusting one's actors and other creative colleagues was never more apparent to Hirsch. Martha Henry and Heath Lamberts had been in Reaney's *Names and Nicknames* at the MTC, and Douglas Rain had done several radio "collages" for Reaney. Three more adult actors, four singers, and twelve children rounded out the cast. With Reaney onsite the script evolved as the actors felt out their parts, and the work of designer Eoin Sprott and composer Alan Laing was woven in. Hirsch and Sprott had decided that the only way to provide sets for forty-two scenes was to use projected graphics, photos and film clips, some of which Sprott collected himself in the countryside surrounding Stratford. The excitement of the collective creation lingers in the memories of the participants. Sprott remembers, "I had screens everywhere. I had screens in the corners, triangular screens, main screens for these projectors that I had borrowed from Lincoln Center. It was revolutionary for me because you could change the scenery overnight by just changing the order of the photographs or using different photographs, and also montages of colour. We would change the projections and the actors, especially Dougie Rain, would do something different. So it changed from rehearsal to rehearsal."

Silverman had been offered an orchestra for the production but decided to make do with just himself and a percussionist. "We ended up memorizing the score and playing some sixty or so instruments between us, moving VERY quickly in the pit." Reaney wrote and re-wrote, and watched Hirsch add in the magical effects he wanted: "A thing you can't write but which an imaginative director writes for you was the beautiful effect with the empty rocking chair at the end of the christening scene. Two rocking chairs rocking all by themselves after Martha Henry has just departed, setting them secretly in motion just before she left."

As usual Hirsch was sharing his nervousness in a decidedly un-Stratfordian way. "This excursion into a poet's mind may well become one of the most debated productions of the year," he told the *Toronto Telegram* in May. "I'm positive it's going to horrify the staid steady customers. They'll say it's insane and unintelligible and psychedelic and obscure ... only they'll forget to say these things about themselves." The prospect, wrote the journalist, seemed to give him a certain painful pleasure, or pleasurable pain.

Hirsch's *Richard III* opened the season on June 12, a visually splendid production designed by Desmond Heeley in black, red, purple and gold, with electronic music composed by Stanley Silverman. But Bates' detached, almost psychopathic Richard bewildered or offended many reviewers. *Time* simply thought him miscast, and most Canadian reviewers longed for a more traditional "bunch backed toad" of a Richard. Why such a pathetically small hump and so perfunctory a limp? What was Bates up to when he tossed his dagger to an equally unsympathetic Richmond in the final act, effectively committing suicide? (The idea was not entirely new, having been suggested by George Bernard Shaw many years before, and would be seen again at Stratford when Brian Bedford played Richard under the direction of Robin Phillips.) Walter Kerr was one of the few to see Bates' performance as part of a coherent directorial vision. "Mr. Bates," he wrote, "does not begin as most Richards do, asking that we be amused by his guile or outraged by his brazenness. He begins reasonably. Death is part of logic, a necessary digit in the equation. His inflections are cool, casual, no more brutal than twentieth-century everyday life." He found not just sound and fury but sense in the final meeting of the armies, as the robotic soldiers moved and wheeled and thrust their spears in clanking lockstep. "In and among them," Kerr wrote, "with nightmare precision, range the principals, prisoners of the monstrous metalwork they have created. Evil is a robot. Set it in motion and it will devour you.... Mr. Hirsch's deployment of his actors reinforces the sense of a patterned, predestined universe again and again." Kerr found much to admire in this *Richard*, but missed the passion of more traditional productions, complaining that "it could use one unprogrammed heart."

No one could accuse Alan Bates of lacking heart on the evening of July 25th, however, when he leapt to his feet at the end of *Colours in the Dark* and led a prolonged standing ovation that only ended when the notoriously shy James Reaney was persuaded up on stage to take a bow. Hirsch had managed to pull together the script, design, music and actors in a way that delighted audience and most reviewers. There was much talk of Canadian plays finally having established a beachhead at what was in effect Canada's (English-language) national theatre, and in the general euphoria that accompanied the Centennial this seemed plausible. The year also saw successful productions of *Lulu Street* in Winnipeg, George Ryga's *The Ecstasy of Rita Joe* in Vancouver, and John Herbert's *Fortune and Men's Eyes* in Toronto (the latter had been workshopped at Stratford in 1965 but rejected because of its explicitly homosexual content). Yet despite the good press notices *Colours in the Dark* did not do well at the box office, averaging a sixty-four-per cent house over its short run of twelve performances.

In general the Festival season that year was a strong one, notable for Jean Gascon's opera *Cosi fan tutte*, Langham's *Anthony and Cleopatra* with Zoe Caldwell and Christopher Plummer, and another Langham production, Gogol's *Government Inspector*, with William Hutt in the title role. Hirsch's *Richard* did well at the box office, at least partly because of its star leading man, but Hirsch was bitter about the critical reception it received. "You can't keep doing Shakespeare as he was done 100 years ago," he told the drama critic from the *Boston Herald* two weeks after the play opened. "You search for meaning in terms of what is going on now. But this gets you into trouble because part of our audience expects the same style of production they used to see when they were young."

This resonated with Michael Langham's reflections on his own efforts "to bring our interpretations into key with the 1960s" during the last years of his leadership at the Festival. He cited Hirsch's *Richard III*, as well as several of his own productions, as having been "strongly resisted by both the press and the middle-aged public of Ontario....I already had the impression that in Establishment Ontario the twentieth century was culturally invalid."

When Langham took his leave of the company he had led since 1955, on the final night of its tour at Expo, he passed responsibility for its future to "John and Jean." The two were already planning their first season, amidst speculation about how the duo might work together. Arnold Edinborough, writing in the *Shakespeare Quarterly*, hoped that Gascon and Hirsch would not only maintain the high standards Langham had achieved at Stratford, but move the Festival forward. He saw in Hirsch a director "who will respect the text and will be concerned about the relationships in a play," and while he expressed impeccably Upper Canadian misgivings about Gascon's "mannered tradition of the *Comédie Française*," he thought that the "polarity" might be profitable.

During the final months of Langham's time at Stratford, Hirsch set several things in motion that would have strong impact in the following season. With his support Stratford hired the MTC's Bill Wylie as its general manager, in line with Langham's determination to modernize the Festival's administration. He got the Festival to expand Langham's policy of hiring bright young Canadians as assistant directors and give bigger roles to recent graduates of the National Theatre School. Finally, he suggested that Peter Raby, a young Englishman brought in by Langham to be Stratford dramaturge in 1966, adapt Alexandre Dumas' *Three Musketeers* for the Festival stage next year.

Raby, who had successfully adapted *The Government Inspector* for Michael Langham, was happy to work with Hirsch. "He would *fizz* in rehearsals," Raby recalled of Hirsch many years later. "He planned, very carefully, but there seemed to be more surprises when he was around. He was widely read in Canadian and American and European literature – fiction and poetry as well as drama – and so he was very attuned to a whole range of literature as well as to performance ideas." The two sat down and roughed out their approach. Then Raby, whose contract was season-to-season at the time, went back to England and started work. "Once he had outlined his vision of it," Raby remembers, "he very much left me to get on with it and trusted me to do so."

Hirsch spent a lot of time that fall travelling, conferring with Gascon and the Stratford administration about the coming season (in addition to *The Three Musketeers*, Hirsch would direct *A Midsummer Night's Dream*) and visiting the Shacks and his friends in Winnipeg. He also dropped in on his friend Jacques Beyderwellen in Montreal and found he had a new boyfriend, a twenty-year-old artist named Bryan Trottier. Born into a military family, Bryan had moved a great deal while growing up and had begun but not finished his studies at Montreal's École des Beaux-arts. When he met Hirsch Bryan was making a precarious living as a graphic artist and enjoying the burgeoning gay lifestyle of the 1960s. For young men like Bryan, being gay was different than for men of Hirsch and Beyderwellen's generation. Gay liberation as a political movement was still a few years away, but official repression of homosexuality was on its way out. In December a new and charismatic justice minister, Pierre Trudeau, would introduce changes to the Criminal Code with the

Designer David Hayes, John Hirsch and Jules Irving during rehearsals
for *Saint Joan* at the Vivian Beaumont Theatre in December 1967.
Photographer unknown, photo courtesy of Mrs. Priscilla Pointer

comment that "there's no place for the state in the bedrooms of the
nation." Bryan had known he was gay since adolescence and had
already had a number of affairs with men, as well as with some
women; his relationship with Beyderwellen was affectionate but not
exclusive. He found Hirsch intriguing and enjoyed his tales of work
and travel when they met at Jacque's Montreal house. But Hirsch was
never in town for very long and in any case was preoccupied with his
next production at the Beaumont, George Bernard Shaw's *Saint Joan*.

Jules Irving had taken on board some lessons from *Galileo*'s
success the previous year. Despite the Beaumont's original mission
to build a repertory company, Irving calculated that the short-term
survival of the theatre would be best reinforced by importing actors
for roles that demanded classical training. Hirsch had two of the
best in Tony Van Bridge and William Hutt, hired to play the Bishop
of Beauvais and the Earl of Warwick, respectively. He also had, for
the second time, a black actress in a lead role: Diana Sands, best

known for playing Sidney Poitier's sister in the film *Raisin in the Sun*. Initially Hirsch ran up against his old enemy, Method acting, in rehearsals with Sands. The story is told that Hirsch actually resorted to tying Sands to a chair in order to make her deliver the text as simply as possible.

On November 24, in the middle of rehearsals for *Saint Joan*, Hirsch found himself racing to Ottawa, where he was to be one of the first recipients of the newly created Service Medal of the Order of Canada. The event, as Hirsch told the story, turned into a Marx Brothers-type farce. Reluctant to sacrifice any rehearsal time, he allowed just enough time to get to the airport from a morning rehearsal, catch a plane for the investiture, then race back to New York the same night in order to start rehearsals on time the next morning. The plan began well. At the last minute the stage manager handed him a set of tails and accoutrements in a box and bundled him into a taxi for the airport. But when Hirsch checked into a hotel in Ottawa to dress, he found that many of the shirt's buttonholes were worn away, and it was impossible to keep it closed. With no time to acquire another shirt he struck upon the idea of using "a Napoleonic pose with my right arm clutching my shirt to keep it from opening," and hopped another taxi to Rideau Hall, the Governor General's residence. There, realizing he couldn't shake hands without exposing his bare chest, he used his left hand, explaining to everyone he met that he had pulled a muscle in his right arm. When his name was called, he approached the dais, shook Roland Michener's extended right hand with his left, and once again repeated his story. Returning to his seat, Hirsch said to his neighbour, another naturalized Central European Jew, "You see, this is God's way of reminding me that in His eyes I am still just a Hungarian-Jewish orphan."

There was general relief at the Beaumont when *Saint Joan* opened to good notices on January 4, 1968. Predictably, much was made of Diana Sands' being black: at a press conference she squashed a journalist who asked her what it was like to play a "black Saint Joan," retorting that the only character she had any intention of playing was the one Shaw wrote, full stop. But the reliance on foreigners

Striking "a Napoleonic pose with my right arm clutching my shirt to keep it from opening," Hirsch receives the Order of Canada from Governor-General Roland Michener, November 1967.

was noticed. Critic Glenn Loney was not alone when he asked, in a summary of the Beaumont's offerings that year, "But where does that leave American talent? Are there no native directors as able as Hirsch or Quayle (whose *Tiger at the Gates* followed *Saint Joan*), no actors as polished as Van Bridge or Hutt?"

Hirsch, however, was about to do his own version of reciprocity. He had discovered a young American he wanted to bring to Stratford. Christopher Walken had never played any Shakespeare before, but he was handsome, moved gracefully (he was originally a "hoofer"), and had been acclaimed in recent New York productions. Hirsch proposed Walken as the male lead in *Romeo and Juliet*, to be directed by Douglas Campbell. The risk of an unknown Romeo was reduced by giving the role of Juliet to Geneviève Bujold, a rising international star in both French and English. Walken would also take on a smaller role as Lysander in Hirsch's *A Midsummer Night's Dream*. The *Dream* was scheduled to go on tour to several Canadian cities in early March before opening at Stratford in June, so it was Hirsch's top priority after *Saint Joan* had opened. Yet, as a freelance director must, he was already nailing down the next season in New York. Having triumphed in the subsidized world of the Beaumont, he was ready to try something new. His agent was working on his next contract, a new play by *Catch-22* author Joseph Heller, which was scheduled to open in October at the Ambassador Theater. For the first time, Hirsch would be working on Broadway.

Meanwhile, Peter Raby had returned from England with a rough draft of the *Three Musketeers*, and he and Hirsch worked on it at the Festival offices and at the house rented for Hirsch in the nearby village of St. Mary's. Raby was exhilarated by the process. He knew the actors he was writing for and could write to their strengths and that of the company as a whole. Hirsch was willing to try things out as they went along and for the most part the cast responded to that approach. Raby later commented that "without their readiness to explore a new way of working, of arriving at instant characterizations with little or no help from the script, the enterprise would have collapsed like a balloon." For example, there was a debate about a line for the female villain, Milady de Winter, played by Martha Henry. Would it be just too melodramatic for her to say, at the moment of her execution, that she was too young to die? "Martha Henry said that she would risk it," he recalled, and the same spirit of risk-taking prevailed all through rehearsals.

The technical preparations were as epic as the subject matter. Fight director Paddy Crean happily took on the task of making the action as fast-paced as possible, taking full advantage of the Festival Stage's many levels and exits. There were 250 costumes to design as the final script's forty scenes required innumerable costume changes. Designer Desmond Heeley made a major contribution to keeping costs down when he arrived from New York with four tea-chests full of materials he had picked up for $500. (Hirsch nonetheless went well over budget, keeping the props staff busy as he experimented with ever more objects that had to be carried on and off stage.) Heeley remembers enjoying the "directorial panache" with which Hirsch directed the play, but also his care in making full use of the main stage: "John was very much like Langham in this," Heeley says. "He made sure that everybody in the audience got their money's worth."

A different set of risks was being taken – often by the same actors – in rehearsals for *A Midsummer Night's Dream*. Hirsch had a clear vision of the production he wanted and that vision was something few in the Stratford public would have seen before. He was again influenced by Jan Kott's ideas, particularly about the essential eroticism of the play, and by the attitudes to sexual and social changes occurring in the late 1960s. His pre-rehearsal notes for the design team are expansive and detailed: "Light the Court darkly at the opening – a sense of Gothic and gargoyles" contrasts with a forest "where all fantasies can be realized.... The fairies are flower children, animal-like with the intense concentration and co-ordination of squirrels, full of swift, sudden movements, moving as one. Light is their only enemy – they are children of the freed loins of Night, moon-ripened and moon-governed. They lead a life of total sexual experience...." Some of that experience was decidedly homoerotic, with the fairies – a mostly male and athletic group – occasionally

"The year sex came to Stratford." *A Midsummer Night's Dream*
with Barbara Bryne as Puck, Martha Henry as Titania, and
Christopher Newton as Oberon.
*Photo by Douglas Spillane, courtesy of Stratford
Shakespeare Festival Archives*

gathering at the stage corners to hiss at the various pairs of lovers.
Costume designer Leslie Hurry was allowed to forget Athens and
Elizabethan England and to clothe some of the characters in distinctly
kinky ways. The play opened with Kenneth Pogue's Theseus – a dirty
old man rather than a noble duke – being laced up in a corset, while
Marilyn Lightstone's Hippolyta carried a riding crop and casually
revealed thigh-high boots beneath her black velvet dress. As Titania,
Martha Henry wore one of the scantiest costumes ever seen on the
Festival Stage. Kenneth Welsh remembers that he and the other
young men playing the Mechanicals used to position themselves at
the tunnel entrance just to watch her. For her part, Henry remembers
the discomfort of having to hold in her stomach ("not something
you want to have to worry about when you're playing Titania!" she
laughs) but otherwise loving Hirsch's take on the play: "Now I can't

imagine Titania considered without a sexual, sensual component – the text seems so clearly to go in that direction."

When the play opened on June 5, 1968, critical reactions ranged from the delighted to the disgusted. Arnold Edinborough was among the delighted, declaring that "This was the year that sex came to Stratford…. Never was a Bottom more lovingly stroked than in this production of *A Midsummer Night's Dream*." Individual performances, ensemble scenes, costumes and music all received praise, but it was Hirsch's overall vision that marked something new on the Stratford stage. The *Boston Globe*'s Kevin Kelly said that, "despite all the easy chatter about love and its comic pretences, there is a kind of terror gliding by at the same time…. If Shakespeare was writing about love, he was also writing about love's tyranny, its dismay, its shifting illusion and its gross obsession, and Mr. Hirsch presents all this to us with uncommon insight."

A member of the current Stratford company, Stephen Ouimette, remembers it as the first play he ever saw and the one responsible for his decision to become an actor. Then a high school student from a small Ontario town, he had come in a big yellow school bus with his class. "It was one of those matinees, with 2,000 students behaving badly. I remember the lights going down and I don't think I breathed for the whole show. I was absolutely enraptured. I still tell that story because when we do student matinees and get these rowdy groups of kids, I always think about me sitting in that theatre in awe. I think, well, there is at least one person out there who is getting it, so it's worth doing for them."

Did it go over the top? Undoubtedly: both Arnold Edinborough and the *New York Times*' Walter Kerr agreed that presenting Theseus as a geriatric lecher had no basis in the text. But Hirsch was also expressing something that was in the theatrical air: while still producing a satisfying entertainment, he had given the *Dream* a good shaking-up, and introduced a gay element – not a men-in-frocks pantomime but an overtly sexual production – at a time when the theatre was opening up to a more visible and diverse presentation of sex on stage. *The Boys in the Band* and *Hair* had just arrived on

Broadway (both premiered while Hirsch's *Dream* was doing its pre-Stratford tour in March and April) and *Oh! Calcutta!* was only a year in the future.

As always in the theatre, not all of the sex was on the stage: it had surfaced in Hirsch's life in ways that might have come out of *The Boys in the Band*. Jacques Beyderwellen and Bryan Trottier arrived in town to see the new season's offerings, and were staying with Hirsch at his house in St. Mary's. The trip was a treat for Bryan from Beyderwellen, but as it was for a week, Beyderwellen had to do a bit of business travel in Southern Ontario. On one of the evenings Beyderwellen was away, Bryan and Hirsch ended up in bed. There was no hiding it when Beyderwellen returned, and some dramatics ensued. The jilted lover briefly threatened suicide and disappeared into the night, which inevitably was a dark and stormy one. A half hour later he came back, rain-drenched and complaining that he couldn't find a rope, and the evening ended in laughter. The friendship between Hirsch and Beyderwellen survived the incident, and Bryan and Hirsch were together – barring a few "commotions" in Bryan's words – until Hirsch's death over two decades later.

On stage, the rest of the season went well for both Hirsch and Stratford. Gascon's *Seagull* and William Hutt's *Waiting for Godot* got good reviews, though disappointing houses, while Gascon's *Tartuffe*, with William Hutt in the title role and Douglas Rain as Orgon driving each other to superb performances, was in all the critics' opinions (except for the grumpy Nathan Cohen) one of the best productions ever mounted at Stratford. Douglas Campbell's *Romeo and Juliet*, on the other hand, was weakened by Christopher Walken's evident lack of experience with Shakespeare and the fact that Geneviève Bujold was replaced on relatively short notice by a young Montrealer named Louise Marleau – a fine actress, but one who didn't speak English at the time, and had to learn her part phonetically.

Things were going less well for Hirsch and Gascon, however. The two were discovering that despite a personal friendship they were in Hirsch's words, "opposite in temperament, background and aspiration." Hirsch was a morning person, while Gascon was an evening person; Hirsch made up his mind quickly, while Gascon was famous for putting decisions off until the very last moment; Hirsch tended to separate his work from his social life, while Gascon thought of his colleagues as family, and loved to socialize with them. Neither could understand the other's administrative style. As their differences surfaced divisions between pro-Jeans and pro-Johns began to appear in the company, sometimes around issues where there actually was no problem between the two directors. Keith Turnbull, who was Hirsch's assistant director on *The Three Muske-teers*, sensed that many in the cast and production staff preferred Gascon's "classical" approach to plays and were uncomfortable with Hirsch's innovations and risk-taking. "Re-writing *Three Musketeers* on a daily basis, going bananas with the props, everything ... it really was the antithesis of what Stratford was about. The actors had never worked off a script that hadn't been published, where the lines could change. So this was all very radical. And for that to go on in the golden horseshoe of that theatre was sacrilege to some people."

A "generation gap" may also have been at work. Hirsch wasn't shy about promoting young actors, particularly those he had taught at the National Theatre School. One of the recent NTS graduates, James Blendick, played Porthos in the *Musketeers*. He remembers, "I think John found it much easier to work with young people because we were far more open to any kind of vision – we would try anything. Whereas a lot of the senior actors were fairly entrenched in their way of working, they knew what worked for them." (Blendick was another Winnipegger who had come into the theatre because of Hirsch. In 1962 Hirsch was casting a musical revue for the MTC when he spotted Blendick singing with a trio called the Swing Tones in the Chan's Moon Room supper club. Blendick was surprised when Hirsch asked him if he'd ever thought of working in the theatre: "I'd never *been* in a theatre," he laughs. The revue, *Bonfires of 1962*, was a success and led to Blendick going on to NTS.)

Hirsch often felt the need to vent with "his people" and was glad to have Bill and Betty Jane Wylie in town. Deeply engaged in a long overdue reorganization of the Festival administration, including the introduction of computer-based accounting, the new general manager and his wife frequently found Hirsch on their doorstep after evening rehearsals. Betty Jane fed Hirsch salami and pickles, and the couple listened as Hirsch paced, telling them his troubles and complaining about whatever was bothering him, including his differences with Gascon.

Yet despite the tensions, Stratford was in good shape that first summer after Michael Langham's departure. Hirsch and Gascon still had much to share and enjoy, as was evident in some of the peripheral events organized at Stratford. Peter Raby remembers working with Hirsch to put together a Dumas evening, a process that began on a Saturday morning and ended in the performance on Tuesday evening: "John worked very fast and had an instinctive sense of what was theatrical and dramatic and gripping. He made a kind of collage about Dumas' life, with extracts from letters, memoirs, other people's memories and so on. I knocked it into shape, and Jean Gascon and others read it wonderfully." Gascon and Hirsch also agreed on bigger projects for the Festival's future, such as a theatre school (Hirsch's pet project and a consistent theme of his over the years) and a permanent winter home for the company.

The Three Musketeers was the box-office hit of the season, with Douglas Rain's D'Artagnan moving from country-bumpkin innocence to cynical experience as cannons roared, trumpets sounded and swords pierced bodies and cheeses. The risks all paid off: Milady's "But I'm too young to die" held the audience night after night. As a result the CBC asked Hirsch to direct a two-hour television version of the play for broadcast in 1969. The shoot was done with most of the original cast, but Douglas Rain had commitments in England and had to be replaced by the young Kenneth Welsh.

Hirsch finished the summer on a terrific high. He had a successful season at Stratford behind him, a New York production immediately ahead of him, an invitation from Israel's Habimah Theatre to direct a Chekhov play in Tel Aviv and a new lover who looked like a "keeper." Bryan entered Hirsch's life bit by bit, travelling between Montreal and New York, where he helped Hirsch find an apartment and began to meet Hirsch's New York friends and colleagues like the Chelsea Theater Center's Bob Kalfin and designer Eoin Sprott. It was an exciting time for both, with lots of parties and openings to attend and the fun of a great city to explore together. Some tensions emerged early, notably Hirsch's impatience with what he saw as Bryan's lackadaisical approach to building a career. He pushed Bryan to paint more and to make greater efforts to sell his work. Later that year he helped Bryan get some freelance graphics work with the Festival doing programs and posters.

Hirsch had by then taken Bryan home to Winnipeg to meet Sybil and Pauline Shack. Sybil was by this time comfortable with her adopted brother's homosexuality and accepted Bryan as his partner. For his part, Bryan remembers the mother and daughter as "tiny little women with big hearts" who took every opportunity to feed him.

Hirsch's partner Bryan Trottier in 1968.
Photo courtesy of Bryan Trottier

He was less enchanted by Winnipeg and spent little time there, although he enjoyed meeting some of Hirsch's old friends.

Hirsch's rehearsals for *We Bombed in New Haven* were soon underway at the Ambassador Theater. Joseph Heller's play had premiered two years before at the Yale Drama School, and like the author's bestselling *Catch-22* had an anti-war theme. Heller was experimenting with Pirandellian techniques when he wrote the play, with actors carrying scripts and stepping out of their roles to address the audience directly. Reviews of the Yale production were sharply divided and initial enthusiasm by several producers for a new work by Heller had melted away. The Shubert Organization, which owned the theatre, hired Hirsch in hopes that he could make it work, a role he would take on with difficult productions several times in the future. Bryan accompanied Hirsch to some of the rehearsals and was startled one day to hear a female voice heckling Jason Robards from the back of the audience: "You call that *acting?*" It was Lauren Bacall, who at that time was in the process of divorcing Robards (and was soon to appear on Broadway in *Applause* with Len Cariou as her leading man).

We Bombed in New Haven opened in mid-October and ran for eighty-five performances. Once again, reviews were mixed. It is hard to know what another director might have done better with the play and with the cast Hirsch was given; it has been revived occasionally since then, but is generally regarded as dated agitprop.

In the meantime, a major hitch appeared in the planning for the 1969 Stratford season. After the *Musketeers* had proved to be a hit Hirsch had set Peter Raby a new dramaturgical challenge: to work up a musical based on a Roman satire, Petronius' *Satyricon*. The sprawling story used the misadventures of a former gladiator and his wayward boyfriend to criticize social practices and skewer recognizable people in Rome in the late first century AD. Hirsch was intrigued by what he saw as political and economic parallels between Petronius' era and the late 1960s. "This is not an age of torches," he told Herbert Whittaker, "but it is an age of glitter and sheer froth.... I find a great parallel with the fragmented age of Petronius. I have a feeling that we are at the tail-end of a civilization.

So were they." As with *Musketeers*, Raby agreed to work on the script from his home in Britain, collaborating with composer Stanley Silverman on the songs. Things began to falter in the late autumn when Raby received a cable asking him to fly to the Virgin Islands to work on the script with Hirsch for a couple of months. Raby already had some scenes roughed out, but was not prepared either to leave or to uproot his young family again. He resigned from the project, which was already fixed – somewhat rashly, for a new musical – in the Stratford schedule.

Faced with that crisis, Hirsch turned to an old friend. In a move that suggested an increasing takeover by the "Winnipeg mafia," Stratford had hired Tom Hendry as its literary manager, a new post at the Festival that included and extended some of the functions of dramaturge. Now Hirsch needed Hendry to save *The Satyricon*. Hendry did some research and came back to Hirsch early in the New Year, telling him that trying to follow the original was hopeless. Instead he proposed to focus the musical on current social trends and business scandals, including some from Stratford that he'd read about in the local press. In contrast to Raby's panoramic treatment of *Musketeers*, Hendry chose only one event from the original, a party at the mansion of the wealthy merchant Trimalchio, transposed it to the 1930s, and made it the setting of the entire show.

It was a scramble to deliver script and musical score in time to cast the various parts, and eyebrows were raised as Hirsch detailed the people he wanted to hire outside of the usual Stratford mold: a stand-up comedian, five tap dancers, singers who could handle both music hall and rhythm and blues, and a professional stripper, Jeri Archer, who went by the time-honoured stage name of La Belle Poitrine. More eyebrows, particularly Bill Wylie's, were raised as Hirsch added special effects and sets, going well over the planned budget. Stanley Silverman made use of every kind of music from Wagnerian opera and cheesy burlesque to acid rock and protest songs performed by a stage band in sequined jackets, and threw in electronic tape for good measure. Eoin Sprott again contributed projections, this time on a single giant screen, "happening" style.

Hirsch was fully aware that it was all vastly tasteless, blithely asserting to reporters that "to put tastelessness on the stage takes taste." But there was also some degree of sheer cussedness at work. Hirsch had on several occasions spoken publicly about his discomfort with staid, anglophile Stratford – and with the Festival Board – and he appears to have decided, with Hendry's help, to give it a poke in its collective eye. Unfortunately Hirsch and Hendry were also at odds by this time over the script. Keith Turnbull remembers constant re-ordering of scenes, each of which had implications for the rest of the production. A deleted scene meant that an expensive set or group of costumes had to be junked, while changes in scene order meant re-doing notes for stage managers and dressers overnight in order to be ready for a new run-through the next day. Betty Jane Wylie had taken to hosting poolside barbecues for cast and staff on weekends when the season got underway. She remembers the initial tension between the Stratford regulars and some of the outsiders, particularly several New Yorkers who were somewhat patronizing about the small town they found themselves in. Moreover, the tap dancers and one of the singers were black, representing more black talent than Stratford had ever seen apart from the brief visit of Duke Ellington's band in 1957. Despite the chaos the company did come together over the course of the rehearsal period, and there were some particularly memorable cast parties (one interviewee for this book swears he saw the fencing master Paddy Crean drink champagne out of Jeri Archer's shoe at one of them). But once again the production staff found it hard to accept Hirsch's working methods, and there were flashes of rebellion from them as the opening approached.

Hirsch's late-night rants at the Wylies' house continued and his differences with Gascon was growing. He had several other projects in mind including a new Reaney play, but found it hard to get decisions from Gascon. Rumours of backbiting began to circulate and the conflict between the pro-Jean and pro-John factions became more pronounced. According to William Hutt's biography, Hutt reported to Gascon that Hirsch had viciously criticized Gascon's directing during a dress rehearsal while the company was on pre-season tour.

James Blendick and Jeri Archer (La Belle Poitrine) in
The Satyricon, 1969.
Photo by Douglas Spillane, courtesy of Stratford
Shakespeare Festival Archives

(Hutt may have been the victim of misinformation himself. None of the four people interviewed for this book who were at the rehearsal in question can remember Hirsch doing any such thing, and all doubt he would have criticized Gascon to an entire cast.)

Hirsch's most controversial casting decision was to choose Kenneth Welsh to be his Hamlet. Though he had recently been well received as D'Artagnan in the televised version of *The Three Musketeers*, which millions of Canadians saw broadcast on March 19, Welsh was still very inexperienced to be taking on Hamlet. The interpretation was also risky. Welsh remembers Hirsch saying that he didn't want "a melodious Hamlet, he didn't want a melancholic Dane, and he didn't get it. We came out with all guns firing."

When *Hamlet* opened at Stratford in June the reviews ranged from lukewarm to hostile. Most critics felt Welsh was simply too young to take on the part and didn't like the anger and youthful energy that characterized the production. Hirsch called a thoroughly demoralized Welsh the next morning and invited him to go for a walk on the Festival grounds. As they walked Hirsch said that Welsh had played the part exactly as he had hoped, adding, "I am very happy with what you've done and so should you be. Don't worry about the critics, you are playing this part beautifully and just keep on doing it the way you are doing it." Welsh was overcome by the support: "Suddenly I felt very liberated by what John had said, and the kindness he had shown."

Despite the reviews, *Hamlet* was the top draw that summer, in a season that included two well-received productions by Gascon and an excellent *Measure for Measure* directed by David Giles.

The Satyricon also did well at the box office, particularly (according to several reviews) among local farmers who came to get a peek at naked women and probably hadn't bargained for semi-naked men as well. The cast were delighted to find that line-ups for tickets went round the block and bemused at the appearance of the "morality squad" at the back of the theatre most nights. But with few exceptions the critics found the whole thing tasteless and inappropriate to Stratford. One critic summarized: "Billed as a burlesque based on Petronius,

Juvenal, Tacitus and Minsky, it was all Minsky.... Forty twirling buttocks do not make a drama, but Canada's staid middle class loved it."

One could shrug off the critics, but not the numbers. Despite the crowds queuing at the Avon theatre *The Satyricon* had exceeded its production budget of $109,000 by $84,000, and with a relatively short run it was impossible to make this up at the box office. (*The Satyricon* was resurrected a few years later when the director Richard Foreman took some of Hendry and Silverman's songs and created a review called *Dr. Selavy's Magical Theatre*. The show ran successfully off-Broadway in 1972-73 and has been revived several times since then.)

But by the time the figures had been added up at the end of the season, Hirsch was long gone from Stratford, having resigned from his associate directorship on July 5, the day before *The Satyricon* opened. According to Jean Gascon, he and Hirsch knew – "in fact, everyone knew!" he commented – that their working relationship had broken down, and they were only too aware of the factionalism their differences were causing in the company. They finally asked the Board to decide which of them it wanted to lead the Festival. While they waited for the decision, Gascon invited Hirsch to his office where he had a bottle of champagne in his fridge. The two sat sipping their champagne until word came back: the Board had chosen Gascon. Hirsch duly offered his resignation.

There is a "Hirsch story" in circulation that on *The Satyricon*'s opening night Hirsch showed up in the bar of the Avon wearing an orange muumuu, with a rose in his teeth. The story is true – both Keith Turnbull and Ken Welsh were there. Hirsch didn't mention what had happened with the Board, and Welsh remembers that Hirsch seemed much more concerned with finding his car keys. "Muumuus don't have pockets, of course," says Welsh. "I asked how he was, and he gave this big sigh and said, 'Oh my God, I've lost my car keys. I've lost everything.'" It was pretty sad, but I didn't know what had happened. (Welsh also says that a lot of people were wearing muumuus at Stratford that year. "It was the sixties, remember.")

The resignation was duly announced. When a writer from the *Toronto Star* interviewed Hirsch in his office shortly afterward, she described him as slumped in his chair, looking as though he hadn't been to bed the night before. Hirsch gave the story his own spin, telling her he was tired and it was high time he moved on. "I've been making decisions for the last twenty years that were affecting the future of Canadian theatre," he told her. "In the last sixteen years [i.e. since the Festival opened] I've been the only director who has managed to put on a new work for three consecutive seasons. In the last two I have mounted eight works, six here and on tour, and *We Bombed in New Haven* for Broadway, plus lecturing, auditioning and talking to writers. Now I want to be frivolous, irresponsible and selfish for a while – namely to sit and contemplate my navel." A month later he told the Montreal *Gazette* that his resigning from being co-artistic director at Stratford had nothing to do with his incompatibility with Gascon; despite different ways of working they still liked each another as human beings (and in fact, they continued to meet and work together in the future). Rather, he said he needed to work in five-year cycles, and was opposed to artists carving out a secure niche for themselves and staying there forever. "I am an activist," he asserted, "I must change the status quo. This makes me, I suppose, an irritant." He finished the interview on an upbeat, saying he hoped to be asked back to Stratford at some point.

In late September Hirsch returned to New York. The New York stage was full of revivals that year, and Jules Irving had hired Hirsch to direct two as part of an "All American" season at the Beaumont: William Saroyan's *Time of Your Life*, and *Beggar on Horseback*, a hit from 1920s Broadway by Marc Connelly and George S. Kaufman. The first was scheduled to open in November, the second in May the following year.

By this time the Beaumont had hired a dramaturge, the future *New Yorker* theatre critic John Lahr, who worked closely with Hirsch on *Time of Your Life*. The son of Bert Lahr – known to millions as the Cowardly Lion in *The Wizard of Oz* – John Lahr had become a public figure at twenty-nine after publishing a bestselling biography of his father earlier that year. Lahr's diaries from the period cast

Hirsch as a mentor and counsellor to whom Lahr confided the pressure that celebrity was putting on him. Hirsch was pragmatic about the price of fame in New York. "You can't keep your virginity in a brothel, you can't have a Trappist monastery on 42nd Street," he told Lahr. The younger man found Hirsch a mixture of wisdom, tenderness and sweet-sour humour. One diary entry, a long passage about Lahr's ambiguous attitude towards success and competition, concludes, "I say to Hirsch, my fear is that it will all be taken away. Hirsch answers: 'It will be.'"

He also counselled Lahr to take risks with his work and not to think in terms of what he might lose but what he might gain. "A nest, what is it?" Hirsch asked, then answered his own question: "Fifty thousand twigs and a lot of shit to hold it together."

Rehearsals for *Time of Your Life* went smoothly, with Hirsch in tune with his cast and completely comfortable with the play. He immersed himself in the details. Priscilla Pointer, Jules Irving's wife, was in the cast and remembers Hirsch's attention to detail with the barroom setting, right down to making sure that beer was sprinkled on the floor before each show.

Time of Your Life turned out to be the most popular and best received play of the Beaumont's 1969-70 season. Although Clive Barnes thought the play trivial, he judged the production a milestone for the Beaumont: "The director, John Hirsch, has done his job superbly and the cast is great. They are beginning to act like a national theatre – it is only the repertory they lack." *Time* was impressed with Hirsch's updating of the play, noting that, "When cops enter the bar and beat the black jazz pianist bloody, the scene has a truncheon-like impact that was totally lacking in 1939."

The final weeks of the year found Hirsch in Tel Aviv rehearsing Chekhov's *The Seagull* at Habimah, Israel's national theatre. He'd been invited by David William, a young actor-director with whom Hirsch had been friendly since they met at the 1965 Commonwealth Arts Festival in Glasgow. (Through Hirsch, William had been invited to Stratford to direct *Twelfth Night* in1966; he would return to Stratford as its artistic director in 1990-93.) Now William was running

Habimah, the main stage of which was undergoing refurbishment. He originally invited Hirsch to open the refurbished theatre in October 1969, but warned him to prepare for slippage in the schedule, as administrative delays and confusion were rife. "One of the myths the Six Day War promoted is the Efficiency of Israel," he told Hirsch in a letter in March 1969. "This is only a feature of the Army."

Working with the Habimah company was almost surreal. Formed as an offshoot of the Moscow Art Theatre in 1918, the company had emigrated to Palestine in 1928, and Tyrone Guthrie had directed it in the late 1940s. One of the great stars from Moscow days, Hanna Rovina, was still in the company at the age of ninety-two, and her dresser – even older – was still with her, appearing suddenly in the corridors like a ghost. As Hirsch told the story many years later:

> I walked into the first rehearsal, and there were all these people, some of them from when the Moscow Art Theatre was started. An old man said to me, "I understand that Tyrone Guthrie recommended you for this job.' I said yes. 'My name is Finkel,' he says. 'I am the Laurence Olivier of Israel.' I said, 'Nice to meet you.' 'I have taken this very small part only because of Guthrie recommending you.' I said, 'Thank you.' And so it went. And then I came to a tiny old man sitting on a tall chair, grinning, totally bald, and I said to the stage manager, 'Who is he?' And the stage manager said, 'He plays the dog in *The Seagull*.' I said, 'There is no dog in *The Seagull* that I know of.' 'There is a dog, a dog barks across the lake: this is he…. This man is in an old folk's home. He cannot remember lines, but he can bark." And they brought him to the theatre, to bark, on cue, then went home happily – he was still working.

Hirsch found the company one of the most difficult he had ever worked with, although it provided rich material for future storytelling. Nonetheless he and Bryan enjoyed Israel, taking side-trips to Jerusalem and other places whenever possible, and made lasting friendships. Their open relationship was now standard operating procedure, though Hirsch occasionally suffered bouts of insecurity and possessiveness. When Bryan began an affair with a handsome paratrooper whose name, Shahaf, was the Hebrew word for seagull, he told Hirsh, "You've got your Seagull, and I've got my seagull."

As William had warned, the schedule slipped. Rehearsals started late and there was a further delay when Hirsch went back to New York in early January to rehearse *Beggar on Horseback* at the Beaumont. When *The Seagull* finally opened in March most of the reviewers disliked the production. Hirsch never directed in Israel again, although Shimon Finkel, who took over Habimah as artistic director that year, invited him to return. Nor did Hirsch ever tackle another play in a language he didn't speak.

Back in New York, the glow from *Time of Your Life*'s success did not carry over to *Beggar on Horseback*, which was problematic from the start. The story is a fable about the perils of trading one's artistic principles for success. The hero, a young composer, is tempted to "sell out" to Tin Pan Alley by a wealthy industrialist whose daughter he (the composer) happens to love. Jules Irving, having acquired the rights to the play, wanted to update it and add new songs, with music by Stanley Silverman and lyrics by Lahr. The eighty-year-old playwright Marc Connelly, initially flattered by the idea of a revival, grew increasingly resistant to these changes. One of Lahr's diary entries describes a variety of tensions at work and a strange moral world reigning at the theatre:

> Connelly wants to pull "Cottage for Two" from Beggar. It's one of the best songs and musically the most complete parody of the 20s. Connelly who likes the other songs which have no relation to the text dislikes this one. Cottage is the only one written for a specific moment. Jules checked Connelly's contract. Stupidly he has been allowed control of everything that goes on. Stanley [Silverman], furious, comes in quietly and finally says he's quitting. That the song is better than the

show, that everybody likes it. "It's like a smorgasbord and everybody is eating my pretzels" he says. Jules is sympathetic but without any legal grounds he can't 'get tough.' He plots the situation. He likes the song, best moment in the show, but hates the play. He tells Stanley and me he's going to have to play poker. He's going to use Stanley's threatened resignation and the fact that not only Stanley but part of the band, perhaps even the stars will leave or at least be unnerved. Will Connelly be bluffed? The old codger is not senile and he's tough.

The situation grew increasingly fraught. At one rehearsal Lahr observed a half-joking Irving "passing notes giving odds that John Hirsch is going to have a breakdown." Hirsch didn't, but he never got a handle on the play. Instead he reverted to the showbiz effects of *The Satyricon*, hiding the essential weakness of the book with Busby Berkeley-style choreography and eye-popping Art Deco sets and costumes by *Satyricon*'s designer, Michael Annals.

Connelly did not attend the opening and the play was a commercial and critical failure. The *Village Voice* condemned it as "so big, and so ugly, and so empty….It seems to turn into what it is trying to satirize."

The critical ups and downs of Hirsch's life were echoed by domestic tensions with Bryan. Although Bryan travelled frequently to Montreal, where his parents and sister still lived and where he continued to be involved with Jacques Beyderwellen and his crowd, he spent more and more of his time at the apartment Hirsch had rented on 82nd Street. They continued to explore New York's neighbourhoods and markets, go to a wide range of cultural events and spend time with friends like Eoin Sprott, John Lahr (when he wasn't at his other home in London) and Stanley Silverman and his family. Under some pressure from Hirsch, who worried about his passivity and tendency to drift, Bryan picked up occasional contracts as a graphic artist, doing posters for rock festivals and the occasional commercial job, including a cover for *Screw* magazine. He pursued his painting, though not in as organized a fashion as Hirsch would have liked. And even less to Hirsch's liking, Bryan was busy with drugs and sex.

The scenario was a classic one and Hirsch referred to it often in his letters: an older man with an established career trying to make a life with an attractive, much younger, economically less successful lover, a situation ripe for insecurity on one side and resistance (passive or active) on the other. Hirsch's jealousy and pain is visible in his letters to Bryan during these years:

> Do you think of me now when I am not there? What do they do to you? Do you kiss them with closed eyes...Why aren't you here? I am not ROD and DAVID and Margo and Jack and Pellig and Roland and all the rest and I want to cry.... And why did I hit you? Because I DO CARE and why do I run from you or nag you when you are there? Because I run from myself....

Yet the attachment was deep and the relationship continued. With Hirsch constantly working, in meetings, or travelling, Bryan spent a lot of time in the apartment or out walking on his own. One day when he was sitting on a park (he says he was on LSD at the time, but lucid) he struck up a conversation with a smartly dressed young woman. Knowing no more about her than that her name was Susan and that she worked in advertising, he invited her home to meet Hirsch. She became part of their circle of friends, and in 1972 she and Eoin Sprott married, with Hirsch as their best man.

Weekends often found Hirsch and Bryan at the country house of Bob Kalfin, where Hirsch had free rein in the kitchen. Shopping and cooking with Hirsch was "a trip," according to Kalfin: "Hirsch would go to the beach and gather seaweed and make this incredible steamed thing with chickens and clams and lobsters and corn and seaweed all thrown into the same pot." The friendship had a business side to it as well. Hirsch and Kalfin were both deeply involved with the Theater Communications Group, whose network of regional theatres had grown immensely in the late 1960s. Moreover, Kalfin had been on the lookout for a play Hirsch could direct at the Chelsea Theater Center for some time, and finally found one thanks to John Lahr. One of Lahr's London friends was the playwright Heathcote Williams, whose *AC/DC*

had won the 1970 *Evening Standard* Award when it was presented at
the Royal Court in May 1970. Lahr first tried to interest Jules Irving in
the play, but when Irving said no, Lahr took it to Kalfin, who acquired
the rights to *AC/DC* and scheduled it to open February 1971.

Before that, however, Hirsch had another big opening to look
forward to: the new Manitoba Theatre Centre building in Winnipeg.
Hirsch was to direct the first production in the new theatre in
November 1970 and he and Eddie Gilbert had agreed on Brecht's *A
Man's A Man*. Gilbert had shepherded the 785-seat concrete-and-
glass building through its construction phase after the Richardson
family had finally pulled the plug on the old Dominion Theatre. As
it turned out Gilbert was no longer artistic director at the MTC when
Hirsch arrived for rehearsals. After four successful years running
MTC Gilbert had married and "retired" to a farm in New Brunswick
in 1969. He was succeed by the young Kurt Reis, whose political
activism (he could frequently be found hanging out at student
demonstrations at the University of Manitoba) got him fired by the
Board within a year. Reis was replaced by an equally young Keith
Turnbull, Hirsch's assistant director at Stratford, who had been
directing at the MTC Warehouse for a year. The Board hedged its
bets by making Hirsch consultant artistic director for the season.

Winnipeg was glad to have Hirsch back and his big, provocative
production of *A Man's A Man* attracted substantial crowds. Opening
night was accompanied by a gala attended by Governor General
Roland Michener.

Hirsch scarcely had time to savour the hometown enthusiasm
before he had to return to the Beaumont to direct Synge's *Playboy
of the Western World*. This time he had brought with him two
Stratford actors, Martha Henry and James Blendick, both of whom
were also scheduled to act in his production of *Antigone* later that
year. *Playboy of the Western World* opened in January 1971 to mixed
reviews, but by that time Hirsch was preoccupied with another
production: *AC/DC*.

When he first received the three-hundred-page script back in
the fall, Hirsch had found it incomprehensible. After Bob Kalfin

engaged someone to look up the many scientific, electronic, and technical terms and provide an index and footnotes, Hirsch read the play again and found it exciting. He asked Kalfin to invite the playwright to New York to shape it and was impressed when Heathcote Williams – an astonishingly gifted poet, playwright and songwriter – arrived from London with Jean Shrimpton, one of the day's most famous international models. The pair struck Hirsch as two wraith-like figures out of an Arthur Rackham fairy-tale book. He described Williams as "a changeling with flaming red hair and very white, almost transparent skin wearing a big black cape." The cutting and clarifying took place at the Chelsea Hotel, with Jean Shrimpton spending hours typing in front of the fireplace.

Written at a time when Marshall McLuhan's theories on media and culture were very much in vogue – his bestselling *The Medium is the Message* was published in 1967 – the play deals with the effect of media, especially television, on the human mind. It begins with a threesome making love in a pinball arcade and ends with brain surgery performed with a corkscrew on the protagonist in his shabby one-bedroom apartment. Hirsch saw it as a horror play, an electronic Grand Guignol expressing both pessimism and euphoria about the technological future. The sets broke new ground for the New York stage: twenty-five TV screens set up by a San Francisco-based collective called Video Free America ran a barrage of images ranging from Cape Canaveral lift-offs to a flickering electroencephalograph tracking neurons firing in the brain, along with pictures of current political figures like Spiro Agnew and Jerry Rubin. The special effects were impressive but put a huge strain on the theatre's budget. Kalfin authorized the expenses in "damn the torpedoes" fashion, but was worried. His theatre was heavily subsidized, with substantial backing from city, state and federal government grants, the Ford Foundation and the Rockefellers, and he cherished its ability to experiment without commercial pressures, but he had a board and a budget, and both had their limits. He also wondered if the local audience in Brooklyn that he had been carefully building would stay with him on this.

When the play finally opened reviews were savage from mainstream critics like Clive Barnes, who wrote, "I suspect the only mind blown was that of the playwright himself." But it netted three Obie Awards, including Best Director for Hirsch. Perhaps more important, because it indicated the support of the regional theatre movement, *AC/DC* prompted a special award for the Chelsea Theater Center from the New England Theatre Conference for "continuing to produce some of America's most exciting theatre."

Hirsch was now as busy as a freelance director can possibly be. Before beginning rehearsals for *Antigone*, he realized a long-time ambition to direct an opera. The opera was Verdi's *Un Ballo in Maschera* (The Masked Ball) at Lincoln Center's State Theatre, which opened on March 21 with New York City Opera's maestro Julius Rudel conducting and the Canadian tenor Louis Quilico in the role of Renato. The courtly Rudel remembers that Hirsch came "well prepared and acquitted himself honourably," and the production ran in repertory during the spring and fall of 1971. Hirsch was also busy with the usual meetings a freelance director has to do, teeing up contracts years in advance of the actual production.

In May, *Antigone* opened at the Beaumont. Though Clive Barnes panned it, Martha Henry won the Theatre World Award for best debut on the New York stage and *Time* magazine stated, "The revival at [the] Beaumont Theatre is of Olympian stature, the finest work that has ever been done there....Martha Henry's Antigone is a female javelin seeking death and wielding it." Backstage it was a low point. James Blendick remembers resentment among the company at the hiring of Canadians, and Hirsch's demanding style of directing was provoking increased resistance from its more entrenched members.

Moreover, Hirsch and Martha Henry were not getting along with one another. She found him distracted during the rehearsal period and she didn't agree with his concept of Antigone. Today she reflects, "I didn't believe in myself as a sex object – that was the crux of the matter." She had formed her own sense of Antigone as "earnest and committed...which at that point in my life went along with brains and no makeup" and she suspected she was being asked to "sex it up" for commercial reasons, to appeal to a New York audience.

She refused to wear what she calls a "Farah Fawcett" wig the costumes department had made for her, even after Hirsch had called time out and taken her for a long walk in Central Park to talk it over.

Until that time, Henry had always trusted Hirsch's ability to push her creatively and had put him in a special category in her mind, beyond comparison with other directors. At Lincoln Center she was working with "people who *did* compare [to] him, and found him 'difficult,' 'impatient,' 'demanding,' 'eccentric,' 'intolerant.' Odd. 'It's fine for you,' an actor said to me, "he doesn't do *that* to *you*.' By the time we got to *Antigone* he was doing 'that' to me too." They argued and made up several times, but in the end, "A door seemed to close and I didn't work again with John for six years."

Around that time Hirsch and Jules Irving also had a serious argument, and Hirsch understood he wouldn't be working at the Beaumont anymore. A sympathetic letter from John Lahr, by then in London working on his biography of playwright Joe Orton, tells Hirsch "you paid the price for talking up and taking issue with the Leader.... So now you are cut-off from Mama Beaumont, and I agree with you, the separation can only be healthy. You'll get work because you're too good not to work."

Except Hirsch didn't feel like working and had planned a small "sabbatical" for himself. At the end of the summer he and Bryan left for Rome, where they stayed for a couple of months. The next stop was Turkey, where they spent several balmy October weeks travelling around in rural buses, visiting ruins, fishing ports, and hillside villages before returning to Istanbul. They found the city exhilarating, but travel brought out some tensions between the two, partly the result of the seventeen-year age difference. They had a blazing argument after a quick visit to Athens, and Hirsch went back to New York. Bryan returned to Montreal, where a friend suggested he take a sabbatical from Hirsch's sabbatical and invited Bryan to travel with him to Egypt. Bryan did so, but instead of returning to Hirsch in North America he hit the "hippie trail." He spent several months in India before moving to Paris, where he lived in a commune and became part of a *ménage à trois* with a couple he knew from Montreal.

FRAIDIE MARTZ AND ANDREW WILSON

Hirsch was hurt by Bryan's defection, but the two wrote one another frequently over the next twenty months. Their correspondence highlights the differences in the two personalities. Hirsch's letters are full of movement, recounting travels, meetings, productions, people he has met. Bryan's letters – distinguished by his beautiful calligraphy, sometimes in different coloured inks and accompanied by small sketches and graphics – are more whimsical, often reflecting on books he has read and films he has seen. Money was a constant problem. His efforts to make a living as an artist were only occasionally successful, with an occasional exhibition or the sale of a painting. Over and over, the letters return to their love for each other, and their desire to find some way to live together. In late summer of 1973 Bryan explains, "You are the strongest person in every way I've ever known – it is a challenge to keep up with you, and I knew you can't slow down – I knew we must take 'breathers' from one another…."

Hirsch replies with his worries about Bryan's financial and emotional dependence on him. "Maybe a tiny job," he suggests, "just to get used to living in your own place and as a try at real independence." Hirsch worries about Bryan's passivity, describing him as "a kind of quiet housekeeper…a bit of a ghost aware of the need of the owner for a familiar. A second cat. All this in no way to hurt you, love, but to give you a push, please, for some motion. But I also know that perhaps it is impossible for you to live any other way. I hope not. I do miss you and love you, thinking of you and still knowing that there must be some way for us."

The two met only a few times during this period when Bryan made the trip home to Montreal to see his parents and when Hirsch was travelling. For Hirsch had begun another journey of his own, both geographic and spiritual, that would result in one of his defining productions, *The Dybbuk*.

The Dybbuk had been on Hirsch's mind for many years, having once considered it for Theatre 77 but rejected it as too ambitious for the company. Several of his colleagues over the years had suggested it as something he should direct. But the real spur occurred during one of his trips to Winnipeg in 1971, when he made a speech to the Jewish Historical Society. After speaking at some length about the Chekhov and Shakespeare plays that most interested him at the time, Hirsch took questions from the floor and was stopped short when a small, elderly woman challenged him: "If you're so interested in what's going on in the world, and so interested in history, how come you've never done a Jewish play?"

The question started Hirsch rethinking what it meant to him to be Jewish. He recognized that he still carried the burden of contradictions, the result of his experiences. The active, vocal anti-Semitism he had encountered in Europe, the taunts of "Christ-killer" as a young boy had left him with feelings of guilt: "When my family was destroyed, and my whole world collapsed, in a perverse way it seemed quite logical to arrive at the conclusion that indeed all those people were right....It took me a long time to get rid of that feeling."

Hirsch finally read S. Ansky's *The Dybbuk* for the first time. A pioneering Jewish ethnographer, Ansky wrote *The Dybbuk* in Yiddish in 1914, cobbling it together from various Hasidic stories and tales he had collected in the early part of the century. Though Konstantin Stanislavsky, the director of the Moscow Art Theatre, saw early drafts and gave the project his support, Ansky never saw it performed by a professional company. In the huge disruptions of the First World War and the Russian Revolution, he dedicated himself to providing relief to the hard-hit rural Jews of Galicia. It was only after Ansky's death in 1920 that *The Dybbuk* saw its first performances with a cast that became the nucleus of the Habimah. In the next three decades the play became the most celebrated work in the Jewish theatrical canon and was performed all over Europe and America in the original Yiddish as well as English and Hebrew translations.

The concept of the *dybbuk* spoke deeply to Hirsch, resonating with memories of his murdered brother István and the story of his uncle Rezsō who had committed suicide over an unhappy love affair. A *dybbuk* is a clinging soul of someone who has died without fulfilling his or her destiny. Because it has unfinished business on earth, it comes back and possesses a living person in an attempt to fulfil its destiny. The idea of destiny denied by a broken promise – a breach in the moral order of the universe – is at the heart of the play. Although betrothed by their fathers before birth, Chanon (there are various spellings but this was the one used in Hirsch's production) and Leah grow up in separate towns, unaware of each other's existence. But when Chanon, a poor theological student, appears in the town of Brenits, Leah is drawn to him as he is to her, each recognizing the other as their *bashert* (intended). Their love is thwarted, however, when Leah's father, Sender, arranges for Leah to marry another, wealthier man. The desperate Chanon uses his knowledge of Kabbalah to help his case. He dies in a mystical trance and returns to his bride in the form of a *dybbuk*, entering Leah at the moment when she is to be wed.

Hirsch spent much of the winter of 1972-73 in New York thinking about *The Dybbuk* and reading widely about Jewish history and culture. He also began to explore the possibilities of staging it, first with Eddie Gilbert at the MTC and also with Gordon Davidson, the director of the Mark Taper Forum in Los Angeles and a fellow member of the Theater Communications Group. Both were enthusiastic and Hirsch knew that one way or another he would direct the play sometime in the near future.

The spiritual questioning provoked by *The Dybbuk* became a major preoccupation for Hirsch. At a time when many in the theatre were questioning Western religions and spending time in ashrams in India, Hirsch worried that living in New York was contaminating his mind and spirit. He wrote at the time, "All I can think of [is] where my next job was coming from and will I be as famous as X whose photograph [was] in the *New York Times*." He resolved to pursue a different goal, nothing less than "finding out how to become a better human being and how to make sense of my existence." Slowing his career down, he only directed three productions in 1972 and 1973: *A Midsummer Night's Dream* at the Guthrie Theater in July 1972, *Lulu Street* at the Lennoxville Festival in Québec later that summer, and *Guys and Dolls* at MTC.

In the spring of 1973 he left on an extended trip financed by a

Canada Council travel grant and carrying with him a paperback copy of *The Dybbuk*. He spent the first part of his trip in Hungary, renewing his acquaintance with the city of Budapest and visiting some of the leading individuals in the theatre. Overall he was unimpressed with the theatre scene there, finding that "the social realism of the 1950s [had] turned into a very awkward and imitative effort at avant garde." During his visit he paid for Bryan to come for a three-week visit from Paris, where he was still living hand-to-mouth in his commune. Bryan was enchanted by Budapest's fading grandeur and greatly enjoyed the trip. They talked about getting back together when Hirsch had finished his travels but left it un-resolved. Hirsch then pushed on to Czechoslovakia, where he was depressed to see how the heavy hand of Brezhnev's Soviet Union was stifling the creativity that had made Czech theatre so interesting in the 1960s.

If Eastern Europe was stifling, Asia was everything he had hoped for. In those days before the Soviet occupation of Afghanistan and the Islamic Revolution in Iran, crossing borders was easy and Hirsch ranged far and wide in his travels, visiting Turkey, Israel, India, Iran, Afghanistan, Singapore, Indonesia and Japan over the space of several months. Reading *The Dybbuk* on his journey, it became clear to him that he was seeking places where, as in the *shtetl* of nineteenth century Jewry, religion, ritual and spirituality were still living forces. He found what he was looking for in several places, always by chance. In Iran, he followed a funeral procession and ended up visiting an Armenian Christian community, which despite generations of living within a Muslim society had preserved its language and religion. He was struck by the parallel to the Jewish communities living in Russia and Poland.

His most powerful experience was in Bali. Letters and interviews recount his enchantment with a culture where people prayed in the "most natural and lovely way" at all times of the day. Art and spirituality came together: in the morning, people went to work carrying little baskets or trays filled with leaves, flowers and fruit to place in front of the gas pump if they worked at a gas station, or on top of a cash register in a store. And he watched with delight the delicacy with which women would place their little trays at the two ends of the bridge they crossed every day. He admired the collective sense of responsibility to family and village that he saw everywhere, and particularly the manner in which death was treated, as a rite of passage rather than a personal tragedy.

A particular event resonated with his memories of Catholic ritual in his hometown of Siófok. Since poor Balinese lack the funds to do a full Hindu funeral each time a loved one dies, groups of families often band together to do a collective funeral. Hirsch had the luck to witness the culmination of the funerals when the ashes of the dead (Hindu ritual insists on cremation) are brought in jars to a central place. After much feasting, singing and dancing he watched a long column of men and women wearing multi-coloured sarongs carry twenty-foot towers through the village and beyond until they reached neighbouring fields of high grass. The towers were topped by the jars, each of which also held a small bamboo boat with a candle in its centre. The procession ended at a beach of black sand where the towers were set down and the boats removed. "By then it was about seven o'clock and the sun was going down," he recounted years later, still under the spell of the ritual. "When the tide moved out hundreds of little boats sailed out to sea with all their candles burning. More dancing followed. And then the towers were burned. The whole beach, a mile or so long, was ablaze, and when you looked out at the sea you saw these tiny flames moving further and further away."

In observing such rituals Hirsch found a profound concordance between the "exotic" cultures he was visiting and that of his child-hood. Though far removed in time and space, he found that "an over-riding and on-going celebration of life itself was expressed in ritual and prayer." The experience evoked memories of his grand-father putting on his phylacteries every day to pray, even in the darkest days of the Budapest Ghetto. The daily ritual of thanksgiving had made no sense to Hirsch as a young teenager; now, in his early forties, *The Dybbuk* helped make the meaning of his grandfather's worship clear: it provided a clearly defined moral order and thus a

Marilyn Lightstone in the exorcism scene from *The Dybbuk*, early 1973.
Photo by Robert C. Ragsdale

great comfort to the people who lived in it. He described the play as a highly moral tale and said, "today, when there is a conscious overthrow of moral values, a mockery of justice, this play makes sense. It explains why it's important to stick to certain moral precepts, because a small pin pulled somewhere risks the collapse of the whole structure."

Although Hirsch had originally hoped to find someone else to do the adaptation he eventually decided to do it himself. After completing his trip in August he went to ground at his Winnipeg home and set to work, having agreed with Eddie Gilbert – who had returned as artistic director – to direct the play at the MTC the following January. (Hirsch also made a separate engagement to mount the play in Los Angeles at the Mark Taper Forum, using the same script, music and design, but a mostly American cast.) As ever, Sybil and Pauline Shack welcomed him home. Surrounded by the love of his adopted family and deeply engaged with the material, Hirsch found this work a deep and gratifying experience: "It gave me a tremendous sense of personal liberation because I could explore complex states of mind, heart and background; and it was the ideal medium to transform this intensely personal experience externally onto the stage."

The play that emerged differed considerably from Ansky's original. From the start Hirsch set out to "make it more accessible to not only a Jewish but also a non-Jewish audience." Justifying his changes on the grounds that Ansky was not a playwright and the play lacked structure, Hirsch reshaped it in several ways. Most strikingly, he had the lovers Chanon and Leah talk and meet towards the end of the play, whereas in the original they meet only once and never speak.

As the play took shape Hirsch enlisted several old friends to help with the project. He enticed designer Mark Negin to return to Winnipeg from England. In preparation Negin did a great deal of library research and based his design both on medieval manuscripts and on photos taken in the 1930s of wooden synagogues in Poland, almost all of which had been destroyed in the Holocaust. Hirsch also hired Alan Laing to write the music and got Tom Hendry to contribute lyrics for original songs.

At the same time as he was preparing for *The Dybbuk*, Hirsch was negotiating on two fronts of major importance. One was the future of his relationship with Bryan. Letters between the two flew back and forth across the Atlantic as they continued what Bryan called their "Turkeytalks" in honour of the tensions that had broken them up after their sojourn in Istanbul. They eventually agreed that Bryan would return to Canada and that once *The Dybbuk* had opened they would give living together another try.

The other negotiation was for the most daunting job Hirsch had ever been offered: head of drama for CBC television. This is described in the following chapter, but it formed a backdrop to the period described here, with Hirsch finally accepting the CBC's offer at the end of November.

Shortly after the CBC contract was signed, rehearsals began in Winnipeg for *The Dybbuk*. Advance ticket sales were the largest ever at the MTC and Eddie Gilbert approved a much larger budget than usual, expecting to recoup some of the expenditure by touring the production in Ontario and Quebec. Composer Alan Laing remembers Hirsch being "at his most demanding" in this production, constantly changing his mind: "John originally intended the production to be spare, but halfway through the rehearsals he was adding all kinds of sound effects and such, to the point where my sound recordist had a breakdown. When I (who was also creating the sound) asked him why this was happening, he replied, 'Alan, things change!' – which has since been a watchword with me." In view of the short time span Negin was joined by Maxine Graham to work on the sets. Visually the play was framed by three irregularly shaped timber arches, which bore richly coloured cloth hangings in the interior scenes and stood in stark relief when the action changed to the town square. Hebrew letters projected on scrolls, huge candles, and other striking design ideas were introduced to mark the different scenes, and Hirsch's staging enhanced the visuals with a series of vividly imagined tableaux.

The Winnipeg cast included a mix of seasoned professionals from all over North America, local actors Hirsch had known since Theatre 77 days, and very young actors to play the part of religious students. Among those Hirsch auditioned for these parts was fifteen-year-old Celeste Sansregret. Describing herself as "four foot eleven with full benefit of the doubt," Sansregret remembers being auditioned in a group: "He wanted to see how people were going to look in a tableau. I probably looked suitably pious." She got the part, but with no experience of Judaism in her Winnipeg Catholic upbringing she soon attracted Hirsch's individual attention. In an early rehearsal, as she knelt in front of the Torah scrolls emoting all the piety she could muster, a couple of long arms grabbed her from behind, "the way you pick up a cat under its front paws. He picked me up, put me on my feet, put his hand on my chest and got me rocking back and forth. He said, 'When you are a Jew, *this* is how you pray.' This was my introduction to Judaism."

The Dybbuk opened to excellent reviews and full houses in Winnipeg, and this continued when the production went on tour later in the year. Both the *Toronto Star* and the *Globe & Mail* gave it superb reviews when it opened at Toronto's St. Lawrence Centre on September 10, and critics in Ottawa, Montreal and smaller centres followed suit as the tour continued. When the play opened at the Mark Taper Forum in Los Angeles on January 30, 1975 with a fresh cast (the exception being Marilyn Lightstone who played Leah on both sides of the border), the praise continued. Stephen Farber in the Sunday *New York Times* judged, "Hirsch has discovered the fire and poetry beneath the surface of this extraordinary play. The result is that *The Dybbuk* seems as pertinent as if it has been written yesterday." It won three Los Angeles Drama Critics' Circle Awards, including one for Hirsch as director.

It is ironic that just as Hirsch's star as a director of theatre was at its highest, he had now taken on a completely different role in his move to the CBC. Aside from *The Dybbuk* he would direct only one other play between 1974 and 1979.

[Seven]

CBC: The Storm Maker

ON NOVEMBER 2, 1973 Hirsch wrote to Bryan from Toronto about "a possible offer from CBC. They want somebody to rethink, reorganize and regenerate their whole drama programme. The job is huge. ..." He had already had several interviews and knew he was on a short list of three people.

The Canadian Broadcasting Corporation was in one of its periodic stages of renewal, with new heads being hunted to rejuvenate its different services. Once again the Winnipeg connection proved its value. One of the three-man headhunting team was a young journalist named Peter Herrndorf, who by then was a special assistant to one of the CBC vice-presidents. Herrndorf had come to Winnipeg from Holland with his family after the Second World War. He knew all about Hirsch from his parents, who were enthusiastic season ticket holders at the Manitoba Theatre Centre. After graduating from the University of Manitoba he did a law degree at Dalhousie and joined the CBC as a reporter in 1965. Herrndorf has since had a distinguished career in the nation's cultural industries; though not an artist himself, he has an evident knack for managing creative personalities and institutions. So it would prove in his relations with Hirsch over the next decade.

Herrndorf and his colleagues Thom Benson (another Winnipegger, who had been with the CBC since 1947) and Robert McGall had already written a document known as the Drama Study, which laid out a five-year plan for revitalizing drama programming. They then spent eight months looking for someone to run television drama, flying to New York, Los Angeles, London and all over Canada in the process. Although Herrndorf had thought of Hirsch as a strong candidate from the beginning, he was not the first choice of the team. However, after two other candidates in Los Angeles and London respectively turned the job down, Herrndorf and his team made an offer to Hirsch.

Hirsch was flattered but cautious. He knew that the television drama department was in bad shape. There had been a "golden age" when CBC dramas had drawn large audiences and made consistent sales to other countries, but it was long past. Talented directors like Paul Almond, Ted Kotcheff and Norman Jewison had departed by the late 1960s for Hollywood along with many of the country's best screenwriters and technicians, and no organized effort had been made to train their replacements. By 1973 only *The Beachcombers* – a weekly half-hour drama set on the coast of British Columbia – attracted a respectable audience. The Drama Study provided a road map to a new "golden age" by investing much more in developing new shows, hiring the best Canadian writers and working with the theatre community to bring new Canadian plays to television audiences. Crucially it aimed to increase original programming from seventy to one hundred and thirty hours per year (not an impossible target: by comparison, the BBC broadcast five hundred hours of original drama at the time). Underpinning these efforts would be a greatly increased multi-year budget. The CBC management had adopted the Study as policy, and it was the basis of the job that Hirsch was being offered.

It sounded good. Hirsch told Bryan,

> The temptation is great. There are a great many young writers, film makers and actors around who should be gathered in and their work shown to the country. The CBC could be a real weapon in the fight for an independent Canada and these very vital young people could have a voice which through the CBC could speak to 15 million people. I would have a chance to get the best out of them and to shape the direction of a very important but just now moribund part of the CBC.

(There were other things on Hirsch's mind at the time: the letter also contains an anguished plea for Bryan to make up his mind and re-join Hirsch in Canada.)

Still, Hirsch's previous experience with the CBC made him cautious. He hired a young lawyer named Garth Drabinsky, who had only graduated from University of Toronto's law school earlier that year. Drabinsky – an extraordinary figure who has made, lost and remade a couple of fortunes in the North American film and theatre industries – duly arrived at the CBC for a meeting with Herrndorf and two other lawyers to negotiate Hirsch's contract. Herrndorf tells the story with retrospective relish: "Garth was obstreperous, insulting, impossible…. It was all a game to him, and if insulting lawyers and contract people enhanced his client's situation, that was okay with him." After an hour the other two lawyers walked out, leaving Herrndorf to try to deal with the young legal pit bull. Herrndorf told Drabinsky he had a vested interest in Hirsch: "I want to keep the CBC from destroying what John is about, as much as you do," he said. "So why don't we draft a contract that not only protects John in normal contractual terms but protects him from the CBC?" Drabinsky agreed, and together they drafted a pair of contracts which Herrndorf's two colleagues accepted a few days later, though both refused to meet with Drabinsky again. The first contract, between Hirsch and the CBC, covered Hirsch's position as a salaried employee. The second was between the CBC and a new company Drabinsky had set up called Flugle Productions, which would furnish Hirsch's services as a "creative consultant to the CBC and as a freelance producer/director of certain television dramatic productions."

The company's name was a private joke of Hirsch's. Flugle Street (sometimes spelled Floogle Street) was a classic vaudeville sketch from the 1930s, in which a hapless straight man tried to find his way to the improbably named street. Hirsch later commented about the additional contract, "It guaranteed me enough money to go into a sanatorium afterward." In the same month Drabinsky renegotiated Hirsch's *Dybbuk* contract with MTC in a similarly abrasive manner, causing a major headache to then-manager Thomas Bohdanetzky, but netting Hirsch additional royalties.

At the end of November Hirsch wrote Bryan that he had taken the job and was now "tied body and soul" to the corporation. The terms were attractive, offering a four-year contract, freedom to continue directing plays, and enough money to buy "a reasonable house" in Toronto. The contract also permitted him to hire three people of his own choosing: a production manager, someone to train and develop new talent, and an administrator "so all the bureaucratic bullshit will be taken care of by other than yours truly...."

Despite his due diligence, Hirsch should probably have known better. Everything depended on the CBC following through on the recommendations of the Drama Study. Although Herrndorf and his colleagues were negotiating in good faith, Thom Benson later admitted in an interview that, having worked at the CBC for decades, "in my heart I knew that the promises in the [Study] were only a beautiful dream. We promised Hirsch a rose garden and we knew that it was full of aphids." The promised stability was almost immediately compromised by the arrival of a new management team at the level above Hirsch's, which when faced with shrinking resources would give priority to news and current affairs budgets rather than drama or variety programming. Moreover, the idea of multi-year funding – a dream of generations of CBC executives – was a non-starter, then as now. For a variety of reasons, not least the opposition of Canada's commercial broadcasters, the CBC relies on a mixture of annually approved parliamentary grants and strictly limited commercial advertising. This makes serious long-term planning almost impossible.

Hirsch moved to Toronto after *The Dybbuk* opened, and stayed with Michal Schonberg for his first three months in town. Schonberg was a fellow Central European who had come into Hirsch's life at Stratford in 1968. Hirsch and Jean Gascon had greatly admired the Czech experimental films exhibited the previous year at Expo 67, and when they learned that these were for sale for a dollar and the cost of removal they had the Festival purchase them. Schonberg arrived in Stratford with the exhibit and became friendly with Hirsch. The Festival's plan to remount the exhibits at Stratford came to an end in August 1968 after the Soviet invasion of Czechoslovakia and they were eventually disassembled and sold, but Schonberg remained in Hirsch's life as a friend and colleague. By the time Hirsch started working for the CBC Schonberg had married and begun to teach theatre and media studies at the University of Toronto. Hirsch and Bryan were invited to the wedding and frequently came to celebrate Rosh Hashanah and Chanukah at the Schonbergs' house.

He had a last bit of business to do in Winnipeg, however, appearing in January as an expert witness in a court case brought by the Crown against the distributors of the film *Last Tango in Paris*. Appearing for the defence Hirsch argued that the film should be judged as a whole, not by its controversial sexual scenes between Maria Schneider and Marlon Brando. Legal papers from the time quote Hirsch providing a metaphor to buttress his argument:

> The film in its entirety may be regarded as the coat, the sexual scenes are the buttons. Now buttons have an essential role to play in a coat. But they are not the coat, and it would be transparent error to treat them as if they were. The viewer who condemns *Last Tango* merely on the basis of its sexual episodes has judged the buttons and not the coat.

The appeal was successful, and contributed to changing media law in Canada.

Hirsch reported for duty at 790 Bay Street on March 1, 1974 and set up on the fifth floor in a corner office, which he decorated with a cheap poster of a cartoon vulture saying, "One of these days I'm going to kill something!" In the early days he held frequent departmental meetings, a mix of pep rally, seminar and religious revival to which all staff was summoned. David Helwig, hired in May as the department's Literary Manager, wrote years later of these meetings:

> The one I remember most vividly was in an ugly window-less room, everyone sitting in ugly standard issue chairs, Hirsch delivering one of his set-pieces about how he alone

could do nothing, solve nothing. We must do it…The endless arm took a great sweep through the air and came toward
us, the middle finger rising and falling to emphasize his
words. 'Ladies and gentlemen,' the soft, precise, insistent
voice said, the rabbi teaching, 'we are in a whore-house here.
And people are getting fucked. And you cannot just sit and
listen to the blind piano player.' What a performance it was,
the whole thing. Fix it, do it, make it wonderful.

Helwig was a writer of fiction and poetry who had been teaching
literature at Queen's University but had also written for radio and
television. The newly-appointed casting director, Muriel Sherrin,
soon became a key member of the team. Organized and imper-
turbable, Sherrin was another Winnipegger, who had worked briefly
at the MTC and later on for the Canada Council. Years later she
would play a notable role at the Stratford Festival. She came as part
of a package with husband Robert who since working with Hirsch on
children's plays at the MTC in the mid-1960s had spent three years
as artistic director of the Neptune Theatre in Halifax. Providing continuity and organizational memory was John Kennedy, a long-time CBC
staffer who as the department's business manager would be invaluable
in helping Hirsch handle the complex organization he had joined.

Hirsch's strategy for making the Drama Study a reality had three
strands. The first was providing training in television production
for new writers, producers and directors. There simply weren't
enough good scripts available, nor were there people to move them
along the production process to create finished programs. At a time
when the use of videotape was increasing (it was much less expensive
than film) the department had only three experienced videotape
directors. In mid-summer Hirsch set up the first of what he hoped
would become regular training sessions under the guidance of
George Bloomfield, a CBC producer who had gained considerable
experience in live-to-tape production during the 1960s. Bloomfield's
first "students" were mostly theatre directors from Toronto's
alternative theatre scene, many of whom are now familiar names in

Canadian theatre history like Ken Gass, Stephen Katz, Martin Kinch and Paul Thompson. In September David Helwig held a television writing workshop, inviting some of the country's best or most promising writers including Sharon Pollock, David Fennario, Larry Fineberg, Tom Cone and George Walker – all of whom eventually had scripts produced by the department.

The second strand was to revive the tradition of "anthology" programs on CBC Television, which presented new Canadian dramas shot either in videotape or film. Hirsch's team scheduled a new anthology, *Performance*, to begin in December. As the department's "flagship" program it would run at nine o'clock on Sunday evenings.

Finally Hirsch aimed to create some popular TV series to challenge the American cop dramas, sitcoms, and soap operas that captured over eighty per cent of English Canada's viewing audience.

Hirsch was well aware that these ambitions were beyond the current capacity of the department. Since training programs would only bear fruit at some time in the future, he had to hire talent – a lot of it. "I can walk on water," he told an interviewer, "but to do it I need fifteen people who can hold their breath for fifteen minutes standing under the surface holding me up. People who can do that are scarce, so they command a lot of money."

He looked for talent not only in Canada but in the United States and especially in the U.K. A number of British writers, producers and directors arrived in fairly short order – ironically, given Hirsch's past and future problems with English imports. Some, like Peter Wildeblood, were interesting and accomplished individuals who would make lasting contributions to the CBC. Wildeblood had a long history of successful television and West End theatrical productions in London; he was also a courageous, openly gay man whose book *Against the Law*, which included his account of being jailed for his sexuality, contributed to changing the U.K.'s laws on homosexuality. Other British imports only stayed long enough to do one or two productions, sometimes leaving a trail of disgruntled Canadians muttering about "colonial attitudes." But Hirsch was right about the scarcity and high price of such individuals. He personally pursued Irene Shubik, a top script editor and producer who would later conceive *The Jewel in the Crown* for the BBC. She finally declined after what she later called "the longest courtship in history." In a letter to her Hirsch admitted that he simply couldn't compete with the fees she was earning in the U.K.

Running a theatre is hard enough, but running CBC Television's drama department was like playing three-dimensional chess. Head office was in Ottawa, where the prime concerns were managing the political vicissitudes of the federal government, walking the ever-lasting tightrope between French and English, and defending budgets. The regional offices held a great deal of power and jealously guarded their autonomy against the centre; individual program areas (Current Affairs, Variety, etc.) defended their territories as did the various technical divisions: film staff kept totally separate from those who worked with videotape. And finally there were the producers and directors – some long-term staff, others on contract – who worked on their individual projects with a constantly changing roster of writers, researchers and assistants. As a freelancer in the theatre, Hirsch had answered to an artistic director and worked on projects consecutively. At MTC and Stratford he had answered to a board and rehearsed, at most, two plays simultaneously. Now his accountability ran in several directions and at any given moment he was responsible for literally dozens of projects and hundreds of thousands of dollars.

In his memoir about the period, *Magic Box Fix Everything*, David Helwig describes the scene that Hirsch would walk through during his early days there: "In every corner of the fifth floor, groups of people were planning productions of many kinds, some going into studio immediately, some only hypothetical...." In one corner a group was planning a soap opera. In another Perry Rosemond was starting to work with a small team on a new sitcom called *King of Kensington* set in the ethnic melting pot of Toronto's Kensington Market. Rosemond got his start in the entertainment business with Hirsch on Winnipeg's Rainbow Stage as a young man in the 1950s (there is a photo of him flourishing a scimitar in the musical *Chu*

Chin Chow) and had gone on to direct and produce a variety of television shows in Canada and the United States. Hirsch had brought him back from Los Angeles expressly to create a successful sitcom, something that had eluded the CBC since *The Plouffe Family* in the 1950s. Across the floor a group of people were developing a new cop show, *Sidestreet*, with one of Hirsch's British imports as story editor. And off by themselves, Stephen Patrick and Ralph Thomas were deep in production of the new anthology series *Performance*.

Hirsch had poached Patrick and Thomas from the Current Affairs department in hopes that they would bring urgency and political punch to television drama. With Hirsch's blessing the two began to hire some of Canada's best filmmakers and writers to make sixty- or ninety-minute programs. When *Performance* began in December 1974 it quickly gained respectable audiences. It also provoked Hirsch's first serious controversy at the CBC with the February broadcast of a one-hour drama called *Baptizing*, based on a short story from Alice Munro's collection *Lives of Girls and Women*.

The film was directed by Allan King, himself no stranger to controversy. His award-winning documentary about an institution for disturbed children, *Warrendale*, had been cancelled at the last minute by the CBC in 1967. *Baptizing* pulled in 1.5 million viewers but also offended some of them with its depiction of teenage sexuality. This provoked a petition from concerned citizens in Red Deer, Alberta, who felt the CBC was encouraging young people to believe that sex "is being done as the NORMAL thing in today's society." Responding for the Corporation in a letter addressed to the daily *Red Deer Advocate,* Hirsch apologized – barely – for upsetting people, but invited readers to tell him what they would like to see on *Performance*, concluding with a theme he would repeat frequently in coming years: "The CBC is your network, and we want, as much as possible, to make it even more so."

Performance also served Hirsch's plan to bring theatre directors and their companies into television production, working with veteran executive producer Robert Allan. One of the first was Paul Thompson and Theatre Passe Muraille, who did a videotaped production of their *Farm Show,* a collective creation about life in the rural community of Clinton, Ontario. The clash of cultures between alternative theatre and TV people was immediately apparent. Thompson and his company wanted to tape the show in front of a live audience out in a farm community and after much argument Allan finally agreed to bring a rural audience into CBC's Jarvis Street studios by bus. In a later and more technically assured production, *1837,* the fiercely political Passe Muraille company went on strike to protest against CBC's decision to interrupt the program with commercials. Hirsch himself had to come down to negotiate with the company, agreeing that the show would be broadcast without commercials, but would also have to be cut from ninety to sixty minutes.

The job involved frequent travel in Canada and overseas. Hirsch's files from that period contain many travel schedules drawn up by his secretary, several with notes admonishing him not to book flights himself. His most frequent foreign stop in the early years was London, where in addition to meetings with the BBC and independent producers he would see friends like Alan Bates and John Lahr, and catch up on what was being produced in the theatre.

Within Canada he could frequently be found at the offices of the Canada Council in Ottawa and at meetings of the federal Advisory Arts Panel. The latter could be interesting – or at least, the get-togethers after the meetings could be. These gave Hirsch a chance to talk with people who were making headlines in their various disciplines. In the list of attendees at one meeting one sees Hirsch's name along with fellow panel participants like writers Michael Ondaatje and Roch Carrier, dancer Anna Wyman, water-colourist Bruno Bobak, sculptor Joe Fafard, double bass virtuoso Gary Karr, composer Gilles Tremblay and filmmaker Jean-Pierre Lefebvre. Hirsch was at the top table of the Canadian arts establishment but typically he was ambivalent about it. The playwright Sharon Pollock, another Advisory Arts Panel member, recalled meeting Hirsch in Charlottetown at another meeting:

> …He had just come from what he said was the best theatre
> he'd seen in years. He'd been at the Saturday night wrestling

in town. He asked me what I was doing there. I guess I thought I was working on behalf of the artists of Canada. He said, "Then go home and write. That's what you're supposed to be doing. Don't get co-opted into the bureaucratic process. Your job is to write the best plays you can."

Between the constant meetings, the travel and the paperwork Hirsch's days were now brutally full. By this time he and Bryan were now living together in a rented house in Toronto's Rosedale district. Bryan remembers Hirsch frequently coming home in a fury, unwilling to talk about the day's events, usually with several scripts or other documents that he had to read. The "Turkeytalks" occasionally flared up, as Bryan's still unsettled lifestyle clashed with Hirsch's now highly regulated schedule. A terse letter from Hirsch tells Bryan, "For four months you've had time to get keys to the outside door. It is not the fact that you come in at 5:00 in the morning – but that you woke me. I have a hell of a time at work… I need uninterrupted sleep." The other matter that continued to drive Hirsch crazy was Bryan's lack of aggressiveness in pursuing his artistic career. He often gave away or destroyed his paintings, and his most lucrative work tended to be the result of Hirsch's contacts. Yet they were also enjoying Toronto and building up a shared social life. They began to throw dinner parties together and started to look for a bigger house.

Hirsch's first twelve months on the job were frustrating ones. His department was trying to do its job with antiquated equipment and leaky studios. Hiring experienced outsiders was expensive but so was using inadequately trained staff: productions frequently went over budget because they took longer than scheduled, or substandard material had to be re-written or re-shot. His concerns about training were not being taken seriously, he felt, despite many meetings and memos in which he had argued that failure to invest in training now would land the department in the same sorry state five years later. As spending cuts began to be imposed, memos landed on his desk from senior executives with increasing frequency, taking him to task for not balancing approved budgets and reminding him of missed targets for reduced spending. Most of all he hated having to put his limited budgetary eggs in one basket, particularly in the development of new series. Gearing up to start production on *Sidestreet*, the new police drama, he felt "like the monkey with the one note in the orchestra – if you don't hit it, you're fired. But, you know, there are fifty million monkeys down there [in the U.S.], all of them hitting police series, and out of that we only see probably the best one."

As so often in the past, Hirsch went public with his frustrations. In February he told one interviewer that it was like being stuck in "a squirrel cage, running and running and never being able to consider what we are going to do next year." The threat to quit was clear: "I'm asking, give me the money, give me the ability to plan, give me the commitment to training and development. If I don't have the money and the commitment then I can depart in good conscience without any rancour and say I've tried, but this thing is too big or impossible for anyone." He turned up the volume in April when he spoke at the annual Alan B. Plaunt lecture, named after one of the early governors of the CBC. Trumpeting the success of *Performance* in attracting audiences, he attacked senior CBC management for getting "scared" every time there was a controversy: "I'm from show business," he said, "and as long as they mention you, you should be thankful." Winding up his talk, he attacked the Corporation for having abandoned its promise to increase drama content to one hundred and thirty hours per year. "If the CBC means business, it has to go at it in a big way," he concluded, calling for television viewers to write to their MPs and the CBC president.

This time there was a reaction from upstairs, specifically from Denis Harvey, an executive two steps above Hirsch in the hierarchy (Harvey was another of the new brooms headhunted by Herrndorf at the same time as Hirsch). Being questioned about his public behaviour left Hirsch angry and shortly after he drafted a memo to Harvey: "I have been a shit-disturber all my life and I don't intend to change because I have achieved a hell of lot by being one." The Corporation, he charged, "spends its time behaving as if the Treasury Board and hardware, etc., are the most important things in its life." Programming and creativity were not encouraged or even talked about: "There is no communication except when the shit hits the fan. In short, no news is good news; good work is taken for granted, never mentioned, never rewarded." Again he invoked the promises of the Drama Study and the success of *Performance*: "The public reaction has been remarkable, and it has been positive, if only I can convince the Corporation of that." It is not clear if the memo was ever sent. A handwritten note by Hirsch's secretary, Gloria Golden, reminded Hirsch that Denis Harvey was actually "on your side" within upper management and asked "Do you still want it to go?" Hirsch scrawled "HOLD" over her note.

For a while Hirsch toned down his public pronouncements and he and the CBC management found a degree of mutual tolerance that held for the time being. Good audience ratings were certainly part of it, but the environment around him had improved. He now felt well supported by his senior management team. Muriel Sherrin had proved so effective as Drama's head of casting that other departments in the Entertainment division used her team's services, and in a memo Hirsch wondered if Drama could charge for this. John Kennedy had indeed shouldered a great deal of the "bureaucratic bullshit" that Hirsch had feared when considering the post and maintained a certain degree of calm on the fifth floor. And still in his corner was Peter Herrndorf, now head of Current Affairs and occupying the office directly above Hirsch's. Herrndorf frequently came down the back stairwell to give Hirsch a hand. "I spent probably a third of my time in Hirsch's office," remembers Herrndorf, "as he was either looking for advice about how to persuade the CBC to let him do certain things or try to keep the CBC from destroying his best ideas."

And for all his frustrations Hirsch was also having a lot of fun. He had always loved film and the job allowed him to meet directors whose work he admired. Sometimes the meetings went awry. He opened a letter to Don Shebib, director of the seminal *Goin' Down the Road*, "After your little scene this morning, I would like to point out to you that if you have anything to tell me beyond 'go and screw yourself', I would be most interested in talking with you." Others led to fruitful collaborations. A meeting with the exiled Czech director Jan Kadar, whose *The Shop on Main Street* won the 1965 Academy Award for Best Foreign Film, resulted in Kadar being hired to direct a one-hour drama for the CBC. Broadcast in 1976 and introduced by playwright Arthur Miller, *Mandelstam's Witness* told the story of Nadezhda Mandelstam and her long campaign to protect the legacy of her husband, Osip, the poet who died on his way to the gulag after criticizing Stalin. The show was a prestigious affair for CBC Drama, winning an international Emmy.

Also fun was the shaping of complete seasons, working with his senior producers to choose scripts, directors and actors. Starting in September 1975 the *Performance* season provided a wide range of mainstream and alternative Canadian plays, along with some international ones. On one evening it would be a Canadian historical play like *Lulu Street*, Ann Henry's play about the Winnipeg General Strike that Hirsch had commissioned eight years earlier. On another viewers saw Donald Pleasance in the satirical *Captain of Köpenick*, a role Pleasance had brought to the London stage a few years earlier. Most critics agreed that Hirsch's choices had been good ones and the productions of a high standard, one noting that "Hirsch has shown he knows the plays and the groups making up most of current Canadian theatre, and more importantly, he has brought some of them to television, most for the first time."

There were some rumblings that the Canadian content was Ontario-centric and that Hirsch should have tried harder to find scripts from other parts of the country. The Vancouver-based playwright Beverley Simons, whose work never reached the national network, alluded to this in a 1975 play called *Prologue*, in a passage where a chorus of characters discussed a sleeping playwright (presumably Simons herself): "Not good enough for Soap... Or Sitcom... Oh, John Hirsch... Oh, Canada Council."

Québec, however, was well served by Hirsch, at least in terms of talented people hired by English Drama. Hirsch was able to take advantage of a slowdown in the Québec film industry to hire Claude Jutra, whose 1971 *Mon Oncle Antoine* makes every shortlist of best films ever produced in Canada.

On his first visit to Toronto to talk about working at English TV Drama, Jutra became aware of the gulf between television and theatre that Hirsch was attempting to bridge. Running into a crowd of television people in Nicholson's, the Greek restaurant that was the main CBC hangout at the time, Jutra told them he'd like to see a play and meet some local actors while he was in town. Could anyone recommend a show? No one could. He then ran into Hirsch at a drugstore and asked the same question.

> So Hirsch started, "Well, first there is Tarragon Theatre, they're doing this, it's a new play," and he'd tell me the whole cast. And I said, "It's just for tonight, tell me one play to go and see." "Well," he said, "go and see Passe Muraille, they're very interesting." I went to see them. And I cast the whole film with the cast of that play.

Passe Muraille's director at the time, Paul Thompson, remembers it well, since Jutra's hiring decisions gutted a very good company of actors that had gelled during the run of *The West Show*. He remembers complaining, "Hirsch is stealing my actors by offering them real money!"

Hirsch's domestic situation was settling into the shape in which it would continue for the rest of his life. In late 1975 he and Bryan and several cats moved into the home they would share for the rest of Hirsch's life. 187 Hudson Drive was a large house on the edge of a ravine in the Moore Park suburb. Hirsch and Bryan loved it the moment their real estate agent showed it to them and Hirsch had no problem paying for it. The two-contract arrangement with CBC – enforced by Garth Drabinsky's sharp legal elbows on behalf of Flugle Productions – made Hirsch more than comfortable. He also continued to invest wisely, the legacy of Sybil's advice since the 1950s.

Although the two were now a firmly established couple, Hirsch was always discreet in public about his relationship. In an interview in January 1975 he alluded to the loss of his family in Hungary when he told the *Los Angeles Times*, "I have never married. There are, basically, losses you never recover from." Hudson Drive gave

Hirsch and Bryan the space to create a new family from their expanding circles of friends and acquaintances. The connection to the Shacks in Winnipeg remained strong, with a physical reminder as cuttings from Ma Shack's jungle of houseplants sprouted a healthy second generation in Toronto. Hirsch continued to phone Pauline and Sybil Shack each Sunday morning and to visit them in Winnipeg as often as possible. Sybil, who by now had a national profile as a writer on education and human rights, frequently came to visit on business trips to Toronto, and there was a steady stream of Winnipeg friends dropping in.

A number of Winnipeg friends moved to Toronto to further their careers. One of these was the documentary filmmaker Gail Singer, who helped establish a tradition of long Sunday lunches at Hudson Drive. These generally involved many guests and much "competitive cooking" and kibitzing; one visitor remembers passionate arguments about the correct way to cook a goose and where the best ingredients could be bought. Food had always been important to Hirsch, and now that he had his own kitchen, he could fully indulge his passion for both cooking and feeding people, which he identified with both his Hungarian and Jewish heritage. He and Bryan started a tradition of Passover seders, more food-based than religious, to which Jewish and gentile friends were invited.

New acquaintances came and went, some becoming fixtures at Hudson Drive. One was Magda Zalán, an exiled Hungarian journalist who arrived in Toronto with her four-year-old son Andy in 1975. Hirsch was one of two people she knew in Canada, and he helped her with contacts and references. She was struck by the way Hirsch compartmentalized the different parts of his life, only learning that he was head of CBC Drama several months later when he took her out to a play. At first she was confused: "Everybody seemed to know him, but everybody, from the ushers to the secretary to the performers, called him by his first name – something you would never see in Europe with someone important." Then the penny dropped: "Jancsi," as she knew him, was a big deal in this town. That was also the night Zalán learned that Hirsch was gay and had a long-term partner. Because the invitation came at short notice, giving Zalán no time to find someone to look after her son, Hirsch offered her "the best babysitter in town, absolutely reliable, and free of charge." That turned out to be Bryan. Andy and Bryan enjoyed each other's company and the "service" was repeated many times over the years. Bryan built a treehouse for Andy in the garden and took him and his friends from daycare on "expeditions" in the ravine behind the house. There were other outings such as a visit to a flea circus, where Hirsch and Bryan were enraptured by the spectacle of tiny insects pulling carts and performing tricks long after Andy had lost interest.

Zalán, who eventually found a job as a journalist on CBC's Hungarian service, found it hard to get a handle on Hirsch. On the one hand he was paternalistic, frequently lecturing her on how to make her way in her new country. On the other he had great ideas and was generous with time and contacts. He encouraged her to begin organizing a series of literary cafes and attended all of them. "He was more friendly with the performers than he had ever been to me," she wrote in a memoir about her early days in Canada. "After the last show of the subscription season he invited us all for a Hungarian bean soup party at his house. The guests left charmed. I stayed behind helping to clean up the mess." Zalán expected some praise from Hirsch, but instead got another lecture about making an even better series. Crushed, she nonetheless heeded the advice and eventually produced a literary café series at the St. Lawrence Centre. The first of these was organized around the writings of one of Hungary's most distinguished exiles, the poet George Faludy. Hirsch, who was friendly with Faludy, directed the evening and the performers included a distinguished group from Hirsch's theatre and television circles.

The truce at work held for the rest of 1975, and while Hirsch never actually settled in his surroundings, he expressed some sense of ownership. The vulture poster on his office wall was now accompanied by an eclectic selection of objects including a blue-and-green blanket from Mykonos, a throw rug from India, a brass Tibetan calendar, and a sketch of Albert Einstein.

In September both *Sidestreet* and *King of Kensington* premiered.

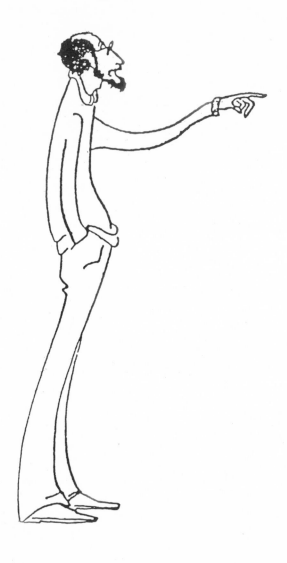

Original caption accompanying drawing: "John Hirsch directing
The Dybbuk at the Mark Taber Forum, Los Angeles, 1975.
Courtesy of the creator Sylvie Drake

The cop show got favourable reviews; the sitcom didn't. The latter was not entirely unexpected: the hastily produced pilot had been judged dismal months before. The first episodes of the regular series showed considerable improvement, but had not yet settled in and were still struggling with some built-in challenges. The shows were shot live in several takes, and went to air a week later. The scriptwriters also had to insert references to current news events and make them funny as well as topical. Despite the criticism Hirsch continued to support Perry Rosemond and his production team and to defend the show's budget. He liked Al Waxman in the lead role as the Jewish shopkeeper – a friendlier, more *mensch*-like presence than the hardedged characters in current U.S. sitcoms like *All in the Family*. He also liked the King's WASP wife and multi-ethnic crowd of friends and business acquaintances, and believed that Canadians would come to like the show. As the show developed Hirsch's confidence was vindicated. It attracted good audiences and – accolade of accolades – actually sold to stations in the United States. It also made a star of Al Waxman: back in Winnipeg his photo went up on the wall at Kelekis restaurant – in the company of Hirsch and Perry Rosemond.

Although it got better reviews *Sidestreet* had a more turbulent time "backstage." Although Hirsch had supported the idea of a cop show that played down violence and emphasized more of the reality of community policing, he wasn't happy with what he saw in the first episodes. The show wasn't slick or fast-paced enough and he didn't have confidence that the initial production team could make the necessary improvements. David Helwig, who took over as story editor after the first few episodes, had a tough few months as Hirsch frequently intervened, forcing writers and editors to work crazy hours.

As new scripts were shot Hirsch got happier with the series. A few episodes stood out, notably one in which the great Québec actress Monique Mercure played a Métis woman battling slum landlords. The show found the right balance of traditional cop show drama (an arson scene) and social issues (the housing problems of urban minorities), carried off with believable dialogue and crisp editing. Like *King of Kensington*, the series established one of its leading actors, Donnelly Rhodes, as a television star.

The Drama department had a constant stream of people coming and going by this time. Larry Mirkin, a young American who had assisted Hirsch while he was re-staging *The Dybbuk* in Los Angeles, arrived in mid-1975 to work as a story editor. He found a department in flux, with a marked divide between old guard ("suits and ties") and new hires ("people like me with hair down to their shoulders and colourful shirts and pants"). When a friend wrote from Los Angeles asking what it was like, Mirkin wrote back, "It's a different place. There are at least 80-90 people in the department, and as far as I can tell only four of us are Jewish. We have a good story editor named Anne Frank who is not Jewish and a good publicist named Maureen O'Donnell who is." Another American hire was Stan Colbert, who stayed in the department for many years as an executive producer before leaving to establishing one of Canada's premier talent agencies and later to head the publisher HarperCollins. Colbert was sometimes accused of making programs "slicker" and more "American" during his time at the CBC, but as this often meant making them faster-paced, he fit well with Hirsch's sense of how to capture audience share for CBC Drama.

Lawrence Mirkin remembers a kind of competition between the two top executive producers, Ralph Thomas and Stan Colbert:

> In general, I think that Stan's work never hit the high artistic quality that the best of Ralph's work did, but Stan's work was more consistent. No question that many of Ralph's docudramas were relevant socially and executed at a high level (the ones that missed often missed greatly, but you have to expect that with an anthology series.) But Stan and the *King of Kensington* folks tended to bring in the larger numbers. I think that John was just fine with the idea that some shows should get numbers and others should display outstanding excellence, even if his ideal program would have done both things simultaneously.

Performance continued to get good reviews and audiences, and provided employment for some of the best film directors in Canada, but another Hirsch initiative did neither. The weekly half-hour *Peepshow* was intended to showcase work by the new writers and directors that the Drama Department had been training. In fact, cutbacks had forced Hirsch to cancel his training sessions and the show appears to have been at least partly a way for Hirsch to hide training within the production budget. The tactic backfired. While most of the films and videotaped programs were at least interesting – examples include work by David Cronenberg and the satirical troupe Codco, and Theatre Passe Muraille's *Country Fable* about a farmer's infatuation with Mary Tyler Moore – few were ready for prime time, and the videotaped plays looked particularly bad on screen. Hirsch found himself painted into a corner. He had no alternatives to fill the Thursday evening slot and had to grit his teeth while the network aired inferior work produced under his command. His strategy of providing a fast track for theatre people into television production was slowly sinking. The skill sets and professional cultures were too different, the technology too unforgiving, and CBC management never got behind the idea.

Hirsch's frustration level began to mount again as budgets came under increasing pressure within the corporation. Then in March 1976 members of the Association of Canadian Television and Radio Artists picketed the CBC Toronto offices, their placards protesting the decision to cast an American, Kathleen Widdoes, in the part of the Canadian suffragette Nellie McClung. Hirsch argued in vain that twenty-four Canadians had been considered for the part, but none had been suitable or – more importantly, given the difficulties of booking scarce studio time and technical staff – available for the already-scheduled shoot. The story escalated, with hostile coverage from the country's top radio show, CBC's *Morningside*. When Widdoes was denied a work permit CBC had no choice but to give in, and Hirsch not only didn't get the actress he wanted but lost his scheduled studio time. The Nellie McClung program was eventually made when Kate Reid became available to play the lead. After the adverse publicity died down Widdoes went on to work frequently at Stratford.

More bad publicity ensued when Hirsch attempted to "interfere" with *The Beachcombers*, asking for cuts in a script that he found too slow-paced. This was a bigger issue than it sounds. The CBC's internal structure reflected and sometimes amplified some of the country's regional tensions. David Helwig had already been sent out to make suggestions about improving the series and had not exactly been welcomed. There may also have been something personal at work. Hirsch and Bruno Gerussi, the show's star, had never gotten along very well, and it may be that the sight of Gerussi onscreen simply rubbed Hirsch the wrong way. It was even rumoured that he tried to kill the series. In any case, the B.C. operation, which had been producing its popular show for three years before Hirsch was appointed, told Hirsch he didn't understand "the B.C. pace" and suggested he butt out. Hirsch suggested that B.C. follow orders. Again the story went public. A "committee to save the CBC from itself" was formed in B.C. and quickly found support in other parts of the country. Hirsch also went public, charging that the CBC was threatened by balkanization and defending his right and duty to edit productions. The controversy eventually died out and *The Beachcombers'* ratings continued to climb during Hirsch's time at the CBC.

Complaints about Hirsch's interference were not limited to the regions. Many producers in Toronto resented his frequent demands for re-writes and re-shoots, and some said so at a meeting held in early July. Hirsch stood his ground, saying that things needed to be tightened up; too many productions were badly planned, inadequately supervised, and unresponsive to requests for improvements. He reiterated these points in a memo sent the following week, concluding, "I ask for your cooperation and support, and please understand that the 're-Hirsching' is not because I enjoy 'fixing' or in some of your minds 'interfering', but because the standards that I have discussed with you before a shot was shaped, simply haven't been met. I am determined that we should see that all adjustments are made to shows before they hit the air."

It was time that Hirsch and the CBC took a rest from each other.

On July 15, 1976 Hirsch sent a memo to all staff in TV Drama, telling them that he would be away until early September and Muriel Sherrin would run things until he returned. Until then, he assured them, "My mail will be forwarded to me once a week and you can expect answers to them." Hirsch was off to direct *The Three Sisters* at Stratford, his first time back there in seven years.

After Hirsch left Stratford in August 1969 Jean Gascon had continued as the Festival's artistic director. The genial Gascon was a much-loved figure at Stratford and had directed some wonderful plays there. But by 1973 box office sales were stagnant and the stresses of running the Festival – as well as a long-running problem with alcohol – were affecting Gascon's health. There was no obvious successor and the search committee couldn't find a Cana-dian available or acceptable to the Board. Hirsch was still very definitely *non grata* with some board members. Memories were still fresh of *The Satyricon*'s bare buttocks and financial overrun, and of Hirsch's ungentlemanly criticisms of the Stratford establishment. In fact, he was still at it. In an interview published in the *Canadian Theatre Review* in 1974 he again criticized Stratford as

> essentially a colonial institution covered with a nationalistic Canadian blanket… I think that if the theatre could order 30 of those animated dummies from Disneyland and if they could program them for 36 plays of Shakespeare and get different designers every year to put costumes on them and get recordings of them from England (Olivier and Richardson), they would still pull in three million dollars.

Where were the new leading actors, he asked? Where were the exciting reinterpretations of *Lear* or *The Winter's Tale*? If Hirsch's words were unkind to Jean Gascon, their real target was the Festival Board.

When the Festival announced that the job would go to Robin Phillips, a young English director with a brilliant reputation, it caused a nationalist outcry. Hirsch quickly joined forces with other Canadian directors, who demanded a meeting with the Stratford

Board. This was held in April, where a smaller delegation presented a letter drafted by Robertson Davies, who had been carefully chosen in his capacity as a senior cultural nationalist and former Board member (Hirsch was travelling at the time and did not attend the meeting). The letter is careful and conciliatory; in fact, it reads less like a manifesto than a strategic planning document complete with a numbered list of recommendations. Phillips isn't even mentioned by name, the directors having accepted that the contract had been signed. They were more concerned that as the most heavily subsidized theatre in the country, Stratford should start to act as a national theatre rather than as a splendid island unto itself. Keith Turnbull, one of the signatories, attended the meeting and remembers that its tone was polite until it became clear that the directors intended to release their letter to the press. At that point things turned acrimonious, and twenty-seven years later Turnbull's overriding memory is the Board members' arrogant dismissal of their recommendations.

Though shaken by the outcry over his appointment, Phillips duly arrived to take up his position at Stratford. Over the next two years, as Hirsch was rebuilding CBC's Drama Department, Phillips made major strides in revitalizing the Festival. His first season in 1975, though not a complete success, provided ample evidence of his talents. The high point was a *Measure for Measure* that jettisoned the Festival's traditional theatricality and saw the lead actors – Martha Henry, William Hutt, Nicholas Pennell, and a new Phillips recruit, Brian Bedford – mesmerize audiences with nuance and understatement.

In preparing his second season Phillips made an effort to meet the criticisms in the Davies memo, scheduling a new Canadian play by Larry Fineberg and hiring Tarragon Theatre's Bill Glassco to direct *The Merchant of Venice*. Though he had been warned off Hirsch by some board members, Phillips decided early on he couldn't ignore him. Although early overtures left the impression that Hirsch was determined to keep his distance, Phillips persisted. In a letter to Hirsch in April, 1976 Phillips stressed "how much I hope you personally will gradually be drawn back to this organization and that we will find a way of involving you that will give you satisfaction and pleasure." The timing of the letter is important. Barely two months before the Stratford Season was to open there was no mention yet of *The Three Sisters*.

At the time Hirsch was committed to directing something very different as his "mini-sabbatical" from the CBC. He and Leon Major, who by that time was running Toronto Arts Productions, had been talking for almost a year about producing a new musical at the St. Lawrence Centre. Called *Vaudeville*, the show was supposed to recreate an old-time vaudeville show with, as Hirsch put it, "some additional pizzazz." By June, commitments had been made to several actors and production staff, the hall had been booked, and financing had been arranged for the production and a subsequent tour.

At that point Hirsch pulled out, citing a variety of problems including difficulties in getting the first-class cast he needed to make *Vaudeville* a success. Major was furious, his company out of pocket, but he could do nothing. Garth Drabinsky was still representing Hirsch's interests with his usual tenacity and a final contract had still not been signed. (Hirsch wrote in a semi-apology to Major soon after, "I wish I had just negotiated with you alone rather than through Garth...but he did not understand that our relationship, based on the past, is not that of Louis B. Mayer and some Hollywood director. I regret what happened there.")

Other correspondence suggests that Hirsch's concerns about the show were genuine, but his decision to bail out was also based on an offer that came out of the blue sometime in June. Phillips, who was already directing an incredible six plays simultaneously that season, had suddenly found himself having to take over *The Way of the World* from another director. *The Three Sisters* was the final show in the season with the designer and cast already in place. Hirsch had a reputation as a genius with Chekhov: would he consider taking it on? He would, and gladly, despite the late date. After two years of memos and budget battles at the CBC, directing Chekhov would be like "sending my soul to the dry cleaners."

Hirsch was almost evangelical about Chekhov. He believed it was important for Canadians to see Chekhov plays, not least because they dealt with people like themselves who live in relative isolation from the rest of the world and who hanker after metropolitan cultures rather than aspiring to "attain some degree of authentic self-awareness." Chekhov also portrayed like no other playwright the theme of spiritual discouragement in the face of social change, a perennial interest of Hirsch's.

And there was the sheer theatricality of the play. He loved the way *The Three Sisters* functioned as both a symbolic work and a detailed observation of a family under deep stress. The three Prozorov sisters are trapped in a dull provincial town by the death of their father, a distinguished general in the Imperial Army. Dreaming of the glittering social life they had lived in Moscow years before, they pin their hopes for escape on their brother Andrei, whom all expect to have a brilliant career as a professor at a great university. These dreams are shattered when Andrei marries an initially shy local woman, who ends up dominating the sisters and their brother.

Phillips had assembled a splendid cast for the three lead roles. Olga, the oldest sister who teaches school and has missed her chance at marriage, was played by Martha Henry. Marti Maraden took the role of twenty-six-year-old Irina, suffering the devotion of a boring suitor. Masha, a passionate soul unhappily married to a kindly but dull headmaster, was played by Maggie Smith. This was Smith's first season at Stratford, and the beginning of Phillips' policy of bringing international stars to Stratford.

As with *The Cherry Orchard* Hirsch had directed a decade before, much in the play resonated with his personal experience and with the world he had lost in pre-war Hungary. The Prozorovs lived the kind of life he remembered in Siófok: the close-knit family, the visitors dropping in, the musical evenings. Masha, he told Maggie Smith, reminded him of his bluestocking grandmother Tekla, with her intellectual brilliance and quick temper. The play also reminded him of his early years in Winnipeg and of the crowd of young actors and intellectuals at Child's Restaurant who longed to be in London or New York – anywhere but Winnipeg. "Anyone who has spent a winter on the prairies," he said, "knows exactly what *Three Sisters* is about."

A FIERY SOUL

Once again Hirsch prepared meticulously before rehearsals began. He brought Larry Mirkin with him from the CBC as dramaturge to work on the script, and made a variety of revisions to the translation, some of them based on recent academic research on Chekhov. He brought a great deal of information to early rehearsals to steep his cast in the physical and social context of the play: the quality of light, the look of the birch trees, the way people touch, descriptions of clothing and household goods.

As Martha Henry had not parted on the best of terms with Hirsch five years earlier after playing *Antigone* for him in New York, she was a little apprehensive when rehearsals began. But Hirsch was on "best behaviour" in this production. Some of it may have had to do with having Maggie Smith in the cast (Robin Phillips, too, was observed to be "careful" with her in the first season), but perhaps more importantly, he had a top-flight cast and a script he totally believed in.

Marti Maraden, who was somewhat intimidated by the eminence of Henry and Smith, found Hirsch "kind and absolutely supportive, but relentless to make me do what he wanted me to do." Today a distinguished director herself (as is Martha Henry), Maraden judges that all the intellectual preparation allowed him to take the cast to the next, necessary stage: "The era, the time, Chekhov, Russia – he completely got all of that and made us aware of it, but he really directed very emotionally, which was what the play needed." She particularly remembers working privately with Hirsch on the Act III fire scene, when a fire breaks out in the town and the sisters stay up till the early morning, waiting as news comes in. In Hirsch's staging, Maraden had to speak most of her lines from a rocking chair until she leaps up from it, weeping in despair. Then he did something risky, as Maraden recounts:

> When he realized that he could allow a certain degree of anarchy in the great fire scene — Irina breaking down as she loses belief in her dreams and her future, Masha insisting on confessing her love affair with Vershinin, Olga desperate NOT to hear her – John decided to trust us to do it differently each night. Sometimes in my flailing despair, I

233

would end up in Masha's arms, sometimes in Olga's. The only rule was that after Natasha's entrance with her candle and Masha's joke that the way she walked around with that candle she might have started the fire, we were all to land in a heap on top of each other on the floor, laughing hysterically. When John made the final decision to allow us this degree of improvisation, he draped his long, long arms over his head, elbows akimbo, and said, "Alright, alright, I'll let you do it differently every time, because every time it's wonderful. Just don't hang from the chandeliers!"

At the end of the opening night, on September 1, the audience sat in silence for a moment before breaking into thunderous applause. Maraden describes the feeling backstage: "The three of us Sisters went into the wing, stage right, embracing each other and weeping – we were so in it that we didn't understand that we were being asked to go back out on stage again." Most critics agreed with the *Toronto Star*'s Gina Mallet (who later became one of Hirsch's most implacable critics) that *The Three Sisters* was the best play in a very good season.

It was also the last time Hirsch would direct a play at Stratford until he became the Festival's artistic director in 1981. There were no artistic differences with Phillips. Today Phillips says without hesitation, "this was a *great* production of a *great* play [his emphasis]." The problem was personal. There had been tension between the two from the moment Hirsch arrived in Stratford. In Phillips' memory his attempts to make friends with Hirsch were to no avail. On one of the rare nights they had dinner together Hirsch went on at some length about how Phillips, as an Englishman, could never understand a Hungarian Jew like him. Phillips interrupted, "John, I live with a Jew whose Hungarian grandfather stowed away on a ship in order to escape to New Zealand." Phillips says this both surprised and mollified Hirsch for a while, but the détente didn't last. Rumours circulated that Hirsch was criticizing the way Phillips was running the Festival; that the two had argued when Phillips refused to let Hirsch fire some cast members; and that Phillips was jealous when

Maggie Smith wondered publically where Hirsch had been all her life. Martha Henry remembers becoming aware of the conflict later, but says Hirsch "never, ever" criticized Phillips during the rehearsals.

Whatever the truth of the rumours, the final straw came days before the opening of *The Three Sisters*, when Hirsch gave an interview to the *Globe & Mail*'s John Fraser. Discussing the *Vaudeville* debacle, Hirsch mentioned that he regretted its falling through, in part because he had hoped "to make some money" from it. In an almost parenthetical comment, Fraser wrote that since Phillips would be paid "a handsome sum" for each production, directing seven of the season's ten productions would net him more money than "any director in Canada's history."

Three Sisters 1976: Maggie Smith, Martha Henry and Marti Maraden.
Photo by Robert C. Ragsdale, courtesy of Stratford Shakespeare Festival Archives

It wasn't true – Phillips was on a straight salary – but Fraser didn't check the facts before he went to print. Phillips blew up when he read the article, called Fraser at 6:00 in the morning and demanded to know the source of the information. Fraser replied, "I think, professionally, that I mustn't tell you, Robin, but you're a smart man and can figure it out," which Phillips took to be an indirect confirmation that Hirsch had deliberately slandered him. Phillips then called Hirsch, who denied the charge. According to him it was Fraser who'd asked the question about Phillips' earnings and all Hirsch had done was recall that when he'd worked at Stratford in the 1960s artistic directors got an extra payment for each show they directed. Phillips didn't believe it and decided that Hirsch would never work again at Stratford while he was artistic director.

When Hirsch arrived back on the fifth floor at the CBC he returned to the three-dimensional chess board of television programming, in which the opening square was always the script – or the search for one. He still read dozens each month and was generally unhappy with what he read. In November 1976 Hirsch published an open letter in the *Globe & Mail* that began, "Dear Aspiring Young Television Writer. Our country desperately needs you, but before you enter the glamorous world of the little screen, please read the sign on the gate: Beyond This Place There Be Monsters." The piece was a particularly Hirschian mixture of sober analysis of the Canadian market for television scripts, exposition of how scriptwriting is done, criticism of the commercial competition (he asked readers to consider, "How healthy it would be if CTV and Global provided you with 80 hours apiece of programming outlets") and appeal to the best in people: "We need your energies, your wit, and your writing. We will help you as much as we can, but we cannot do it alone."

Ralph Thomas, who met regularly with him on potential scripts, remembered Hirsch throwing a script on the floor and then falling on it, saying "I can't express how bad this script is in any other way." The brutal frankness was hard for many people to take, as were other aspects of Hirsch's management style. As a result, there was a constant stream of new faces on the fifth floor as people left – some of them "hating Hirsch" as Thomas recalled – and were replaced. Those who stayed had to find their own ways of dealing with their unpredictable boss. Thomas found his own form of resistance: "He described me as an 'anal-retentive WASP' [because] basically all I ever did was sit and say nothing and sometimes smile, and that drove him crazy… We drove each other nuts and managed to make some good programmes." The histrionics and the arguments were indeed hard to take, but that "probably made me a better producer, made me a better writer, made me a better artist."

In contrast, David Helwig had become more confrontational with Hirsch during his time in the department: "After all, he said we had to fight these things out. There was always a lot of dramaturgical talk in the air, about the purpose and structure of scripts, and I had learned from it, and from John himself, as he intoned the words, 'What is this about? Why is it interesting?'" Helwig finished out his two-year contract and went back to Kingston, where he continued a career that mixed teaching and writing (he returned to the CBC occasionally as a scriptwriter). Though they didn't part on the best of terms Hirsch sent him a thank-you note, and Helwig later reflected, "John Hirsch changed my life. I've never met another human being who existed on such a large scale, what they call a sacred monster, I suppose."

The monster certainly emerged from time to time. Writers, director, and actors suddenly fell out of favour, sometimes after arguments or conspicuous failure, but just as often for reasons that weren't clear to anyone. Some were blackballed like the actor Barbara Hamilton; although she had done many dramas for the CBC, Hirsch simply didn't like her. At the same time Hirsch gave opportunities and a helping hand to many people, especially to talented individuals at the beginning of their careers. One was Des McAnuff, the current artistic director at the Stratford Festival. A polymath writer, director, and musician in his mid-twenties, McAnuff was just about to leave for New York when he dropped in at the CBC to pick up a script he'd had produced there. He was surprised when Hirsch spotted him in the reception area and came over to say hello. The two chatted for a moment. McAnuff was pleased to hear that Hirsch had read and liked the script and surprised to find that Hirsch knew a lot about his work in the Toronto alternative theatre scene. When McAnuff mentioned that he was off to New York, Hirsch was enthusiastic about the idea and gave him a twenty-minute rundown about what was happening in the theatre there. He particularly recommended that McAnuff get in touch with Bob Kalfin at the Chelsea Theater Center, where he had directed *AC/DC* five years earlier. McAnuff did so a few weeks later and was impressed to find that Hirsch had already called Kalfin to recommend him. The contact resulted in McAnuff's first directing assignment in the United States, the surrealist *Crazy Locomotive* at the Chelsea Theater Center.

Hirsch's battles with other parts of the CBC continued. Some of his worst were with the late Jack Craine, a long-time staff man who as Director of TV Programming was his immediate boss. A memo to Craine in early 1977 begins, "Perhaps our conversation the other day left you confused… We will never have our own native television directors without you putting aside some programming volume to be used for their graduate training. Unless you allow me this volume we will be condemned forever to use people from the BBC and United States." It didn't help when the CBC sent his administrative head, John Kennedy, on an extended educational leave to Quebec to learn French. Hirsch made sure his back was covered as much as possible by promoting Muriel Sherrin. She now became Assistant Head of TV Drama, and took on increasing responsibilities for script development and production.

Hirsch lost another important ally when Peter Herrndorf moved to CBC headquarters in Ottawa. Herrndorf remembers that it had been growing harder to run interference for Hirsch: "As time went by his frustration level with the CBC grew, and the CBC's frustration level with him grew." Yet to the viewing public Hirsch and his department were riding high, with some of the lustre of the "golden age" reappearing. Several of the most important scripts of Hirsch's tenure at CBC were arriving on the nation's television screens or making their way through the production pipeline. One of the best was

Dreamspeaker, written by Anne Cameron and directed by Claude Jutra for the *Performance* series. The film tells the story of a disturbed eleven-year-old boy who runs away from a psychiatric institution and finds shelter with an elderly Native shaman (played by George Clutesi) on Vancouver Island. *Dreamspeaker* not only did well with Canadian audiences but was also successfully sold to networks in other countries. When it was re-broadcast on the public broadcasting network in the U.S. months later the *New York Times* gave it a great review ("...crammed with memorable images and scenes. The style is spare. The impact is devastating"). Hirsch triumphantly sent the review to CBC president Al Johnson – cc-ing Jack Craine in Programming – with the note: "I thought you might be interested in reading the attached review. Isn't it marvellous?"

Several memos and travel schedules show that from early on in his time at CBC Hirsch had been pursuing Kate Nelligan, a Canadian who had become a leading actress with Britain's Royal Shakespeare Company. He finally hired her to star with Donald Sutherland in *Bethune*, a biographical drama about the doctor-hero of the Spanish Civil War and the Chinese Revolution. The star of *M*A*S*H* had been trying to arrange a feature film on the life of Bethune for some time, but after the Chinese government rejected his request to film in China he accepted an offer from the CBC to produce it as a ninety-minute drama for television. It took time to finalize a script and find a time to shoot the production between Sutherland's other commitments, but *Bethune* was broadcast in October 1977. (Even for such prestigious projects Hirsch had to fight for the CBC's scarce technical resources. In a memo to the Director of TV Production Hirsch complains bitterly that breakdowns in videotape equipment had been holding up production for almost a week: "Eric Till has wasted two nights being unable to do anything in VTR because of these breakdowns. I must have Eric as soon as possible to work on *Riel* and at this rate he will never finish *Bethune*.")

Hirsch's contract permitted him to act as executive producer on individual dramas, stipulating that he would be paid extra if he did more than one in a year. His first such production was a ninety-minute play based on the life of the actress Sarah Bernhardt, broadcast in 1976. For the lead character he hired his Mother Courage of a decade before, Zoe Caldwell. The show was nominated for an international Emmy in 1977.

When next he took on the executive producer role Hirsch called on another friend from MTC days, Gordon Pinsent. Since leaving Winnipeg Pinsent had become a familiar face on Canadian TV in the late sixties as *Quentin Durgens, M.P.* and had written, directed and starred in a successful feature film, *The Rowdyman*. He and Hirsch had stayed in touch over the years and Pinsent knew all about Hirsch's problems with the CBC. Hirsch once sent him a letter saying, "Running the department is like working in an atomic research lab manipulating a pair of mechanical arms through a glass wall a foot thick, rather than dealing with problems with your own hands."

Possibly to balance the stream of programs about ethnic minorities that TV Drama had been producing, Hirsch asked Pinsent to write a Christmas story set predominantly in Anglo-Saxon Southern Ontario at the end of the nineteenth century. The story Pinsent produced – an elderly man's reminiscences about Christmas as a boy – met the bill, but as the scheduled shoot approached no script was forthcoming. Always busy, Pinsent was trying to write the show at the same time as he was appearing in a musical version of *The Rowdyman* at the Charlottetown Festival. He remembers that Hirsch eventually had to go to Charlottetown to work personally on the script with Pinsent in order to get it done. It was worth it. *A Gift to Last* was a hit, and Pinsent (working with Peter Wildeblood) extended it into a series that ran on CBC until 1979 and that sold well abroad.

More old friends showed up when Hirsch took on an international co-production based on a short story by Mavis Gallant. Hirsch had always been a fan of Gallant's and had hoped to commission something by her as early as 1968, when he was still at Stratford. In 1975, he met Gallant in Paris to talk about "His Mother," a story she had published in the New Yorker about an elderly woman in Budapest whose life revolves almost entirely around letters from her émigré son. Having secured Gallant's agreement and the necessary rights, Hirsch put together a deal between the CBC, its Hungarian equivalent and a production company called International Cinemedia Center, which had recently filmed *The Apprenticeship of Duddy Kravitz*. He hired one of Hungary's best directors, Károly Makk, to direct the film, with a script by Suzanne Grossmann and a cast that included Gordon Pinsent and Donnelly Rhodes.

As executive producer Hirsch attended some of the shooting in Budapest, and Pinsent remembered it as painful for him: "I could see John hovering, taller than any of the bystanders, not wanting to be a nuisance on another director's turf – well, wanted to, dying to, would have drawn blood to." Just before the film was released Hirsch wrote to Gallant, "on the whole, it is better than most of the shows made for television....The performances are good, and there are even remains of your sensibility, if one looks very hard!"

By this time Hirsch's cousin Anna, the daughter of his uncle Gyuri, had moved to Canada with Hirsch's help in 1970, settling with her husband in Halifax. Gyuri came to visit once a year and Hirsch enjoyed seeing his Hungarian family more frequently. Another figure from his Hungarian past came back into his life unexpectedly in 1975. Ora Markstein, his friend from the Aschau displaced persons camp in Germany, had spent two decades in Israel with her husband and son, but found life there very hard. When the Marksteins arrived in Canada Hirsch did what he could to help them, putting them in touch with friends in Hamilton where they finally settled. He was delighted when Ora – a talented artist – began to sculpt in soapstone and he came to Hamilton to open her first show in Canada.

Hungary remained important to Hirsch as part of his identity. He once remarked, "I can be in Hong Kong, Paris, any totally strange country – guess what I do? I don't know why I do this but it is an absolutely conditioned response. Every time I feel unhappy, abandoned, unloved, rejected, depressed, melancholy, which for a Hungarian is practically an everyday thing, I look for the first Hungarian restaurant and after the soup I feel okay....It is totally part of me and part of who I am." He now set about strengthening his connections with Hungary, having made friends there during the making of *His Mother*.

One of his new friends was Peter Molnar Gal, the doyen of Hungarian film critics. Molnar remembers meeting Hirsch in 1976 at a dinner organized by several of Hungary's young filmmakers. On behalf of a mutual friend Hirsch brought Molnar Gal a book of poems by George Faludy, whose writings were banned by the Communist government. They arranged to meet again at Hirsch's hotel the next day. There they were joined after a short time by a handsome young pianist Hirsch had met in the hotel sauna. By the time the visit was over Molnar Gal had lent Hirsch the keys to his summer house in Visegrad, a picturesque town forty kilometres north of Budapest, where Hirsch and the young man could spend time during Hirsch's visit. Although homosexuality was illegal in Hungary at the time and gay men had to be very discreet, Molnar Gal comments, "John had no problems with his homosexuality and the socialist system. They ignored each other."

On subsequent visits Molnar Gal frequently accompanied Hirsch to the theatre. Hirsch was already thinking about his return to stage directing when his contract with the CBC finished, and was interested in finding Hungarian plays that he might bring to North America. (One that excited him was Gyula Hernady's *Grand Hunt,* and Hirsch did in fact bring it to North America a few years later). Molnar Gal also took Hirsch to gatherings of artists and intellectuals from among his wide circle of acquaintances. Although Hirsch was meeting government ministers and heads of cultural institutions in his capacity as head of CBC Drama ("they all asked how much I earned," Hirsch told him) and could have played the visiting big shot, he rarely told people who he was. Molnar Gal remembers going to a cast party with Hirsch and watching him get into a deep discussion of the play with the actors "as if he were just another bearded theatre professional in a sweater."

Through Molnar Gal Hirsch met Andras Hamori, a young theatre critic who was also working on film and TV documentaries. Hamori, who is now a well-known producer of feature films (*eXistenZ, Sunshine, The Sweet Hereafter* and many more), found in Hirsch a mentor;

for his part, Hirsch saw huge potential in Hamori and urged him to come to North America. The two began to correspond in English and, when Hamori defected from Hungary a few years later, he lived in the basement suite at Hudson Drive for his first two years in Canada.

Meanwhile Ralph Thomas and Stephen Patrick had been working on a new anthology program, *For the Record* (actually called *Camera 76* in its first season), which aimed to produce "docudramas" on topics of current social and political interest. They continued to hire Canada's best film directors and Hirsch had found the money to hire an experienced script consultant for the series: Ben Barzman, a former Hollywood screenwriter who had been banned by the House Un-American Activities Committee in the 1950s and who had since worked in the U.K., France and Quebec.

The first program in the series, *The Insurance Man from Ingersoll*, started things off with an appropriate bang. It was based on investigative journalism into corruption in Ontario's construction industry, but also took a powerful swipe at the press's reporting of such issues. Director Peter Pearson, a veteran of both the National Film Board and the commercial industry, consciously evoked political thrillers like Costa Gavras' *State of Siege* in the way he paced the film, but also appreciated the uncredited work of Barzman for "teaching us scripting pirouettes learned from his 70 produced movies." The program got the highest ratings the CBC had ever had for a Sunday night drama, and for the next nine years *For The Record* would continue to receive good ratings with several productions per year.

Pearson's relationship with Hirsch was never an easy one. In his unpublished memoir "My Life: The Movie," Pearson recounts an early screening of *Kathy Karuks is a Grizzly Bear*, another highly popular film in the series, which tells the story of a long-distance swimmer. Pearson recalls that Hirsch "hated the first edit and ripped me in his guttural Hungarian-Canadian. 'Peetaire, I hate telling you dis,' – he said, much relieved at telling me this – 'but you haff no firkin' talent. This piece of shee-it should be flushed down the toilet. You can't write, direct, cast, edit – anythink.'"

Looking back, Pearson suggests that part of his problem with Hirsch was one of style: "I'm a bit of a joker. I wouldn't take him as seriously as he took himself, and he was insulted by that. But I made three films under him, and they were good films."

Ralph Thomas adds another explanation: it took time before Hirsch learned to "read" a film's rough cut. "It was a problem for the first few years," remembers Thomas. "There are very few people who can read a rough cut. People say 'Oh yeah, I'll know what the film looks like' but until you have all the tracks and the music and some sort of reasonable mix, most people have no sense of what the film will ultimately be like. So I made a rule that if John was going to a screening, I had to be in attendance. But sometimes I'd be out of town or doing something else and I'd get a phone call from my associate producer saying 'John insisted on seeing the film' and I'd say, 'why did you allow that? And of course the answer was, 'How could I not let him? If he wants to see the film he sees the film.'"

Hirsch's involvement was often exasperating, but along with the exasperation one finds in people's reminiscences a consistent note of appreciation for his backing up artists against the Corporation's risk aversion. Allan King recalls bringing Hirsch the script for *Maria*, which was written by Montreal playwright Rick Salutin and told the story of a young woman trying to organize her fellow workers in a clothing factory. Hirsch observed that the story was "a socialist-realist tract," to which King replied only with a raised eyebrow and wary silence. "Well, why not?" Hirsch said after a moment. "We've never done a socialist-realist tract," and gave the project the green light. Later on, when shooting still photographs in preparation for filming, King realized that the faces of the actors "disappeared" against the strong colours of the bolts of cloth they worked with. His solution was to film in black and white, but he had little hope of getting permission for this at CBC, where "no one, but no one, shot in black and white any more. *Verboten*! I went to see John and described the problem and bless him, he just swallowed hard and said, 'Well black and white are colours too, aren't they?'"

The biggest risk arose from another Peter Pearson project, *The Tar*

Sands. Hirsch disliked the project from the moment Pearson and Ralph Thomas pitched it to him. They proposed to film a drama about the massive Syncrude development in Northern Alberta, building the story around provincial premier Peter Lougheed as he negotiated a high-stakes deal with the international oil industry. Hirsch was unconvinced that it ought to be a drama, whether it might be better dealt with by Current Affairs. Nonetheless, by this time Hirsch and Thomas had a good working relationship and the program got the green light. Kenneth Welsh took on the role of Lougheed and shooting began.

Then, as the production neared completion the Corporation began to get nervous about *The Tar Sands*. Lougheed was a powerful figure and tensions between the West and Central Canada were running high at the time. The show was pulled from its scheduled broadcast date of February 13, 1977. The CBC's president, Al Johnson, viewed it. Lawyers reviewed it. Hirsch fought for it and was backed up by both Denis Harvey and Herrndorf. It finally aired on September 12 to excellent reviews. On September 13 Peter Lougheed announced he would sue for defamation and a legal epic began that would drag on until 1982, when the CBC and Lougheed settled. While not backing down on the content of the program itself, the CBC apologized "for any personal distress" to Lougheed, paid him $80,000 and agreed never to show the program again (which to this day it hasn't; it can't even be viewed at the CBC archives).

Oddly, at the same time that *For the Record* was rocking political boats Hirsch took on a job for the federal government producing a major stage show in Ottawa for the 1977 Canada Day celebrations. A similar show had been planned in 1976 and then cancelled for lack of money. Everything changed in November 1976, when the Parti Québécois took power in Quebec for the first time. The Trudeau government suddenly found a lot of money for anything that might bind the country together, including $3 million for Canada Day events. Trudeau appointed Bernard Ostry, yet another Winnipegger who had become prominent in Central Canada, as head of the Canada Committee. Ostry and his wife Sylvia had known Hirsch for years. Sylvia had actually grown up mere blocks from the Shacks' house in North Winnipeg before going on to be a prominent economist and public servant. For his part, Bernard Ostry had been an academic, a television moderator, and an advisor to the Trudeau government on communications policy. He was now running Museums Canada with the rank of deputy minister. Ostry had little time to prepare the event and called on friends and colleagues to help with various parts of the project. He asked Hirsch to put on a three-hour show on Parliament Hill, which would be simultaneously broadcast to the nation on CBC television.

Hirsch's first problem was finding the talent to make an entertaining show while meeting the political requirement of representing the country's happy diversity. It wasn't hard to find ethnic and First Nations dance troupes and a politically acceptable trio of MCs for the evening was easily drawn from Hirsch's friends and colleagues: "Bruno Gerussi for the Italian vote, Al Waxman for the Polish and Jewish vote, and Jean Gascon for those Canadians who don't watch television," as scriptwriter Allan Gould put it. But hiring Gascon highlighted an additional wrinkle in the talent problem. Almost all of the interesting talent in French Canada was either separatist or afraid of being tagged as a *vendu* (sell-out), and was thus "unavailable." Working through the CBC Variety division Hirsch managed to hire one genuine francophone star, the sixteen-year-old singer René Simard ("he's asking for $15,000," says a memo from the negotiations) and one would-be disco star, Patsy Gallant ("she will settle for $5,000," says the same memo), but that was it.

Hirsch ran into trouble when he hired another friend, lighting specialist Johnny Desantis, to come up from the United States to lend a hand. The National Association of Broadcast Employees and Technicians protested the use of an American to light up Canada Day, forcing Hirsch to issue a press release saying that he had personally flown Desantis up to Ottawa and that Desantis had given his advice for free as a personal favour. This was an out-and-out lie, but not something that could be investigated further in those pre-Freedom of Information days, so the story ran out of steam. Other stories took its place when the Québec legislature refused to pass a motion wishing Canada "happy birthday" and former prime minister John Diefenbaker protested in Parliament that the federal government was turning the celebration into a "Liberal party event."

Small "p" politics were even worse behind the scenes, as the creative team led by Hirsch continually clashed with the various government agencies involved, particularly the Department of Public Works. When Hirsch authorized the creation of a 145-foot Canadian flag to be unfurled from the Peace Tower at the end of the show, he received a memo advising "there may be some political problem about spending this kind of money for a decoration that will be seen for about one hour and that we should at least inform Bernard Ostry before we proceed with this expenditure." Hirsch got his way on that one, but not on a crucial fight with the Department, which refused to fund the construction of a roof to protect the performers and equipment in case of rain.

Of course, it rained. Jean Gascon opened the evening with a speech in English and French, but the singer Juliette (another CBC Variety star) got only halfway through her set when the heavens opened. The Prime Minister and VIPs fled at the first drops, but the 70,000-strong crowd stayed put, and their patience was rewarded a half hour later when the rain stopped. The stage was mopped off, the Shumka Dancers of Edmonton showed off their Ukrainian folk moves and René Simard and Patsy Gallant got huge ovations for gamely singing *a capella* when some of the electrical equipment couldn't be restored. The crowd greeted the spot-lit unfurling of Hirsch's banner with a spontaneous rendition of *O Canada* and the evening closed with stupendous fireworks. Hirsch was quoted next day to say, "Natural disasters get people together," but all in all it was a close-run thing.

Hirsch was now approaching the end of his four-year contract. Nervous as always about what might follow, he negotiated an additional few months with the CBC on a consulting basis. His correspondence file also shows that he took advantage of his remaining access to the CBC letterhead. It contains dozens of references for young actors including several from the cast of *The Dybbuk*, a letter recommending Donald Sutherland for the Order of Canada and support for applications by Tom Hendry and Ralph Thomas for Canada Council grants. There is also a letter to Garth Drabinsky, who had outgrown personally overseeing Hirsch's business affairs; using the newly created tax incentive for Canadian films he had already produced his first feature film, *The Silent Partner*, starring Elliott Gould, Christopher Plummer and Susannah York. Drabinsky had applied for a Canada Council grant to fund a research assistant for a book project, and wanted Hirsch's support. Hirsch replied that while he understood Drabinsky hasn't time to do the research himself, he thought Drabinsky was already enough of a "tycoon" to do without a government subsidy. "What will be left," he asked, "for us poor paupers who are out in the world of freelance, no-lance, depending on the kindness of strangers?"

When Hirsch finally packed up his office at the beginning of March 1978 he welcomed reporters for a final interview as head of TV Drama. The interview was a by-now-typical Hirsch farewell. On the one hand, he was proud of the successful new series, the greatly improved ratings, the foreign sales and critical recognition. On the other, he was still annoyed about the frustration of his plans to make CBC a training centre: "The whole country is still suffering from a lack of trained talent," he said. "I wasn't able to change that much. It still needs to be done. It's one of the most important on-going problems." He reminded them of the broken promises about increased funding and increased hours of broadcasting, noting that both had come to naught. "If I had to give you another metaphor for this place," Hirsch told *Toronto Life*, "it would be coitus interruptus. They kept getting me all excited and then they took everything away."

Larry Mirkin, who went on to work in a wide range of television and film projects in Canada and abroad, has a kinder judgement of Hirsch's time at the CBC. For him, Hirsch's time there was an essential stage in the history of Canadian cultural industries. "I don't think that it's appreciated how much that John and the people in that department then and who followed shortly after him accomplished to make this possible," he comments.

Today we still have problems with funding and we have problems – as everyone does around the world – in creating excellence and sufficient popularity at the same time. But we do have a critical mass of talent and of crews and our audiences love good Canadian programs. We actually have a television drama industry where one didn't exist 35 years ago. The CBC isn't now the only game in town, and although there is always this tension between ratings and critical acclaim, we are actually, relatively speaking, consistently competent in the drama that is produced in this country. All of this has many seeds in what John and others did in those years at the CBC TV Drama Department.

Hirsch with Pierre Trudeau and Pierre Juneau, circa 1978.
Person to left of Hirsch unknown.
Photo by Fernand R. Leclair
Library and Archives Canada

[Eight]

Director at Large (Again)

A FREELANCE CAREER can take time to restart, and 1978 was a quiet year for Hirsch in terms of work. He did another Canada Day show with a bigger budget but similar weather conditions, including not only rain but an electrical storm as well. Hirsch did well out of it financially. In a letter to his young friend Andras Hamori in Budapest Hirsch described it as "fun to do" and proudly mentioned the live audience of one hundred thousand plus the one million people who watched on television.

A number of possibilities presented themselves. An inquiry from the Vancouver Playhouse about his interest in becoming its artistic director in 1979 came to nothing, and Hirsch complained about it to the *Vancouver Sun*, saying that it was "typical of the cavalier way in which directors are treated in this country.... In Canada – unless you happen to be a newly-arrived Englishman who has the kind of veneer to impress the Establishment – they treat you as if they were doing you such a favour by considering you for a job that you should get down on your knees and thank them for even suggesting it." (Playhouse board member David Y.H. Lui replied to the charge somewhat vaguely. He couldn't remember if the search committee had decided Hirsch was too expensive or "if they simply forgot to call him and tell him.")

While relieved to be out of the CBC, Hirsch found himself watching from the sidelines as some of his Toronto friends were busy reshaping the entertainment industry in Canada. Three in particular stood out. Moses Znaimer, the partner of Marilyn Lightstone, Hirsch's lead actress in *The Dybbuk*, was revolutionizing local television with CityTV after several years with the CBC. Hungarian-born Robert Lantos had just released his first major feature film, *In Praise of Older Women*, based on the novel by Stephen Vizinczey (another Hungarian who had spent time at the CBC). And Garth Drabinsky had projects on the go in both motion pictures and live theatre. The meals and conversations with this group were important to Drabinsky at the time: "I recall John at one of these in a white suit and sandals, sitting there like a rabbi, pulling at his beard dispensing wisdom. It was a sort of Jewish entertainment-entrepreneurial intelligentsia, and of course Robert had the Hungarian connection with Hirsch as well. We were full of piss and vinegar, and always enjoyed the discussions."

Drabinsky was about to make his first foray into American commercial theatre as producer of *A Broadway Musical*. The show opened at the Lunt-Fontanne Theatre on December 21, 1978 after a troubled rehearsal period. Always supportive of Drabinsky's projects Hirsch came down for the opening. Drabinsky remembers, "John got up at the end of the show, and he simply looked at me and shook his head. The optimistic side of me always believed that it had a shot at getting some good reviews, but as soon as I looked at John's face, I knew I was fucked. I closed the show on opening night." Devastated, Drabinsky swore he would never go back to Broadway again – but did so a few years later with a string of Tony-winning hits, starting with *The Kiss of The Spider Woman*.

As it turned out, Hirsch's first concrete invitation for work in this new phase of his life came from south of the border, when Gordon Davidson invited him to direct *The Tempest* at the Mark Taper Forum in Los Angeles, with Anthony Hopkins as Prospero.

Under Davidson the Mark Taper Forum had become a power-house in American theatre, premiering award-winning plays like *The Shadow Box* and *Children of a Lesser God*. Davidson had enjoyed working with Hirsch on the Los Angeles production of *The Dybbuk* in 1974. When the smaller roles were being cast for *The Dybbuk* Davidson portentously announced that he was going to break his usual practice as artistic director and insist that Hirsch hire "a particular actor."

Hirsch bristled, until he heard the punch line. Davidson's father had just retired after a career of teaching theatre, but had never had a professional stage role. "I got him an Equity card as a birthday present so that he could try to find work as an actor," Davidson recalls. "John laughed, and without a moment's hesitation cast him in a tiny role. And for the next five years, my father got small parts in plays."

By the late 1970s Davidson had decided to try bringing high-quality Shakespeare productions to the Los Angeles stage using experienced directors and classical actors. Given an ample budget Hirsch put together a strong creative team, hired his old friend Stanley Silverman to compose the music and invited one of the best-regarded American designers, Ming Cho Lee, to do the sets.

Lee had seen Hirsch at the annual conferences of the Theater Communications Group (TCG), the organization representing North America's 170 non-profit regional theatres, but he had never spoken to him. In Lee's memory, Hirsch had by that time become known, admiringly or otherwise, as "the rabbi of the theatre" for his improvised and often polemical speeches. Lee usually agreed with what Hirsch had to say, particularly his oft-repeated charge that regional theatres had become safe and boring since the nervy days of the 1960s and early 1970s, but was hesitant. He asked around, and was told that while Hirsch was thought to be unpredictable and occasionally difficult it was worth the risk because of what one could learn from working with him. Lee accepted the job.

At their first meeting Hirsch described *The Tempest* as Shakespeare's *Magic Flute*, and said he wanted the set to emphasize its magic and fantasy. This intrigued Lee, who despite his track record as an innovator had begun to feel stuck in a Brechtian rut of spare, sculptural designs. There was an uncomfortable moment when Hirsch produced a sketch, something designers usually hate. But Hirsch's idea of a set resembling the Radio City Music Hall rainbow circle felt new and fresh, and Lee took away the sketch to work on it. Lee was touched when Hirsch gave him a present, an Art Nouveau ashtray, which he explained was an example of the style he was looking for. It was the beginning of a fruitful association between the two.

When rehearsals began Anthony Hopkins accepted Hirsch's idea of an impatient, intellectual Prospero rather than an effortlessly wise, benevolent one as the role is so often presented. In an interview with Michal Schonberg just after the show opened Hopkins praised Hirsch's understanding of the play and his staging ideas. But the two were not a good match emotionally and the brevity of the rehearsal period – three weeks – made things worse. "John and I have had an interesting relationship," Hopkins commented. "We'd talk and then it would all go to pieces.... It's been a rather traumatic experience." Hopkins was just coming out of a dark period in his life, struggling with stage fright and alcohol, and found Hirsch's directing approach at odds with his need for encouragement and precise instructions. "John is a very fluent talker, and knows his business intellectually. There are some directors who are martinets and sadists and John isn't like that, but we had problems.... I needed to work very quietly and very slowly and if you've got a director saying [he briefly takes on Hirsch's tone and accent in an uncanny imitation] 'No no no no, you must do it this way!' – well, I can't work that way.... When you see out of the corner of your eye the gestures and shadow movements of anxiety and despair from the director who is supposed to be leading the company, then that really is the most awful thing to happen. And that happened one day and I went home."

The frustrations ran both ways. Bryan remembers Hirsch coming back to their rented apartment "in a state, unable to talk about it." Hopkins was also hard on the two young actors playing Miranda and Ariel, Stephanie Zimbalist and Brent Carver. Two weeks after the play opened Hirsch wrote to Carver, telling him "I admired your behaviour and work during the trying weeks of rehearsal. Remember, whatever Tony does, ought not to affect you as a performer; if he behaves unprofessionally, that's his problem."

In the end, *The Tempest* came together and Hopkins himself described it as "a fine production." Silverman's atonal music and Lee's set framed a restrained, subtle performance by Hopkins and strong ensemble playing by the cast. While generally admiring the high production standards of the show and applauding the Mark

Taper Forum for bringing Shakespeare back to the city, some of the critics disliked Hirsch's interpretation of the play, notably the *Los Angeles Times'* Sylvie Drake, who was disturbed by what she called its "coldness and resistance to emotion."

For Hirsch it was a solid re-entry into directing for the stage. Shortly afterward Hirsch was hired as consulting artistic director at the Seattle Repertory Theater. The "Rep" was part of a wave of non-profit regional theatres that had come up in the wake of the MTC. It was organized in 1963 by a group of prominent Seattle citizens as a resident company for the eight-hundred-seat playhouse built for the 1962 World's Fair. By 1979 the Rep was a well-heeled operation in a city with double the national average of theatre attendance. Its board was impressed with Hirsch's curriculum vitae and tried very hard to get him. Hirsch set a lot of conditions. Since he was already committed to two productions in the following twelve months and didn't want his hands tied, he would only be "consulting" director. That meant having a resident director who would do a lot of the work, and he had one in mind, Daniel Sullivan, who had worked for him as an actor at the Beaumont in New York. "At that point I was a gypsy director trying to make a living at the various regional theatres," recalls Sullivan. "The Seattle folks knew me and when John couldn't commit on a full-time basis, he had the idea of bringing me into the Rep." Hirsch finally signed a three-year contract and flew to Seattle to plan his first season with Sullivan.

Hirsch never put down roots in Seattle, but enjoyed his extended visits there. Although the rain got a little oppressive, the changing quality of the light pleased him and he found the people had a civic pride that reminded him of Winnipeg. He rented an apartment and quickly got to know the city's markets and restaurants. Bryan maintained the house in Toronto, but came out frequently to the west coast to visit.

Ever conscious of the need to build up a buzz, Hirsch did this via a by now well-practiced routine with the newspapers, promising excitement and excellence in the upcoming season. Although he and Sullivan would place a great emphasis during their tenure on employing local actors and designers, for his first production, Shaw's *Saint Joan*, Hirsch hedged his bets by bringing in people he could count on. For music and design he hired his *Tempest* collaborators Stanley Silverman and Ming Cho Lee. The theatre building was a problem, with a cavernous auditorium that ate actors' voices and made any kind of intimacy difficult to achieve. Lee dealt with the problem by designing an overhead lighting grid that swept out over the audience and pulled them into the action onstage, but he struggled to complete detailed drawings on time. When Lee wanted to go home to New York for his birthday Hirsch simply refused to let him leave Seattle before the design was finished. "He got everyone together for a party and they gave me a birthday cake, but he still wouldn't let me go!" remembered Lee. Sullivan recalls that Hirsch actually resorted to locking Lee in a room at one point.

For the title role of Saint Joan, Hirsch brought in the Canadian actress Roberta Maxwell. The hall posed as much of a problem to her as to the designer. "The part required enormous physical stamina and I run on a very short and thin wire in that respect," she said in interview some years later. Hirsch's solution was to bring chicken soup to the theatre and feed her a large bowl before each performance. "It must have worked because I went on at top volume from the moment I stepped on the stage."

The local critics loved *Saint Joan* and the Rep was roundly congratulated by local newspapers on its coup in hiring Hirsch. The rest of the season also went well for Hirsch and Sullivan, closing with a bang in April with Hirsch's production of the musical *Pal Joey*. In between, however, Hirsch went home to Canada to direct two very different productions at the National Arts Centre in Ottawa and at the Young People's Theatre in Toronto.

The first, Christopher Durang's *A History of American Film*, had premiered on Broadway the year before. A musical, it covers four decades of Hollywood in a series of sketches and songs. It was the kind of production in which Hirsch usually excelled, with a well-crafted script and lots of room for interesting staging and effects, including a California earthquake that closes the show. The National

Arts Centre had both the budget and the technical resources for Hirsch to do what he wanted and he was also given an energetic cast and a skilled design team.

Susan Benson designed the costumes for the show. Born and trained in Britain, Benson had worked in Canadian regional theatre and Stratford, but also had a parallel career as a painter and portraitist. She and Hirsch clicked from the beginning, partly, she thinks because of Hirsch's love of fine art and artists. She remembers going to Hudson Drive and being bowled over by some of the paintings he had on his walls: "I knew Ivan Eyre's work, and when I went to John's house and saw this painting John owned – blimey, I thought!" Benson remembers *American Film* as a challenging production that required the cast to take on several roles each. "Every few minutes they were off and changing their costumes," she remembers, "so technically it took a lot of planning. I sat there most of the time with my fingers crossed that they'd make their change okay for the next scene." The show turned out to be every bit the crowd-pleaser Hirsch had aimed for and he hired Benson to design his next production, *Twelfth Night*, at the Young People's Theatre in Toronto.

John Bluethner, who as a fourteen-year-old had been in Hirsch's *Andorra* at the MTC, was his assistant director on *Twelfth Night*. Bluethner had already had a year as an actor at Stratford under Robin Phillips and was struck by the difference in approach of the two directors. Phillips, it seemed to Bluethner, brought a cool, controlling intelligence to his plays using a variety of techniques to get the performance he wanted (in an interview, Bluethner at first used the terms "mind games" and "manipulative," then struggled to find a word that didn't have a pejorative sense, concluding, "You'd have to have spent a year at Stratford to know what I mean"). In contrast, Hirsch was exploratory and passionate, coming at each character as if he or she was a real person. "Hirsch was always trying to get the actors to flesh out everything that was going on *offstage* for the characters," remembers Bluethner. It was a very Stanislavskian approach in rehearsal, where he'd go into parsing every line. What is the motor in the scene? What are each character's changes? Where is the climax and how do you get there? It was an incredible education."

Assistant directors are often in an unhappy position of being given very basic jobs like taking notes, but Hirsch liked to give them a lot of responsibility once he felt he could trust them. Bluethner paints a vivid picture of how this worked out as rehearsals progressed: "One of the problems with Shakespeare is you have to keep it moving. You can't have a lot of down time in scene changes. So Hirsch set me to working with the smaller parts, whose job it was to change the furniture. In minor roles you're the one who runs on, or if you're standing there when the scene goes dark you grab a stool and off you go. We worked on timing, getting it faster and faster. I was still intimidated by John, and the tension was growing, as it always happens on a show the closer you get to opening nights. I worked a lot with the younger actors, and I thought we'd got the scene changes down. Then we finally were doing it in a run[through] and he turned around and started screaming at me, 'They're too slow!' So I yelled back at him, 'Look, I worked really hard with them, and I'll work with them again and we'll get it down!' And he stopped and he said, 'Oh.' (Pause.) 'Okay.' If I hadn't stood up to him he wouldn't have had any respect for me."

Twelfth Night got excellent reviews with the *Globe & Mail* describing it as a "jewel of a production." In fact, this period of Hirsch's professional life was markedly successful, and across a wide range of material. He did two more musicals in the next twelve months and also took an uncharacteristic detour into commercial "dinner theatre" with an original review called *Flying*. This came about after Hirsch took on an agent, Catherine McCartney, for his Canadian work. He'd met McCartney during his time at CBC, when she represented Al Waxman in the negotiations for *King of Kensington*.

McCartney, who sometimes works as a producer, was struck by Hirsch's love of "screwball comedy" films from the 1930s and 1940s: "He used to do the routines and sing the songs – I was always telling him, NO, John, please not the singing!" When he mused about adapting the film *Flying Down to Rio* for the stage she put him in

Ink and drybrush portrait of John Hirsch by Charles Pachter.
From the collection of Martin Knelman
© Charles Pachter 1979, used by permission of the artist

touch with two other clients, composer Joey Miller and lyricist Stephen Witkin, whose musical *Eight to the Bar* was a hit at the 1978 Charlottetown Festival. Hirsch flew out to Charlottetown to catch the show, liked what he saw and started talking with the partners about what they might do together. That led to another couple of McCartney clients, the sister-and-brother act Donna and Andrew Best. The Bests were two prodigiously talented black teenagers who were in a Toronto R&B band called Soul Express.

Miller remembers that Hirsch fell in love with the Bests and their talent, and was determined to work with them. He and Miller put together a twenty-minute program of song and dance numbers for the Bests and their band, found a venue and invited some influential friends. "It was all very much like in those old movies John loved. Hey, let's put on a show!" recalls Miller. "But first he needed see how the kids would work in front of an audience, and their discipline, and whether they could learn to act and could be choreographed to do a different, less contemporary kind of dancing."

One of the invitees, Garth Drabinsky, was skeptical: "I knew Hirsch had this zest for comedy and musicals and so on, but it seemed like the antithesis of what he stood for," he says today. Nonetheless, the showcase was impressive and with Drabinsky's backing McCartney was able to "green light" a full show. It took about a year to put together. Having roughed out a story line with Hirsch and Witkin, Miller scoured CBC archives and sound libraries to find songs that when put together would give the show a narrative arc. "It was one of the first jukebox musicals, like the ABBA *Mamma Mia* show. John was an important part of the writing, making sure that the songs fit the storyline and were right for the kids."

With the show coming together McCartney booked it to play at one of Toronto's most prestigious nightclubs, the Imperial Room at the Royal York Hotel. There was a short, frenetic rehearsal period of about three weeks, which Miller remembers as both joyful – "there was none of that sitting with actors who are asking 'what am I doing here?' like you often get in shows" – and high-pressure, with Hirsch pushing everyone to the limit. But it all paid off. *Flying* sold out most evenings during its ten weeks at the Imperial Room in the summer of 1980, and then moved to the Bourbon Street Café for another ten weeks. With a few cast changes, it then went to the Village Gate in Manhattan and ended up playing for a year in Atlantic City.

Hirsch was delighted by what he liked to call his "jiggle-show," but it was only one of many projects and activities he had on the go during that period. His profile in the United States theatre community had risen with his election to the Theater Communications Group executive in July 1979. Over the next few years, as supply-side economics and conservatism gained ground under Ronald Reagan, Hirsch would speak frequently in defence of non-profit theatre and against the government's slashing of the National Endowment for the Arts.

In the latter half of 1980 Hirsch directed two European plays, one a political comedy and the other an allegory from Tsarist Russia. The first was Gyula Hernady's *The Grand Hunt*, which he had seen in Budapest during one of his visits while at the CBC. After several false starts he finally commissioned an adaptation he liked from Suzanne Grossmann, who had adapted the Mavis Gallant story *His Mother* for CBC Television. He then worked out a deal that saw the production open at the Shaw Festival in Niagara-on-the-Lake and then move to the National Arts Centre, and finally Seattle. In a press release from the Seattle Rep, Hirsch referred to the difficulty of producing interesting theatre in a time of recession. "Fine theatre is expensive. By sharing the rich resources between theatres, in the form of highly regarded productions such as *The Grand Hunt*, we can continue to present well-rounded seasons."

The Grand Hunt takes as its starting point an historical event: the attempt of the last Hapsburg emperor, Charles I of Austria (who was also, confusingly, Charles VI of Hungary), and his wife, the Empress Zita, to regain the Hungarian part of his throne in 1921. This is as far as historical reality goes in the play. In the first of many plot twists the royal couple are assassinated by mistake, and scheming courtiers attempt to replace them with two hapless imposters, neither of whom knows the other is an imposter. Hirsch particularly liked the play's echoes of the sophisticated café culture to which his grandmother had exposed him even though he was too young to understand the details. He told an interviewer, "It harkens back to the thirties when Hungary was famous for its urbane, light comedies with a special sardonic tone about how things were. The first thing Hungarians are taught is how to read between the lines. Out of that comes the particular Central European humour, which is based on the fact that you doubt everything because you are not told the truth.... You never trust the surface." He speculated that since Vietnam and Watergate had pushed North Americans toward a more cynical and therefore realistic view of politics, audiences would relate to the play's tone and content in ways they might not have even a decade before.

The play garnered good reviews when it opened in August 1980 at the Shaw Festival in Ontario. Seattle reviewers were even more impressed when it opened there in November. The *Post-Intelligencer* said:

> It has dazzling speed, splendid costumes, droll writing ('A dead enemy is almost a friend'), brilliant acting and a flavour rarely found on the American stage. Spies stand at doorways clicking their heels. Shots ring out. A king wears a tunic weighted with oversize medals. A count causes death with a nod to men in long leather coats. It's all cosy, creepy and – wondrously – funny too.

They were less effusive about *Strider: The Story of a Horse*, which opened at the Rep in October. Tolstoy's allegory about cruelty and exploitation from the horse's point of view, first adapted for theatre by the Gorky Theatre in Leningrad, had a successful run at Bob Kalfin's Chelsea Theater Center in 1979. The Seattle critics were ambivalent, with one writing that Hirsch had given the play "a big, strong loud, dynamically paced staging – and the poor horse has been bled to death in the process. The show has style but no pathos – spectacle but no soul. But despite its difficulties, *Strider* is an incredibly wonderful play – one that shouldn't be missed." Others were savage, calling Strider "Black Beauty in drag" and "what one might expect if Walt Disney tried to interpret *War and Peace.*"

Hirsch's reaction to the hostile reviews in Seattle was uncharacteristically even-tempered. His position at the Rep and his relationship with Seattle seemed to work well for him. He and Sullivan introduced some changes to the company, but not revolutionary ones. They used fewer "imported" stars and employed more local actors than the previous artistic management, and introduced frequent workshops to encourage new works. One of his most memorable ones took place in 1981, when he invited author Studs Terkel to participate in workshopping his 1980 book of oral history, *American Dreams: Lost and Found.* (Seven years later Hirsch would direct his own adaptation of the book in Atlanta.)

Despite Hirsch's interest in new plays he rarely found scripts he liked or felt he could direct, and it often led to the charge back in Canada that he did little to encourage Canadian playwrights. One script he did like was *Thimblerig* (originally *Dud Shuffle*), a play by Winnipeg writer Alf Silver. Having workshopped the script in Winnipeg in 1979 at what later became the Prairie Theatre Exchange Hirsch brought the script to Seattle, where Sullivan directed it in a second workshop production. *Thimblerig* finally played in MTC's Warehouse Theatre in January, 1982.

New plays can come about in unexpected ways. In 1980 Gordon Davidson and Hirsch were at a Theater Communications Group convention at Princeton University. Looking back, Davidson paints the scene as a rabbinical one: "Hirsch and I were strolling the ivy-covered walkways with hands clasped behind our backs, stooping slightly and discussing such light-hearted matters as the purpose of man's existence and what plays we were going to do the following season in our respective theatres when the scripts that were coming in didn't seem to mean anything." Davidson had been planning a season of plays about Los Angeles, and Hirsch came up with an unlikely idea. Why not create a stage version of *Number Our Days,* anthropologist Barbara Meyerhoff's Oscar-winning documentary film (and later a book) about a community centre for elderly Jews living in the Venice Beach district on L.A.'s Westside? While amused by their bickering and *kvetching* Hirsch had been touched and intrigued by the characters' preoccupation with values and their arguments about moral and political questions. Davidson had seen the film and agreed it would make good theatre. On Hirsch's recommendation Suzanne Grossmann was hired to create a script. Davidson scheduled the play for the 1981-82 season and assembled a cast of elderly Jewish actors – many of them with years of experience in Hollywood films – for rehearsal.

Marti Maraden, who had last worked with Hirsch in his *Three Sisters* at Stratford, was called to join the cast at the last minute, to play a part that had grown greatly as the script developed. Maraden describes an alarmingly volatile rehearsal process as the script was being re-written almost daily. While she remembers feeling fortunate to be in the company of some gifted and renowned actors, it also became clear to her that some of them had memory and concentration problems. Maraden was constantly improvising lines to cover when other actors forgot theirs, and frequently got caught in the crossfire as an increasingly stressed Hirsch lost his temper. She remembers, "I was always in the washroom holding little old ladies in my arms who were crying and I'd say, 'He does this to everybody, tomorrow he'll love you, don't let it hurt too much….' And then he would be so funny and so affectionate." As the opening approached Hirsch reverted to his habit of adding "business" when he had doubts about a script or a cast; at one point he added a group of roller skaters such as one finds on the Venice Boardwalk.

The reviews, when the play opened, were mixed. While unconvinced by the script, the *Time* reviewer said, "the production itself is impeccable, and the cast proves again that one thing Los Angeles is not lacking is superb actors." Yet it was the Mark Taper Forum's biggest success that season.

By this time Hirsch had been appointed artistic director at the Stratford Festival in 1981 (see the following chapter), bringing to a close his three years of freelancing and consulting at the Seattle Repertory Theater. In his final contribution to program notes at the Rep Hirsch wrote, "I have had two marvellous years in this city, which is one of the most civilized communities in the country.... I thank you for your hospitality, warmth and the bouquets as well as the bricks." Mentioning the prevailing tide of "sometimes mindless cutting" in the nation, he warned the city to look after what it had: "In these days of violence and madness on a grand scale, it is the function of the arts to remind us of values that are corrective, of ways of living which are different from the frightening reality that surrounds us. Seattle is what it is because of the Rep and other institutions that make it so."

It had been for the most part a period of professional success for Hirsch and a happy time in his life generally. People who had known him in other places and situations noticed the difference. When John Bluethner came to work with Hirsch at the Toronto Young People's Theatre in 1980, for example – having not seen him for fifteen years – he found Hirsch to be more relaxed than he had expected. He speculates, "It may have been simply because it wasn't his theatre, so all he had to do was direct."

Eddie Gilbert, Hirsch's successor at the Manitoba Theatre Centre, echoes and amplifies Bluethner's insight. Gilbert quotes the maxim attributed to British humourist Max Beerbohm to the effect that people are either born hosts or born guests. In his mind Hirsch was by nature a guest, "someone whose real gift was to shine and to entertain. But John also felt some kind of an obligation to be the host, the person who lets other people's talents find employment." This was at least one of the reasons Hirsch took on big jobs that involved managing institutions – and why he was about to return to the Stratford Festival.

Nine

The Winter of His Discontent

ON A SNOWY SUNDAY morning in December, 1980 Hirsch got a phone call from Julian Porter. Hirsch knew that Porter was a top Toronto lawyer, well connected politically and half of a Toronto "power couple": his wife Anna – another Hungarian who had left her native country in 1956 – was a major force in Canadian publishing. The Porters lived a few blocks away and Hirsch had met them at cultural events like the George Faludy celebration he had directed in 1978.

Porter told Hirsch he was calling from Stratford and had some urgent business to discuss. Could he come by at 4:30 that afternoon, with two colleagues? That would be fine, said Hirsch.

Hirsch had been in Seattle for the past few weeks and just arrived back in Toronto to start rehearsals for *A Funny Thing Happened on the Way to the Forum* at the St. Lawrence Centre. But he had a pretty good idea of what Porter wanted to talk about. For over a year he had been hearing directly and indirectly about the Festival's efforts to find a successor for Robin Phillips. But he didn't know the latest news, for it was only the afternoon before that the Festival's annual general meeting – normally a sparsely attended formality – had ended in an uproar, with one of Stratford's leading actors yelling "You pig!" at the Board's president.

As was described in Martin Knelman's account of the affair, *A Stratford Tempest*, the story went back to May 1979 when Robin Phillips told the Stratford Board that he would be resigning as artistic director in November 1980. The Phillips years at Stratford had been successful ones artistically and financially, and the Festival had grown dependent on him. There was no heir apparent among any of the visiting or assistant directors hired over the past six years. Phillips himself was ambivalent and ambiguous about leaving; instead of a clean break, he allowed (encouraged would be putting it too strongly) the Board to think about some form of shared directorate.

Although the Board duly created a search committee, by the opening of the 1980 season there was still no successor. Giants like Hume Cronyn and Michael Langham didn't want the job; the actor/director John Neville had serious reservations about the Stratford board; William Hutt never got a clear offer and could never quite bring himself to demand a job that could have been his. A few directors who had never worked at Stratford before were also contacted. These included John Dexter, an Englishman who was currently working at the Metropolitan Opera in New York. No one from the search committee called Hirsch.

After a summer of increasingly desperate meetings and phone calls the Festival announced at the end of August that a two-tier artistic directorship had been adopted, a solution so complicated that many of the people involved didn't fully understand or believe in it. Far from being replaced, Phillips was included in both tiers. The attitude of the Board was clearly expressed by its president, Robert Hicks, who said, "Phillips has got to be the fulcrum."

Unfortunately Phillips was now exhausted and thoroughly unhappy with the Stratford Board. There was a complicated back story to this. Months of effort to engineer a British tour of *King Lear* starring Peter Ustinov had fallen through, and Ustinov eventually sued the Festival over it. Phillips now declined to be the Festival fulcrum and the two-tier solution collapsed barely two weeks after being announced. On September 18 the two tiers became a four-person "directorate." Inevitably nicknamed the "Gang of Four," the directorate was composed of Martha Henry, Festival dramaturge Urjo Kareda, and directors Peter Moss and Pam Brighton.

Robert Hicks stated that the Board was "totally committed to this new cohesive group." Except, alas, it wasn't. While the directorate started putting in long days pulling together the 1981 season – choosing the plays, calling actors and directors, and working up a budget – senior Board members and the newly hired executive director, Peter Stevens (former general administrator of the U.K.'s National Theatre), were talking to John Dexter about becoming Stratford's next artistic director. Stevens had worked with Dexter in the U.K. and was certain he would accept the offer.

The directorate included Hirsch in its plans. Martha Henry called him with a flattering offer. Maggie Smith had said Hirsch was one of the few directors she was willing to work with in the coming season. Could he suggest a play for Smith that he would like to direct? He could: Victorien Sardou's *Madame Sans Gêne*, a play from the 1890s that had been a star vehicle for both Sarah Bernhardt and Ellen Terry. Henry took this back to Smith, who was finishing up a successful season at Stratford in *Much Ado About Nothing* with Brian Bedford and the one-woman show *Virginia*. Smith first said no, then changed her mind a few days later. Dropping by Henry's office in the Festival theatre Smith said that her husband, the playwright Beverley Cross, thought the play was perfect for her and had offered to write a new adaptation of it for performance at the Festival.

By the end of October 1980 the directorate had roughed out a plan for the 1981 season. It was late to be doing this kind of work and many artists were already booked elsewhere for the following summer. Nonetheless, the directorate presented the Board with a plausible program of eleven productions, much of it based on verbal commitments with directors and principal actors. Unbeknownst to them, however, Peter Stevens then ran his own numbers on the program, which he took to the executive committee of the Board. According to his calculations the Gang's planned season would lose $1.3 million. Moreover, he questioned many of the plays and directors they were proposing, and indeed their qualifications as the Festival's artistic leadership. His solution: hire John Dexter immediately. Panicked by the numbers, the executive committee agreed. Stevens called Dexter, who flew up from New York for a meeting with several Board members at a Toronto airport hotel on November 2.

Dexter agreed to accept the job, but with a few caveats. First, he had several commitments that would prevent him from working full-time for Stratford until April. Second, he rejected any formal arrangement that included the Gang of Four, although he wanted to keep them "involved." And what about a work permit? The men from Stratford agreed to his terms and assured him that they could fast-track a work permit through the federal Department of Immigration in Ottawa.

On November 10 Kareda and Henry were given the bad news in the Festival Theatre's VIP lounge. They and their two colleagues were being fired after less than two months on the job. Sorry, but.... Compensation would of course be paid. And by the way: would they, for the good of the Festival, be kind enough publically to support Dexter?

They wouldn't. Martha Henry's husband, Douglas Rain, called the *Toronto Star* almost immediately and the story went hugely, embarrassingly public. And hugely political. The Board, despite the furore over Robin Phillips' appointment in 1974, had assumed that it could ride out the nationalist storm Dexter's appointment would cause.

For many in the Canadian acting community, this was the Brit that broke the camel's back. Actors Equity announced a boycott of the Festival, a threat which could cripple its coming season. In Ottawa Immigration Minister Lloyd Axworthy took note of the outcry and declined to fast-track the requested work permit for Dexter. Instead he had his officials review the case. Axworthy had recently been elected as the Member of Parliament for Winnipeg-Fort Garry and was well acquainted with the Manitoba Theatre Centre. He was surprised to learn that Hirsch hadn't even been interviewed for the job and became annoyed at the Festival's assertion that Dexter's permit had to be granted immediately if the 1981 season was to be saved. On November 27 the Department of Immigration announced that the work permit would not be granted "at this time" on the grounds that the job had been offered to Dexter without first ensuring that no Canadian was qualified for it. (Interestingly, as late as November 30 Dexter was telling friends that the job was "fairly definitely" his, "though this is not for release for some considerable time yet.")

Then came the Annual General Meeting on December 6. Unlike previous AGMs this one was packed. About four hundred members attended, many of them local people who had paid their $25 membership on that day in order to voice their feelings. Outgoing president Robert Hicks had to endure speaker after speaker calling the Board's integrity into question. The worst came after the Board handily defeated a non-confidence vote with the help of 633 proxy votes (the final tally was 874 to 305), and used the same absent majority to elect an entirely Board-nominated trio of new members. When Hicks tried to adjourn the meeting, Richard Monette leapt to his feet and into Canadian theatrical history. A leading actor in the company, who would eventually become its longest-serving artistic director, Monette yelled at Hicks, "You pig!" Hicks, blinking into the auditorium lights, asked, "What is your name, sir?" As two security guards walked purposefully towards Monette, the actor declaimed, "We have all spent our lives in this theatre. We have given of our time and art. You talk about money all the time. You have no morals. I don't know how you can sleep!" Hicks adjourned the meeting.

That evening the newly-elected Board created a new search committee headed by Julian Porter and gave him a list of five Canadian directors to talk to, headed by Hirsch. Porter was one of the newly elected members and thus untainted by previous events. By his own admission he also knew very little about Stratford, or indeed about what an artistic director actually did. He was also unaware that at least some of the executive committee members – and, crucially, Peter Stevens – fully expected the committee to find that none of the five were available at this late date, reopening the door to John Dexter. Porter instead took the assignment at face value and was determined to come back with a new artistic director.

After the meeting ended Porter attended a party for the Board, where one member told him a story at some length about Hirsch ordering twelve satin tails for a dance routine "at quite some expense" and then deciding to cut the scene. A decade later, the memory of *The Satyricon* evidently still lived on with some of the Board. Nonetheless, after further conversations Porter had the feeling Hirsch was his man and resolved to see him as soon as possible.

Which is what brought Porter to Hudson Drive the following day, along with Peter Stevens and the new Board president, John

Lawson. The meeting was inconclusive and highlighted the different agendas in play. Porter, eager for a quick result, overstepped his authority and offered Hirsch the job, to Stevens' considerable annoyance. As Martin Knelman described it, Hirsch played "the reluctant sage" and asked for time to think about it, but was actually caught in a difficult position. On the one hand, having been a leading figure in the nationalist protest against hiring Phillips seven years earlier, "he might put himself in the indefensible position if he turned down the position in the Festival's hour of need.... The Board would be able to use his reluctance as an excuse for getting Dexter in, and it might be a very long time before the Board offered the job to a Canadian again." On the other hand, after his experience at the CBC he wasn't sure he wanted to manage a complex, high-profile institution like Stratford. He had once very much wanted the job. Today, however, his part-time arrangement with Seattle was working out fine. He knew he didn't like Stratford as a place to live, and his bad memories of the Board were reinforced by its latest shenanigans. There was every possibility that he could fall flat on his face if he took over a season so late in the day. And yet...Canada's most important theatre was on the brink of collapse. There really was a danger that there would be no 1981 season if he didn't step up.

Hirsch wrote to Porter two days later. Yes, he was available, but (like Dexter) only partially, given his existing commitments for 1981. Porter had further talks with Robin Phillips and William Hutt. There was a popular groundswell in Stratford in favour of Hutt as artistic director and several Board members asked him to think about taking the job on an interim basis. But Hutt wanted to keep Phillips in the picture in some capacity and that meant keeping Hirsch out of the picture. Moreover, the offer of a one-year interim directorship was insulting. Hutt finally declined.

Although Porter and Hirsch had agreed not to speak publically about the situation, the press was hot on the story's trail. When Hirsch took his phone off the hook a CBC reporter got an elderly neighbour to walk through the snow to take a message to him. As pressure grew Hirsch broke the agreement first, confirming to the

Montreal *Gazette* that he had indeed been offered the job. Porter then confirmed Hirsch's confirmation. There were more talks behind the scenes at Stratford, with Stevens trying hard to convince the Board to stick with Dexter and tough it out with Immigration. But on December 18 the Board voted unanimously to offer the job to Hirsch.

Although he was putting in long hours rehearsing *A Funny Thing Happened on the Way to the Forum*, Hirsch immediately started to plan the next season. He spoke to Muriel Sherrin, who had by this time left CBC and had her own business as a freelance producer and consultant. Sherrin was someone he trusted and he knew her organizational abilities. She was willing to stand in for him at Stratford during the first few months while he completed his contract in Seattle. They would stay in constant touch by phone, with Hirsch providing direction and Sherrin pursuing the details. Hirsch also called on his friend Michal Schonberg, asking him to be his literary manager. Schonberg agreed and obtained leave from the University of Toronto, where he was teaching in the Drama Department.

Hirsch then started calling possible leading actors and directors to see who was still available for the 1981 season. One of the first on his list was John Dexter. Dexter declined the offer in a letter dated December 24, emphasizing that he bore Hirsch no ill will. "To put it more bluntly," Dexter wrote, "I think we were both being negotiated with and manipulated at the same time." John Neville also declined. But others were available, as Hirsch went through his contact lists. Jean Gascon, by then director of theatre at the National Arts Centre, quickly agreed to direct *The Misanthrope* and another play. Brian Bedford said he would be happy to take the lead role in *The Misanthrope* but on condition that he could direct as well. Hirsch offered him *Coriolanus* and was able to get his old Winnipeg protégé Len Cariou – at that time riding high on Broadway as the original Sweeney Todd – to lead the cast.

Another piece in the puzzle fell into place at the St. Lawrence Centre, where Susan Benson was designer for *A Funny Thing Happened on the Way to the Forum*. In the final days before the January 1 opening Hirsch asked her to be head of design at Stratford. Though she was now used to working with Hirsch she was unprepared for the offer. "I was a little taken aback, not being one to believe in going too far too fast and I thought perhaps I wasn't ready for it," she recalls. But the urgency of the situation won her over: "I could see a lot of the good people in the permanent staff losing their jobs if the theatre closed."

A Funny Thing Happened on the Way to the Forum opened on New Year's Day and proved a resounding critical and commercial success. Five days later Hirsch signed his contract with the Festival, committing to three years at an annual salary of $75,000. The Festival would provide a house for him when he started full-time on July 1.

In the meantime his troops started arriving in Stratford. Muriel Sherrin and Michal Schonberg said goodbye to their respective families (both had children) and drove out to start work at the Festival on January 15, renting a house together. Schonberg describes Sherrin as being almost constantly on the phone during that month and remembers her imperturbability in what were extremely trying circumstances.

By the end of January, after a marathon of telephone calls and meetings, a season had been put together. Gascon's readiness to help was a godsend. He would direct *The Misanthrope* and Dürrenmatt's *The Visit*. Another godsend: with Gascon directing, William Hutt agreed to lead the cast of *The Visit*. Hutt was crucial to providing continuity within the acting company's illustrious past, since Martha Henry and Douglas Rain had made it known they wouldn't be coming back to Stratford until the Board had made a full apology to Henry. Peter Dews, then director of the Chichester Festival in England, came on board to direct *The Comedy of Errors* and *The Taming of the Shrew*. The latter would provide a second lead role for Len Cariou. At Muriel Sherrin's urging Leon Major put aside his annoyance at Hirsch's leaving him in the lurch in 1976 and agreed to direct Gilbert and Sullivan's *H.M.S. Pinafore*.

The process was full of stops and starts. Hutt had agreed to do *The Visit* only if a leading lady of international stature could be found to play the aged billionairess around whom the story revolves.

Sherrin got a verbal agreement from the French movie star Danielle Darrieux, then waited in vain for Darrieux's agent to sign the contract. Weeks passed. Finally, fearful that Hutt would pull out of the production, Sherrin finally managed to sign Alexis Smith, another actress better known for her movie career than the stage but without Darrieux's international reputation. More panic ensued when it took longer than expected to find a director for *Wild Oats*, an eighteenth century comedy recently revived by the Royal Shakespeare Company. The Australian director Derek Goldby, who had been working at the Shaw Festival, finally saved the production by agreeing to take it on.

The scramble to put on the season was just as hard on the production side, as Susan Benson recounts: "It was a hell of a time, trying to find designers in January when the shows were due to open in late May, early June. We had no designers, no design assistants. In the end, it was a relatively small group plus the resident production staff who were getting that together under extreme circumstances."

It was hard to keep a lid on costs, since the Festival was now in a poor negotiating position. Actors had to be offered higher salaries than usual, as did the other unionized workers. Programs had to be done in a rush, incurring overtime charges. There were additional costs related to the previous year's furore. The Festival had to make payments to Peter Ustinov for the abortive *Lear* tour, to John Dexter and the Gang of Four for their loss of earnings, and to Peter Stevens when the Board decided to let him go in March. Revenue was also going to be squeezed since the final line-up was eight plays over twenty-two weeks, compared to the previous season's fifteen plays over twenty-eight weeks. And finally, the most important question: after all the bad publicity, would the audiences come? Advance ticket sales were well below previous years' levels.

Hirsch arrived in May in such an overworked, ominous atmosphere, the Seattle Rep having released him two months early. His schedule instantly filled up. There were meetings to attend, phone calls to make, decisions to be made every hour of the day. Bryan came and went in the first few weeks, but found it hard to be in the house with his distracted, driven partner – when Hirsch was in the house, which wasn't often. And unlike in Toronto, where he had friends and many distractions if he wanted them, there was nothing for Bryan in Stratford. He retreated to Toronto, on call if Hirsch needed him but usually just visiting on weekends.

It weighed on Hirsch's mind that the season had been shaped almost entirely by expediency – who was available and what they would accept – than by what he would have chosen. Hirsch should have been more gracious to the people who were helping him out but graciousness wasn't his strong suit. Susan Benson commented, "I'm not sure John understood what people went through to get it done."

Leon Major, who had directed *The Gondoliers* at the Avon Theatre in the early 1960s, found himself at odds with Hirsch over *H.M.S. Pinafore* almost from the beginning. The show was Hirsch's idea. He'd seen the New York Shakespeare Festival's *Pirates of Penzance* the year before, which had featured pop star Linda Ronstadt. "During the rehearsal period we had many arguments about how it should be done," recalls Major. "He really wanted *Pirates*, not *Pinafore*, and I couldn't give him *Pirates*. The casting was done with singers, not rock stars. We couldn't rewrite the orchestration to accommodate electronics, so we had to do it with the score we had. It was not a good combination, the two of us."

Hirsch felt less inclined to interfere with Jean Gascon, but didn't like what Gascon was doing with *The Visit*. Composer Alan Laing remembers Hirsch's visible disapproval of Jean Gascon's approach to the political satire. "Where Hirsch would have produced a very strong dramatic piece, Jean was gentler, more humane and subtler. I knew in advance that John would hate it, and indeed he did."

William Hutt wasn't happy with *The Visit* either, but for different reasons. Alexis Smith proved unequal to her role, undermining the efforts of Hutt and the rest of the company. But there was more to it than that. He found the changes at Stratford unsettling: "After twenty-five years at the Festival," he told an interviewer, "to come back and have the entire staff new…it's a culture shock." Moreover, not to have been offered a Shakespearian role seemed demeaning to someone of his stature. With Major and Gascon, Hirsch seemed ungrateful and ungracious; with Hutt, he was failing to look after one of the Festival's greatest assets.

Hirsch had put himself on the line and felt horribly exposed. In Seattle he had been praised and appreciated wherever he went. In Toronto his *A Funny Thing Happened on the Way to the Forum* had been one of the biggest successes in the St. Lawrence Centre's history. In Stratford he felt like he had parachuted into enemy territory: Phillips territory. The compact town contained areas where he never felt comfortable, not least its best restaurant, the Church, a mere block from the Avon Theatre. The Church was owned by Phillips's partner, Joe Mandel, and Phillips was often there with a crowd of friends: it was sometimes referred to as the "Court-in-Exile." The lack of welcome wasn't entirely in Hirsch's imagination. Michal Schonberg remembers a certain "hostile undertone" during his first months, and facing questions that were less than friendly when he gave a talk at the public library.

If Hirsch wanted to be surrounded by friendly faces in Stratford, he would have to import them. Among the early visitors was Andras Hamori, his young friend from Budapest, who had finally defected from Hungary. His first order of business after dropping off his bags at Hudson Drive in Toronto was to visit Hirsch. When Hirsch picked him up at Stratford's little railway station, Hamori got the strong sense that Hirsch had something on his mind that he was hesitant about saying. Finally Hirsch came out with it: did Andras realize Hirsch was gay? It seemed an odd question to Hamori – of course he knew, and he had just met Bryan – but he realized they had never talked about it before. Hirsch pursued his line of thought: had Bryan mentioned that there was "someone else" in the house at Stratford? Yes, came the reply. "So you won't be surprised…" Hirsch said, then corrected himself – "Actually, you *will* be surprised" – as they drove up to the house. Hamori still laughs heartily at the memory: "At that moment the door opened and this creature came out in a kimono with his arms full of flowers, which he then tossed down on the driveway screaming, 'Welcome to Canada!' It was Jacques Beyderwellen."

The flamboyant businessman and playwright had appointed himself Hirsch's major domo, ensuring that Hirsch's meals were cooked, his clothes washed, and his house filled with flowers. Though Beyderwellen had always been welcome at Hudson Drive, he had never felt entirely comfortable there, caught between Hirsch and Bryan. Now he had found a role that was perfect for him. Beyderwellen was financially self-sufficient and happy to entertain himself when Hirsch wasn't around. Hamori found himself wondering what the neighbours thought: "Jacques was probably the most feminine man I ever met. And Stratford is the straightest small town in Canada. The people around there probably thought it was the end of the world."

Despite the jitters, the conflicts and the rush to get the plays up and running, the season was far from the debacle that Hirsch had so feared. In mid-June the opening week's productions – Jean Gascon's *Misanthrope*, Brian Bedford's *Coriolanus* and Leon Major's *H.M.S. Pinafore* at the Avon Theatre – all proved to be solid productions worthy of the Stratford Festival. As the other five productions opened over the course of the summer it was clear that audiences had not massively abandoned Stratford. The best box office performance was the Gilbert and Sullivan, with attendance rates of ninety-two per-cent over the course of its run; the lowest was *Coriolanus*, at sixty-one per-cent, despite some good reviews for both the production and the performance of Len Cariou. The financial results were dire, with a loss of just over a million dollars, but that had been expected. The Festival had survived and could hope to bounce back in the following years.

Stratford breathed easier. Local businesses that depended on the Festival hadn't done badly. Michal Schonberg had the impression that the town got friendlier to the new Festival regime after the first plays opened and it was clear the sky hadn't fallen in. "It became less hostile," he thought, "because people realized that like it or not, Hirsch was there to stay."

The new regime was going to have to do without Muriel Sherrin, however. She had always said she was only there to help out for the one season, and despite pressure from Hirsch she stuck to her guns and left when the season finished. Schonberg stayed on, however, and Hirsch started to hire what he hoped would be a stable management team for the future. He brought in Gerry Eldred from Ballet Canada to be his executive director and Richard Dennison from the National Theatre School to be his production manager. Both men had worked at the Manitoba Theatre Centre, though neither during Hirsch's time there. The inclusion of Dennison signalled Hirsch's determination to push ahead with a training program for young actors, tentatively called "Shakespeare 3" since it would be based at the Festival's third stage.

More changes were coming at a different level. Many of the current Board members were due to retire and Hirsch wanted to ensure that he would have a Board he could work with. In the early autumn he called Peter Herrndorf, who had left the CBC and was now the publisher of *Toronto Life* magazine. "I've got an assignment for you," said Hirsch. "I need you to go on the Board of Stratford." Herrndorf listened as Hirsch explained that he had worked out a deal to elect three or four members who would be "his people" with the job of protecting him from the organization and from the rest of the Board. Herrndorf was amused to be given an "assignment," but agreed. He remembers, "The bulk of the Board thought it was a little odd that an artistic director needed to have 'his own Board members.' In the past the Board members had been Stratford members, not Board members for a particular regime." At the next Annual General Meeting Herrndorf was duly elected, along with David Silcox, an art historian and well-connected cultural bureaucrat who was about to become Assistant Deputy Minister for Culture at the federal Department of Communications. Silcox would prove particularly important in fundraising over the next few years.

By this time Hirsch had already announced his next season. By and large it had a reassuring feel to it. Brian Bedford would be back to direct Noel Coward's *Blithe Spirit*, which would transfer after its Stratford run to a commercial theatre in Toronto. Derek Goldby would return to direct *Julius Caesar* and *The Merry Wives of Windsor*.

A welcome piece of news was that Michael Langham had agreed to direct Shaw's *Arms and the Man*, his first production at Stratford since 1970. After the box office success of the Gilbert and Sullivan the previous year Brian Macdonald would direct *The Mikado*. There would be a contemporary play from Northern Ireland, *Translations* by Brian Friel, whose *Freedom of the City* had been a great critical success during Hirsch's years at the CBC. The Shakespeare 3 Company – twelve young actors and four senior ones who would work together over the summer in a kind of apprenticeship arrangement – would perform two plays in a brief run at the end of the season. And Hirsch himself would direct two plays: *Mary Stuart* at the Avon and *The Tempest* on the Festival Stage, with Len Cariou returning as Prospero.

Hirsch was not able to work things out with William Hutt. On November 20 Hutt sent Hirsch a cordial letter thanking him for "the efforts you have made to make the Stratford 1982 season interesting for me" but saying that he had decided to take a year away from the Festival. Hutt's biographer suggests that Hirsch's offer of roles in *Translations*, *Damien* and the secondary role of Gonzalo in *The Tempest* was deliberately calculated to provoke a refusal. This seems unlikely – Hirsch wasn't that subtle a psychological game player – but he certainly didn't make Hutt an offer equal to his stature. His relationship with Hutt by this time was complicated and contradictory compared to when they first worked together in the 1960s. People who knew both speculate that there were just too many differences, including their different ways of living with their homosexuality. Hutt was discreet and contained in his relationships compared to Hirsch's exuberant promiscuity, but he famously descended into uncharacteristic cattiness by describing Hirsch as "a contradiction in sperms." But there may have been other reasons why Hirsch didn't offer Hutt a bigger role – such as Prospero – that season. Paul Thompson speculates, "Look at both of Hirsch's Properos over the years: Anthony Hopkins and Len Cariou – intense, burly, medium-height guys. Hirsch just didn't *see* a tall, patrician actor like Hutt in his *Tempest*." Whatever the reasons Hirsch went through a similar negotiation dance with Hutt the following year, and again Hutt did not accept what Hirsch had to offer. Hutt never did work again at Stratford while Hirsch was there.

There were more frustrations to come. Maggie Smith let Hirsch know that she wouldn't be back to Stratford for the time being. Hirsch replied to her by letter: "I understand your loyalty to Robin, and honour it.... [I] hope that someday, while we are still able to walk, and work, we'll get together to do something beautiful." Possibilities with Alan Bates fell through due to a communications mix-up. Hirsch wrote an apology and invited him for the following year, playfully promising, "You can play practically anything except Titania."

Another blow was the resignation of Susan Benson as his head designer in April. Benson had been working flat out for almost a year and half and Hirsch seemed to assume that she would take any problems in stride. Schedule changes found her trying to deal with *The Merry Wives of Windsor*, *The Mikado* and *Mary Stuart* all at once. It was impossible. Hirsch would have to find new designers for *Mary Stuart* while there was still time. Moreover, Benson didn't feel she was in control of the design department and felt that Hirsch sometimes undermined decisions she made, particularly hiring decisions. She was much happier when she was back to working on a project-to-project basis. Tanya Moiseiwitsch agreed to take on *Mary Stuart*'s costumes and Hirsch was able to bring Ming Cho Lee up from Yale to design the set.

On the domestic front Jacques Beyderwellen had returned to Stratford for the season, again playing his role as chatelaine of the artistic director's house. Close friends like Andras Hamori had taken to calling him "Madame Jacques" and delighted in Beyderwellen's ability to cook everything from Indonesian *rijsttafel* to ratatouille. When Bryan came to Stratford on weekends he sometimes "felt he was paying a visit to mum and dad." Much of Hirsch's social life in Stratford continued to revolve around out-of-town guests, but Hirsch was also getting to know the town better and was now on a first-name basis with many local people. This was a double-edged sword in the case of local merchants, since it made him even more aware of how much the town's economic health depended on the Festival. He also had come to appreciate the countryside surrounding Stratford. He liked to take guests in his beige VW Rabbit on shopping expeditions to the farmers' markets and small shops that are one of Southern Ontario's most attractive features. In a radio program he did for the CBC many years later he mentioned with great affection a favourite stop, the Blue Moon Hotel between Stratford and Kitchener, which had begun in the 1830s as a stop for stagecoaches: "The beer comes in pitchers, the food is first rate Waterloo home cooking. My favourites are pigtails and ribs served with sauerkraut. It tastes heavenly even though the ingredients are earthy."

Most important, Hirsch was back to doing what he loved most: directing plays. His thinking about *The Tempest* had developed since his production in Los Angeles three years earlier. He later wrote that his "identification with the character of Prospero was very strong, coming on the play as one did in middle age, when one has to confront giving things up." Fundamental to this production was his vision of Prospero as a man nearing middle age who has run away from his responsibilities: "Shakespeare says that if you want to regain your sanity, you have to run away from society. It's essential for our spiritual well-being. But it's a paradoxical self-exile and flight because it is also the duty of the ruler to stick with it, and you cannot co-opt your responsibility. What is good for your soul, finally, must be of benefit to the society in which you live." Len Cariou remembers his excitement at Hirsch's interpretation of the play and worked out a tightly controlled Prospero whose mix of anger and existential anguish bespoke a man in mid-life crisis.

Hirsch was determined to make this *Tempest* a much larger, layered, and more magical production than the one in Los Angeles, and worked with designer Desmond Heeley and lighting designer Michael Whitfield to take full advantage of the Festival Stage's possibilities. At the same time he spent hours with the cast on the complexities and ambiguities of the text. The late Richard Monette, who played Sebastian, was particularly struck by what Hirsch called the "moral declension" in the play:

Among other things, this referred to the gradations of evil seen in my character, Sebastian, and in Antonio, played by Colin Fox. Antonio embodies aggressive evil, John said, while Sebastian is only passively evil. As he spoke of this, I couldn't help thinking – though he made no reference to it – of the difference between those who actually ran the concentration camps and those who just stood by and let it happen.

As he so often did, Hirsch brought in an expert to talk to the cast. Monette remembered a talk by the psychiatrist, Vivian Rakoff, who spoke to the cast about how Shakespeare's plays "allow us to delve safely into areas of human experience that could well destroy us in real life." The usual Hirsch stories emerged during this period – Miles Potter, playing Caliban, remembers Hirsch throwing boxes of Kleenex at him during a particularly fraught rehearsal – but for the most part the production worked its way smoothly toward opening night.

It was different in the rehearsals for *Mary Stuart* over at the Avon stage. Hirsch was very hard on the lead actress, Margot Dionne, and as rehearsals progressed the famous finger-clicking became accusatory rather than simply impatient. Ming Cho Lee, who hadn't seen this side of Hirsch before, found it disturbing to be around as he worked on the sets. Also unhappy was R.H. Thomson, whose career as a leading man on the Canadian stage was taking off during these years. He admired Hirsch's breadth of knowledge and constant stream of ideas but couldn't get what he needed from him as a director. He would look back on *Mary Stuart* as some of the worst work he ever did. There were also mutterings about expenditures on the production, again with negative comparisons to the Phillips era. Robin Phillips and his designer Daphne Dare had worked out a "black box" approach for the Avon Stage, an easily stored structure which could support sets for several different productions, permitting a crew of ten to take down a matinee set and replace it with the one for the evening performance. The *Mary Stuart* set required

Miles Potter as Caliban, Ian Deakin as Ariel and Len Cariou as Prospero
in *The Tempest*, summer 1982.
*Photo by Robert C. Ragsdale, courtesy of the Stratford
Shakespeare Festival Archives*

another six crew members – each with a minimum four-hour call – to do a changeover. Hirsch told an interviewer that people had described the black box as looking "like a cross between an Elizabeth Arden beauty salon and a mortuary. That blackness and those mirrors, after a while it became so depressing. No doubt," he added, "it did save money." But having hired one of North America's top designers, Hirsch wasn't about to limit Ming Cho Lee's creative possibilities with penny-pinching.

The season, when it opened in June, marked a respectable debut for Hirsch in his full role as a working artistic director. Overall attendance rates were about the same as the previous year at about seventy-five per-cent, although with many more performances revenue was considerably higher.

With eighty-per-cent houses Hirsch's *Tempest* got the best audiences of the five Shakespeare plays that summer. The visual power of the production was there from the start, as huge sails in green silk descended over the stage and the abandoned helmsman's wheel spun crazily in the flickering light. The critics were sharply divided. The veteran British critic Robert Warren thought it "the first coherent version of the play that I have seen, the only one to wield the disparate elements of the play into a unity." Another British reviewer, writing for the *Financial Times,* dismissed it as "one of the most extravagantly vulgar things I have ever seen." There was similar division on Len Cariou's Prospero. Of Cariou's epilogue, delivered in simple clothes that emphasized his renunciation of his magical powers and total control of the island, the *Times'* Irving Wardle wrote, "I have heard it better spoken, but never with a better sense of what Prospero has given up." The role that got the most praise was Nicholas Pennell's Stephano, a satirical portrayal of a thoroughly incompetent man tasting power that fully reflected Hirsch's ideas about the play's moral declension.

Michael Langham's *Arms and the Man* and Brian Bedford's *Blithe Spirit* were both well received, but the season's greatest success was again Gilbert and Sullivan, with Brian Macdonald's *Mikado* pulling in ninety-six per-cent houses. Audiences enjoyed the beautifully realized production, and it added a certain piquancy when word got round that one of the bit roles satirized Hirsch's least favourite Toronto critic, Gina Mallet. The box office disappointment was *Mary Stuart*, with the lowest attendance of all the shows at fifty-seven per cent. Mallet panned it with an article entitled "A Limp Martyr on a Set from Speer."

From the outside observer's point of view the Festival had pulled back from the brink but had not yet found an overall style or sense of itself. Of the roughly one hundred actors in the company in 1980 only fifteen were onstage in the 1982 season, and there were no commanding figures around which it could coalesce. Len Cariou, the biggest "name" in 1981 and 1982, had been glad to help out at Stratford and to take on some roles that interested him, but didn't see a future for himself there. Though still attached to Winnipeg (like Hirsch, he continued to visit his family there regularly) he was now a confirmed New Yorker and shared Hirsch's discomfort with the small Ontario town. "Everybody knew when you went to the bathroom!" Cariou laughs today. "I found it really disconcerting."

When the accounts for the season were tallied it became clear that, while the financial situation was much improved from the previous year, it was still not good. Gary Thomas, the head of administration who had started work under Jean Gascon and would continue under several artistic directors after Hirsch, comments that tough economic times complicated matters considerably. "Those were difficult years," he comments, "with a recession and record high interest rates. Theatres always suffer during tough economic times because people pull back on ticket spending." He reflects on the cycles he has seen in the Festival's history: "When it started to have good years it would seem to build momentum. And when the momentum went down, it was hard to get it back – it took a while every time that happened. In the early eighties, it lost momentum and it was hard to turn the ship around and get it righted again." Thomas, a reticent man by nature, chooses his words carefully when describing the working relationship with Hirsch, saying simply that "Hirsch was very demanding and very passionate about what he was doing." Thomas felt fortunate to have both Gerry Eldred and Michal Schonberg in the picture. Both had Hirsch's ear and both were skilled at communicating Hirsch's wishes in more reasonable terms than Hirsch himself would have expressed them.

A great deal of Hirsch's time in the next few years was taken up with fundraising. The files are full of his letters to the federal and provincial governments, to funding bodies like the Canada Council and to wealthy individuals. He and his Board were noticeably successful on the fundraising front. There were major donations from Imperial Oil and from individuals like the former president of Maclean-Hunter, Floyd Chalmers, and real estate developer Mark Tanz. But on the other side of the equation, expenditures climbed well ahead of revenue for the next two years.

Although Hirsch proved to be an effective fundraiser it was not a role he enjoyed. He felt aggrieved that he had to beg for money and liked to tell the following story about one of his Sunday morning phone calls to Ma Shack back in Winnipeg. When she asked, as she always did, what he had done that week he replied,

On Monday I was in the capital trying to convince a Deputy Minister that unless we had an additional $700,000 subsidy, the theatre was going down the drain. That afternoon I asked the head of a corporation for $200,000 for a project. The next day I spoke at a cocktail party to raise funds for additions to the Festival Theatre. Wednesday I was talking to the Department of Tourism people, telling them how important it is to promote the Stratford Festival. The day after that I talked to a man who is a multi-millionaire asking for $300,000 to start a 'Young Company.' My mother paused on the other end of the phone and said, 'Isn't it a pity. All this education and you end up being a *schnorrer* [beggar].'

The punchline was pure Borscht Belt; the anger, pure Hirsch.

* * *

When the season ended at Stratford in late September 1982 Jacques Beyderwellen returned to Montreal and Hirsch moved back to Toronto, returning to the house in Stratford only when he had to stay for extended meetings or other work assignments. Andras Hamori was now living downstairs at Hudson Drive while he tried to find his professional feet in Toronto. When Hamori lasted exactly one day in a job Hirsch helped him find at the CBC, Hirsch was not surprised or annoyed. In fact, he laughed when Hamori dismissed the national broadcaster with, "I didn't leave Hungary to get back into the socialist system." Hamori soon found a job working in film production for Hirsch's friend Robert Lantos and began his rapid climb in the industry.

Hamori loved having a ringside seat at Hudson Drive with its constant steam of dinner guests from Hirsch's different "mafias": Jewish, Hungarian, Winnipeg and gay, with some people representing more than one category. He enjoyed the secular seders Hirsch and Bryan had started doing at Passover and the fact that the house was a kid-friendly zone. Hirsch and Bryan both loved having children around and related well to them. Martin Knelman's daughter Sara and son Josh were frequent visitors. The latter recalls thinking of Hirsch and Bryan as fixed, solid features in his childhood: "John would listen to an eight-year-old like me with the same seriousness as he'd give to an adult. They both would. I never thought of them as anything but a warm, together couple."

Andras Hamori saw the couple but he also noted what he called the "cage aux folles" aspect of the house: "There were always good-looking young men around – theatre students from Hungary, makeup artists who just needed a place to stay for a few days." When Hamori started adding to the mix by bringing girlfriends home, Hirsch reacted like a proud father. He and Bryan both became friendly with the women in Hamori's life, happily adding them to the ever-changing mix at the house.

When Hamori announced that his mother was coming from Hungary to visit him, Hirsch called "a family meeting" with Bryan and Hamori to discuss how they were going hide Hirsch's homosexuality from the visitor. Though Hamori didn't think it would be a problem, Hirsch was worried, since homosexuality was still both officially and socially taboo in Hungary. Hamori remembers:

> John decided he would wear a three-piece suit with a vest. I asked why, and he said 'Because gay people don't wear three-piece suits, they wear jeans and sweaters.' I said fine and Bryan said fine. My mother arrived and John started to wear this really ugly, brown three-piece suit. After a few days my mother asked if Bryan and John were gay. I said, yeah. And my mum said, 'So why does John wear a suit? Gay people don't wear suits.' I told this to John and he said 'Thank God!' and went back to the big beige sweater that he always wore and his green corduroy pants.

Hirsch was less happy with another, part-time member of the ménage. Bryan had become intimate with Tony Brown, who was a celebrity in Toronto's "gay ghetto" around Church and Wellesley Streets. Six-foot-four, black and strikingly handsome, Tony worked for years as a female impersonator in nightclubs. Hirsch was wary of Tony and didn't make him particularly welcome when he came to visit. It bothered Hirsch that Tony frequently stayed in the house whenever he was away at Stratford, but given his own sexual activities he could hardly accuse Bryan of infidelity.

Hirsch and Bryan spent their vacation in Haiti that winter. The early months of 1983 kept Hirsch busy with public appearances. Much of this was related to fundraising. The afternoon before a speech at the University of Western Ontario he told an interviewer that he had become "much more aggressive in light of the terrible financial situation." But he was also there in a role he had played for years, as an advocate for the arts. At a time when major government subsidies had been given to the manufacturing and extractive industries in the U.S. and Canada, Hirsch argued for continued government support to the cultural industries. His main point was that Canada needed to maintain and develop production capacity in Canada, particularly in film and television. He told the interviewer:

> There are always cries about free enterprise and that subsidies are socialist and so on – but I always ask, 'What about Dome?' and 'What about Chrysler?'[1] People start screaming when the government puts money into the cultural industries, but nobody screams when they pour billions of dollars into private industry by way of subsidies. And if we are to preserve a reasonable balance between what we produce and what we get from the United States, we obviously have to protect to some extent, and to promote to a great extent, and to subsidize to a reasonable extent, what we produce in the cultural industries.

Even while running the Festival Hirsch made the occasional attempt to return to the film industry he had entered while at CBC. A notice in the trade magazine *Cinema Canada* from this time shows him in negotiations to direct a short film based on a script by Stratford's long-time fight master Paddy Crean. The film was never made, but another project that would be more successful came along as Mordecai Richler showed up at Stratford with film producer Robert Lantos and director Ted Kotcheff to talk about the script of Richler's *Joshua Then and Now*. The CBC had invested in the film and had asked that Hirsch do some story editing on the screenplay. Hirsch was amused by the idea of giving Mordecai Richler notes on his own story, but worked on the screenplay with Richler for several days.

Hirsch continued to speak at public events as often as possible and never missed an opportunity to get publicity for the Festival. When he met Ronald Reagan at a public function in Washington he offered the American president a job at the Festival, suggesting the former actor might like to play King Lear, with Charlton Heston as his fool. In many of his public appearances he spoke about the need for training young actors and other professionals. Speaking at

Columbia University in 1983 at the Theater Communications Group conference for dramaturges and literary managers, he returned to concerns he'd had about mass media and language since the late 1960s. "The actors I work with now," he commented, "are of a generation which learned from television. Not even the movies.... They don't really know what language is – the sensuality of language, the total connectedness between the head and the heart and the groin doesn't really occur to them. You have to take them back to learn to taste language."

Antoni Cimolino, now General Director of the Stratford Festival, was just out of theatre school around this time and remembers this emphasis on language when he auditioned for Hirsch in the Festival Theatre:

> I was doing Hamlet's fourth soliloquy: "What is a man / If his chief good and market of his time / Be but to sleep and feed...." When I got to where it says that God did not give us our human qualities "to fust in us unused," Hirsch stopped me and said, "Unused. Un*used.*" Then he said, "You think you have a talent?" He was not the gentlest of auditioners and at that point I thought, "Oh God, just get me out of here." But then something inside of me rebelled and I told him, "Yes, I have a talent." And he said, "Good, good.... What if you don't get to act for the next forty years? *That's* unused. Now say it again." I did the speech and when I got to the word it had all the colours of the rainbow, it was so inhabited for me and real. He turned around and he said to the other person who was with him, "Well, now we're starting to get somewhere."

Cimolino didn't make it into the company this time but would later on in the 1980s.

Seana McKenna was part of the generation of young actors who came into the Festival during Hirsch's directorship. She reflects now on the change of style that Hirsch was looking for in the company.

"Before, I think there was a different sensibility that we Canadians associated with elegance and class. I'm from an Irish and Polish background and I think he appealed to me because his aesthetic seemed Eastern European – he wanted passion, fire, cracks in the armour. He wanted rawness, he wanted mistakes, he wanted spontaneity. I used to regale my parents with John Hirsch stories – they loved them." Hirsch's insistence on tying plays to contemporary concerns was part of his overall approach, remembers McKenna. "He insisted you take responsibility for the play and why we were doing that play *now*. It didn't matter if it was written in 1580 or 1720. Why are we doing this play with this audience in this year? Not this decade, this year – *this month*." At the same time she remembers the damage Hirsch could do to some people's confidence with the bluntness of his criticism. "His ferocity put a lot of people off. I never felt it was mean-spirited; it was his obliviousness to the effect he was having on people."

She and other actors (notably Martha Henry and R.H. Thomson) have reflected on Hirsch in the context of the old question about whether it is essential for a director to have experience as a working actor. McKenna does not come down on one side or another of the question, but comments on Hirsch's approach: "He didn't actually know how we did what we did. You might say that he had an idea of the painting he wanted to see, but he didn't know how to help you put in the best strokes. So he used to say, "You're the actor, *you* make it better." Part of me liked that, because I had a certain freedom. He wasn't going to give me a line reading."

Hirsch was pleased when Michael Langham accepted his invitation to run the Festival's Shakespeare 3 Company (which Langham quickly renamed the Young Company). This was an important development. Langham was not only one of the world's best directors of Shakespeare, he was an experienced educator after years of teaching at the Julliard School in New York.

Hirsch was also concerned with getting Shakespeare more widely into Canadian schools. Having worked out a deal with the CBC to televise several of the Festival's Shakespeare productions, he turned this into a joint venture with the newly created CBC Enterprises to market an educational package that included four videotaped plays and accompanying teaching materials (the plays are still available on DVD).

Hirsch placed a great deal of emphasis on the Festival's program of concerts and lectures that accompanied each season's plays. The Celebrity Lecture Series, organized by Michal Schonberg and held on Sunday mornings at the Festival Theatre, started with Northrop Frye and ranged from authors like John Kenneth Galbraith and Peter C. Newman to show-business figures like Peter Ustinov. Arthur Miller lectured twice during this period, which also included leading Shakespeare scholars from Britain, Canada and the United States. One of the high points for Hirsch was to be able to bring his favourite singer, Ella Fitzgerald, to sing on the Festival Stage in July 1983. He later described the way Fitzgerald, now frail and nearly blind after several eye operations, "transformed herself in a marvellous way" when she began to sing. Somehow she was still the same person-ification of artistry and hope he remembered listening to on U.S. Armed Forces radio in 1945. "If you look in the face of a great per-former at the moment he or she is performing," he commented, "you'll always see a child of six, maybe seven. And she looks like five. She *believes*."

Hirsch's relationship with the Festival Board never warmed up very much, despite the election of people like Herrndorf and Silcox at the previous AGM and new members in 1983 like Murray Frum, the Toronto realtor and husband of journalist Barbara Frum. In contrast to his days at the Manitoba Theatre Centre, when he some-times played the prima donna in order to enliven board meetings, Hirsch was no longer making the effort. He would put his case for whatever he wanted forcefully and push them to make greater efforts in fundraising, but he refused to engage with questions that he considered encroached on his prerogative as artistic director. Julian Porter remembers some Board members asking why the Festival didn't tackle *Othello*, only to be met with a putdown: did they really want to take a day out while Hirsch explained *theatre* to them? "It was a sort of 'you know nothing about this and how am I ever going to educate you?' type thing, says Porter." The old Hirsch, the entertainer who had so adroitly managed the board of the Manitoba Theatre Centre, was rarely in evidence.

At just over $12 million for twelve productions the budget for the 1983 season was the highest yet by a considerable margin. Hirsch had decided to direct one Shakespeare comedy, *As You Like It*, and Molière's *Tartuffe*. Michael Langham's Young Company would present two plays and *The Mikado* would return to the Avon and be joined by *The Gondoliers*, both directed by Brian Macdonald. Hirsch also hired Des McAnuff to direct *Macbeth*.

In the decade since Hirsch had recommended him to Bob Kalfin at the Chelsea Theater Center McAnuff had made a name for himself in the United States, notably directing Shakespeare for Joseph Papp in New York. McAnuff remembers being thrilled at the idea of sharing directing duties for the Festival Stage with Hirsch and Michael Langham. "I was only thirty, and that was young by Stratford standards," he comments. "In a sense I was tutored by them, not so much directly but by attending auditions with them and watching them work with the young actors in the company that were trying to get into Stratford. It certainly had a big impact on my work since then." He wasn't happy with some of the casting decisions that had been made before he arrived, but otherwise felt free to pursue his ideas about *Macbeth*. Given his age at the time he thinks Hirsch took quite a chance on him: "John attended my first rehearsal where I read my manifesto about the play to the company, but after that he really had little involvement. He came to a dress rehearsal and we talked about the relationship between Lady M and Macca [Macbeth], but for only five, ten minutes. I don't recall even getting notes from John."

Before the season was finished Hirsch invited McAnuff to come to Stratford as an associate director. McAnuff was also weighing an invitation to become artistic director at the La Jolla Playhouse in California. McAnuff finally chose La Jolla, where he would originate a number of successful productions that made their way to Broadway.

Briefly assailed by second thoughts McAnuff asked Hirsch if it was a serious career mistake to pass up Stratford at this time. Hirsch replied, "Don't worry, you'll need something important to do in your fifties."

Of Hirsch's two productions that season *As You Like It* provoked the most comment. His reflections on the play during the previous winter had dovetailed with his overall conception of Shakespeare's comedies as progressions from darkness into light (in visual terms), from bondage to liberty (in political terms), and from fragmentation to wholeness (in psychological terms). He was strongly influenced by psychologist Bruno Bettelheim's 1967 book *The Uses of Enchantment*, which proposes that the darkness of traditional fairy tales – particularly the abandonment, violence and death so prevalent in the stories collected by the Grimm brothers – provides a symbolic means by which children can deal with their fears. The opening scene of Hirsch's *As You Like It* confronted audiences with an especially dark vision coloured by his experience in wartime Europe. To the sound of a Viennese waltz the lights came up on a wintry urban scene in which a shivering boy stands chained by the neck to a man playing a hurdy-gurdy. Soldiers roughly escorted a chained prisoner across the stage, scattering passersby, but the audience's attention remained focused on the child as he began to sing a plaintive "It was a lover and his lass," holding his hand out in hopes of a coin. This prologue-to-the-prologue segued into the harsh world of a totalitarian court.

As You Like It got generally favourable reviews from the newspaper reviewers, notably from Arnold Edinborough in the *Financial Post* ("witty, romantic, colourful, well-conceived and executed") and the *Guardian*'s Gerald Kaufman ("brilliant"). Reading the reviews today one is struck by the extent to which Canadian critics were still under the spell of Maggie Smith's Rosalind in the 1977 Stratford production; Roberta Maxwell's spunky tomboy seems to have been chiefly criticized on the grounds that she wasn't Smith.

Once again Hirsch had delivered a respectable season and the Board invited him to extend his contract for two years, which Hirsch accepted. But he – and everyone else at Stratford – was only too aware of Robin Phillips' latest venture: a new repertory company at the Grand Theatre in London, Ontario. It seemed like the Court-in-Exile had moved from talk at the Church Restaurant to opening a front barely an hour's drive from the Festival Theatre. The Grand's opening season featured a full range of plays from the rock musical *Godspell* to *Hamlet*, with a roster of actors that included Brent Carver, Martha Henry and William Hutt. Critical reaction to the first season was excellent and critics noted that, whereas Stratford was playing it safe with "standard high-school text plays" like *As You Like It*, Phillips had taken risks like putting on the relatively rarely performed *Timon of Athens*. Stories circulated about Hirsch's rage at the situation. One such story, which was repeated in at least one history of the Festival, was that Hirsch arranged to have a box of cockroaches smuggled into the Church restaurant and then called the health inspectors, but this seems to be just another Stratford rumour. (Bryan Trottier hadn't heard the story and laughed when asked about it: "That's something John might *say* but I can't imagine him doing it – he liked food too much.")

As it turned out, Phillips' ambitious plans ran into the same economic reality that Hirsch was confronting. The Grand Theatre Company was built on the assumption that Phillips could pull in the same eighty-plus per-cent houses that he achieved at Stratford in the 1970s – and without stars like Maggie Smith or Peter Ustinov. The reality was cruelly different. The most popular show, *Godspell*, only got seventy-seven per-cent while *Timon of Athens* attracted only thirty-six-percent houses. The season resulted in a loss of $1.4 million on a budget of $4.4 million and Phillips resigned after his first season in February 1984.

Meanwhile at Stratford the deficit was causing growing concern. Peter Herrndorf took on the job of heading a committee of board members and staff to review the Festival's financial performance over the past decade, examine the problems it faced and make recommendations for the future. The committee would table its report in May 1984.

As the Canadian winter set in Hirsch and Bryan again went south to the Caribbean island of Hispaniola, but this time to the Dominican Republic where they would return year after year. Their stays always began at the Hostal Nicolas de Ovando, a gracious colonial-era building in the capital, before heading to the north coast in a rented car.

While staying in the town of Puerto Plata they heard an improbable-sounding story about a "Jewish" town in the area. The story was true. In 1938 the country's dictator Rafael Trujillo had offered shelter to Jewish refugees from Europe and about eight hundred from Austria and Germany were able to take advantage of the offer. They were given land in the small coastal town of Sosúa, where they built a synagogue and established a dairy industry. Today a major tourist destination, Sosúa was still relatively quiet when Hirsch and Bryan first showed up. Hirsch was amazed to see street names like Calle Herzl and was occasionally gripped by the idea that he might knock on a door to one of the whitewashed houses and find his brother or parents behind it. He bought land there with the hope of building a house, though this turned out to be one of Hirsch's few bad business deals. The house was never built and Bryan today refers to it as "a folly, but a beautiful one."

Part of the country's attraction was sex, which could be easily purchased for cash or "presents" on the street or in brothels. Hirsch was open about his adventures to his close friends, and several – gay and straight – urged Hirsch and Bryan to be careful. The shadow of AIDS was beginning to darken across the North American gay community. Eric Steiner, a colleague from his CBC days and the partner of Hirsch's friend Steven Jack, was the first in their circle to be diagnosed with the virus in late 1983 (Steiner died of AIDS ten years later). Hirsch and Bryan listened to their friends' advice, but like many gay men at the time, ignored it.

Hirsch arrived back in Stratford tanned and relaxed after his holiday. Susan Benson was touched when he dropped by her design desk with a basket of seashells he'd collected for her. It was part of Hirsch's unpredictability. Just as there could be critical comments and flashes of anger there were also thoughtful presents when one wasn't expecting them. Steven Schipper was one of the assistant directors whom Hirsch hired during this period. Schipper remembers having lunch at a cafeteria when Hirsch showed up and ceremoniously handed him a script as if it were a silver platter. Hirsch told him, "Here is a present for you: *Little Red Riding Hood* by Evgeny Schwartz, the most produced play in the Soviet Union." Despite Hirsch's mock seriousness it was nothing less than the truth. Schipper checked it out and learned the 1936 play was indeed a theatrical mainstay in the Soviet Union.

Hirsch had reason to be pleased as he began work on the new season. Good things were happening to the Festival infrastructure that year as a result of the Board's fundraising efforts. Most notably, a $6-million expansion of the Festival Theatre provided much-needed rehearsal and storage space. But despite these bright spots Hirsch was getting a lot of bad financial news as the new season geared up. Advance ticket sales were almost a half-million dollars below target by the end of April, and cash flow was suffering. Peter Herrndorf's committee reported back in May and laid out the situation facing the Festival. There was no room to move on ticket prices, which had already risen sharply. Box office targets had to be more realistic and, unless the Festival decided to do more crowd-pleasers and hire international movie stars, budgets had to be based on expectations of seventy- to seventy-four-per cent houses (the report noted that Broadway had averaged seventy-four percent over the previous five years). To those still fixed on the success of the Phillips years Herrndorf argued those years had been inherently unsustainable. A recession, an illness, the withdrawal of stars – all of these could sink a season financially. This had indeed been demonstrated in 1979 after Phillips had partially withdrawn due to illness and the Festival suffered the only loss of his tenure; it was also a year in which the only imported star, Peter Ustinov, played in a limited, late-season run of *King Lear*. In its summary the report laid out in stark terms the choices facing the Festival: "It can attempt to mount a major campaign to *increase its revenues* from government and private donors; it can *tighten its belt on the expenditure side* in a significant and painful way; it can proceed with a judicious blend of increasing grants and donations ... and reducing costs; or, finally, it can *change* its artistic,mandate."

Herrndorf remembers that Hirsch understood the report's message, "but I don't think he cared. He cared about putting on a great production, so he would use whatever resources he could lay his hands on." Brian Rintoul, who worked at Stratford as an assistant director that year, remembers Hirsch demanding a change to the sound design of *A Streetcar Named Desire*, which Hirsch was directing at the Avon Theatre. Hirsch listened to the original recording and pronounced it "crude." He wanted more of the soundscape one would find in the streets of New Orleans. The production team created a tape that increased the number of individual sound cues from seventy-five to two hundred, pulled in "reality" from the French-speaking market stalls in Ottawa, and remixed and rebalanced everything to make it sound like it was coming through an apartment's wall. The cost was over ten thousand dollars for something that most audience members would only register subliminally, but Hirsch was delighted with the result.

For the 1984 season Hirsch had programmed six Shakespeare plays, including the fourth *Midsummer Night's Dream* of his career. The *Dream* opened the season on June 10 and was probably the most controversial production of Hirsch's directorship at Stratford. Once again Hirsch and designer Desmond Heeley created a striking prologue, which began as the audience was still coming into the theatre. To the sound of pastoral music, a trio of rustics swept up leaves on the stage. After a while the music and the set darkened, the rustics fled as if fearing a storm and – after a brief, thunderous blackout – a battle scene erupted between soldiers led by Theseus (Nicholas Pennell) and Amazons led by Hippolyta (Patricia Connolly), ending with the defeated Hippolyta borne off at spear-point. The show ended with what critic Roger Warren called, "one of Mr. Hirsch's touches of theatrical magic: the shimmering light representing the 'field-dew consecrate' with which the fairies bless the place not only spread across the entire huge stage but was reflected all over the roof of the theatre as well."

As might have been expected, the *Toronto Star*'s Gina Mallet found little to praise ("Was this *Macbeth* we saw before us? No, a *Midsummer Night's Dream* rendered as a violent nightmare"). And while the sets and many of the performances and staging ideas were generally admired a number of reviews questioned Hirsch's reading of the text. Was this implicit critique of the sexual status quo stretching the text beyond what it could or should bear dramatically? Ray Conlogue, generally a fan of Hirsch's, commented that "Hirsch's reading of the script is so strong and so bitter that a real problem arises with the reconciliation at the end, which is essential in any romance.... Hirsch's sensibility about this is strong: he admits the idea of social reconciliation, but he looks upon it with sad-eyed dolefulness, as if he does not really trust it. In this, he and the playwright are at odds."

Critics were beginning to question Hirsch's leadership at the Festival. Nationalists noted that no Canadian plays had been performed during Hirsch's tenure; was this the same director who had brought James Reaney's *Colours in the Dark* to the Stratford stage? In fact, Hirsch had made it his policy not to produce Canadian plays at Stratford, arguing that the regional and "alternative" theatres around the country made better choices and produced Canadian plays better than Stratford could.

More seriously, Hirsch was accused of yet again playing it safe with a season heavy on Shakespeare comedies, three Gilbert and Sullivan musicals and – with works by Molière, Tennessee Williams, Beckett and Rattigan – nothing new or recent. Michael Billington, who had come over from the U.K. to cover the season for the *Guardian*, thought the productions on offer were of good quality but wondered about the programming strategy. Noting that Stratford operated on the same scale as the U.K.'s National Theatre but with much less of a subsidy, Billington judged that as artistic director Hirsch faced "a classic dilemma. Play safe and he is accused of caution; take risks and the box office may fall. What worries me (and it is a problem as common in Britain as it is in Canada) is the increasing reliance on the handful of Shakespeare plays that are set texts in schools." Ralph Berry, writing in *Shakespeare Quarterly* after the 1984 season, looked at the audience figures and delivered a harsher judgment: "Those unfilled seats are the precise measure of Stratford's current difficulties. And, as has now become clear, of John Hirsch's failure as Artistic Director."

The criticism went beyond the by-now-predictable potshots taken by his most vociferous critic Gina Mallet. For the past four years she and Hirsch had conducted a kind of feud that reflected little credit on either, except in its entertainment value for readers. (When she left the *Toronto Star* in July 1984 Mallet couldn't resist a parting swipe at Hirsch, telling her readers, "I want to have fun. I want to complain that there is a conspiracy against me because I was born in England, not Hungary.") What seems clear is that there was a clash of aesthetic at work. The view that Hirsch was simply the wrong type of person to be leading Stratford was most tren-chantly expressed by Keith Garebian in a 1986 article later re-edited and published under the title "John Hirsch's Bad Taste." Garebian's critical ideals were clear: he proudly accepted the label of "elitist," expressing his preference for "playwrights such as Shakespeare, Shaw, Williams, Coward, Wilde, Chekhov, Orton and Stoppard; for directors such as Robin Phillips, Christopher Newton and Derek Goldby; and for performers such as William Hutt, Heath Lamberts, Maggie Smith and Brian Bedford." Summing up Hirsch's work at Stratford, he concluded, "Unevenness is not necessarily a fatal trait in itself, but when it is combined with gross tonal flaws and textual distortions, it produces damnable subsidized rubbish." As an example, Garebian cited Hirsch's *As You Like It* as a "perverse mutation of pastoral – a sort of Shakespeare meets the Sick Soul of East Europe," and argued that Hirsch was perverse in his reading of the play in the light of twentieth century barbarity: "What was Hirsch thinking of? The Tsars? Pogroms? Nazis?"

In fact, that *was* what Hirsch was thinking of as he interpreted the centuries-old text in the light of his own experience. That experience had been dealt a strong reminder in 1983 with the release of *None Is Too Many: Canada and the Jews of Europe 1933-1948*. The book, by historians Irving Abella and Harold Troper, uncovered the mix of general xenophobia and outright anti-Semitism behind the Canadian government's systematic exclusion of Jews as immigrants or refugees after Hitler's rise to power. Hirsch made no bones about infusing his productions with whatever interested him at any given moment and of the historical development of plays as new directors and theorists analyzed and produced them. "In the nineteenth century," he told an interviewer, "*As You Like It* might have been filled with rabbits and cuckoos and Beerbohm Trees [stylized, expressive acting]. That's how they saw the play. But I live in a different time.... I work out of my guts, and I work out of my own past and I see what I see. And that's why I love to do those plays."

Hirsch's spikey, political, visually over-the-top productions were never likely to fit well at Stratford. Keith Garebian accurately represented the prevailing aesthetic. As an institution Stratford has generally preferred its classics to be served up elegantly, with wit and understatement, as they might have been done in England – or by Robin Phillips. Except, of course, that is not "how plays are done in England"; British theatre is much more diverse than that, as are its theatre critics. Garebian's acid judgement of Hirsch's *Midsummer Night's Dream* ("Hirsch's literal minded extravagances put the production squarely into a baroque tradition of sensuality, rather than into a more delicate, subtle world of fancy's images") sits uncomfortably with the judgements of two established British critics who came to visit that year. Michael Billington didn't rave about the production but neither was he outraged or shocked by it: "John Hirsch's production of the *Dream* was pleasurable without being transcendental." For his part Roger Warren thought it "a production of stunning impact."

Writing in *Toronto Life* in 1989 Martin Knelman had a different explanation:

> Hirsch came out of a tradition in which the theatre was a passionate instrument for idea-mongering, social change, political debate.... In European countries, including Hungary,

Jewish artists and audiences played a central role in developing that kind of theatre – and they were a formidable influence
in creating American culture, both high and low. You can
see it in the rhythms of Broadway theatre, Holly-wood
movies, and even American television. It isn't possible to
separate what's Jewish from what isn't Jewish; it's all part
of the fabric.

Knelman was not alone in arguing that, although theatre in Britain
had moved on since the 1960s, Stratford in the 1980s remained at heart
a colonial institution with a preference for anyone-for-tennis-style
theatre. "Hirsch," he concluded, "was a bull in Stratford's china shop."

The 1984 season again produced a loss, with a shortfall of $740,000
in box office revenue. The thirteen plays and four concerts had been
budgeted for attendance of seventy-three per cent, but the total was
only seventy. The accumulated deficit had now risen to $3.3 million.

By this time Hirsch had announced he would be leaving after
the 1985 season, when his contract concluded, and the Festival once
again set up a search committee to look for a new artistic director.
Like Michael Langham and Robin Phillips before him, Hirsch
approached the end of his tenure convinced that the job was too big
for one person. What was needed, he told an interviewer, was an
association of top directors, citing the structures at the National
Theatre or RSC in Britain. (This is arguable as both of those institutions have tended to function best under a single leader.) He
believed the talent would have to be found outside Canada since
the country still didn't have directors with the mix of intellect and
experience who could take on the challenges of the Festival stage.

In this respect Hirsch had done no better than Phillips or Gascon
before him in "growing" Canadian directors. All had hired Canadians
to work as assistant directors on individual productions, but few of
these had graduated to the Festival Stage let alone to the artistic
directorship. In a thoughtful article about the problem Ray Conlogue
took Hirsch to task for his "reluctance to give a trainee director The

Big Chance." Hirsch countered that the RSC sometimes employed assistant directors for as many as six years before they got a crack at their own production.

In any case, one of the strongest contenders to replace Hirsch was already at Stratford that season. John Neville played Shylock in *The Merchant of Venice* and lent his considerable comic talent to the Young Company in *Love's Labour's Lost* as the grandee Don Armado (the production was a memorable one by Michael Langham, and did very well at the box office). A Canadian resident since 1972 Neville had a formidable track record as an actor and as a prudent manager of theatres, having served as artistic director at Edmonton's Citadel Theatre and the Neptune Theatre in Halifax.

Although Hirsch had brought Neville to Stratford in the first place, the two had never been comfortable with each other and the relationship got no better in the following months. When the search committee produced a shortlist that included John Neville, Hirsch instead backed John Caird, who though born in Canada had made his career in Britain; in the first half of the 1980s, Caird co-directed a number of blockbuster productions at the Royal Shakespeare Festival, including *Nicholas Nickleby*. In the end, John Neville got the job. This meant Hirsch would have to spend his final year at Stratford rubbing shoulders with someone he didn't like. In a story that is strangely reminiscent of Robin Phillips' early encounter with him, Hirsch told a friend that he'd tried to make overtures to Neville, inviting him over for a meal. "I made a nice dinner and a plum cake," Hirsch complained, "and John was just nasty – he left before the end of dinner!" Several interviewees for this book reported that when someone said in John Neville's hearing, "John Hirsch is his own worst enemy," Neville replied, "Not while I'm alive."

Once again, the Winnipeg connection proved its value to Hirsch when Peter Herrndorf was elected chairman of the Board in November. Herrndorf set himself several major objectives. The first was to finish Hirsch's tenure with an operating surplus (the deficit, at a record $3.4 million, was a bigger problem that would have to be dealt with later). The second was to ensure a smooth transition between Hirsch and Neville. Herrndorf recalls, "I spent most of my year as chair negotiating as peaceful a co-existence as you could muster between John Hirsch, who by that time had gotten pretty unhappy about the way it had all ended, and Neville, who was pretty eager to put an end to the Hirsch regime and begin the Neville regime." A third objective, reported in the minutes of an executive committee meeting in January 1985, was to "re-establish credibility with the public" and to attempt to reverse the fall in audience figures.

Herrndorf's determination to end the 1985 season with a surplus meant he would have to ride herd on the finances in a way no Board president before or since has ever done. Effectively becoming the Festival's CEO he held regular meetings with senior staff every Saturday, alternating between Stratford and the offices of *Toronto Life* where he was still the publisher.

It was in effect a managerial *coup d'état*. Herrndorf recalls having a heart-to-heart talk with Hirsch at that point, telling him that he could no longer be "his" Board member and that there might be times in the coming months when the two would disagree. There were indeed such times, though their friendship survived them. Herrndorf did not interfere with Hirsch's choice of plays or directors, but nonetheless clipped his wings by significantly scaling back the next season from thirteen to nine productions.

On the plus side for Hirsch, two of those productions would be directed by first-rank directors he admired. Michael Bogdanov, then an associate director at the National Theatre in Britain, would direct *Measure for Measure*, while the versatile Ronald Eyre, known for television and opera productions as well as the stage, would direct Gogol's *The Government Inspector* at the Avon in a new translation by Michal Schonberg. There would of course be a new Gilbert and Sullivan, *The Pirates of Penzance*. Hirsch himself would direct *King Lear* with Douglas Campbell in the title role, and another Tennessee Williams, *The Glass Menagerie*.

The Board hesitated for some time over Hirsch's proposal that the Festival take *Lear* and *Twelfth Night* on tour to several American cities after the regular season was over. Hirsch's main argument was that the company needed to raise its profile in the United States, where ticket sales – always important to Stratford – had been falling over the previous four years. When the Board finally approved the project the rumour mill inevitably – and probably with some reason – ascribed the tour to Hirsch's concern about employment after Stratford, calling it "John Hirsch's audition tour."

There was also the problem of what to do for John Neville during Hirsch's last season. An arrangement was worked out: Neville would take charge of the Young Company in 1985, giving him the chance to lay some groundwork for when he did eventually take over, while maintaining some distance from Hirsch.

The cast assembled for Hirsch's last Shakespeare play at Stratford was a particularly appropriate one for the occasion. It included some of the young people Hirsch had brought along in the Young Company like Colm Feore (Oswald) and Seana McKenna (Cordelia). A different generation was represented by James Blendick (Kent), whom Hirsch had "discovered" singing in a Winnipeg nightclub in 1962 and who had been in several Hirsch productions at Stratford in the late 1960s and in New York in the 1970s. The longest association was with Douglas Campbell in the title role. An original member of the Stratford company, Campbell had been a friend and supporter of Hirsch's since the early days of the MTC and had acted in Hirsch's first Stratford production, *The Cherry Orchard*. Campbell's elder son Benedict was also in the cast as Edmund.

Hirsch saw a continuity (thematic, if not chronological) between Lear and Prospero, the protagonist in his first Stratford production as artistic director. For Hirsch, Prospero was a ruler who learns about the nature of power in middle age and has a chance to put into effect what he learns, while Lear was someone who at the age of eighty admits, "O, I have ta'en too little care of this" (Act 3, Scene IV) and lives to see his country devastated by the effects of his misrule. But Hirsch was also working out something both personal and political. In *King Lear*'s violence and cruelty Hirsch saw echoes of what had happened to his family and what he had personally witnessed in the 1940s. He told an interviewer later that year, "I felt supersensitive and fragile when I began directing King Lear because the play evoked my childhood memories of the Holocaust and because I was directing in the middle of the Keegstra, Zundel and Mengele affairs.[2] So the play became a cathartic experience for me."

Hirsch told the same interviewer that he was upset when some colleagues at Stratford "thought it funny to tell me some so-called Jewish jokes." It was, he said, the first time he had ever experienced anti-Semitism among theatre folk in Canada.

Despite all the connections between the cast and director, the rehearsal process did not go smoothly. Brian Rintoul, who was back for his second season as Hirsch's assistant, describes a clash between Hirsch and Benedict Campbell over an idea Hirsch had introduced to the play. In the scene where Gloucester is blinded Hirsch had added a young boy in the scene as an observer. (The image was reminiscent of the prologue to Hirsch's *As You Like It* two years earlier). Rintoul remembers:

> John was taking a lot of time with the young boy – which was John's version of the play – and the time he was taking with him was time he wasn't taking with people who were doing the play Shakespeare actually wrote. Finally Ben snapped and said a lot of things that perhaps would have been better left unsaid and stormed out. I can still see it: John had just said something to this kid, and his hand was in the air, and when Ben snapped John didn't drop that pose, his eyes just moved to Ben. And he stayed there after Ben stormed off, thinking "What can I do?" and his only response was "Who's his understudy?" Of course, Ben went for a walk along the river and came back, and life went on.

There was a much bigger problem brewing between Hirsch and his *Lear*. Many years later Douglas Campbell said that the friendship between the two was cooling by this time. In his opinion Stratford had changed Hirsch for the worse. The love and passion for theatre

Douglas Campbell as King Lear and Nicholas Pennell as
The Fool in *King Lear*, summer 1985.
*Photo by David Cooper, courtesy of the Stratford Shakespeare
Festival Archives*

was still there, but "power did not sit well with Hirsch. He became what he didn't want to be....So much anger to get rid of, so many chips on his shoulder." The personal tension was amplified by artistic differences. The way Rintoul remembers it, Hirsch wanted a reflective Lear to emerge over the course of the play and for much of the rehearsal process was able to get what he wanted from Campbell. But as the opening approached Campbell lost confidence in Hirsch's interpretation and went back to the booming, actorly style that had served him so well on the Festival Stage for so many years. The two quarrelled – different witnesses swear that one or the other man was actually looking for a fight at that point, and perhaps they both were – and the show the audience eventually saw when it opened on May 26, 1985, was noticeably unbalanced between an overwhelming Lear and a lower-key supporting cast. Nonetheless, Seana McKenna, who played Cordelia, remembers the production as extraordinary, with many line readings that remain in her mind over two decades later. "Some people might have said, 'Oh, it's too big, this *Lear*, it's bombastic.' It was passionate. When that Lear's heart cracked, you knew that it would resound through the universe."

Hirsch's final season did not still the criticisms of his leadership and it was frustrating on a personal level. Other productions were better received than his *Lear* and *Glass Menagerie*, although the touring *Lear* later in the year got a good reception in the United States (the *Los Angeles Times* judged that "In the big things and the small things, this is a major Lear.") David Giles' production of *Twelfth Night* was solid, reassuringly traditional Shakespeare, with good performances from a strong ensemble cast, while Ronald Eyre's *The Government Inspector* got excellent reviews and houses. Hirsch had hoped that Michael Bogdanov's *Measure for Measure* would inject some edgy excitement into the season and it certainly had the effect of dividing the critics. Reviewers either loved or hated its half-hour-long cabaret-style prologue, traffic and helicopter sounds, strobe lights and armed police ranging up and down the Festival Theatre aisles.

The final figures for the season showed that attendance had fallen a further five per cent from the previous year to sixty-five per cent. That would have spelled a publicly disastrous end to Hirsch's tenure as artistic director but for the cost-cutting efforts Peter Herrndorf had put in place and the intervention of an important figure from Hirsch's Winnipeg past. Unbeknownst to Hirsch Herrndorf had been talking with Kathleen Richardson, who had made the Manitoba Theatre Centre possible with her anonymous purchase of the Dominion Theatre in the late 1950s. Herrndorf recalls: "We came to an understanding that up to a certain amount Kathleen would play the role of 'angel' so that we could complete the fiscal year with a small surplus. It was important symbolically that, even if the surplus was a dollar, there was a signal that the ship had been righted somehow. So, in the thirty-six hours before the end of the fiscal year, I told Kathleen how much we needed and she said okay and wrote a cheque." The Board was able to declare a surplus of $24,901.

Compared to the mess of 1980-81 the changeover from Hirsch to John Neville went relatively smoothly. There was a bit of sniping-by-interview afterwards, mostly from Hirsch, but Neville held the media high ground much as Hirsch had in 1981 as the man who was going to rescue the Festival. Neville was able to announce a reconciliation with the Festival's past, with Martha Henry and William Hutt returning to the Stratford stage and Robin Phillips directing a play in the coming season. In sharp contrast to the "safe" programming of the past two years, Neville would build his first season around three of Shakespeare's less-performed romances – *Cymbeline, Pericles,* and *The Winter's Tale* – and the historical play *Henry VIII.* (As it would turn out Neville, too, would have to trim his artistic sails in subsequent seasons.) With his English accent and courtly manners Neville seemed a better fit than his predecessor with the town of Stratford.

As with any regime change there was a certain amount of "which side are you on" politics. One actor describes it as being like the child of a bad divorce: people felt they had to position themselves with the new artistic director or suffer the consequences of being too much identified with the outgoing one. Hirsch knew about this and it troubled him, but there was nothing he could do about it. Once his last season was underway he was increasingly "out of the loop" and irrelevant. He might have expected it, but it still hurt. He spent much of the time during his final weeks packing up material for his archives.

Hirsch left Stratford in October. It was a quiet leave-taking without any fanfare. Susan Lemenchick, who had been working as his secretary for a year and half remembers the last time she saw him. She was several months pregnant at the time with her first child. "John stopped at my desk," she remembers, "and placed on it a lovely ceramic unicorn music box wrapped in Kleenex. All he said was, 'For the baby.' Then he smiled at me and departed. I did not know it was his last day in the office. I'll never forget that moment or the kindness in his eyes."

Ten

Our Revels Now Are Ended

ONE AFTERNOON IN LATE 1986 Hirsch and Andras Hamori were walking near 42nd Street in New York. Hamori by this time had left Hudson Drive far behind him and was now an established film and television producer, working with Robert Lantos in Alliance Entertainment. He and Hirsch remained close and met whenever and wherever their schedules permitted.

As they strolled down the street they stopped by a street vendor who was selling hats. Hirsch tried several on, negotiated the price down to eighteen dollars and chose one that he attempted to pay for with a twenty-dollar bill. As Hamori remembers it, "The vendor said he didn't have change and Hirsch said he wasn't falling for that old trick – the guy should go and get the necessary change and Hirsch would mind the hats while he did so. After a little while a bespectacled gentleman stopped by the stand and said, with a worried look on his face, 'John, are you okay?' John said, 'Hi Arthur, want to buy a hat?'" It was Arthur Miller, whom Hirsch had known since his time at Lincoln Center. Hamori smiles as he remembers Hirsch starting to explain this unexplainable situation. "Arthur had this half-sorry, half-understanding smile as if he was saying: 'Sure, sure....'"

Miller's concern for an unemployed colleague was unnecessary. The telephone had not exactly been ringing off the hook with offers of work, but Hirsch could afford to take it easy for a while. He was in very good financial shape; a summary by his investment advisor in February 1986 shows that Hirsch had almost a million dollars in various bonds and investments. Sybil Shack's sisterly lessons about prudent investment all those years ago in Winnipeg had paid off handsomely. He could afford to take time off and have a "sabbatical" after five years of heavy pressure.

As had happened when he left the CBC in 1978, Hirsch initially got more attention in the United States than in Canada. The month after he left Stratford the City of Chicago – an important market for the Stratford Festival – made him an honorary citizen. He told an interviewer: "I love Canada; it's a beautiful country, a country of great decency and civic virtues, but I have to get out periodically to escape a love of failure, a kind of negativism I find there." He remained critical of the Reagan government, but lauded the "tremendous sense of energy" in the United States and its "on-going belief in potential and a strong sense that things can and will happen."

He spent some time reflecting on his experience at Stratford and concluded that during the five years of running the largest theatre in Canada he had changed, "from my original shape into a kind of *Tempest* monster." Only now, he felt, could he acknowledge how much he had hated being the head of an Establishment Theatre. For an artist who was subversive by nature ("as are most artists," he mused) running a conservative institution and taking on the role of administrator was a recipe for stress and conflict. "It was like putting dynamite under the very thing you're trying to maintain.... Fire and ice: mutual annihilation."

Hirsch's first jobs after Stratford were as a teacher rather than as a director. Ming Cho Lee had been on the faculty of the Yale School of Drama since 1969 and he arranged for Hirsch to come to the school as a guest lecturer starting in the spring of 1986. The two worked out a course for both directing and design students in which they emphasized collaboration in the director-designer relationship by bringing together teams of two from each stream to work together during the seminar. Hirsch asked each student to bring a box containing things they wanted to see, feel, or touch in the play, which they would present to their working partner as well as to the rest of the class.

Hirsch explained the exercise both in terms of ritual and as a practical point of departure:

Directors working with designers and vice-versa, go through an initial period of courting, which means you are dancing around each other. And if you are bearing gifts when you are dancing and showing off your feathers, you are titillating the person who will enter into this marriage with you. So you spread your tail, you do all sorts of funny noises etc., and out of this comes a kind of collaborative thing, but you've got to have things that you show off. In nature, birds bring little pebbles and they put it in front of the male or vice-versa, and that's what I want you all to do. Just begin the mating dance and bring gifts.

He also asked the students to create a "portrait gallery" when they began working on the project in order to visualize the characters in the play. Lee still uses this approach with his first-year design class. The first seminar went down very well with students and faculty and Yale asked Hirsch back the following year.

The Yale job led to Hirsch's appointment later that year as a visiting professor in the Drama Department of the University of Cali-fornia, San Diego, and at the Meadows School of the Arts at Southern Methodist University in Dallas. He always hoped to return to the faculty of the National Theatre School, but despite some discussions with Paul Thompson, who became the School's director in 1987, it never worked out.

As well as a new stage in his career as a theatre educator 1986 saw Hirsch enter the movies as an actor in a motion picture called *Sword of Gideon*, with a cast that included Michael York and Rod Steiger. The movie was based on George Jonas' book about the aftermath of the massacre of Israeli athletes at the 1972 Olympics and was produced by Hirsch's friend Robert Lantos for CTV and Home Box Office (it was later remade by Steven Spielberg under the title of *Munich*). Hirsch played a retired Mossad agent whose son is assigned to avenge the massacre. Looking at the film today the casting seems perfect. Hirsch is believable and compelling as an embittered, cynical man who feels he has been used by his old employer and fears the same will happen to his son. It was a small

A FIERY SOUL

part that Hirsch enjoyed playing, not least because his scenes were shot on location in Israel.

He took Bryan along to Israel for the filming and enjoyed spending time with Robert Lantos and other people in the film world. Over the next few years Hirsch stayed close to that world and got involved in several projects as potential writer or director, though none got a green light while he was well enough to pursue them.

But for the most part 1986 was a quiet year for Hirsch. The relationship with Bryan had settled into an affectionate routine. The passion was gone, but the happy home life they had built together at Hudson Drive remained solid, though Hirsch was still prone to blow up at Bryan occasionally. Magda Zalán, the Hungarian journalist who had known them since the mid-1970s, remembers, "John would yell in Hungarian when he was upset and Bryan would yell back with the Hungarian he knew – all cooking words: 'Goulash! Palancinki! Paprikash!' Which would make John laugh and then the argument would be over." Bryan's boyfriend Tony was now living in the downstairs suite, mostly staying out of Hirsch's way when he was in town and migrating upstairs to Bryan's bedroom when he wasn't. Hirsch could see the advantages of the arrangement: when he and Bryan were both away there was always someone in the house to feed the cats and water the plants.

He and Bryan went again at the end of the year to the Dominican Republic, and as became their practice invited friends to join them. This year the Hungarian critic Peter Molnar Gal, a friend of Hirsch's since his CBC days, came for the Christmas holidays. On New Year's Eve the group ventured out to the beach where there was a fiesta going on. "Prostitutes, petty thieves, sailors and all sorts of folks gathered and danced on the concrete," Molnar Gal recalls. "With his height, Hirsch stood out quite a bit in this environment and several girls asked him to dance. One rather feisty girl grabbed him around the waist and he danced with her, with a lot of fire. Soon everyone stopped around them, applauding Hirsch and his partner."

At the same time Molnar Gal was concerned by Hirsch's sexual activities. "I watched the way he lived his life on overdrive, how he

313

John Hirsch and Bryan Trottier's Christmas card from
the Dominican Republic, 1986.

brought back young men to his cabin on the beach indiscriminately
and without protection." AIDS was by now gaining destructive speed
among gay men, with a growing toll of death and illness among
those working in the theatre and other creative fields. The death of
the movie star, Rock Hudson, in October 1985 after "coming out"
about his homosexuality and his AIDS diagnosis a few months earlier
had raised awareness about the disease. Gay activists were in the
forefront of prevention programs and groups like the AIDS Committee
of Toronto and AIDS Vancouver had gained a high profile in Canada.

The holiday over, Hirsch resumed his teaching duties, first
spending a month at Yale and then going down to Dallas for his
second stint at Southern Methodist University (SMU). The SMU
Drama Department was very pleased with Hirsch, not least because
of the people he brought with him into the program. On his recommendation they had hired British director Ronald Eyre, who proved
an extremely popular teacher (the two had become friends when
Hirsch brought Eyre to Stratford to direct *The Government Inspector*
in 1985). Hirsch also brought Ming Cho Lee down from Yale for a
short seminar, introducing the school to another world-class theatre
professional, and again one that the students liked very much.

As for Hirsch, the reviews from students at SMU were mixed.
Aaron Posner was a graduate student in the theatre program at the
time and had been assigned as assistant to the visiting professor. He
remembers his first impression of Hirsch in class:

They were doing a read-through in a big circle and as they would read John would stop and comment and harangue. And then they would read a little bit more and he would make another comment. And within five minutes I was enthralled – this is fascinating, this is brilliant! And I remember sitting there in the circle thinking, how can I get him to know that I'm smart and *I get it* and I understand what he's saying?

Fortunately Hirsch quickly decided he liked Posner and could work with him. Posner speculates that it may have been partly a kinship based on their being two Jews in a very Gentile environment.

As Hirsch's assistant Posner took on the role of loyal adjutant that others had played so often in Hirsch's past. And Hirsch needed an adjutant because many of the students disliked Hirsch's temper and demanding manner. The project this term was A *Midsummer Night's Dream*, and Posner remembers Hirsch laying out his credo for the type of acting he wanted. "I've directed *Midsummer Night's Dream* four times," Hirsch told them.

I know the play backwards and forwards. If you get up and do a generic Lysander or a generic Hermia or a generic Oberon you have absolutely no way of interesting me for a moment. But if you will, with courage and generosity and abandon and fullness, tell the truth about your life, about what you bring to Lysander, what you bring to Hermia, what only you can bring to Puck, then I am engaged and enthralled – I'm yours.

Posner adds, "And HE SAID LIKE THIS! IT MUST BE *YOURS*! IT MUST BE WHAT YOU HAVE TO OFFER!'" Today Posner credits Hirsch as one of the most important influences in his career as a director, which began the following year when he established the Arden Theatre Company in Philadelphia.

When Hirsch's teaching term ended the School offered Hirsch a new contract not only to teach in 1987-88 but to evaluate the drama program, which was contemplating deep organizational change. His duties also included creating a new mission statement for the school and advising on the recruitment of new staff. To help him with the report Hirsch hired a recent graduate of the School, David Bassuk, who was working at Lincoln Center in New York. Bassuk spent three days in Toronto with Hirsch, which he remembers as "three days that changed my life." Together they produced a visionary document based on Hirsch's thoughts about the social and spiritual value of theatre and its responsibilities to its local community. It echoed the ideas of Roger Planchon that had so influenced Hirsch when he was setting up the Manitoba Theatre Centre in the late 1950s and also reflected Hirsch's identification with an activist strand of Jewish thought (Bassuk's working notes include Hirsch's words: "For a Jew, there is a basic premise that everything that exists is not good enough. It can be made better"). As it turned out the report went far beyond what the university was expecting and nothing more was heard of it. But working with Hirsch had inspired Bassuk: when he finished the report and went back to New York he had decided to leave Lincoln Center and try to find some way of applying some of what he had learned from Hirsch. They stayed in touch and in few months they would work together again.

By this time Hirsch had two contracts in hand to direct plays, one a revival in Toronto and the other a new play in Atlanta. The revival was George Abbott and John Cecil Holm's comedy *Three Men on a Horse*, a Broadway hit that had played at Toronto's Royal Alexandra Theatre in May 1935. Hirsch was going to direct it in the same theatre, now owned by the Mirvishes. The play involves horse racing, bookies and an innocent suburbanite who discovers he has an amazing ability to pick winners. Hirsch had an actor in mind for the lead, having just seen Stephen Ouimette in the highly successful *B-Movie, The Play* at Toronto Workshop Productions. Ouimette remembers being called out of the blue by Hirsch, who asked what he was doing next Saturday morning. "I told him I usually watched the *Pee-wee Herman Show* and Hirsch said, 'Why don't you come over and we'll watch it together? And I have something to ask you.' So I went over on Saturday morning and we laughed our heads off and he asked me to do *Three Men on a Horse*.'"

With *Three Men on a Horse*, which opened on September 4, Hirsch was back in thematic territory he had always loved, playing with the mythology of urban America and the theatrical devices of vaudeville. Steven Ouimette had heard all about Hirsch's ferocious reputation but found him much gentler and less troubled than he'd expected. "When he was just freelancing, maybe he was a happier person," Ouimette speculates. "I remember seeing him on stage during the rehearsals of *Three Men*. He was just playing with my hat, doing crazy things to it, not showing me but I think inspiring me to think creatively about the props in the show, or things I could do, giving me freedom to explore. And I just jumped on that, I took every opportunity to go on the set when people weren't working and try and plan crazy kind of physical comedy bits."

Hirsch had his own real-life version of urban farce shortly before rehearsals began in June 1987, when he almost got arrested at a Shoppers Drug Mart in Toronto. He had been out to dinner at a Hungarian restaurant with his friend Gail Singer and the Winnipeg artist Esther Warkov, and stopped in at the store to pick up a prescription. Singer got into an argument with the store staff over a sale item – four rolls of two-ply toilet paper advertised in the storefront window for ninety-nine cents, but which turned out to be offered at that price if a box of facial tissue were purchased at the same price. Voices were raised as Singer accused the store of false advertising. Hirsch added to the situation by taking out a felt pen and writing THIS IS A LIE next to the offending sign, at which point a security guard appeared and bundled Hirsch into a back room with Singer and Warkov in tow. Police arrived but declined to lay charges. Hirsch and Co. were banned from the store and the story gained a bit of notoriety when Martin Knelman reported it in the magazine *Toronto Life*.

Three Men on a Horse got excellent reviews from the Toronto papers. Hirsch followed up two months later with another success in Atlanta at the Alliance Theater Company. The production was a stage version of Studs Terkel's bestselling book *American Dreams: Lost and Found*, which Hirsch had workshopped with Terkel at the Seattle Rep in 1981. Working from the stories Terkel had gathered while talking to people across the country about their definition of the American dream, Hirsch put together a script in which ten actors played nineteen characters. These included a former beauty queen, a coal miner's daughter, broadcasting magnate Ted Turner, a Daughter of the American Revolution, and a Klan member. The settings ranged from sharecropper farms and Indian reservations to wartime detention camps for Japanese-Americans and the pre-dominantly African-American neighbourhood of Bedford-Stuyvesant in Brooklyn.

In his initial notes to the cast Hirsch described the play as "diagnostic theatre." Its purpose was to say to audiences, "Let's get together for two and a half hours and I'd like to tell you how the world looks to me. This is what we are today, an unequal society. Do something to make it better."

The Theatre's artistic director, Robert J. Farley, was surprised when Hirsch asked him to arrange a conference call with Studs Terkel at the *Chicago Tribune*, where the celebrated author still worked. "The switchboard put us straight through and Terkel picked up his phone immediately," recalls Farley. Hirsch wanted to add some characters who weren't in the book, notably Ted Turner, because he was a prominent figure in Atlanta. "Terkel and Hirsch talked about it and Terkel told him to go ahead," says Farley.

The production, mounted in the company's Studio Theatre in November 1987, came together in what Hirsch regarded as an ideal melding of design, script and cast. Designer Michael Stauffer's set extended out into the lobby, so that before taking their seats the audience first passed through a collection of American cultural icons: flags and computer printouts, cans of Coca-Cola, a bank of television screens and the Statue of Liberty with a vacuum cleaner hose over her shoulder. Before the play started the actors mingled with the audience as if they were part of it and the separation of spectators and players only began when the production's musical director and pianist, Stan Keen, started in with "America the Beautiful."

The reviews were enthusiastic though the production's social criticism seems to have gone over some of the local critics' heads. Hirsch left Atlanta pleased with both the production and the way he he had been treated as a visiting director. The feeling was reciprocated as artistic director Farley wrote to him on opening night, "The work you and this acting company have done so strongly reaffirms my commitment to the theatre, and reminds me that every once in a while it truly is worth all the effort we pour into this crazy business."

Later that month Hirsch and Bryan accompanied Sybil Shack to an awards ceremony at the Ontario Institute for Studies in Education. Now seventy-six years old and long retired as a high school principal, Hirsch's sister was as busy as ever in Winnipeg as a writer on education and as a human-rights activist. The Institute had made her a Fellow in recognition of her contribution to education in Canada, particularly in teachers' rights and the education of girls.

The Winnipeg connection remained a strong one. Ma Shack was now in her mid-nineties, but still vigorous, baking bread each day. Hirsch continued to call her each Sunday and to visit whenever he could. On those visits to Winnipeg Hirsch sometimes had a quiet chat with Ogden Turner who had been on the original Manitoba Theatre Company Board in 1958 and was still a leading member. The MTC's fortunes had risen and fallen over the years, having had a succession of artistic directors. Steven Schipper, the young director whom Hirsch had brought to Stratford in 1982, met with Hirsch at the Westin Hotel during one of these visits. Schipper had just been hired as an associate director at the MTC and was surprised when Hirsch told him he should be preparing himself to become its artistic director. Although Schipper was eager to work there he assumed that his career path would eventually take him back to Central Canada. But Hirsch knew what he was talking about and two years later the Board hired Schipper for the top job, and he became the MTC's longest-serving artistic director.

Shortly after Sybil's visit Hirsch received an emergency call from New York, where the producers of a new musical were in trouble. Two and a half million had been invested in a musical version of Chaim Potok's novel *The Chosen*, which had also been a successful film. But the production had serious problems: the first director had jumped ship and been replaced by one of the producers; one of

Hirsch with his adoptive sister Sybil Shack, 1987.
University of Manitoba Archives

the leads had to be replaced; the previews had been so bad that the opening had to be postponed ... the list went on. The producers thought the director needed support from a consultant, one with both experience in musicals and some understanding of the show's religious themes. Hirsch accepted the job and flew to New York, hiring David Bassuk as his assistant. In mid-December Hirsch wrote a note to himself: "Just 15 days [to go]. Do your best and don't get so involved that it could tear your heart out. But it is Chaim Potok. A lovely book. Warm and worth a lot. How [can] the present dog's breakfast be sorted out? *Wer weiss?* [Yiddish for 'Who knows?'] Just for the money?" He told himself not to worry about it and concentrate on the work. Over the next two weeks he, Bassuk and Potok desperately re-wrote scenes in the morning and worked with the cast in the afternoon.

The Chosen is about two Jewish boys, the sons of rabbis from very different streams of Judaism, who become unlikely friends in 1940s New York. The story reflects many themes, including dissension among American Jewish communities over the establishment of the state of Israel. Despite his worries about the production Hirsch loved working with Potok, who as well as being a bestselling author had a Ph.D in philosophy and was actually an ordained rabbi. After rehearsals they kept talking, sometimes about literature and politics but most often about the issues brought up in the play.

But as Hirsch wrote to a friend in February 1988, "despite my ministration, the patient died." *The Chosen* got terrible reviews and closed after only eight performances. (A decade later Aaron Posner would work with Potok on a new stage version of *The Chosen*, which has been performed frequently since it opened in 1999.)

Hirsch had a busy year to look forward to. He would spend much of the first half teaching at Yale and Dallas, then in early summer start rehearsals for *Coriolanus* at the Old Globe Theater in San Diego. August would see him back in Toronto to direct a new play by the B.C.-based playwright Frank Moher, and in the fall he would again go to Yale for the second seminar that year. Finally he would direct Ben Jonson's *The Alchemist* in November at the Yale Repertory Theater in New Haven.

Hirsch always centred his seminars on a specific play and his March seminar at Yale was about *The Dybbuk*. Three afternoon-long sessions were taped and transcribed by the theatre scholar Elizabeth Osborn, leaving a unique documentation of Hirsch's eclectic teaching approach. Hirsch goes deep into the play's historical context and its relationship to the Kabbalah, discusses aspects of his own production of the play and relates it to both his personal history and the political history of the twentieth century. He tells folktales from Eastern Europe, but also pulls in other art forms, from *The Tempest* (as an example of dealing with magic on stage) to *The Cabinet of Dr. Caligari* (as an example of the visual style in which the first productions of *The Dybbuk* were framed in 1920s Moscow).

As always he talked about his personal history – Siófok, the deaths of his family members in the Holocaust, his coming to North America – and his current political and social concerns. He repeated his conviction that the classics were not "museum pieces" to be simply re-clothed in this or that period costume. The *ideas* were the thing and ideas were nothing if they could not be applied to reality. He closed by asking his students

> to focus your attention on theatre as a forum for ideas, as a place where essential human issues are discussed in a theatrical way, in an entertaining way, in a gripping and involving way. Where both your intellect and your emotions are touched in a way that will make you feel and think....So the whole *business* of the theatre, with all the fame-fortune-glamour thing, will be balanced with something – to use a nineteenth century word – *nobler*.

He showed what he meant two months later when rehearsals began in San Diego for *Coriolanus*. It was his first time directing this – one of Shakespeare's least popular but most political plays. Hirsch intended to direct the play as a media-age spectacle, moving Shakespeare's seventeenth-century play – itself an interpretation of a story from the fifth century B.C. – to America in 1988. He was fully aware that the immediacy of the setting meant that his production would quickly date itself, but so what? In his notes to the cast he said, "There is a live camera on the stage because I want to make clear to the audience that what they see on the stage is what they see every day on their screens. I want to bring the production as close to their experience as possible."

Hirsch acted as his own dramaturge, pruning within scenes to emphasize the political aspects of the play. His concept was that Coriolanus, the soldier-hero of Rome's war with the neighbouring Volscians, had much in common with Oliver North, the former Marine lieutenant colonel charged with selling arms to Iran and channelling the funds to the Contras in Nicaragua. North had been a prominent witness in the televised Congressional hearings on "Contragate" in 1987, and had actually been indicted the month before Hirsch started rehearsal. He would later be convicted on several charges, including lying to Congress, though these convictions were later reversed on appeal. Hirsch was fascinated by the ambiguity of American attitudes towards North. Although he had lied to Congress, broken the law and apparently kept his activities from the President, North was an admired patriot to many, a Rambo-like figure who kicked foreign ass in covert operations.

When *Coriolanus* opened at the Old Globe in August the audience found itself facing two huge banks of television monitors flipping between scenes of modern battle footage, urban squalor, clips from *Wheel of Fortune* and the testimony of Oliver North at Congressional hearings. The production clearly aimed to push buttons with the audience. In Byron Jennings Hirsch had a suitably handsome, crewcut Marine as the hero. The icy, calculated performance of Elizabeth Shepherd as his mother Volumnia was based on Rose Kennedy, and the southern drawl of Dakin Matthews' Roman senator, Menenius, inevitably reminded people of Senator Sam Ervin's chairmanship of the Watergate hearings. The enemy Volscians were portrayed as Latinos, emphasizing their foreignness (at least in the All-American terms of the media) and reminding audiences of the Contra side of the Iran-Contra scandal. In keeping with the Rambo flavour he wanted Hirsch had worked closely with his designer, David Jenkins, to produce spectacular effects like the hero's departure from Rome in a helicopter and – swinging up to the parapets on a crane hook, automatic rifle in hand – blowing open the walls of Rome with grenades.

In some ways the production was an object lesson in how to enrage theatrical traditionalists. The text changes excited considerable comment, as did Hirsch's permitting actors in smaller roles to ad-lib in contemporary English. The critic John Simon found the production "scrupulously executed, lavish and often impressive," but judged it "ruinous to Shakespeare" and complained of a looting soldier yelling an un-Shakespearean "S—! I thought this was silver." And yet the reception from reviewers and audiences was enthusiastic. The *Los Angeles Times* judged, "Hirsch took a sizable chance when he decided to go this far out on a limb – and he won."

The theatre scholar R.B. Parker noted that praise came from both ends of the political spectrum, with some reviewers from the Right seeing it as a salutary warning about what might happen if the U.S. failed to support its military. "From the scholar's point of view," Parker wrote, "the text was vandalized. Yet it was done intelligently, not carelessly, with a particular aim clearly in mind – to focus on the play's politics; and it worked well in production, as even reviewers who lamented the alterations admitted.... Not an interpretation for all seasons, certainly; but one brilliantly calculated for the political climate of Southern California in the summer of 1988."

The play sold well during its six-week run and the Old Globe's artistic director, Jack O'Brien, talked with Hirsch about directing *Pericles* the following year. Hirsch was delighted with *Coriolanus*. As with *American Dreams* in Atlanta he had greatly enjoyed working with a well-funded regional theatre that was willing to take chances. "I think it's my best work so far," he told the *Los Angeles Times*. "I became very bold and creative and pursued my vision to the very end. I guess the older you get, the more courageous you get because you have less time to lose. I'm looking forward to exploring more and more with greater courage – and joy."

He expressed his sense of having no time to lose more than

once during the course of 1988. In a long interview with Robert Enright, editor of the Manitoba-based magazine *Border Crossings,* he said, "The older I grow, the more I realize the incredible beauty of the world and already I'm raging about the fact that I'll be going soon. I haven't really drunk enough and thought enough and loved enough and worked enough and made enough connections. I've wasted a lot of time. So now, when I'm confronted with this incredible world that I live in, instead of diminishing, my hunger for it increases."

It is tempting to read a sense of foreboding in these words. The death toll due to the AIDS epidemic was climbing steeply year on year, and the toll was particularly high in the theatre and other creative professions across North America. In Toronto Bryan remembers going to three funerals in one week, all of them friends or acquaintances who had been diagnosed with AIDS. "It was like having a sniper on the loose," he remembers. "All of a sudden, someone else would be gone. He could have been living a wild life, or he could have been living the most monastic existence imaginable. There didn't seem to be any sense to it."

Several friends and colleagues noticed that Hirsch had developed a cough that was often with him. His friend Gail Singer recalls first noticing it when they attended a play at Stratford shortly after he had been teaching in Texas. She told him to see a doctor, but Hirsch insisted it was just an irritation caused by the dust in Dallas. Doctors were for sick people; he had a life to get on with.

And that life was a full one. He saw everything that the Toronto theatre community produced, went to the movies with Bryan as often as possible and always had several books on the go. He also continued to visit art galleries, buy and sell paintings (and occasionally donate them) and maintain friendships in the art world. The painter Charles Pachter, who had become a friend in the 1970s, remembers that Hirsch always came to his openings and had a lively interest in whatever was new and interesting on the art scene. He recalled Hirsch's fascination with a graphics program that Pachter was experimenting with on his home computer: "He sat in front of the monitor and immediately composed an image, patiently learned the mechanics and vowed he wanted to get one."

Above all he had a busy and varied career to attend to. In September he directed Frank Moher's play *Odd Jobs* at Toronto's Canadian Stage Company and followed it up in November with *The Alchemist* at the Yale Repertory Theater in New Haven. Seana McKenna was in *Odd Jobs* and remembers Hirsch saying that he was looking back at his career and trying to understand the frequent storminess of his work as a director. "He was actually questioning why actors had a problem with him or he had a problem with actors. He didn't understand it. My husband had been his Caliban, and he said, 'Miles was such a wonderful Caliban, what's the problem?' I said, 'Well John, you threw cardboard boxes at him....'"

Hirsch continued his educational work, doing another session at the Yale Drama School and publishing an article on theatre training for *American Theatre* magazine. And more projects were on the way. In October he signed a contract with the producer Michael Frazier to direct a production of *B-Movie, The Play* Off-Broadway by February 1990. He started talking to the Old Globe Theater about casting for *Pericles* and to Robert Lantos about a film project. In early December Lantos sent him a letter telling him, "believe it or not, it now looks like we can get *Eye of the Spider* off the ground in the first half of 1989."

Early December was also the time when CBC Radio started to broadcast a series of four programs hosted by Hirsch on his favourite singer, Ella Fitzgerald. As Hirsch spins favourite records he mixes biographical material about Fitzgerald with his own personal reminiscences, describing certain songs as Proustian madeleines that instantly conjure up specific moments in his life: listening to Ella in 1945 on U.S. Armed Forces Radio in a freezing Budapest apartment; getting her autograph when she played at the Don Carlos Casino near Winnipeg in 1949; bringing her to Stratford as part of the 1983 Festival. He also looked back on 1988, telling listeners, "I had a great year. It was a re-discovery of myself, a year of growth and a return of a touch of frivolity even. It comes from going from job to job, place to place. A footloose and fancy free time, which at my time of life is a gift."

In late December Hirsch and Bryan went south for another vacation in the Dominican Republic. Hirsch by this time had decided that the land he bought there had been a bad investment and he spent part of the time trying to arrange its sale and to find an apartment instead. He also spent some time preparing his next teaching project at Southern Methodist University, which was to be another 1930s Broadway hit, *You Can't Take It with You*. The comedy is about the encounter between two New York families – one conservative and the other full of chaotic, creative dreamers – and Hirsch had always thought it represented much that was hopeful in the country.

As it turned out he never completed the production. When Hirsch first arrived in Dallas in early February 1989, all seemed well. But after a week or so he started to lose energy and focus. Frank Savino was the only professional actor in a cast otherwise made up of students, playing the part of Grandpa Vanderhof. Savino was bewildered by the rapid change in Hirsch: "I lived in the same apartment where the school was putting us up, and I started to go and help him dress in the morning, and drive him in. Some mornings he couldn't even tie his shoes." Worried, Savino called Bryan, who flew down to Dallas and was shocked to find Hirsch too weak to get in and out of the bathtub by himself. Bryan also learned that Hirsch had been to a clinic, which had diagnosed *Mycobacterium avium* complex, one of the most common opportunistic infections associated with AIDS. Completing the teaching project was out of the question. Hirsch was just well enough to travel and he and Bryan quickly boarded a plane for home.

In Toronto Hirsch's friend Michal Schonberg was waiting at the airport to drive Hirsch straight to Mount Sinai Hospital. Hirsch was feverish and dehydrated when he checked in and quickly lost weight, to the extent that when Sybil arrived soon after she described him as "a barely living skeleton." But after a few weeks he stabilized and began to feel stronger. He wrote to the director Ronald Eyre, "An awful lot of people called and visited.... The food was godawful but my friends organized a catering service and once all the tubes were out of every orifice of my body I was able to eat quite well."

His four mafias – gay, Hungarian, Jewish, Winnipeg – were rallying around, with friends and colleagues from Hirsch's various professional and personal circles making the trip to his big, sun-filled private room.

His agent Catherine McCartney came early on. "When I visited him the first time, everyone had to wear green gown and mask and gloves when they went to see him," she recalled. "He had this little board and chalk and he did the bit from the *What's My Line* game show – would you sign in, please. I started to laugh and he said, 'Oh, it's Catherine.' He knew my laugh."

Martin Knelman remembers that it was like a Kaufman and Hart play with Hirsch holding court over a constant stream of visitors. Some of the visits or offerings that arrived were from the Canadian equivalent of royalty. "Barbara Frum sent soup that she made herself and it was treated as holy," Knelman laughs. "It was supposed to be saved for his dinner. And one of the attendants accidentally gave it to him for lunch. Big crisis!" Len and Heather Cariou came up from New York, bringing a small leather-bound *Tempest* as a gift and sharing the latest Broadway gossip.

Other visitors were less famous but had long associations with the patient. Catherine McKeehan had crossed his path several times, first as a high school student volunteering at the Manitoba Theatre Centre and later on as stage manager on *Three Sisters* at Stratford in 1976. She had always been in awe of him, but screwed up her courage and went to the hospital.

Tom and Judith Hendry were there, and Bryan, and a famous American actress – Stephanie Zimbalist, I think. I had to fling myself into the room and he looked over to see what the commotion was. Seeing me, he said in this dreamy voice, pointing, "I've known her since she was fifteen years old." Knock me over with a feather! He was the "god," after all, and somehow he remembered when I first started hanging around MTC. His extended family, I guess.

In April Hirsch was well enough to go home. Hudson Drive had never looked better to him and he took great solace from watching the raccoons and other wildlife coming up into the back garden from the ravine. He and Bryan hired a Hungarian woman who came in three times a week to cook the comforting Central European food he loved so much. He was well enough to have a party to celebrate his fifty-ninth birthday on May 1 – a roast goose feast with his seder gang – and to go out to Tom Hendry's birthday on June 7 ("He reminded me that I was a year older than he was, as he'd done since I met him at university," recalls Hendry). During June and July he worked several days a week with theatre academic Leslie Thomson on a theatre student's guide to *A Midsummer Night's Dream*.

Letters and phone calls continued to arrive and Hirsch spent a great deal of time writing to well-wishers. It was a time of fence-mending. Martha Henry wrote to say, "I've been thinking of you daily. It's been a long time since we've seen each other and I just want you to know that I love you and want you to get well." Henry was by this time artistic director of the Grand Theatre in London, Ontario, and asked if Hirsch might be interested in directing something there when he was better – perhaps *Glengarry Glen Ross*, she suggested? Hirsch replied in an emotional letter, "You know how much I cared and care about you, even though we have not been working together or even talking over these last few years....The invitation warms the cockles of my heart."

Other offers of work were coming in. The Old Globe proposed that he do *Measure for Measure*. Daniel Sullivan, who was by then artistic director at the Seattle Rep, offered to work with him in case he needed help or couldn't finish it. Hirsch was heartened by such offers, but told everyone he needed to take it easy for a while. He remained interested in theatre and film and politics, reading as widely as always and talking on the phone to keep abreast of events and gossip. In a letter to Jean Gascon's widow, Marilyn (Gascon had died the year before), he said that Muriel Sherrin frequently phoned or dropped in to talk about friends and colleagues: "You can rest assured that all of it is kind and not an ounce of bitchery passes our lips."

His health fluctuated, with some good days and some bad ones. On one of his good days he had a visit from Des McAnuff, who made a detour on his way back to California after touring *A Walk in the Woods* in the Soviet Union. Over tea Hirsch spoke to McAnuff about Stratford and its importance as a cultural resource in North America, and told him he had a responsibility as a Canadian to work there again. With a string of award-winning productions behind him in the United States Stratford was not particularly on the younger director's mind at the time, but he was moved that Hirsch wanted to talk to him about it. With some trepidation, McAnuff said he was more interested in making motion pictures, at least in the medium term.

> Instead of throwing me out of the living room, he got on the phone and he called various friends in Canada and mentioned a number of people that I should get in touch with. It was like a flying saucer changing directions ninety degrees in mid-flight – off he went talking about the Canadian motion picture scene and motion pictures in general, and the conversation went on for the rest of the afternoon.

No one remembers Hirsch mentioning the word AIDS, though most of his friends correctly suspected the cause of his illness. For the most part he maintained a degree of optimism about the future. He wrote to Elizabeth Osborn, "It is clear to me that I have been driving myself with extraordinarily compulsive force ending up at death's door. If I can get healthy and go on living I simply must change....I was pretty stupid not to pay enough attention to my physical and mental well-being."

At the same time Hirsch had done a remarkably good job of putting his house in order, particularly with regard to looking after his partner. Bryan had never had a steady job or income and Hirsch didn't fully trust Tony, who still lived in the basement and maintained his relationship with Bryan. Without telling Bryan Hirsch asked Michal Schonberg to set up an annuity that would give Bryan enough to live on, and in periodic payments rather than a lump sum. Looking back on it, Bryan says, "I was astonished when I found out about the annuity. John was right, I really couldn't have survived without it."

In July Hirsch became extremely ill and returned to hospital. His severely compromised immune system was unable to stave off the opportunistic infections (in his case Cryptococcal meningitis) that attack people with full-blown AIDS. Bryan came to visit every day, spending hours at Hirsch's bedside, and again friends rallied round. But this time there was no recovery. There were better and worse moments, but Hirsch was sinking. His breathing got heavier and he drifted in and out of coma.

On the afternoon of August 1, Gail Singer visited the hospital, passing Tom Hendry who was just leaving. Singer had brought some fresh raspberries, a fruit Hirsch loved but could no longer eat, so she squeezed some of them into his mouth. After he had swallowed the juice he told her, "I've seen the other side." What did you see, she asked. "There's a white light…quite nice. And it's okay." He drifted back into sleep and she left. A bit later Marti Maraden arrived with David Silcox and his wife, Linda Intaschi (she had been Hirsch's stage manager on *Number Our Days* in Los Angeles in 1982). Maraden's diary for August 1 reads, "John is curled on his side, his head facing upward, tubes everywhere, beads of sweat all over. He opens his eyes when we speak, but I doubt he knows who we are. His breathing is very laboured."

That evening, John Hirsch died. He was buried on August 3, 1989 following a short religious ceremony with a eulogy by the scholarly Reform rabbi Gunther Plaut.

Two months later a committee of Hirsch's friends organized a tribute evening for him at the St. Lawrence Centre featuring many of the artists he had worked with over the years. In a running order Hirsch would surely have loved, it began with a vaudeville routine – "Flugle Street," performed by Stephen Ouimette and Douglas Campbell's son Torquil – and ended with Shakespeare. The artist Charles Pachter noted some of his impressions in his diary:

> Bryan Trottier greeted us at the door. I gave him a hug….
> The crowds started to arrive, and the tribute evening began.

It was beautifully organized and orchestrated by Muriel Sherrin, Gordon Pinsent, and Michal Schonberg. I was moved by the tributes, each thoughtful, some humorous. There were choice Hirsch anecdotes from actors, producers, theatre people who waxed eloquent, nostalgic, passionate about John. Nicholas Pennell recited an Auden poem, Douglas Rain did Dylan Thomas. David William, the new Stratford artistic director, was disarming, impressive, a great story teller. This was the first opportunity for Toronto audiences to see and hear him. John would have approved. Salome Bey sang "Mon Pays." Seana McKenna was funny and ribald describing a rehearsal with John, and doing the best imitation of him. Gordon Pinsent's Winnipeg reminiscences were heart-warming. Al Waxman was low-key, Michael Langham eloquent, Brian Bedford's closing soliloquy from *The Tempest* was perfect.... It's now 1:30 AM and as I write this I'm still thinking about the power of the theatre to move us when it's good.

Epilogue

"All your better deeds / Shall be in water writ..."
—Francis Beaumont and John Fletcher,
in *Philaster, or Love Lies a-Bleeding* (Act V, Scene 3)

DANIEL SULLIVAN, a friend and colleague of Hirsch's through several decades of his life, once quipped that, "During the 1980s, North American actors had to bring three things to any audition: a classical piece, a contemporary piece and a John Hirsch story." Part of Hirsch's legacy is surely the stock of stories that theatre people tell about this complicated, often contradictory man, generally with laughter, occasionally with a degree of pain or bewilderment.

The private Hirsch reminds one of *As You Like It*'s melancholy Jacques, with a personality "compounded of many simples, extracted from many objects" and wrapped in "a most humorous sadness." He was an intellectual, someone who read widely and deeply enough that he could talk for hours about art theory or philosophy, but could make friends with a three year-old. He loved feeding people, gave thoughtful presents and was generous with his time and contacts, but he could also (in his friend Mark Negin's phrase) be "tighter than a camel's arse in a sandstorm." Hirsch was very much a product of the four "mafias" in which he claimed membership, but with a few twists and contradictions: He was an expatriate Hungarian whose greatest comfort was a bowl of *bableves*; a non-Yiddish-speaking *mensch* who took decades to embrace his Jewishness fully; a sensual man whose sexuality was illegal for more than half his lifetime; and a grateful, enthusiastic Winnipegger who phoned home every Sunday and delighted to see his photo on the wall of the Kelekis family's restaurant.

When Martha Henry wrote a memorial piece about Hirsch in late 1989, she quoted several phrases from a letter he sent her shortly before he died, while he was still at home at Hudson Drive:

> Theatre in this country, or perhaps everywhere, is somewhat of a snakepit.... I've learned, yet once again, that the theatre is a place for exceptional artists, actors, who live dangerously on the stage.... I just have to remind myself of something I always knew, that every day is a gift and a blessing...come and watch the squirrels, racoons, and our four cats – they do a good show.

Henry commented, "John was in all those phrases at once, often at battle with himself. He was intricate, canny, driven and powerfully talented. No one else will ever resemble him."

Several people interviewed for this book made reference to the ephemeral nature of live stage performances as being "in water writ." A few videos and some film footage exist of plays directed by John Hirsch, and even of Hirsch directing, but the *experience* of sitting in a particular theatre watching the performance of a John Hirsch play is gone forever – as gone as the old Dominion Theatre in Winnipeg where the Manitoba Theatre Centre got its start. A few mouldering reviews by critics rushing to meet deadlines offer only the merest sketches of a vivid moment in time. You really had to be there.

Hirsch left an important and varied legacy beyond the contradictions, the stories and the experience. The most concrete legacy – literally – is the Manitoba Theatre Centre (as of 2010 the Royal Manitoba Theatre Centre) at 174 Market Avenue in Winnipeg. The MTC's Main Stage theatre, built in 1970, was renamed after Hirsch on May 11, 2008 on the fiftieth anniversary of the company that remains one of the most successful regional theatres in North America. He and Tom Hendry, after whom the company's second stage is named, are immortalized in the bronze statue by Ruth Abernathy that stands outside the theatre box office. (There is another, much smaller bronze that sits on the desk of Peter Herrndorf's office at the National Arts Centre. It is based on the sketch of Hirsch by the *Los Angeles Times* critic Sylvie Drake in 1975. Herrndorf, who is the CEO of the National Arts Centre, says he talks to the statue when he has a problem to thrash out, but then corrects himself: "Actually, John does most of the talking and gives me hell when I have to compromise too much.")

Less concrete but well documented is Hirsch's role as an advocate for the arts in general and for theatre in particular in Canada and the United States. Throughout his career he was a powerful voice in favour of public funding for the arts and served on dozens of committees and boards that administered such funding. He was also a notable – if occasionally intimidating – teacher, serving on the faculties of the National Theatre School, Yale and Southern Methodist University in Dallas.

Another concrete part of the Hirsch legacy is the funding he left behind. He often spoke about the importance of training and support for young artists and his will reflected that interest. He left one substantial bequest to the Manitoba Foundation for the Arts, which established the annual John Hirsch Award for Most Promising Manitoba Writer. Another went to the Jewish Immigrant Aid Services of Canada to set up a scholarship for students in the arts and performing arts. A third was earmarked for the Ontario Arts Council to provide for promising young theatre directors.

His legacy as an administrator at CBC Drama is an outstanding one, judged by the quality and quantity of programs produced. He brought the Canadian television production industry to a level of "critical mass" and the careers of countless actors, directors, writers and technicians began or got a huge boost during his tenure. He hated many aspects of the job but took it on and stuck it out because he believed it was important to Canada. It is outrageous that Canadians are still unable to view *The Tar Sands,* the 1977 docudrama Hirsch had misgivings about but which he defended tooth and nail once he had given it the green light.

At Stratford the record is more mixed. Hirsch and Stratford were not a good fit in many ways, though it is impossible to know what the record there would have looked like had he become artistic director in good economic times. But he did step in when the Festival needed him. He re-built the acting company and established the training program for young actors. He also greatly increased funding from government and private sources while changing both the Festival's fundraising stance and attitude of major funders towards the Festival. Most important, he directed some exciting productions himself and hired other directors who did fine shows during his tenure. One wonders if he and Stratford would have been happier with one another had he left after three years, having put the Festival back on its feet, and gone back to freelancing and consulting. He could be a useful and stimulating consulting director, as his time at the Seattle Repertory Theater showed.

Shortly after Hirsch died, the poet and playwright James Reaney sent a letter to the *London Free Press:*

> Sir: Your obituary *You either loved or loathed John Hirsch* (Free Press, Aug. 3) rather misses the point about this man's life, a life so rich and creative that it defies being broken up into a neat list of pluses and minuses, dimples and warts. Since he was never meant to be an administrator adept at big theatre politics, why not concentrate on what he was really good at – putting on plays?

So, what about the plays? Mug's game though it might be, it is possible to do "Hirsch by numbers." Leaving aside juvenilia but including his full-length Winnipeg Little Theatre productions, and allowing for a certain amount of archival confusion, Hirsch directed 126 stage productions, of which twenty-seven were musicals or revues.

He also directed an opera and several television dramas. Of the stage plays, forty-nine were written by American authors including four productions of Tennessee Williams (two of them *Glass Menageries*) and two productions of Saroyan's *The Time of Your Life*. Some of his best productions were American musicals, a form with which he demonstrated a sure hand.

Almost a third of the twenty-two Canadian plays that Hirsch directed were written by himself (mostly plays for children) or Tom Hendry, and he only directed three Canadian plays after 1970. Paul Thompson, a key figure in the rise of Canadian drama, argues that Hirsch's greatest contribution in this area was not as a director but as an advocate with bodies like the Canada Council and the Ontario Arts Council. "I like to make a sports analogy," says Thompson. "Hirsch was like a downhill or slalom skier, doing those international styles beautifully. The Canadian drama that came up starting in the late 1960s was original and indigenous, like snowboarding. He didn't have the muscles for it, and so for the most part he left it to people who did, and was remarkably good at getting money for it."

Hirsch's twenty-five European plays included five Brechts and three Chekhovs, and here his "muscles" certainly showed themselves. He did Chekhov better than anyone in North America and his *Mother Courage* at the Manitoba Theatre Centre fully deserves its legendary status.

Of his thirty-four productions of plays by British authors, seventeen were by Shakespeare – including four *Midsummer Night's Dreams* and two *Tempests* – and five by Shaw, including two *Saint Joans*. Hirsch's strength, and occasionally his weakness, with Shakespeare was that he refused to see the comedies and tragedies as "museum pieces" (his term). He always had to relate them to the things that concerned him at the time, whether it was changing sexual mores (*A Midsummer Night's Dream*) or power politics (*Richard III* and *Coriolanus*).

He insisted that Shakespeare's texts be spoken clearly and with the actor's full understanding of each word, yet he did not regard scripts – classic or contemporary – as sacred. He felt free to take liberties with the script of *The Dybbuk* and had some notable successes when he was working directly on a script with a playwright (James Reaney on *Colours in the Dark*, Heathcote Williams on *AC/DC*, Peter Raby on his adaptation of *The Three Musketeers*). One wonders if his success with Chekhov had something to do with the specificity of the plays in time and place, forcing Hirsch to forget his contemporary concerns and concentrate on the plays that Chekhov actually wrote. Yet even with Chekhov the text wasn't sacred: he chose his translations carefully and rigorously "dramaturged" the scripts.

In one of his last interviews Hirsch talked about aging in a culture that is inclined to discount and ignore mature artists. It annoyed him intensely. "You begin to come into your own when you reach forty," he asserted. "At fifty you know what you are doing; at sixty you're really beginning to cook." He never made it to sixty, so we'll never know exactly what he would have cooked – only that it would have been substantial and generously spiced, served in eye-catching crockery and that a few more Hirsch stories would have spilled over in the process of getting it from the kitchen to the dining room table.

Chronology of John Hirsch's Theatre Productions

Play	Author	Dates	Theatre or Company
Peter and the Snowman	John Hirsch	October 1953	Muddiwater Puppet Company
The Time of Your Life	William Saroyan	December 1953	Winnipeg Little Theatre
Sauerkringle	John Hirsch	February 13, 1954	Junior League Children's Theatre
A Passport for Mr. Braun	John Hirsch	March 1954	Junior League Children's Theatre
The Enchanted	Jean Giraudoux	April 1954	Winnipeg Little Theatre
The Wizard of Oz	L. Frank Baum and Paul Tietjens	July 16, 1956	Rainbow Stage
Our Town	Thornton Wilder	July 31, 1956	Rainbow Stage
Can-Can	Cole Porter and Abe Burrows	June 24, 1957	Rainbow Stage
Do You Remember?	Tom Hendry and Neil Harris	July 1957	Rainbow Stage
Chu Chin Chow	Oscar Asche and Frederic Norton	August 13, 1957	Rainbow Stage
The Italian Straw Hat	Eugene Labiche	October 1957	Theatre 77
Alice in Wonderland	Lewis Carroll, adaptation by John Hirsch	December 20, 1957	Theatre 77

A Funny Thing Happened on the Way to the Forum	Stephen Sondheim	January 1967	Manitoba Theatre Centre
Galileo	Bertolt Brecht	April 13, 1967	Lincoln Center
Richard III	William Shakespeare	June 12, 1967	Stratford Festival
Colours in the Dark	James Reaney	July 25, 1967	Stratford Festival
Saint Joan	George Bernard Shaw	January 4, 1968	Lincoln Center
A Midsummer Night's Dream	William Shakespeare	Tour, March 13, 1968 & Festival, June 5, 1968	Stratford Festival
The Three Musketeers	Alexandre Dumas, adaptation by Peter Raby	July 22, 1968	Stratford Festival
We Bombed in New Haven	Joseph Heller	October 16, 1968	Ambassador Theater
Tyger! Tyger! and Other Burning Things	Eric Malzkuhn	March 5, 1969	Longacre Theater, New York (National Theater of the Deaf)
Hamlet	William Shakespeare	Tour, March 5, 1969, Festival, June 6, 1969 & National Arts Centre, October 20, 1969	Stratford Festival
The Satyricon	Tom Hendry and Stanley Silverman	July 4, 1969	Stratford Festival
The Time of Your Life	William Saroyan	November 6, 1969	Lincoln Center

** ERRATUM **
This insert replaces page 342 in the book.

Death of a Salesman	Arthur Miller	March 1958	Theatre 77
Arsenic and Old Lace	Joseph Kesselring	May 22, 1958	Theatre 77
Box of Smiles	John Hirsch	February 1, 1958	Dominion Theatre
Brigadoon	Lerner and Loewe	July 1958	Rainbow Stage
Hellzapoppin' in Winnipeg	Neil Harris and Goldie Gelmon	July 1958	Rainbow Stage
The King and I	Rodgers and Hammerstein	August 18, 1958	Rainbow Stage
A Hatful of Rain	Michael V. Gazzo	October 20, 1958	Manitoba Theatre Centre
Teach Me How to Cry	Patricia Joudry	December 8, 1958	Manitoba Theatre Centre
Cinderella	John Hirsch and Neil Harris	December, 1958	Manitoba Theatre Centre
The Glass Menagerie	Tennessee Williams	January 1959	Manitoba Theatre Centre
Ring Round the Moon	Jean Anouilh	March 1959	Manitoba Theatre Centre
Of Mice and Men	John Steinbeck	May 11, 1959	Manitoba Theatre Centre
The Wizard of Oz	L. Frank Baum and Paul Tietjens	June 28, 1959	Rainbow Stage
Showboat	Rogers and Hammerstein	July 1959	Rainbow Stage
Cinderella	John Hirsch and Neil Harris	December 1959	Manitoba Theatre Centre
Tea and Sympathy	Robert Anderson	November 1959	Manitoba Theatre Centre

The Reclining Figure	Harry Kurnitz	January 1960	Manitoba Theatre Centre
Volpone	Ben Jonson	March 17, 1960	Manitoba Theatre Centre
Anastasia	Marcelle Maurette	May 12, 1960	Manitoba Theatre Centre
The Pajama Game	Richard Adler and Jerry Ross	July 1960	Rainbow Stage
Carousel	Rodgers and Hammerstein	July 1960	Rainbow Stage
Mister Roberts	Joshua Logan	October 6, 1960	Manitoba Theatre Centre
A Streetcar Named Desire	Tennessee Williams	December 1, 1960	Manitoba Theatre Centre
Biggest Thief in Town	Dalton Trumbo	January 1961	Manitoba Theatre Centre
Dark of the Moon	William Berney and Howard Richardson	March 1961	Manitoba Theatre Centre
Visit to a Small Planet	Gore Vidal	April 13, 1961	Manitoba Theatre Centre
Trapped	Tom Hendry	Summer 1961	Manitoba Theatre Centre
South Pacific	Rodgers and Hammerstein	July 1961	Rainbow Stage
The Most Happy Fella	Frank Loesser	July 1961	Rainbow Stage
The Lady's Not for Burning	Christopher Fry	October 6, 1961	Manitoba Theatre Centre
Arms and the Man	George Bernard Shaw	January 1962	Manitoba Theatre Centre
The Boy Friend	Sandy Wilson	February 1962	Manitoba Theatre Centre

Separate Tables	Terrence Rattigan	March 1962	Manitoba Theatre Centre
Thieves' Carnival	Jean Anouilh	April 13, 1962	Manitoba Theatre Centre
Look Ahead!	Len Peterson	May 11, 1962	Manitoba Theatre Centre
Bonfires of '62	Tom Hendry and Neil Harris	October 5, 1962	Manitoba Theatre Centre
Once More with Feeling	Harry Kurnitz	November 1962	Manitoba Theatre Centre
An Enemy of the People	Henrik Ibsen, adaptation by Betty Jane Wylie	November 30, 1962	Manitoba Theatre Centre
Mrs. Warren's Profession	George Bernard Shaw	January 1963	Manitoba Theatre Centre
Pal Joey	Rodgers and Hart	February 1, 1963	Manitoba Theatre Centre
Summer of the Seventeenth Doll	Ray Lawler	March 1963	Manitoba Theatre Centre
Cat on a Hot Tin Roof	Tennessee Williams	April 1963	Manitoba Theatre Centre
A Very Close Family	Bernard Slade	May 1963	Manitoba Theatre Centre
Private Lives	Noel Coward	October 1963	Manitoba Theatre Centre
Names and Nicknames	James Reaney	October 1963	Manitoba Theatre Centre
The Hostage	Brendan Behan	November 29, 1963	Manitoba Theatre Centre
A Midsummer Night's Dream	William Shakespeare	January 10, 1964	Manitoba Theatre Centre
Pygmalion	George Bernard Shaw	March 13, 1964	Manitoba Theatre Centre

The Gazebo	Alex Coppel	April 10, 1964	Manitoba Theatre Centre
Hay Fever	Noel Coward	September, 1964	Manitoba Theatre Centre
All About Us	Len Peterson, Tom Hendry, Alan Laing	October 28, 1964	Manitoba Theatre Centre
Mother Courage	Bertolt Brecht	December 2, 1964	Manitoba Theatre Centre
The Taming of the Shrew	William Shakespeare	December 30, 1964	Manitoba Theatre Centre
Irma La Douce	Alexandre Breffort and Marguerite Monnot	February 1965	Manitoba Theatre Centre
Who's Afraid of Virginia Woolf?	Edward Albee	April 7,1965	Manitoba Theatre Centre
The Tiger/The Typists	Murray Schisgal	May 1965	Manitoba Theatre Centre
The Cherry Orchard	Anton Chekov	July 26, 1965	Stratford Festival
The Importance of Being Earnest	Oscar Wilde	November 3, 1965	Manitoba Theatre Centre
Andorra	Max Frisch	December 1, 1965	Manitoba Theatre Centre
Mère Courage	Bertolt Brecht	January 2, 1966	Théâtre du Nouveau Monde
The Threepenny Opera	Bertolt Brecht	February 9, 1966	Manitoba Theatre Centre
Henry VI	William Shakespeare	June 7, 1966	Stratford Festival
Fifteen Miles of Broken Glass	Tom Hendry	September 1966	CBC (television)
Yerma	Federico Garcia Lorca	December 8, 1966	Lincoln Center

A Funny Thing Happened on the Way to the Forum	Stephen Sondheim	January 1967	Manitoba Theatre Centre
Galileo	Bertolt Brecht	April 13, 1967	Lincoln Center
Richard III	William Shakespeare	June 12, 1967	Stratford Festival
Colours in the Dark	James Reaney	July 25, 1967	Stratford Festival
Saint Joan	George Bernard Shaw	January 4, 1968	Lincoln Center
A Midsummer Night's Dream	William Shakespeare	Tour, March 13, 1968 & Festival, June 5, 1968	Stratford Festival
The Three Musketeers	Alexandre Dumas, adaptation by Peter Raby	July 22, 1968	Stratford Festival
We Bombed in New Haven	Joseph Heller	October 16, 1968	Ambassador Theater
Tyger! Tyger! and Other Burning Things	Eric Malzkuhn	March 5, 1969	Longacre Theater, New York (National Theater of the Deaf)
Hamlet	William Shakespeare	Tour, March 5, 1969, Festival, June 6, 1969 & National Arts Centre, October 20, 1969	Stratford Festival
The Satyricon	Tom Hendry and Stanley Silverman	July 4, 1969	Stratford Festival
The Time of Your Life	William Saroyan	November 6, 1969	Lincoln Center

Beggar on Horseback	Marc Connelly and George S. Kaufman	May 14, 1970	Lincoln Center
The Seagull	Anton Chekhov	March 1970	Habimah Theatre
A Man's a Man	Bertolt Brecht	November 2, 1970	Manitoba Theatre Centre, Guthrie Theater
The Playboy of the Western World	J.M. Synge	January 7, 1971	Lincoln Center
AC/DC	Heathcote Williams	February 24, 1971	Chelsea Theater Center
The Masked Ball (Opera)	Giuseppe Verdi	March 21, 1971	New York City Opera
Antigone	Sophocles	May 13, 1971	Lincoln Center
What the Butler Saw	Joe Orton	October 25, 1971	Manitoba Theatre Centre
A Midsummer Night's Dream	William Shakespeare	July 7, 1972	Guthrie Theater
Lulu Street	Ann Henry	Summer 1972	Centennial Theatre, Lennoxville
Guys and Dolls	Frank Loesser, Jo Swerling and Abe Burrows	February 5, 1973	Manitoba Theatre Centre
The Dybbuk	S. Ansky, adaptation by John Hirsch	January 11, 1974	Manitoba Theatre Centre, St. Lawrence Centre, Mark Taper Forum
Three Sisters	Anton Chekhov	September 1, 1976	Stratford Festival
The Tempest	William Shakespeare	May 17-July 1, 1979	Mark Taper Forum, Los Angeles

Saint Joan	George Bernard Shaw	November 1979	Seattle Rep
History of the American Film	Christopher Durang	December 3, 1979	National Arts Centre
Twelfth Night	William Shakespeare	February 1980	Young People's Theatre, Toronto
Pal Joey	Rodgers and Hart	April 1980	Seattle Rep
Flying	Joey Miller, John Hirsch and Stephen Witkin	July 1980	Imperial Room, Royal York Hotel
The Grand Hunt	Gyula Hernady	August 1980 November 1980	Shaw Festival, National Arts Centre and Seattle Rep
Strider: The Story of a Horse	Leo Tolstoy	October 1980	Seattle Rep
A Funny Thing Happened on the Way to the Forum	Stephen Sondheim	December 1980	St. Lawrence Centre
Number Our Days	Suzanne Grossmann and Barbara Myerhoff	January 21, 1982	Mark Taper Forum, Los Angeles
The Tempest	William Shakespeare	June 9, 1982	Stratford Festival
Mary Stuart	Friedrich Schiller	August 6, 1982	Stratford Festival
As You Like It	William Shakespeare	June 7, 1983	Stratford Festival
Tartuffe	Molière	August 5, 1983	Stratford Festival
A Midsummer Night's Dream	William Shakespeare	June 10, 1984	Stratford Festival

A Streetcar Named Desire	Tennessee Williams	September 7, 1984	Stratford Festival
Tartuffe	Molière	March 31, 1985	CBC
King Lear	William Shakespeare	May 26, 1985	Stratford Festival
The Glass Menagerie	Tennessee Williams	August 30, 1985	Stratford Festival
Three Men On A Horse	George Abbott and John Cecil Holm	September 1987	Royal Alexandra Theatre, Toronto
American Dreams: Lost and Found	Studs Terkel, adapted by John Hirsch	November 6, 1987	Alliance Theater, Atlanta
The Chosen	Chaim Potok	January 6,1988	Second Avenue Theater, New York
Coriolanus	William Shakespeare	July 28, 1988	Old Globe Theater, San Diego
Odd Jobs	Frank Moher	September 1988	Canadian Stage Company, Toronto
The Alchemist	Ben Jonson	November 1988	Yale Repertory Theater, New Haven

Notes

[1]Dome Petroleum was an upstart Canadian player in the oil industry that built up huge debts in the early 1980s and required federal intervention several times before it was finally bought out by an American major. Chrysler was famously bailed out by the U.S. government in 1979.

[2]Alberta high school teacher James Keegstra was convicted of hate speech in 1984 after teaching his students that the Holocaust was a fraud and that Jews were "power hungry" and "child killers." Ernst Zundel was convicted in Toronto of publishing several Holocaust-denial publications in 1985. The death of Josef Mengele, the Auschwitz "Angel of Death," who had fled to South America after the war, was confirmed in the same year.

Sources

This book is based on several types of source material, including interviews, scholarly journals and books, newspaper and magazine articles, and a variety of materials held in several archives. A complete, footnoted version of the manuscript is maintained by the authors. The following is a summary of key sources organized by chapter.

Within citations, the following abbreviations are used:
ETJ = *Educational Theatre Journal*
GM = *Globe & Mail*
JH = John Hirsch
LAC = Library and Archives Canada
LT = *Los Angeles Times*
NYT = *New York Times*
TH = Tom Hendry
TDS = *Toronto Daily Star*
TS = *Toronto Star*
WFP = *Winnipeg Free Press*
WT = *Winnipeg Tribune*

Unless otherwise attributed, unpublished sources can be found in the John Hirsch fonds at Library and Archives Canada, NAC MG 31 D81.

Chapter 1. A Hungarian Childhood, Interrupted
Hirsch's childhood memories are principally taken from: JH, "In Search of a Theatre," speech to the Winnipeg Junior League on October 27, 1954, published in 1955; interview in *The Country Guide* (Winnipeg), December 1955, page 31; undated manuscript in Manitoba Archives beginning "John Hirsch: Well, obviously there are several..."; JH, "The Garden and the World", University of Manitoba essay;

Elizabeth Osborn, "John Hirsch at Yale" (typescript), January 3, 1988. Most of the poems quoted are in LAC, Vol. 26 f19.

John's cousin Anna Fried was very helpful in verifying, correcting and occasionally debunking some of the details related by Hirsch.

The historical sources used in this chapter include: István Pogány, "Poets, Revolutionaries and Shoemakers: Law and the Construction of National Identity in Central Europe during the Long 19th Century," *Social Legal Studies*, 16 (2007); Sebestyén József Matyikó, *Zsidók Siófokon*, Budapest: Ethnica, 2002; *Somogy Megyei Levéltár, Siófok község iratai* (Somogy county archives, Documents about Siófok), 1941, No. 3789; "Siófok" in Theodore Lavi (ed.), *Pinkas Hakehillot Hungary* (Encyclopaedia of Jewish Communities in Hungary), Jerusalem: Yad Vashem, 1975; Testimony by witness "D.J.", National Committee of Hungarian Jews for Attending Deportees (DEGOB), Protocol # 3562, November 24, 1945; Central Database of Shoah Victims' Names, Yad Vashem.

The opening poem was published in James Reaney's *Alphabet Magazine*, 8 (1966). The Czeslaw Milosz quote is from John Updike, "Survivor/Believer," *The New Yorker*, December 24, 2001.

Chapter 2. Adrift in Europe

Interviews with David Ehrlich and Ora Markstein were invaluable in writing this chapter, as was Marianne Guttman's unpublished memoir dated May 2001.

Other sources include: JH, "Childhood poems," manuscript; "John Hirsch's Ella," CBC Radio broadcast, January 1, 1988; and Hungarian correspondence and legal papers from the LAC Hirsch fonds.

The story of the Canadian Jewish Congress' War Orphans Project is described in Fraidie Martz, *Open Your Hearts: The Story of the Jewish War Orphans in Canada*, Montreal: Véhicule Press, 1996.

Chapter 3. Our Bird of Paradise

Much of this chapter is based on interviews with Sybil Shack and David Ehrlich.

Other sources include: Arthur Adamson, "Memoir of a Poet," *The Winnipeg Connection: Writing Lives at Mid-Century*, Birk Sproxton (ed.), Winnipeg: Prairie Fire Press, 2006, p. 125; Percy Barsky, "How 'Numerous Clausus' was Ended in the Manitoba Medical School," *Jewish Life and Times*, Winnipeg: Jewish Historical Society of Western Canada, 1983; JH, "Reminiscences," *Aurora: New Canadian Writing*, ed. Morris

Wolfe, 1978; JH, "The Elusive Plays of Anton Chekov" (typescript), April 10, 1952, in the Manitoba Archives; JH, "My Life in Canadian Art," *Canadian Theatre Review*, Spring, 1982; JH, "Adoption by a Cold Land," *Maclean's*, April, 1973; JH, "John Hirsch's Ella," CBC Radio broadcast, December 18, 1987; and the University of Manitoba student newspaper, *The Manitoban*, particularly an interview entitled "Portrait of the Artist," January 8, 1952.

The Dryden poem quoted is "Absalom and Achitophel," 1681.

Chapter 4. Apprenticeship: From Child's to *Chu Chin Chow*

The main interview sources for this chapter are Evelyne Anderson, Doreen Brownstone, Tom Hendry, Daphne Korol, Ed Evanko, Mark Negin, Gordon Pinsent, Ted Patterson, and Sybil Shack.

Special mention should be made of Reg Skene's invaluable "Theatre and Community: The Development Toward a Professional Theatre in Winnipeg, 1897-1957," Ph.D. dissertation, University of Toronto, 1983.

Articles and manuscripts include: TH, "Child's Days," *Canadian Art*, 1962; TH typescript beginning "I worked on fund raising..."; TH, "Trends in Canadian Theatre," *Tulane Drama Review*, 10:1 (Autumn, 1965), pp. 62-70; TH, *A view from the beginning*, MTC publication, 1965-66 season; JH, "In Search of a Theatre," speech made to either the Winnipeg Junior League or the Humanities Association, October 27, 1954; JH, *Box of Smiles*, Manitoba Provincial Archives, P120 f10; JH, "Life as an Artist in Canada," *Visions of Canada: The Alan B. Plaunt Memorial Lectures, 1958-1992*, Toronto: McGill-Queen's, 2004; JH, "Hail and Farewell: Five Years as Artistic Director," lecture given on August 25, 1985, Stratford Festival.

Newspaper articles include: Frank Morriss, "Lack of Finish Deplored in Sheridan Performance," WFP, October 14, 1950; Frank Morriss, "Director John Hirsch Scores Ringing Success with Warm-Hearted and Whacky Saroyan Fantasy," WFP, December 22, 1953; Kevin Rollason, "Legacy of giving: Junior League of Winnipeg folds, but leaves lasting fund," WFP, June 30, 2006; "Peter and the Snowman Bring Puppets to the City," WT, October 10, 1953; Ann Henry, "Roundtable holds same old interest," WT, October 5, 1957; Patrick McDonagh, "Students Make Show Biz History," *McGill Daily News Alumni Quarterly*, Winter, 1999-2000.

Other published sources include: Carol Budnick, "The Performing Arts as a Field of Endeavour for Winnipeg Women, 1870-1930," *Manitoba History*, 11 (Spring, 1986); Michael Coveney, *Maggie Smith: A*

Bright Particular Star, London: Victor Gollancz, 1992; Howard Curle, "More than Just a 'Spotlight': Early Television in Winnipeg," *The Winnipeg Connection*, Prairie Fire Press, 2006; Betty Lee, *Love and Whisky: The Story of the Dominion Drama Festival*, Toronto: McClelland and Stewart, 1973; Felicia Hardison Londré and Daniel J. Watermeier, *The History of North American Theater: The United States, Canada and Mexico – From Pre-Columbian Times to the Present*, Continuum International Publishing Group, 2000; Kevin Longfield, *From Fire to Flood: A History of Theatre in Manitoba*, Winnipeg: Signature Editions, 2007; Gordon Pinsent, *By the Way*, Toronto: Stoddart, 1992; Doug Smith, *Joe Zuken, Citizen and Socialist*, Toronto: Lorimer, 1990; E. Ross Stuart, *The History of Prairie Theatre*, Toronto: Simon and Pierre, 1984; Bernard K. Sandwell, "The Annexation of Our Stage," *Canadian Magazine*, 38:1 (November, 1911); Adele Wiseman, *Old Woman at Play*, Toronto: Clarke, Irwin, 1978; Max Wyman, *The Royal Winnipeg Ballet. The First Forty Years*, Toronto: Doubleday, 1978.

The 1957 broadcast "John Hirsch revives pro theatre in Winnipeg," of October 29, 1957, can be found at http://archives.cbc.ca/on_this_day/10/29/.

The Vivian Rakoff quote is from Robert Fulford, "From Russia, with stories: David Bezmozgis captures the essence of immigrant life in his new fiction," *National Post*, May 27, 2003.

Chapter 5. Growing an Orange on the Prairie

The main interview sources for this chapter are Evelyne Anderson, Louis Bako, John Bluethner, Doreen Brownstone, Len Cariou, Chris Dafoe, John Erkel, Eddie Gilbert, Tom Hendry, Martha Henry, Robert Kalfin, Alan Laing, Sybil Shack, Desmond Scott, Robert Sherrin, Eoin Sprott, Betty Jane Wylie ,and Sarah Yates. Additional material came from Sarah Yates' engaging *Manitoba Theatre Centre. The first twenty years: Conversations with MTC people from 1958 to 1978*, Winnipeg: MTC, 1978, which includes interviews with Tom Hendry, John Hirsch, Desmond Scott, and Ogden Turner. Some raw transcripts from these interviews are also available in the LAC Hirsch fonds.

Books, articles and manuscripts include: Michael Billington, *The State of the Nation: British Theatre Since 1945*, London: Faber & Faber, 2007; Roger Currie and Rory Runnells, *Manitoba Theatre Centre: 50 Years*, Studio Publications, 2007; Michael Czuboka, *Juba*, Winnipeg: Communigraphics, 1986; Martin Esslin, "Brecht and the English Theatre," *The Tulane Drama Review*, 11:2 (1966); Fred Euringer, *Fly on the Curtain*, Ottawa: Oberon Press, 2000; L.M. Green and T. Moore, *Standing naked in the wings: anecdotes from Canadian actors*, Toronto: Oxford, 1967; James Forsyth, *Tyrone Guthrie: A Biography*, London: Hamish Hamilton, 1976; Keith Garebian, *William Hutt: Masks and Faces*, Oakville: Mosaic Press, 1995; Tyrone Guthrie, "Guthrie Looks at MTC," *Stage Centre*, 3:2 (October, 1963); TH, "A view from the beginning," *The Preview*, 1965; TH, "Trends in Canadian Theatre," *The Tulane Drama Review*, 10:1 (Autumn, 1965); Martha Henry, "Adieu," *Impact*, Fall, 1989; JH, speech to Junior League, 1960, Archives of Manitoba; JH, "Tennessee Williams," typescript for *Anthology*, CBC broadcast, April 11, 1960; JH, MTC program for *Thieves' Carnival*, April, 1962; JH in "Questions and Answers," *Performing Arts in Canada*, Winter 1965-66; JH, "On Directing in Canada," *Canadian Theatre Review*, 1 (Winter, 1974); Martin Hunter, *Romancing the Bard*, Toronto: Dundurn Press, 2001; Kevin Longfield, *From fire to flood: a history of theatre in Manitoba*, Winnipeg: Signature Editions, 2001; Richard Monette, *This Rough Magic: The Making of an Artistic Director. A Memoir*, Stratford Festival Publications, 2007; Pat Morden, "A Good Block," in Daniel Fischlin and Judith Nasby (eds.), *Shakespeare Made in Canada: Contemporary Canadian Adaptations in Theatre, Pop Media and Visual Arts*, Canadian Adaptations of Shakespeare Project, University of Guelph, 2007; Davi Napoleon, *Chelsea on the Edge: The Adventures of an American Theatre*. Ames, Iowa State University Press, 1991; Aviva Ravel, "The Dramatic World of Patricia Joudry," Ph.D. dissertation, McGill University, Montreal, 1984; Rory Runnells, "On John Hirsch," *Prairie Fire*, Autumn, 1996; Robert Russell, "The Manitoba Theatre Centre," *Canadian Arts*, 1962; Grace Lydiatt Shaw, *Stratford Undercover: Memories on Tape*, Toronto: NC Press, 1977; Paula Sperdakos, "Acting in Canada: Frances Hyland, Kate Reid, Martha Henry and the Stratford Festival's 1965 The Cherry Orchard," *Theatre Research in Canada*, 19:1 (Spring, 1998); Tom Warner, *Never going back: a history of queer activism in Canada*, Toronto: University of Toronto Press, 2002; Judy Waytiuk, "Theatre in Winnipeg after the Manitoba Theatre Centre, 1958-1972," essay, Department of Journalism, Carleton University, Ottawa, 1972.

Information about the Villeurbanne Theatre comes from David Bradby, *Modern French Drama 1940-1990*, Cambridge, 1991 and Yvette Daoust, *Roger Planchon: Director and Playwright*, Cambridge, 1981.

Newspaper articles include: Patricia Bosworth, "Dude: An $800,000 Disaster. Where Did They Go Wrong?" NYT, October 22, 1972; Nathan Cohen, "Red River Wilderness," "Conquering the Wilderness" and "A

Cause for Hope," TDS, January 21-24, 1963; Robertson Davies, "The Cherry Orchard at Stratford: For Chekhov 87 per cent," *Peterborough Examiner*, July 31, 1965; Gordon Jocelyn, "What's New at Stratford? Chekhov!", *Montreal Gazette*, September 4, 1965; Ron Johnson, "Young Toronto Actors Money-Hungry," TDS, September 5, 1959; Ian McAmmond, "The Caravan of Courage," *The Uniter* (University of Winnipeg student newspaper), February 25, 2010; J. Kelly Nestruck, "Cariou, Pinsent, Reeves: All wrapped up in 50 years of history at the MTC," GM, May 10, 2010; Kevin Prokosh, "Acting Its Age," WFP, October 18, 2007; Kevin Prokosh, "She wants you to get with the program," WFP, November 28, 2008.

Other sources include: NFB, *John Hirsch: A Portrait of a Man and a Theatre*, 1965 and George Siamandas, "John Hirsch: Winnipeg's Man of Theatre," (http://timemachine.siamandas.com), Winnipeg Time Machine website.

Chapter 6. Director at Large

The main interview sources for this chapter are: James Blendick, Eddie Gilbert, Desmond Heeley, Tom Hendry, Robert Kalfin, John Lahr, Alan Laing, Alan Mandell, Mark Negin, Stephen Ouimette, Priscilla Pointer, Peter Raby, Brian Rintoul, Julius Rudel, Celeste Sansregret, Stanley Silverman, Eoin Sprott, Daniel Sullivan, Paul Thompson, Keith Turnbull, Bryan Trottier, Ken Welsh, and Betty Jane Wylie. Jean Gascon was interviewed by Michael Schonberg in 1980.

Some of the Hirsch quotes are from interviews conducted by Elizabeth Osborn in 1988. Peter Raby's invaluable *The Stratford Scene 1958-1968* (Toronto: Clarke Irwin, 1968) contains interviews with Michael Gregory, John Hirsch, Michael Langham, and James Reaney. Some quotes from Tedde Moore and Kenneth Welsh are taken from L.M. Green and T. Moore, *Standing naked in the wings: anecdotes from Canadian actors, op. cit.*

Articles and manuscripts include: Herbert Blau, *Take up the bodies: Theater at the vanishing point*, University of Illinois Press, 1982; Robert Cushman, *Fifty Seasons of Stratford*, Toronto: McClelland and Stewart, 2002; André Durand, "André Durand présente Mère Courage et ses enfants," at www.comptoirlitteraire.com; Arnold Edinborough, "Stratford, Ontario – 1968," *Shakespeare Quarterly*, 19:4 (Autumn, 1968) and "Stratford, Ontario – 1967," *Shakespeare Quarterly*, 18:4 (Autumn, 1967); Keith Garebian, *William Hutt: A Theater Portrait*, New York: Mosaic Press, 1988; TH, "Fifteen Miles of Broken Glass," *The Performing*

Arts in Canada, Spring, 1966, p. 22; Martha Henry, "Adieu," *op. cit.*; JH in Arthur Bartow (ed.), *The Director's Voice: Twenty-One Interviews*, New York: Theater Communications Group, 1988; JH, "Adoption by a cold land," *Maclean's*, July, 1973; JH, "How I discovered my roots," *Jewish Life and Times: a Collection of Essays*, Winnipeg: Jewish Historical Society of Western Canada, 1983; JH, transcript from Yale University class, January 3, 1988; Martin Hunter, 2001, *op. cit.*; Richard Bruce Kirkley, "Theatre in Television: theory and practice in English Canadian drama 1952-87," Ph.D. dissertation, University of Toronto, 1990; Berners Jackson, "Retrospect: The Stratford Festival 1958-68" in Peter Raby (ed.), *The Stratford Scene, 1958-1968*, Toronto: Clarke Irwin 1969; Allan Lewis, untitled, ETJ, 21:3 (October, 1969); Glenn Loney, "Broadway in Review," ETJ, 20:2 (May, 1968); Davi Napoleon, 1991, *op. cit.*; Julius Nowick, "The Old Régime at Lincoln Center," ETJ, 18:2 (May, 1966); Julius Nowick, *Beyond Broadway*, New York: Hill & Wang, 1968; John Pettigrew and Jamie Portman, *Stratford: The First Thirty Years*, Toronto: Macmillan, 1985; Donald Spoto, *Otherwise Engaged: The Life of Alan Bates*, London: Hutchinson, 2007; Grace Lydiatt Shaw, *Stratford Under Cover: Memories on Tape*, Toronto: NC Press, 1977; Guy Sprung and Rita Much, *Hot Ice: Shakespeare in Moscow*, Winnipeg: Blizzard Publishing, 1991; Tom Warner, 2002, *op. cit.*; Sarah Yates, 1978, *op. cit.*

Newspaper and magazine articles include: "Theater: The Mills of the Gods," *Time*, May 24, 1971; Clive Barnes, "Theater: Poor Antigone! Sophocles Maltreated in Lincoln Center," NYT, May 14, 1971; Clive Barnes, "Stage: Saroyan dated," NYT, November 7, 1969; Clive Barnes, "Theater: Heller's 'We Bombed in New Haven' Opens," NYT, October 17, 1968; Arlene Billinkoff, "Hirsch wants to be an international director," WFP, September 1966; Nathan Cohen, "Reaney's Colours in the Dark shows up a bleak failure," TS, July 26, 1969; Sylvie Drake, "'Dybbuk': A Message for Now?", LT, January 26, 1975; Robert Fulford, "John Hirsch faces a familiar dilemma of talented Canadians: Here or there?" TDS, December 24, 1966; Stanley Kauffman, NYT, June 9, 1966; Kevin Kelly, "Stratford's 'Dream' fascinating theatre," *Boston Globe*, June 14, 1968; Walter Kerr, "'Yerma' at Lincoln Center," NYT, December 9, 1966; Walter Kerr, "Canadian Production is Highly Stylized," NYT, June 14, 1967; Mendel Kohansky, "Seagull fails to take wing," *Jerusalem Post*, March 13, 1970; Julius Novick, "You must run twice as fast," *The Village Voice*, May 21, 1970; Tom Prideaux, "Joe Heller's Peakaboo with Reality," *Life*, October 12, 1968; Michael Smith, "Theatre Journal," *The Village Voice*, April 20, 1967; *Variety*, August 9, 1967; Herbert Whittaker,

"Oh! Stratford! What are you up to?", GM, June 14, 1969; Herbert Whittaker, "With Hirsch on Broadway," GM, December 3, 1966; Frank Wood, "Reaney, Colours rate standing ovation," *Stratford Times*, July 26, 1967.

Other sources include: Robert Doyle, "Design is a six lettered word," on the website *From Artillery to Zuppa Circus: Recorded memory of theatre life in Nova Scotia* (http://www.library.dal.ca/); James Reaney Jr., "James' Brand New Blog," September 9, 2008 (http://blogs.canoe.ca/brandnewblog); Robert Simpson, "Frank Bayer, Theatrical Production Manager, Dies at 74," *playbill.com*, September 28, 2010; Martha Henry in interview with R.H. Thomson, "Working with John Hirsch," at Theatre Museum Canada's *Legend Library* (www.theatremuseum canada.ca/legendlibrary.html).

Chapter 7. CBC: The Storm Maker

The main interview sources or those who provided personal communications are: Garth Drabinsky, John Erkel, Andras Hamori, Martha Henry, Peter Herrndorf, Stephen Jack, Marti Maraden, Des McAnuff, Lawrence Mirkin, Peter Pearson, Robin Phillips, Peter Raby, Irene Shubik, Ralph Thomas, Paul Thompson, Keith Turnbull, Kenneth Welsh and Magda Zalán. Thanks also to Peter Molnar Gal for his personal communication (original in Hungarian) and to Peter Pearson for sharing his uproarious – and sadly as yet unpublished – memoir, "My Life: The Movie."

Books, articles and manuscripts include: John Fraser, *Telling Tales*, Toronto: Collins, 1986; Allan Gould, "Morningside," typescript, CBC Radio, July 8, 1977; JH, "On Directing in Canada," *Canadian Theatre Review*, 1 (Winter 1974); Martin Hunter, 2001, *op. cit.*; Allan King, "Memories of Maria: A Contribution to the Discussion on 'The Image of the Working Class in Canadian Media,'" *Take One*, December 1, 2001; Martin Knelman, *A Stratford Tempest*, Toronto: McClelland and Stewart, 1982; Davi Napoleon, 1991, *op. cit.*; Malcolm Page, "Hirsch and the CBC," *Canadian Theatre Review*, Summer, 1976; Nicholas Pasquariello, "Jan Kadar," *Cinema Canada*, September, 1980; John Pettigrew and Jamie Portman, 1985, *op. cit.*; Gordon Pinsent, *By The Way*, Toronto: Stoddart, 1992; Sharon Pollock, "Canada's playwrights finding their place," in Don Rubin (ed.), *Canadian Theatre History: Selected Readings*, Toronto: Playwrights Canada Press, 1996.

Newspaper and magazine articles include: Canadian Press, "Birthday bash a smash hit coast-to-coast," *Ottawa Citizen*, July 2, 1977;

Canadian Press, "New unity thrust predicted," *Ottawa Citizen*, June 23, 1977; Stephen Chesley, "CBC Drama – ACTRA Confrontation," *Cinema Canada*, April, 1976; John Fraser, "For Hirsch, doing Chekhov is like a fabulous retreat," GM, August 22, 1976; Brian Gory and Bruce A. McLeod, "Rain pours but big bash just goes on," *Ottawa Journal*, July 2, 1977; JH, "Dear writer, TV drama needs your wit and energy. But beware the monsters," GM, November 13, 1976; JH, "Why must we suffer such a pallid, Victorianized Chekhov?", GM, August 28, 1976; Phillip Hoare, "Obituary: Peter Wildeblood," *The Independent*, November 25, 1999; Frank Howard and Kitty McKinsey, "The Bureaucrates [sic]," column in the *Ottawa Citizen*, 1977; Penelope Hynam, "Interview: Beryl Fox with a cameo appearance by Claude Jutra," *Cinema Canada*, April, 1981; Gina Mallet, "Three Sisters hums with emotion in a superb Stratford production," TS, September 2, 1976; Philip Marchand, "Will the CBC defeat John Hirsch, too?" *Saturday Night*, June, 1975; Jack Miller, "Hirsch finishes the job as CBC drama chief but dream went astray," TS, March 4, 1978; James Nelson, "Hirsch threatens to quit as chief of CBC's drama," *The Province*, February 13, 1975; James Nelson, "Viewers should tell CBC what they like: Hirsch," *Ottawa Citizen*, April 4, 1975; John O'Connor, "TV: Canada's Top Drama on Channel 13 Tonight," NYT, July 11, 1978; *Ottawa Gazette*, "U.S. citizen lights Canada Day show," June 7, 1977; Roy Shields, "CBC drama boss slams producers for dissension," Southam News Services, July 22, 1976; Sylvie Drake, "'Dybbuk': A Message for Now?", LT, January 26, 1975; Val Ross, "John Hirsch bids adieu," *Toronto Life*, April, 1978.

For scholarly discussions of Hirsch's time at the CBC, see Richard Bruce Kirkley, "John Hirsch and the Critical Mass: Alternative Theatre on CBC Television in the 1970s," *Theatre Research in Canada*, 15:1 (Spring, 1994) and Mary Jane Miller, *Turn Up the Contrast: CBC Television Drama Since 1952*, Vancouver: UBC Press, 1987. See also David Helwig, "Magic Box Fix Everything. John Hirsch and CBC TV Drama: 1974-6," at www.davidhelwig.com/excerpts.htm and JH, "A Personal Report by John S. Hirsch on his Four Years as Head of CBC Television Drama (ESD) – 1974-1978," typescript dated July 1978, National Archives MG3I-D81, Vol. 20).

The sources regarding Hirsch's intervention in the "Last Tango in Paris" appeal (R. v. Odeon Morton Theatres Ltd. and United Artists Corp., 1974) are "Brief to dismiss the appeal by Samuel Freedman," CJM, January 29, 1974 and Robert Martin and Gordon Stuart Adam, *A Sourcebook of Canadian Media Law*, McGill-Queen's Press, 1994, p. 521.

Online resources include: "CBC Television Series, 1952-1982," an online database at www.film.queensu.ca/cbc created by Blaine Allan; Pip Wedge, "Pioneer: Benson, Thomas Frederick (1915-2002)," Canadian Communications Foundation, October, 2002 (www. broadcasting-history.ca); Magda Zalán, "How to be a landed immigrant," *The Hungarian Presence in Canada*, March, 2007 (www.hungarianpresence. ca/Culture/Media/Zalan.cfm).

The Beverley Simons quote is from "Prologue" in the collection *Preparing*, Vancouver: Talonbooks, 1975.

Chapter 8. Director at Large (Again)

The main interview sources, or those who provided personal communications are: Susan Benson, John Bluethner, Gordon Davidson, Garth Drabinsky, Eddie Gilbert, Ming Cho Lee, Joey Miller, Stanley Silverman, Gail Singer, Daniel Sullivan ,and Brian Trottier. The interview with Anthony Hopkins was by Michal Schonberg, May 19, 1979.

Articles and manuscripts include: Jules Aaron, *Theatre Journal*, 31:4 (December, 1979); Weldon B. Durham (ed.), *American Theatre Companies, 1931-1986*, New York: Greenwood Press, 1989; Barbara Myerhoff, *Number Our Days: A Triumph of Continuity and Culture Among Jewish Old People in an Urban Ghetto*, New York: Dutton, 1978; Rory Runnells, *Map of the Senses*, Winnipeg: Scirocco Drama, 2000.

Newspaper and magazine articles include Wayne Edmonstone, "Why John Hirsch works south of the border and not here," *Vancouver Sun*, February 15, 1980; Audrey Ashley, "Movie Spoof Makes Grand Show," *Ottawa Citizen*, December 4, 1979; Freddie Brinster, "Rep drains 'Strider' of its pathos, soul," *Bellevue Journal American*, October 24, 1980; Sylvie Drake, "'Tempest' at Mark Taper Forum," LT, May 18, 1979; Ray Conlogue, "Technicolor Twelfth Night is a jewel of a production," GM, February 6, 1980; Ray Conlogue, "Grand Hunt is peculiar comedy," GM, August 16, 1980; Gerald Clarke, "Show Business: Desire Under the Palms," *Time*, February 1, 1982; O. Casey Corr, "Artful blend of deceit and love," *Seattle Post Intelligencer*, November 28, 1980; Richard Eder, "Stage: new approach to 'The Tempest' on Coast," NYT, May 28, 1979; Adele Freedman, "Hirsch looks between the lines for echoes of troubled times," GM, August 4, 1980; Ann Herold, "Numbering the days," *Santa Monica Evening Outlook*, January 15, 1982; Elaine Lipworth, "Sir Anthony Hopkins: the story of my dissolute, lonely, useless young life (and why it was the making of me)," *Daily Mail*, March 1, 2010; Gina Mallet, "YPT's Twelfth Night is a Winner," TS, February 4, 1980;

Murray Morgan "Strider stumbles at Rep," *Tacoma News*, October 31, 1980; Jamie Portman, "If only earthquake had arrived an hour and 58 minutes sooner," *Calgary Herald*, December 6, 1979; Chaim Rosemarin, "Strider: An equestrian drag," *Seattle Sun*, November 5, 1980.

Other sources include: JH, "Notes from Hirsch," in Seattle Repertory Theater program for *Tintypes*, 1982; "Hirsch's new musical comedy revue a hit with audiences," Royal York News (press release), July 22, 1980.

Chapter Nine. The Winter of His Discontent

The main interviews were with Susan Benson, Douglas Campbell, Len Cariou, Antoni Cimolino, Andras Hamori, Desmond Heeley, Tom Hendry, Peter Herrndorf, Steven Jack, Bob Kalfin, Josh Knelman, Martin Knelman, Robert Lantos, Des McAnuff, Seana McKenna, Julian Porter, Gail Singer, Ming Cho Lee, Leon Major, Julian Porter, Brian Rintoul (interviewed by Alon Nashman), Robert Sherrin, Michal Schonberg, Stanley Silverman, Gary Thomas, Paul Thompson and Bryan Trottier. Thanks also to Alan Laing, Peter Molnar Gal, Charles Pachter and Susan Lemenchick for sharing their memories by e-mail.

The definitive source about Hirsch's hiring as artistic director at Stratford remains Martin Knelman's *A Stratford Tempest*, 1982, *op. cit.*

Books, articles and manuscripts include: Arthur Barton, *The director's voice*, New York: Theater Communications Group, 1989; Ralph Berry, "Stratford Festival Canada," *Shakespeare Quarterly*, Summer, 1982; Ralph Berry, "Stratford Festival Canada, 1982," *Shakespeare Quarterly*, Spring, 1983; Ralph Berry, "Stratford and London, Ontario," *Shakespeare Quarterly*, Winter, 1983; Ralph Berry, "Stratford Festival Canada," *Shakespeare Quarterly*, Spring, 1985; John Dexter, *The Honourable Beast: A Posthumous Autobiography*, London: Nick Hern Books, 1993; Robert Gaines, *John Neville Takes Command*, Stratford: William Street Press, 1987; Keith Garebian, *William Hutt: A Theatre Portrait*, New York: Mosaic Press, 1988; Keith Garebian, *A Well-Bred Muse: Selected Theatre Writings 1978-1988*, Oakville: Mosaic Press, 1991; JH in Arthur Bartow, *op. cit.*; JH in "A Classic Debate, *Theatre Communications*, January, 1984; Martin Hunter, 2001, *op. cit.*; Sheila M.F. Johnston, *Let's go to the Grand! 100 years of entertainment at London's Grand Theatre*, Natural Heritage Books, 2001; Richard Paul Knowles, "From National to Multinational: The Stratford Festival, Free Trade, and the Discourses of Intercultural Tourism," *Theatre Journal*, March, 1995; Richard Monette, 2007, *op. cit.*; Roger Warren, "Shakespeare at Stratford, Ontario:

The John Hirsch Years," *Shakespeare Survey* 39 (1987); Herbert Weil, "Stratford Festival Canada," *Shakespeare Quarterly*, Summer, 1986.

Newspaper and magazine articles include: Canadian Press, "Stratford return a shock: Hutt," *Montreal Gazette*, August 6, 1981; Lyle Black, "John Hirsch: the last act," *Hamilton Spectator*, March 30, 1985; Mark Bourdeau, "Hirsch after the tempest," *London Gazette*, February 15, 1983; Brian Brennan, "Authors, directors equal on stages at Stratford," *Calgary Herald*, July 15, 1984; Canadian Press, "President gets job offer," *Toronto Sun*, February 9, 1983; Ray Conlogue, "Driving pace carries frantic Funny Thing," GM, January 1, 1981; Ray Conlogue, "Spidery Bedford superb in delightful Tartuffe," GM, August 16, 1983; Ray Conlogue, "Stratford opens with a weighty Dream," June 12, 1984; Ray Conlogue, "Stratford stage challenges directors," GM, June 23, 1984; Ray Conlogue, "The Inspector Is Greeted With Thunderous Applause," GM, August 10, 1984; Stephen Godfrey, "Hirsch: The man behind the arras," *Books in Canada*, April, 1981; Martin Knelman, "The Merchant Problem," *Toronto Life*, August, 1989; David Macfarlane, "A document in madness," *Books in Canada*, April, 1981; Gina Mallet, "Mary Stuart: A Limp Martyr on a Set from Speer," TS, August 8, 1982; Gina Mallet, "Shakespeare reclaims Dream in second half," TS, June 11, 1984; Jamie Portman, "O Stratford Festival, whither goest thou? Future's grim for Shakespeare showcase," Southam News Service, December 31, 1985; David Prosser, "Food for the Spirit," *Kingston Whig-Standard*, June 23, 1984; Frank Rasky, "Meteoric career for Stratford director," *Canadian Jewish News*, August 15, 1985; Campbell Robertson, "New Artistic Director for the Stratford Festival," NYT, June 27, 2006; Daniel Sullivan, "Stage Review: Stratford 'Lear' Has A Hurricane-force Lear," LT, November 12, 1985; Irving Wardle, "Theatrical Stratfords: Irving Wardle in Ontario," *The Times*, July 1, 1982.

Much of the correspondence and Stratford internal communications quoted are in Library and Archives Canada. Part of the Stratford 1980 Annual General Meeting can be heard at the CBC Digital Archives. See also "The Stratford Festival: The First 50 Years – Wherefore art thou Canadian directors?", broadcast December 7, 1980; and JH, "John Hirsch's Ella," 1988-89, *op. cit.*

Chapter 10. Our Revels Now Are Ended

The main interviews were with David Bassuk, Robert Farley, Andras Hamori, Martin Knelman, Martha Henry, Robert Lantos, Catherine McCartney, Des McAnuff, Seana McKenna, Stephen Ouimette, Aaron

Posner, Frank Savino, Steven Schipper, Michal Schonberg, Gail Singer, Paul Thompson and Bryan Trottier. Thanks also to Peter Molnar Gal, and to Charles Pachter for sharing his diary entries about Hirsch.

Articles and manuscripts include: JH, "Thinking It Over," keynote address to the California Theatre Conference, Stanford University, 1987; JH, "Hirsch at Yale," typescripts dated March 1, 4 and 8, 1988; JH, "First Reading, American Dreams Lost And Found," Alliance Theater Company, October 20, 1987; JH, "The Imperative for Training," *American Theater*, November, 1988; Elizabeth Osborn, "Vision," *Dramatics*, April, 1991; R.B. Parker, "Corrie-Ollie-Anus: Shakespeare's Last Tragedy and American Politics in 1988," in Jay L. Halio, Lois Potter and Arthur F. Kinney (eds.), *Shakespeare, text and theater: essays in honor of Jay L. Halio*, Newark: University of Delaware Press, 1999; William Shakespeare, *A Midsummer Night's Dream*, John R. Brown and Leslie Thomson (eds.), New York: Applause, 1996; Don Shewey, "Power Play: On Coriolanus," *American Theater*, March, 1989.

Newspaper and magazine articles include: Nancy Churnin, "Historical Nightmare Evolved Into a Political Obsession for Playwright Hirsch," LT, August 19, 1988; Ray Conlogue, "Ouimette triumphs in Three Men on a Horse," GM, September 11, 1987; Paula Crouch, "Studio's 'American Dreams' unfurls flag-waving theatrics in grand style," *Atlanta Constitution*, November 6, 1987; Sylvie Drake, "Coriolanus Is Just South of Ollie North," LT, July 30, 1988; Robert Enright, "Father Courage," *Border Crossings*, Fall, 1988; Bill Hagen, "Updated 'Coriolanus' powerful, passionate," *San Diego Union Tribune*, July 29, 1988; Martin Knelman, "This City" (column), *Toronto Life*, June, 1987; Mervyn Rothstein, "Theater: How 'The Chosen' Became a Musical," NYT, January 3, 1988; Arthur Salm, "Most theatre bores Coriolanus' director," *The Tribune*, San Diego, July 22, 1988; John Simon, "Have some class," *New York*, August 22, 1988.

Also quoted is JH, "John Hirsch's Ella", *op. cit.*

Epilogue

The interviews quoted were with Peter Herrndorf, Mark Negin, Daniel Sullivan and Paul Thompson. Hirsch's comment about cooking is from Robert Enright, 1988, *op. cit.* Other sources include Martha Henry, 1989, *op. cit.* and James Reaney, "Hirsch should be recalled for talent as a director," *London Free Press*, August 21, 1989.

Index

Véhicule Press

www.vehiculepress.com